OECD/G20 Base Erosion and Profit Shifting Project



# Tax Challenges Arising from Digitalisation – Economic Impact Assessment

INCLUSIVE FRAMEWORK ON BEPS

OECD
BETTER POLICIES FOR BETTER LIVES

**Please cite this publication as:**
OECD (2020), *Tax Challenges Arising from Digitalisation – Economic Impact Assessment: Inclusive Framework on BEPS*, OECD/G20 Base Erosion and Profit Shifting Project, OECD Publishing, Paris, *https://doi.org/10.1787/0e3cc2d4-en*.

ISBN 978-92-64-49507-4 (print)
ISBN 978-92-64-49483-1 (pdf)

OECD/G20 Base Erosion and Profit Shifting Project
ISSN 2313-2604 (print)
ISSN 2313-2612 (online)

**Photo credits:** Cover © ninog – Fotolia.com.

Corrigenda to publications may be found on line at: *www.oecd.org/about/publishing/corrigenda.htm*.

# Foreword

The integration of national economies and markets has increased substantially in recent years, putting a strain on the international tax rules, which were designed more than a century ago. Weaknesses in the current rules create opportunities for base erosion and profit shifting (BEPS), requiring bold moves by policy makers to restore confidence in the system and ensure that profits are taxed where economic activities take place and value is created.

Following the release of the report Addressing Base Erosion and Profit Shifting in February 2013, OECD and G20 countries adopted a 15-point Action Plan to address BEPS in September 2013. The Action Plan identified 15 actions along three key pillars: introducing coherence in the domestic rules that affect cross-border activities, reinforcing substance requirements in the existing international standards, and improving transparency as well as certainty.

After two years of work, measures in response to the 15 actions were delivered to G20 Leaders in Antalya in November 2015. All the different outputs, including those delivered in an interim form in 2014, were consolidated into a comprehensive package. The BEPS package of measures represents the first substantial renovation of the international tax rules in almost a century.

Implementation is now well underway. The BEPS package was designed to be implemented via changes in domestic law and practices, and in tax treaties. With the negotiation of a multilateral instrument (MLI) having been finalised in 2016 to facilitate the implementation of the treaty related BEPS measures, over 90 jurisdictions are covered by the MLI. The entry into force of the MLI on 1 July 2018 has paved the way for swift implementation of the treaty related measures. OECD and G20 countries also agreed to continue to work together to ensure a consistent and co-ordinated implementation of the BEPS recommendations and to make the project more inclusive. Globalisation requires that global solutions and a global dialogue be established which go beyond OECD and G20 countries.

As a result, the OECD established the OECD/G20 Inclusive Framework on BEPS (Inclusive Framework) in 2016, bringing together all interested and committed countries and jurisdictions on an equal footing in the Committee on Fiscal Affairs and all its subsidiary bodies. The Inclusive Framework, which already has more than 135 members, is monitoring and peer reviewing the implementation of the BEPS minimum standards as well as completing the work on standard setting to address BEPS issues. In addition to its member jurisdictions, other international organisations and regional tax bodies are involved in the work of the Inclusive Framework, which also consults business and civil society on its different work streams.

Addressing the tax challenges arising from the digitalisation of the economy has been a top priority of the BEPS Project and the Inclusive Framework since 2015 with the release of the BEPS Action 1 Report. At the request of the G20, the Inclusive Framework has continued to work on the issue, delivering an interim report in March 2018. In January 2019, members of the Inclusive Framework agreed to examine proposals in two pillars, which could form the basis for a consensus solution to the tax challenges arising from digitalisation. Pillar One is focused on nexus and profit allocation whereas Pillar Two is focused on a global minimum tax intended to address remaining BEPS issues. A programme of work to be conducted on Pillar One and Pillar Two was adopted in May 2019 and later endorsed by the G20 in June 2019. As part of the programme of work, the OECD Secretariat was mandated to carry out an economic analysis and impact assessment of the Pillar One and Pillar Two proposals. In July 2020, the G20 mandated the Inclusive Framework to produce reports on the Blueprints of Pillar One and Pillar Two by the G20 Finance Ministers meeting in October 2020.

This report presents the OECD Secretariat's economic analysis and impact assessment mandated under the May 2019 programme of work, which has been prepared to support the ongoing discussions by the Inclusive Framework around design questions associated with the Pillar One and Pillar Two proposals. It was produced by the OECD Secretariat in consultation with Inclusive Framework members, Working Party No.2, other international organisations, the academic community and other stakeholders. It does not represent the consensus views of the Inclusive Framework, the Committee on Fiscal Affairs or their subsidiary bodies.

# Acknowledgements

This report was produced by the OECD Secretariat as part of a joint project between the Tax Policy and Statistics Division of the OECD's Centre for Tax Policy and Administration (CTPA) and the Structural Surveillance Division of the OECD's Economics Department.

The project was undertaken under the leadership of David Bradbury, Åsa Johansson and Stéphane Sorbe. The analytical work in the project, the main findings of which are presented in this report, was carried out by Ana Cinta González Cabral, Tibor Hanappi, Valentine Millot, Pierce O'Reilly and Sébastien Turban, with valuable input from Alexandre Jutand and the expert contribution of Frank van Tongeren.

The OECD Secretariat would like to thank the delegates of Working Party No. 2 on Tax Policy Analysis and Tax Statistics (WP2) and the Inclusive Framework on BEPS for their extensive comments and inputs. The important contributions of members of the Extended Bureau of WP2 are gratefully acknowledged. The project also benefitted from interaction with Working Party No. 1 on Macroeconomic and Structural Policy Analysis of the Economic Policy Committee.

The project benefitted from the supervision and strategic oversight of Pascal Saint-Amans and Grace Perez-Navarro, the Director and Deputy Director of CTPA, and was carried out with considerable support from the following CTPA divisions: the Global Relations and Development Division, the International Cooperation and Tax Administration Division and the Tax Treaties, Transfer Pricing and Financial Transactions Division. The project also benefitted from the support of Laurence Boone, the OECD Chief Economist, and Luiz de Mello and Alain de Serres, the Director and Deputy Director of the Policy Studies Branch of the Economics Department.

The project would not have been possible without the invaluable administrative support of Violet Sochay, assisted by Marie-Aurelie Elkurd and Alexandra Le Cam. Karena Garnier, Hazel Healy, Natalie Lagorce and Carrie Tyler assisted with the preparation of the report for publication and communications. Additional contributions from Giulia Aliprandi, Krista Bruns, Agnès Cavaciuti, Chris Hayes, Pardis Nabavi Larijani, Angela Marotti de Sciarra, Anna Milanez, Anne Moore, Tom Neubig and Ruairi Sugrue are also gratefully acknowledged. The project has also benefitted from the contributions of Piet Battiau, Bert Brys, Michelle Harding and Kurt Van Dender.

Contributions from the Trade and Agriculture Directorate, the Directorate for Science, Technology and Innovation, the Statistics and Data Directorate and the Directorate for Financial and Enterprise Affairs are all gratefully acknowledged, in particular the contributions of Nadim Ahmad, Silvia Appelt, Christine Arriola, Matej Bajgar, Charles Cadestin, Alessandra Celani, Chiara Criscuolo, Fernando Galindo-Rueda, Jonathan Timmis, Martin Wermelinger and Belen Zinni.

This report has also benefitted from discussions with and input received from representatives of the African Tax Administration Forum, the European Commission and the International Monetary Fund. The project team also thanks participants in the various academic workshops held at the OECD over the course of 2019 for their contributions and insights.

# Table of contents



## Tables

## Figures

## Boxes

# Executive Summary

This report analyses the economic and tax revenue implications of the Pillar One and Pillar Two proposals currently being discussed by the OECD/G20 Inclusive Framework on BEPS (Inclusive Framework) as part of its work to address the tax challenges arising from the digitalisation of the economy. These proposals are described in the Pillar One and Pillar Two Blueprint reports (OECD, 2020[1]; OECD, 2020[2]).

A number of the design elements and parameters of Pillar One and Pillar Two will be the subject of future decisions by the Inclusive Framework. The 'ex ante' assessment in this report, which has been carried out by the OECD Secretariat, relies on a number of illustrative assumptions on proposal design and parameters, without prejudice to the final decisions of the Inclusive Framework.

The assessment in this report relies on the best data available to the OECD Secretariat across a wide range of jurisdictions, combining firm-level and more aggregate data sources, including the newly published anonymised and aggregated Country-by-Country Report (CbCR) data. Extensive work has been undertaken to ensure the highest possible level of data quality. Nevertheless, the underlying data have several limitations and the assessment relies on a number of simplifying assumptions on the proposals and the potential reactions of multinational enterprises (MNEs) and governments. In particular, the underlying data pre-date important recent developments, most notably the 2017 US tax reform, implementation of some aspects of the OECD/G20 Base Erosion and Profit Shifting (BEPS) package and the COVID-19 crisis.

## Effect of the proposals on tax revenues

Pillar One and Pillar Two could increase global corporate income tax (CIT) revenues by about USD 50-80 billion per year. Taking into account the combined effect of these reforms and the US GILTI regime, the total effect could represent USD 60-100 billion per year or up to around 4% of global CIT revenues. The exact gains could differ from these 'ex ante' estimates as they would depend on the final design and parameters of Pillar One and Pillar Two, the extent of their implementation, the nature and scale of reactions by MNEs and governments, and future economic developments. Global gains would primarily come from Pillar Two:

- Pillar One would involve a significant change to the way taxing rights are allocated among jurisdictions, as taxing rights on about USD 100 billion of profit could be reallocated to market jurisdictions under the Pillar One rules. This would lead to a modest increase in global tax revenues. On average, low, middle and high income economies would all benefit from revenue gains, while 'investment hubs' would tend to lose tax revenues.
- Pillar Two would yield a significant increase in CIT revenues across low, middle and high income economies. It would significantly reduce the incentives for MNEs to shift profits to low-tax jurisdictions, which would generate revenue gains in addition to the direct gains collected through the minimum tax itself.
- The combined revenue gains from both pillars are estimated to be broadly similar – as a share of current CIT revenues – across low, middle and high income jurisdictions.

## Effect of the proposals on investment and economic growth

A consensus-based multilateral solution involving Pillar One and Pillar Two would lead to a more favourable environment for investment and economic growth than would likely be the case in the absence of an agreement by the Inclusive Framework:

- Pillar One and Pillar Two would lead to a relatively small increase in the average (post-tax) investment costs of MNEs. The ensuing negative effect on global investment is estimated to be very small, as the proposals would mostly affect highly profitable MNEs whose investment is less sensitive to taxes. The impact of the proposals is expected to fall predominantly on highly-profitable MNEs in digitalised and intangible-intensive sectors in the case of Pillar One and on MNEs engaging in profit shifting in the case of Pillar Two. Overall, the negative effect on global GDP stemming from the expected increase in tax revenues associated with the proposals is estimated to be less than 0.1% in the long term.
- Pillar One and Pillar Two would support global investment and growth through less quantifiable but nonetheless significant channels, which may partly or even fully offset this small negative effect. In particular, the proposals aim to increase tax certainty and could enhance the efficiency of global capital allocation by increasing the importance of non-tax factors (e.g. infrastructure, education levels or labour costs) in investment decisions. To some extent, they would also reduce the need to raise revenues by implementing other (potentially more distortive) tax measures in the constrained post-COVID-19 budget environment. Finally, the proposals could result in additional compliance and administration costs for MNEs and governments. The extent of these costs is difficult to assess and would depend on the final design of the proposals.
- In contrast, the absence of a consensus-based solution would likely lead to a proliferation of uncoordinated and unilateral tax measures (e.g. digital services taxes) and an increase in damaging tax and trade disputes. This would undermine tax certainty and investment and also result in additional compliance and administration costs. The magnitude of the negative consequences would depend on the extent, design and scope of these unilateral measures, and the scale of any ensuing trade retaliation. In the "worst-case" scenario, these disputes could reduce global GDP by more than 1%.

## Implications of the COVID-19 crisis

The full impact of the COVID-19 crisis remains highly uncertain at this stage, but a few likely implications for the impact assessment of Pillar One and Pillar Two already stand out:

- The COVID-19 crisis is likely to reduce the expected revenue gains from Pillar One and Pillar Two at least in the short run as the crisis weighs on the profitability of many MNEs, even though some digital-intensive MNEs have managed to sustain or enhance their profitability since the beginning of the crisis.
- The crisis has accelerated the trend towards the digitalisation of the economy, further increasing the prominence of the tax challenges arising from digitalisation and the need to address them. Accelerating digitalisation will also increase the relative importance of automated digital services (ADS) in the envisaged scope of Pillar One.
- Accelerated digitalisation, increased pressures on public finances after the crisis, and growing public dissatisfaction with tax planning by MNEs are all likely to reinforce the likelihood of unilateral tax measures if a consensus-based solution cannot be secured by the Inclusive Framework. The likely ensuing tax and trade disputes would undermine investment and economic growth at a time when the global economy is at its most fragile due to the COVID-19 crisis. They would compound the negative effect of the crisis and hinder the recovery prospects.

# 1 Overview of main findings

## 1.1. Introduction

1. The international corporate tax system faces growing challenges. While the OECD/G20 Base Erosion and Profit Shifting (BEPS) project represented an unprecedented multilateral effort to tackle profit shifting, many questions over the allocation of taxing rights remain unresolved. Digitalisation and globalisation have highlighted certain vulnerabilities in the existing framework, which allocates taxing rights principally on the basis of physical presence. In addition to this, some BEPS issues remain. In this context, an increasing number of jurisdictions are taking uncoordinated and unilateral actions, contributing to an increase in tax and trade disputes and growing tax uncertainty. The COVID-19 crisis is exacerbating these tensions by accelerating the digitalisation of the economy and increasing pressures on public finances. The fact that many firms have benefitted from direct or indirect government support during the crisis is also likely to intensify public dissatisfaction with tax avoidance by multinational enterprises (MNEs).

2. Against this backdrop, the OECD/G20 Inclusive Framework on BEPS (Inclusive Framework), which consists of 137 member jurisdictions, is discussing proposals for a consensus-based reform of the international tax rules to address the tax challenges arising from the digitalisation of the economy. The proposals, which are described in the Pillar One and Pillar Two Blueprint reports (OECD, 2020[1]; OECD, 2020[2]), fall under two pillars, which are briefly presented in Box 1.1. As part of the Programme of Work approved by the Inclusive Framework in May 2019 (OECD/G20 Inclusive Framework on BEPS, 2019[3]) and endorsed by the G20 Finance Ministers and Leaders in June 2019, the OECD Secretariat was mandated to carry out an economic analysis and impact assessment of the proposals. The aim of this report is to provide this 'ex ante' assessment.

### Box 1.1. Overview of the proposals to address the tax challenges arising from digitalisation

**Pillar One** seeks to adapt the international tax system to new business models through a coherent and concurrent review of the profit allocation and nexus rules. It intends to expand the taxing rights of market jurisdictions (which, for some business models, is the jurisdiction where the user is located) where there is an active and sustained participation of a business in the economy of that jurisdiction through activities in, or remotely directed at, that jurisdiction. Pillar One also aims to significantly improve tax certainty by introducing innovative dispute prevention and resolution mechanisms. The key elements of Pillar One can be grouped into three components:

- A new taxing right for market jurisdictions over a share of residual profit calculated at an MNE group (or segment) level (Amount A).
- A fixed return for defined baseline marketing and distribution activities taking place physically in a market jurisdiction, in line with the arm's length principle (Amount B).
- Improved tax certainty processes to improve tax certainty through innovative dispute prevention and dispute resolution mechanisms (Tax certainty component).

**Pillar Two** addresses remaining BEPS challenges and is designed to ensure that large internationally operating businesses pay a minimum level of tax regardless of where they are headquartered or the jurisdictions they operate in. It does so via a number of interlocking rules that seek to (i) ensure minimum taxation while avoiding double taxation or taxation where there is no economic profit, (ii) cope with different tax system designs by jurisdictions as well as different operating models by businesses, (iii) ensure transparency and a level playing field, and (iv) minimise administrative and compliance costs.

- The principal mechanism to achieve this outcome is the **income inclusion rule** (IIR) together with the **undertaxed payments rule** (UTPR) acting as a backstop (together, the "GloBE rules"). The operation of the IIR is, in some respects, based on traditional controlled foreign company (CFC) rule principles and triggers an inclusion at the level of the shareholder where the income of a controlled foreign entity is taxed at below the effective minimum tax rate. It is complemented by a **switch-over rule** (SOR) that removes treaty obstacles from its application to certain branch structures and applies where an income tax treaty otherwise obligates a contracting state to use the exemption method. The UTPR is a secondary rule and only applies where a Constituent Entity is not already subject to an IIR. The UTPR is nevertheless a key part of the rule set as it serves as a back-stop to the IIR, ensures a level playing field and addresses inversion risks that might otherwise arise.
- The **subject to tax rule** (STTR) complements these rules. It is a treaty-based rule that targets risks to source countries posed by BEPS structures relating to intragroup payments that take advantage of low nominal rates of taxation in the other contracting jurisdiction (that is the jurisdiction of the payee).

3. A number of design elements and parameters of Pillar One and Pillar Two will be the subject of future decisions by the Inclusive Framework. For the purpose of the 'ex ante' impact assessment in this report, a number of illustrative assumptions on proposal design and parameters have been made, without prejudice to the final decisions of the Inclusive Framework. This report presents results for a range of illustrative parameters for both Pillar One and Pillar Two in order to inform the ongoing discussions of the Inclusive Framework around the design of the proposals.

4. The geographic scope of the analysis in this report is very wide, as it covers more than 200 jurisdictions, including all 137 members of the Inclusive Framework. The analysis is based on wide-ranging and thorough data analysis, as well as insights from the economic literature. It has benefitted from extensive interactions with representatives of Inclusive Framework jurisdictions, as well as exchanges with academics, civil society and business representatives and other international organisations. As is the case for any economic analysis, the methodology relies on a number of simplifying assumptions, for example on the design of the proposals and the way MNEs and governments may react to their implementation.

5. The analysis mobilises a wide array of data sources that are combined in a consistent analytical framework. This comprises firm-level data, including the financial accounts of most of the large MNE groups worldwide, as well as a wide range of aggregate data sources, including the anonymised and aggregated Country-by-Country Report (CbCR) statistics collected as part of the implementation of the BEPS package and published by the OECD for the first time in July 2020 (OECD, 2020[4]). Nevertheless, the data underlying the analysis have limitations in terms of coverage, consistency and timeliness. In particular, the data focus primarily on 2016-17 and therefore pre-date some significant recent developments, including the implementation of various measures under the OECD/G20 BEPS project, the 2017 US tax reform (US Tax Cuts and Jobs Act) and most importantly the COVID-19 crisis. The potential implications of the COVID-19 crisis for the impact of the proposals are discussed in the final section of this chapter.

6. The report focuses primarily on the impact of the proposals on tax revenues, MNE investment and economic activity. This chapter (Chapter 1) summarises the main findings of the analysis at a high level.

The following chapters present more detailed results and analyses, covering a wide range of potential Pillar One and Pillar Two parameters. These chapters also contain a full description of the data and methodology underlying the analyses, as well as a wide range of robustness checks carried out on the data and the results. More specifically, Chapters 2 and 3 focus on the tax revenue effects of Pillar One and Pillar Two respectively. Chapter 4 discusses the effect of both pillars on investment and economic activity. Finally, Chapter 5 describes the construction of the data "matrices" underpinning the estimates presented in the other chapters.

## 1.2. Effect of the proposals on tax revenues

7. The effect of the proposals on tax revenues will depend on the final design and parameter choices to be agreed by the Inclusive Framework. Under an illustrative set of design and parameter assumptions, the combined effect of Pillar One and Pillar Two on global corporate income tax (CIT) revenues could increase global CIT revenues by 1.9% to 3.2%, or about USD 50-80 billion per year (Table 1.1).[1]

8. These estimates assume illustratively – while no decision has been taken by the Inclusive Framework at this time – that the US Global Intangible Low Tax Income (GILTI) regime would 'co-exist' with Pillar Two and US MNEs would not be subject to the income inclusion rule (IIR) under Pillar Two. As a result, Pillar Two revenue gains in Table 1.1 do not include potential gains related to the application of Pillar Two by US MNEs, which are assumed to remain subject to the GILTI regime. Taking into account the combined revenue gains of both pillars and the US GILTI regime,[2] the total effect could represent about USD 60-100 billion per year or up to 4% of global CIT revenues.

### *1.2.1. Global tax revenue effects of Pillar One*

9. Pillar One seeks to adapt the international corporate tax system to the digital age through significant changes to the rules applicable to business profits to ensure that the allocation of taxing rights on business profits is no longer exclusively determined by reference to physical presence. It intends to expand the taxing rights of market jurisdictions (which, for some business models, is the jurisdiction where the user is located)[3] where there is a significant and sustained participation of a business in the economy of that jurisdiction, either physically or remotely. It also aims to improve tax certainty by introducing improved dispute prevention and resolution mechanisms.

10. The key elements of Pillar One can be grouped into three components: a new taxing right for market jurisdictions over a share of residual profit (i.e. profit in excess of a certain profitability threshold percentage) calculated at an MNE group level based on a formulaic approach (Amount A); a fixed return for defined baseline marketing and distribution activities taking place physically in a market jurisdiction (Amount B); and improved tax certainty processes through innovative dispute prevention and dispute resolution mechanisms (Tax certainty component).

### Table 1.1. Overview of global tax revenue effects from the proposals

Estimates based on illustrative assumptions on the design and parameters of Pillar One and Pillar Two

| Estimated global tax revenue gains | | In % of global CIT revenues | In USD billion |
|---|---|---|---|
| Pillar One | | 0.2%-0.5% | 5-12 |
| Pillar Two | Direct revenue gains | 0.9%-1.7% | 23-42 |
| | Additional gains from reduced profit shifting | 0.8%-1.1% | 19-28 |
| | Total Pillar Two | 1.7%-2.8% | 42-70 |
| **Total Pillar One and Pillar Two** | | **1.9%-3.2%** | **47-81** |
| US GILTI regime | | 0.4%-0.8% | 9-21 |
| **Total, including GILTI** | | **2.3%-4.0%** | **56-102** |

Note: The estimates in this table are based on the following illustrative assumptions. Pillar One, for which only Amount A is modelled, is assumed to focus on Automated Digital Services (ADS) and Consumer Facing Businesses (CFB), with a global revenue threshold of EUR 750 million, a profitability threshold percentage of 10% (based on the ratio of profit before tax to turnover), a reallocation percentage of 20% and a nexus revenue threshold of EUR 1 million for ADS and EUR 3 million for CFB. Pillar Two is assumed to involve a 12.5% minimum tax rate with jurisdictional blending and a 10% combined carve-out on payroll and depreciation expenses. The US GILTI regime is illustratively assumed to 'co-exist' with Pillar Two. Therefore, US MNEs (which are subject to the GILTI regime) are excluded from the Pillar Two gains in this table. Revenues from GILTI are included in this table based on estimates from the US Joint Committee on Taxation. MNEs are assumed to reduce their profit shifting intensity in reaction to Pillar Two introduction, resulting in additional tax revenue gains. The interaction between Pillar One and Pillar Two is taken into account in this table. Estimates are presented as ranges to reflect uncertainty around the underlying data and modelling. See Chapters 2 and 3 for more details.
Source: OECD Secretariat calculations, and estimates from the US Joint Committee on Taxation for GILTI.

11. Amount A would lead to a reallocation of a portion of the tax base of in-scope MNE groups from jurisdictions where the residual profit of MNE groups is currently located, to market jurisdictions. Not all MNE groups would be subject to this reallocation, as it is assumed that it would only apply to relatively large and profitable MNE groups (i.e. MNE groups with revenues above a certain global revenue threshold, and profitability above the profitability threshold percentage). Although subject to political agreement, for present purposes this work has proceeded on the basis of the technical proposals to define the in-scope activities as Automated Digital Services (ADS) and Consumer Facing Businesses (CFB). By design, the impact of Amount A would fall primarily on large and profitable MNE groups in the digital-oriented and intangible intensive sectors.

12. Based on illustrative assumptions on Amount A parameters (including the profitability threshold to define residual profit), the residual profit of the MNE groups that would be in scope of Amount A could represent about USD 500 billion, of which a percentage to be decided by the Inclusive Framework would be reallocated to market jurisdictions.[4] Assuming illustratively that this reallocation percentage would be 20%, this would imply that taxing rights over about USD 100 billion of profit would be reallocated to market jurisdictions as a result of Amount A. The existing transfer pricing rules would continue to determine the allocation of taxing rights for other MNE profits (i.e. the profits of out-of-scope MNEs and the non-residual profits of MNEs as well as the share of their residual profits not reallocated under Amount A, which is 80% in this illustrative example).

13. On average, corporate tax rates are relatively higher in the market jurisdictions where residual profit would be reallocated under Amount A than in the jurisdictions where it is currently located. Indeed, a substantial share of residual profit is currently located in relatively low-tax jurisdictions. This implies that the reallocation occurring under Amount A would generate a net revenue gain at the global level. The magnitude of this overall revenue gain would be relatively modest (e.g. up to 0.5% of global CIT revenues under the assumptions in Table 1.1) reflecting that only a percentage of the residual profit of the MNEs in scope would be reallocated, and that not all reallocated profit would face a higher tax rate in market jurisdictions than the tax rate it faces where it is currently located.

14. The effect of the other components of Pillar One (Amount B and the Tax certainty component) is more difficult to quantify due to data limitations (e.g. lack of sufficient data on the nature of MNE activities at the MNE entity level, and lack of transaction-level data) and methodological challenges. As a result, quantitative estimates of Pillar One in this report focus exclusively on Amount A. While the effect of Amount B and the Tax certainty component will depend on their design and scope, their impact on global tax revenues is generally expected to be small. This reflects the fact that these proposals seek to support the existing transfer pricing system and prevent tax disputes, in contrast to Amount A, which establishes a new taxing right.

15. Amount B would set a fixed return for defined baseline distribution and marketing functions of MNEs taking place physically in market jurisdictions. Amount B is expected to reduce administration costs for governments and increase tax certainty for taxpayers, and may be of particular benefit to jurisdictions with low administrative capacity. Where the fixed return for baseline and marketing functions exceeds current returns taxable in market jurisdictions, Amount B would contribute to additional revenues in those jurisdictions. A number of jurisdictions with low administrative capacity assess that this is likely to be the case in their jurisdiction, as a result of the challenges they face applying the existing transfer pricing rules effectively. However, at the global level, the revenue effect of Amount B is likely to be modest, as it does not provide market jurisdictions with a new taxing right, but is merely designed to simplify the administration of the current transfer pricing system.

### *1.2.2. Global tax revenue effects of Pillar Two*

16. The various components of Pillar Two would ensure a minimum level of tax on MNE profit. The GloBE rules (i.e. the income inclusion rule (IIR) and the undertaxed payments rule (UTPR), see Box 1.1) would operate as a 'top-up' on existing taxes to ensure that the effective tax rate on MNE profit that would otherwise be taxed below an agreed minimum rate is brought up to this minimum rate, which has to be decided by the Inclusive Framework. A variety of minimum rates have illustratively been explored in the analysis. The results in Table 1.1 above assume illustratively a 12.5% minimum rate. Results for other rates are presented in Chapter 3.

17. The Inclusive Framework also has to decide on a number of Pillar Two design features, including the degree of 'blending' (i.e. the level of aggregation at which the effective tax rate test would be applied). Two main options are considered: jurisdictional blending (i.e. blending the income and covered taxes of all entities from an MNE group in a jurisdiction) or global blending (i.e. blending all foreign income and covered taxes of an MNE group). While no decision has been taken by the Inclusive Framework yet, the results in this report are illustratively based on jurisdictional blending.[5]

18. Another design question that the Inclusive Framework has to decide upon relates to the existence and design of a formulaic substance-based carve-out. Such a carve-out would exclude a fixed return for substantive activities within a jurisdiction from the scope of the GloBE rules. This fixed return could be defined as a certain percentage of expenses on payroll and depreciation of tangible assets. For example, the results in Table 1.1 assume illustratively a 10% carve-out on payroll and depreciation of tangible assets. The analysis in this report considers a range of potential options regarding formulaic substance-based

carve-outs and suggests that their effect on global Pillar Two revenue gains would be relatively small under the assumptions considered.[6]

19. The analysis suggests that the global revenue gains from Pillar Two could be significant. The impact of Pillar Two would fall on MNEs with low-taxed profits, including due to profit shifting behaviour. The exact size of the tax revenue gains would depend on the design of Pillar Two and the agreed minimum tax rate. In addition to direct revenue gains collected through the Pillar Two minimum tax provisions (e.g. the income inclusion rule or the undertaxed payments rule), Pillar Two is expected to generate indirect tax revenue gains by reducing MNE profit shifting.

20. Indeed, Pillar Two would reduce the differences in effective tax rates across jurisdictions, which are one of the main drivers of profit shifting. Reducing these tax rate differentials would reduce MNEs' incentives to shift profit to low-tax jurisdictions. This would likely lead MNEs to reassess their profit shifting strategies, and some MNEs would likely consider that the gains of certain profit shifting schemes would no longer be worth the costs (e.g. financial and advisory costs of the schemes, reputational costs, etc.). The exact scale of the reduction in profit shifting and location of profits in a post Pillar Two world are difficult to anticipate with certainty as profit shifting schemes are very complex and firm-specific. Nevertheless, the reduction of profit shifting is expected to contribute significantly to the global revenue gains from Pillar Two.

### *1.2.3. Interaction of Pillar One and Pillar Two*

21. The effects of Pillar One and Pillar Two would interact, in the sense that the joint implementation of the two pillars would have a slightly different effect from the effect resulting from the two pillars considered in isolation. Assuming that the minimum tax in Pillar Two would be applied after the reallocation involved by Pillar One, the analysis in this report suggests that the interaction between the two pillars would reduce the overall revenue gains compared to a hypothetical situation where there would be no interaction between the pillars. However, this interaction effect would be quantitatively small under the assumptions on Pillar One and Pillar Two considered in this report.

### *1.2.4. Revenue effects of Pillar One and Pillar Two by jurisdiction groups*

22. On average, it is estimated that low, middle and high income jurisdictions would all benefit from revenue gains as a result of the proposals (Figure 1.1). Gains would be relatively small under Pillar One and larger under Pillar Two. The combined revenue gains from both pillars are estimated to be broadly similar – as a share of current CIT revenues – across low, middle and high income jurisdictions.

23. Estimated revenue gains from Pillar One tend to be larger – as a share of current CIT revenues – among low and middle income jurisdictions than high income ones, reflecting that relatively low amounts of residual profit are currently located in low and middle income jurisdictions, which implies that they would gain unambiguously from the reallocation occurring under Pillar One.[7] These results focus exclusively on Amount A, though depending on its ultimate design, some lower income jurisdictions, particularly those with low capacity tax administrations, may also see revenue gains from Amount B. This reflects the fact that these jurisdictions report that they face challenges applying the existing transfer pricing rules effectively, with some MNEs reporting low or negative returns for baseline marketing and distribution activities in their jurisdiction.

Figure 1.1. Estimated effect of the proposals on tax revenues, by jurisdiction groups

Estimates based on illustrative assumptions on the design and parameters of Pillar One and Pillar Two

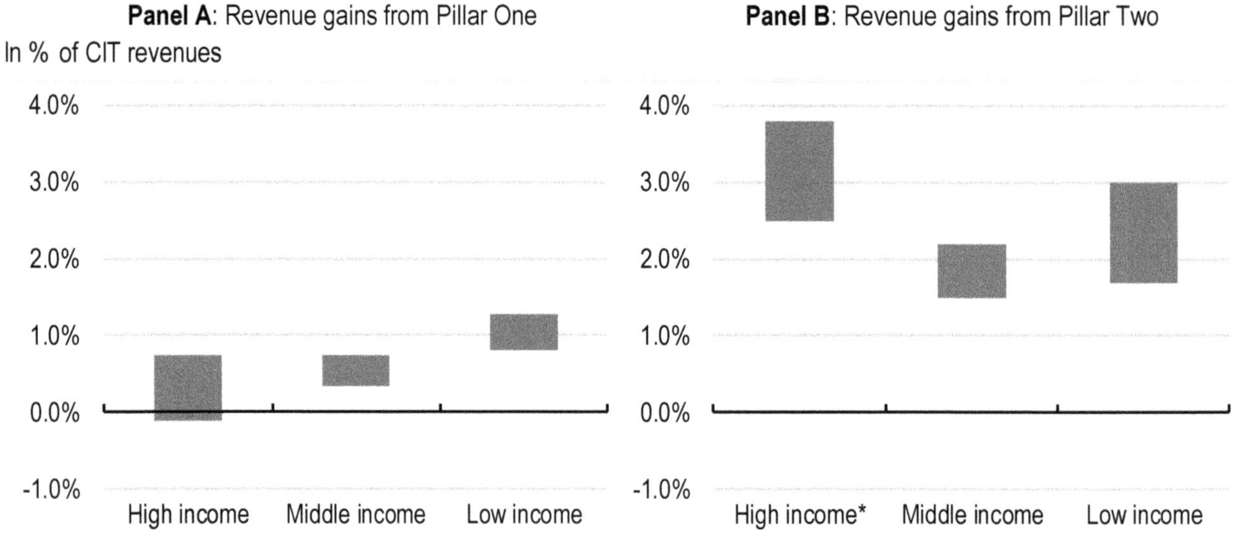


* Excluding the United States (given illustrative assumption that the US GILTI would co-exist with Pillar Two)

Note: The estimates in this figure are based on the following illustrative assumptions. Pillar One is assumed to focus on Automated Digital Services (ADS) and Consumer Facing Businesses (CFB), with a global revenue threshold of EUR 750 million, a profitability threshold percentage of 10% (based on the ratio of profit before tax to turnover), a reallocation percentage of 20% and a nexus revenue threshold of EUR 1 million for ADS and EUR 3 million for CFB. Pillar Two is assumed to involve a 12.5% minimum tax rate with jurisdictional blending and a 10% combined carve-out on payroll and depreciation expenses. The US GILTI regime is assumed to 'co-exist' with Pillar Two. As a result, the United States is not included in Panel B to ensure greater comparability of results (but it is included in Panel A). Pillar Two estimates take into account the interaction with Pillar One and include gains from a reduction in the profit shifting intensity of MNEs resulting from Pillar Two introduction. Estimates are presented as ranges to reflect uncertainty around the underlying data and modelling. Groups of jurisdictions (high, middle and low income) are based on the World Bank classification. Investment hubs (defined as jurisdictions with a total inward FDI position above 150% of GDP) are not included in this figure. See Chapters 2 and 3 for more details.
Source: OECD Secretariat.

24. Revenue gains from Pillar Two are estimated to be significant across all income groups presented in Figure 1.1. The estimated gains tend to be relatively larger among high income jurisdictions, reflecting that gains from the income inclusion rule would accrue to the jurisdiction of ultimate parent of MNE groups, which are often high income jurisdictions. Still, lower income jurisdictions could benefit from significant gains as a result of the reduction in MNE profit shifting expected to result from Pillar Two. The subject to tax rule, which has not been modelled in this analysis due to data limitations, could also support revenues in low and middle income jurisdictions by allowing the source jurisdiction to apply a top-up tax to an agreed minimum rate to certain related-party payments that are subject to low nominal rates of tax in the residence jurisdiction.

25. Furthermore, Pillar Two would put a floor on the competition to attract MNE activities through special tax incentives (e.g. tax holidays), which could bring additional revenue gains to lower income jurisdictions. Indeed, these jurisdictions often have a weak bargaining position vis-à-vis investing MNEs, which can lead them to offer very low tax rates to these MNEs. Pillar Two could enable these jurisdictions to impose at least the minimum rate. The potential resulting gains are not included in the estimates in Figure 1.1.

26. Results for investment hubs[8] are omitted from Figure 1.1 as they generally involve a higher degree of uncertainty than other results and because investment hubs are a relatively heterogeneous group of

jurisdictions. These results are presented in Chapter 2 (for Pillar One) and Chapter 3 (for Pillar Two). In general, investment hubs would tend to lose tax base from Pillar One. The magnitude of the resulting tax revenue loss would depend on the effective tax rate on the residual profit of MNEs that is currently located in their jurisdiction. As this rate is sometimes zero, some investment hubs would lose tax base but not tax revenue. Pillar Two, by reducing MNE profit shifting, would lead many investment hubs to lose tax base (as they would tend to receive less shifted profit after the introduction of Pillar Two).

27. Still, many investment hubs may gain a substantial amount of tax revenues from Pillar Two, especially if they decide to increase the effective tax rate on profit in their jurisdiction when this rate is currently below the minimum rate. The scale of this potential reaction by some governments is difficult to anticipate, as it will depend on a number of strategic considerations and may be influenced by the exact design of Pillar Two. This question is further discussed in Chapter 3, which also presents the potential implications of stylised scenarios on the effect of such tax rate increases on revenue gains across jurisdiction groups.

### *1.2.5. Revenue effects of Pillar One and Pillar Two at the jurisdiction level*

28. Jurisdiction-level revenue estimates of Pillar One and Pillar Two were shared by the OECD Secretariat on a confidential and bilateral basis with most Inclusive Framework members. The OECD Secretariat has provided estimates to more than 115 jurisdictions at their request. After extensive consultation with members of the Inclusive Framework, there was no consensus over whether or not jurisdiction-specific estimates should be publicly released as part of the economic impact assessment. In view of this lack of consensus, no jurisdiction-specific estimates are included in this report. As jurisdiction-specific estimates have only been shared with Inclusive Framework members on a confidential and bilateral basis, each jurisdiction has received estimates for its jurisdiction only.

29. Jurisdiction-specific results were shared in the form of revenue estimation 'tools'. These tools provide jurisdictions with the ability to consider the estimated impact on tax revenues in their jurisdiction of a range of potential Pillar One and Pillar Two parameters (e.g. profitability threshold percentage under Pillar One, minimum tax rate under Pillar Two, etc.) in order to inform the discussions of the Inclusive Framework. Preliminary versions of the Pillar One and Pillar Two tools were shared respectively in October 2019 and February 2020. Refined and updated tools were later shared in June and July 2020, taking into account progress in the design of the proposals, refinements in the underlying data and methodology and feedback from Inclusive Framework jurisdiction officials on the earlier tools and results.

## 1.3. Effect of the proposals on investment and economic activity

30. The proposals would affect MNE investment, innovation and economic activity through a range of channels. The most direct channel is that, by raising additional tax revenues, the proposals would increase (after-tax) investment costs for the MNEs affected. This would likely have a negative effect on investment and activity, but the magnitude of this effect is estimated to be relatively small: less than 0.1% of GDP in the medium to long term (further details are included in Chapter 4).

31. This small negative effect may be partly or even fully offset by the positive effect from other less quantifiable but nonetheless significant channels. In particular, the proposals aim to increase tax certainty, would affect compliance and administration costs in various ways, may enhance the efficiency of global capital allocation, and would reduce the need to raise revenues by implementing other (potentially more distortive) tax measures, as further discussed below.

32. For the purposes of this analysis, the consensus scenario involving the adoption of Pillar One and Pillar Two by the Inclusive Framework assumes the withdrawal of existing digital services taxes (DSTs) as well as a commitment to refrain from introducing such measures in the future. In contrast, the absence of

a consensus-based solution would likely see the proliferation of uncoordinated and unilateral tax measures (including DSTs) continue, which would likely result in an increase in damaging tax and trade disputes. This would undermine tax certainty and investment, with negative effects on global GDP that could far exceed the direct effect of the reform on investment costs, especially in a scenario involving widespread adoption of DSTs and a "worst-case" (i.e. five-time) trade retaliation factor (Figure 1.2).

Figure 1.2. Estimated effect on global GDP in stylised scenarios

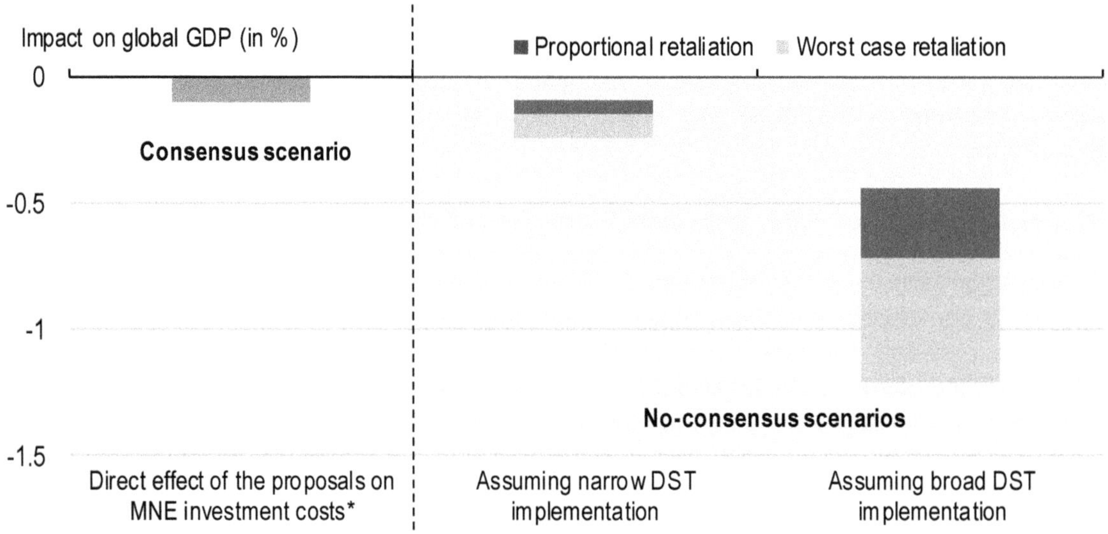


* The proposals would also have positive impacts on GDP through indirect channels (e.g. increased tax certainty, reduced need to increase other distortive taxes) which are not quantified in this figure.

Note: The estimate in the consensus scenario only takes into account the direct effect of the proposals on MNE after-tax investment costs and its implications on MNE investment and ultimately GDP. The range reflects uncertainty on the tax sensitivity of the affected MNEs as well as uncertainty about whether lower investment in a jurisdiction where after-tax investment costs are increased would result in higher investment in other jurisdictions (where some of the investment may be relocated) or not. In the no-consensus situation, two cases are considered: (i) a narrow digital services tax (DST) implementation, where jurisdictions currently subject to Section 301 investigation by the United States introduce a DST, the United States retaliates with tariffs and these jurisdictions counter-retaliate also with tariffs; and (ii) a broad DST implementation, where all jurisdictions except the Unites States, China and Hong Kong (China) introduce a DST and reactions similar to the previous case ensue. In each case, the uncertainty ranges correspond to the range of outcomes between scenarios with 3% to 5% DST rates and 1-time (i.e. "proportional") to 5-time (i.e. "worst case") trade retaliation factors. See Chapter 4 for more details.
Source: OECD Secretariat.

### *1.3.1. Direct effect of the proposals on investment costs*

33. By raising additional tax revenues on the profit of certain MNEs, the proposals would likely increase the effective tax rate on their investment, and therefore after-tax investment costs. Under illustrative assumptions on the parameters of Pillar One and Pillar Two, it is estimated that the effective *average* tax rate (EATR, i.e. the *average* tax rate on the profit derived from a new investment project) on a typical investment project by an MNE would be increased by around 0.3 percentage points on average. The effective *marginal* tax rate (EMTR, i.e. the tax rate on the profit derived from a *marginal* increase in the scale of an existing investment project) would be increased by around 1.3 percentage points on average (see Chapter 4 and Hanappi and González Cabral (2020[5])). These estimated increases are relatively small compared to the current average level of EATRs and EMTRs on MNE investments (about 24% and 25%, respectively). The increases would primarily come from Pillar Two, consistent with the finding that Pillar Two would have larger effects on tax revenues than Pillar One.

34. This small increase in investment costs would likely have a relatively small effect on global business investment. This is because the firms most affected by the additional investment costs would be relatively large and highly profitable MNEs. These firms are estimated to be less sensitive to corporate taxes in their investment decisions than less profitable firms, as discussed further in Chapter 4 and Millot et al. (2020[6]). For example, firms belonging to MNE groups with a profitability rate above 10% are found to be about half as sensitive to taxes as those in groups with a profitability between 0% and 10%. This lower sensitivity may reflect that more profitable firms face fewer financing constraints, and also that they are more likely to benefit from economic 'rents' (e.g. related to market power).[9] Taxes on rents are generally thought to affect firm investment less than taxes on 'normal' profits.

35. As a result, the negative impact on economic activity of this increase in investment costs is estimated to be very modest: less than 0.1% of GDP over the medium to long term. This impact could be even less negative to the extent that some MNE groups that reduce investment in jurisdictions where investment costs have increased may reallocate this investment to other jurisdictions.

36. Indeed, the proposals would encourage some relocation of investment, as investment costs would increase relatively more in jurisdictions that currently offer low effective tax rates (e.g. below the potential minimum rate under Pillar Two). This could affect investment in these jurisdictions significantly, with potential knock-on effects on the CIT tax base and other tax bases (e.g. personal income tax), although this negative effect on investment could be reduced if Pillar Two includes a formulaic substance-based carve-out that excludes a fixed return for substantive activities from the scope of the GloBE rules. In contrast, jurisdictions with tax rates above the minimum rate would face no significant investment loss and may even benefit from higher investment.

37. All in all, by reducing differences in effective tax rates across jurisdictions, the proposals would tend to increase the relative importance of non-tax factors, such as infrastructure, education levels or labour costs, in the investment location decisions of MNEs. This would generally contribute to a more efficient global allocation of investment, in the sense that investment would be more likely to be located where it is the most economically productive, rather than in the jurisdictions that provide the most favourable corporate tax treatment.

### *1.3.2. Other effects of the proposals on investment and economic activity*

38. Beyond their direct effect on investment costs, the proposals would affect economies through several other channels. One important channel is that, by increasing tax revenues, the proposals would reduce, at least to some extent, the need for governments to rely on other (potentially more distortive) tax measures or cuts in government spending to restore public finances after the COVID-19 crisis. As such, the proposals would also support domestic resource mobilisation in developing economies.

39. The proposals would increase global tax revenues through their direct effect (discussed in the revenue section above) and they could further support tax revenues in the longer term by reducing the intensity of corporate tax competition between jurisdictions. This is because the introduction of a minimum tax rate would limit possibilities for governments to use very low statutory corporate tax rates or very generous preferential regimes to attract MNE activity and profit. Indeed, the introduction of a minimum tax rate would lift the floor on the effective corporate tax rate paid by MNEs to an agreed minimum level. The full implications of this on governments' future tax rate and base setting behaviour are hard to anticipate with certainty and will depend on future circumstances. Nevertheless, in the context of the post-COVID-crisis constrained budgetary environment, this could have the effect of slowing or even halting some of the aggressive tax competition that has taken place over the past decades.

40. A potential downside of curtailing the ability of governments to offer very low tax rates is that it may, to some extent, reduce their ability to use tax incentives to pursue specific policy objectives, such as promoting innovative activities or economic development (e.g. via investment tax incentives or tax

incentives for R&D). Under the Pillar One and Pillar Two design and parameters illustratively considered in this report, governments would retain a relatively wide margin to use the corporate tax system to pursue these goals, especially if Pillar Two includes a formulaic substance-based carve-out, as such a carve-out would make it easier to offer low rates to activities involving economic substance. In addition, as discussed further in Chapter 4, the efficiency of these preferential schemes is not always well-established. Finally, governments would continue to have a range of other policy tools at their disposal to support their policy objectives, meaning that they could likely adapt their mix of policy instruments if necessary without significantly undermining their ability to pursue these objectives. As a result, it seems unlikely that the reform would have detrimental effects on innovation or economic development via this channel.

41. Another important question is the potential impact of the proposals on compliance costs for MNEs and administration costs for governments. This impact is difficult to assess comprehensively at this stage, as it will depend on the exact design of the proposals and, in particular, on the extent to which the Inclusive Framework adopts simplification measures in the architecture of the proposals.

42. The new tax provisions under both pillars will increase tax filing requirements, which will have a cost for MNEs and governments (e.g. in terms of time spent and need to adapt existing procedures and IT systems). However, this cost will be moderated by the fact that smaller and less profitable MNEs would be out of the scope of the proposals, and the extent to which efficient design options, such as a centralised and simplified administration system, are to be included in the final design of the proposals. In addition, certain provisions of Pillar One (Amount B and the Tax certainty component) would reduce compliance and administrative costs by simplifying the tax treatment of certain business functions, and preventing tax disputes. It is also important to emphasise that, if a consensus-based solution cannot be secured, compliance costs for businesses would likely increase, as a proliferation of unilateral tax measures would likely give rise to a more fragmented and less consistent international tax system, as well as more frequent tax and trade disputes.

43. The economic impact of the proposals will also depend on who bears the economic 'incidence' of the additional taxes. In theory, the cost of additional taxes can ultimately fall on MNE shareholders (in the form of lower dividends), workers (in the form of lower wages) or consumers (in the form of higher prices). In practice, the incidence may be split between these three categories in proportions depending on the specific situation of each firm, as further discussed in Chapter 4.

44. Finally, the proposals may also affect competition dynamics among firms. By increasing taxes on large, profitable and profit-shifting MNEs, the proposals would likely contribute to a more even tax playing field between these MNEs and other MNEs (e.g. smaller MNEs that do not shift profits) as well as non-MNE firms. This could contribute to mitigating current trends towards greater market concentration, especially in digital markets, that risk undermining consumer welfare, investment and innovation. Indeed, preliminary evidence suggests that profit shifting MNEs use tax savings to crowd out other firms.

### *1.3.3. Impacts on the global economy in case no consensus is reached*

45. The expected effects of the proposals must be compared to the implications of a counterfactual scenario where a multilateral consensus-based solution cannot be secured. The exact nature of this counterfactual scenario is uncertain, but it seems likely that it would not look like the status quo. Indeed, recent years have seen a proliferation of tax and trade disputes, as a number of jurisdictions have taken unilateral action to address the tax challenges arising from the digitalisation of the economy (e.g. by introducing DSTs or similar measures). In particular, this has led to the United States announcing retaliatory tariffs on about USD 1.3 billion of French goods under section 301 of the US Trade Act and to launch several additional section 301 investigations in June 2020.

46. Tax and trade disputes are likely to intensify further if a multilateral consensus-based solution is not agreed. Indeed, in addition to those jurisdictions that have already announced DSTs, a number of

jurisdictions considering DSTs have announced that they will refrain from introducing them if a multilateral, consensus-based solution can be secured. If no agreement is reached, they would likely proceed with introducing DSTs and an escalation of DST-related trade tensions would follow. Several recent surveys confirm that tax uncertainty is a key concern of MNEs and that the perception of uncertainty has been increasing in recent years. A consensus-based solution, which for the purposes of this report assumes the withdrawal of existing DSTs as well as a commitment to refrain from introducing such measures in the future, is expected to provide greater tax certainty than the counterfactual scenario where no multilateral agreement can be secured.

47. A proliferation of DSTs would generate economic inefficiencies. As DSTs are not designed as taxes on corporate profits, but are typically designed more like taxes on turnover, DSTs are more likely to give rise to instances of double taxation. In addition, contrary to profit-based taxes, DSTs would also affect loss-making firms, which could be damaging in the context of a significant economic downturn like the current COVID-19 crisis.

48. These inefficiencies, combined with growing tax uncertainty and the likelihood of further tax and trade disputes, would undermine investment and economic activity. The magnitude of these adverse effects would notably depend on the number of jurisdictions introducing DSTs, the design and rate of these DSTs, and the scale of the tariff retaliation and potential subsequent tariff counter-retaliation by jurisdictions targeted by tariffs. Under stylised scenarios with 'narrow' DST implementation (i.e. only focusing on jurisdictions currently under section 301 investigation by the United States), it is estimated that the negative effect on global GDP could reach -0.1% to -0.2%. In scenarios with broader DST implementation, the negative effect on global GDP could reach -0.4% to -1.2%. The upper end of these ranges corresponds to scenarios with proportional trade retaliation, while their lower end corresponds to worst-case scenarios with trade retaliation factors going up to five times beyond proportional. In most of these scenarios, the negative effect on GDP would be significantly larger than the direct effect of Pillar One and Pillar Two on investment costs (see Figure 1.2 above).

## 1.4. Conclusion and main prospects in the context of the COVID-19 crisis

49. Overall, the analysis suggests that a consensus-based multilateral solution involving Pillar One and Pillar Two would bring significant tax revenue gains to most jurisdictions. In addition, it would lead to a more favourable environment for investment and growth than would likely be the case in the absence of an agreement by members of the Inclusive Framework, while its effects on compliance and administrative costs would depend on the exact design of Pillar One and Pillar Two.

50. More broadly, the analysis suggests that a multilateral consensus-based solution involving Pillar One and Pillar Two could provide a series of key benefits to the international tax system. It would adapt the international corporate tax system to the digital age by ensuring that the allocation of taxing rights on business profits is no longer exclusively determined by reference to physical presence. It would support a more level playing field between highly digitalised and intangible intensive MNEs and other firms, and also enhance the efficiency of global capital allocation. The proposals would likely increase tax certainty, particularly when compared to the unilateral tax measures and escalating tax and trade disputes that would likely result in the absence of a consensus-based solution. The proposals would reduce profit shifting and place a floor on tax competition, which would support the ongoing revenue needs of governments, particularly as they seek to rebuild their economies after the COVID-19 crisis. Finally, the proposals would support the long-term sustainability of the system as the importance of digitalisation and intangibles are likely to intensify further in the coming decades.

51. The full implications of the COVID-19 crisis remain uncertain at this stage. The impact assessment in this report is based on pre-crisis data. Its key messages are likely to remain valid in the post-crisis environment, with nuances discussed in Box 1.2 below. Looking ahead, the COVID-19 crisis will likely

make it even more pressing to address the tax challenges arising from the digitalisation of the economy, for three main reasons:

i. The crisis is accelerating the digitalisation of the economy, making the tax challenges from digitalisation even more acute.
ii. The crisis will lead to a sharp deterioration of public finances in most countries, which will raise questions about how to support tax revenues once the post-crisis recovery is firmly on track.
iii. As many firms are receiving government support during the crisis and many members of society will be asked to make additional contributions and sacrifices to the collective efforts in the context of the crisis, there is likely to be even less tolerance of aggressive tax planning by MNEs than before the crisis.

52. All this suggests that, in the absence of a consensus-based solution, uncoordinated and unilateral tax measures would become even more likely than in the pre-crisis environment. In turn, the negative effects of the ensuing tax and trade disputes would undermine investment and activity at a moment when the global economy is at its most fragile due to the crisis, which could compound the negative effects of the crisis and hinder the recovery prospects.

### Box 1.2. Implications of the COVID-19 crisis for the impact of the proposals

The COVID-19 crisis will affect firms, economies and governments in ways that could modify the expected impact of the proposals, primarily in the short term, but also in the longer term. The full impact of the COVID-19 crisis remains highly uncertain at this stage, but a few likely implications already stand out.

In the short term, the economic crisis is having a strong negative effect on the profitability of most MNEs, reflecting declining consumer demand as well as difficulties with production (e.g. locked-down workers, restrictions on travel, supply chain disruptions). There are some exceptions, including highly-digitalised MNEs that are benefitting from the increasing reliance on digital technologies.

Overall, lower MNE profitability will reduce the amount of residual profit available for reallocation under Pillar One, as fewer MNEs will have profitability above the profitability threshold percentage. It would also reduce the global amount of low-taxed profit and the expected revenue gains under Pillar Two. These effects should largely dissipate over time, as economies and MNE profits recover from the crisis. The timing of the recovery in expected revenue gains from the Pillar One and Pillar Two proposals will depend on the shape and speed of the economic recovery. It will also depend on the design of potential loss carry-forward provisions under both pillars, as MNEs experiencing losses during the crisis could make use of these provisions to offset tax liabilities in the future.

The crisis is accelerating the trend towards the digitalisation of the economy. This will increase the relative importance of automated digital services (ADS) in the overall scope of Pillar One, as envisaged in this report. In 2016, ADS represented about one-fifth of the residual profit of MNEs in the envisaged scope of Pillar One. This share was already on a fast-growing trajectory before the crisis. For example, the residual profit of the top 10 MNEs in ADS sectors was 30% higher in 2019 than 2016. In addition, given that MNEs with a heavy reliance on intangible assets and with highly-digitalised business models generally have more possibilities to shift profits to low-tax jurisdictions than other MNEs, accelerating digitalisation could also increase the revenue effects of Pillar Two.

Finally, the crisis may bring or accelerate other structural economic changes, including potential changes in the sectoral structure of economies, the organisation of global value chains and the competition dynamics among firms. The nature and magnitude of these changes is difficult to anticipate with certainty, but they could also have implications for the long-term impact of the proposals.

## References


Hanappi, T. and A. González Cabral (2020), "The impact of the pillar one and pillar two proposals on MNE's investment costs : An analysis using forward-looking effective tax rates", *OECD Taxation Working Papers*, No. 50, OECD Publishing, Paris, https://dx.doi.org/10.1787/b0876dcf-en. [5]

Millot, V. et al. (2020), "Corporate Taxation and Investment of Multinational Firms: Evidence from Firm-Level Data", *OECD Taxation Working Papers*, No. 51, OECD Publishing, Paris, https://dx.doi.org/10.1787/9c6f9f2e-en. [6]

OECD (2020), *Corporate Tax Statistics*, OECD Publishing, Paris, https://www.oecd.org/tax/beps/corporate-tax-statistics-database.htm. [4]

OECD (2020), *Tax Challenges Arising from Digitalisation – Report on Pillar One Blueprint: Inclusive Framework on BEPS*, OECD/G20 Base Erosion and Profit Shifting Project, OECD Publishing, Paris, https://dx.doi.org/10.1787/beba0634-en. [1]

OECD (2020), *Tax Challenges Arising from Digitalisation – Report on Pillar Two Blueprint: Inclusive Framework on BEPS*, OECD/G20 Base Erosion and Profit Shifting Project, OECD Publishing, Paris, https://dx.doi.org/10.1787/abb4c3d1-en. [2]

OECD/G20 Inclusive Framework on BEPS (2019), *Programme of Work to Develop a Consensus Solution to the Tax Challenges Arising from the Digitalisation of the Economy, OECD/G20 Inclusive Framework on BEPS*, https://www.oecd.org/tax/beps/programme-of-work-to-develop-a-consensus-solution-to-the-tax-challenges-arising-from-the-digitalisation-of-the-economy.pdf. [3]


## Notes

[1] Global CIT revenues are estimated to represent about USD 2.5 trillion in 2019. This is based on OECD and IMF data on CIT revenues in 2016 (the year with best geographic coverage of CIT revenues, with more than 120 jurisdictions covered), extrapolations based on the median ratio of CIT revenues to GDP (i.e. 2.7%) in jurisdictions not covered in OECD or IMF data, and World Bank data on nominal global GDP growth between 2016 and 2019 (assuming a constant ratio of global CIT revenues to global GDP).

[2] Gains from the US GILTI regime are based on *ex ante* estimates from the US Joint Committee on Taxation. See Chapter 3 for more details.

[3] For the purpose of this paper, user/market jurisdictions (henceforth "market jurisdictions") are jurisdictions where an MNE group sells its products or services or, in the case of highly digitalised businesses, provides services to users or solicits and collects data or content contributions from them.

[4] This USD 500 billion estimate assumes illustratively that the MNE groups in scope of Amount A would be those with revenues above a global revenue threshold of EUR 750 million, profitability above a profitability threshold percentage of 10% (based on the ratio of profit before tax to turnover) and activities in ADS and CFB. Estimates based on other potential assumptions on the parameters of Amount A are presented in Chapter 2.

[5] Global blending, which is more difficult to model with the available data, would bring less revenues than jurisdictional blending for a given level of minimum tax rate, as it would allow MNEs to use high-taxed profit in certain jurisdictions to 'offset' low-taxed profit in other jurisdictions.

[6] In particular, it is illustratively assumed in this report that an MNE group that claims the benefit of the carve-out would be required to make a corresponding and proportional adjustment to the covered taxes for the calculation of the ETR. The alternative option (i.e. not making a corresponding and proportional adjustment to the covered taxes) would be difficult to model with the available data. See Chapter 3 for more details.

[7] High income jurisdictions are likely to see higher amounts of residual profit allocated to them under Amount A, but they already have taxing rights over some residual profit of in-scope MNE groups, and will see their taxing rights over these profits reduced where they are reallocated to other jurisdictions under Amount A. Hence, the overall revenue gains from Amount A are estimated to be on average lower for high income jurisdictions than for low and middle income jurisdictions.

[8] In this report, investment hubs are defined as jurisdictions with a total inward FDI position above 150% of GDP. Many of them have relatively low statutory and/or effective tax rates on corporate profit. The jurisdiction groups considered in this report (i.e. high, middle and low income jurisdictions) exclude investment hubs.

[9] The lower sensitivity may also relate to tax planning behaviour, which is expected to be reduced by the proposals.

# 2 Tax revenue effects of Pillar One

## 2.1. Introduction

53. This chapter presents the analytical framework and data sources used by the OECD Secretariat to assess the effect on corporate tax revenues of Pillar One. It focuses exclusively on the effect of Amount A described in the Pillar One Blueprint report (OECD, 2020[1]). The impacts of Amount B and of the processes to improve tax certainty are not modelled due to limitations of the available data, as further discussed below.

54. A number of design elements and parameters of Pillar One will be the subject of future decisions by the Inclusive Framework. The analytical framework presented in this chapter aims to be sufficiently flexible to explore the implications of a range of design and parameter options. The options considered in this chapter are only illustrative examples and should not be seen as prejudging any final decisions to be taken by the Inclusive Framework.

55. The framework presented in this chapter has a wide geographic coverage, spanning more than 200 jurisdictions, reflecting the global nature of the proposals and the wide membership of the Inclusive Framework. To enable this wide coverage, the framework combines a variety of micro- and macro-level data sources into a consistent structure, including a set of matrices that are described in Chapter 5. The framework relies as much as possible on micro-data, and uses among other sources an extensive dataset of the financial accounts of more than 27,000 multinational enterprise (MNE) groups from different sources (ORBIS, Worldscope, etc.), including all major highly-digitalised firms. Extensive benchmarking has been undertaken to ensure consistency across the data sources used in the analysis.

56. While the framework is building on the best data sources available to the OECD Secretariat, it is nevertheless subject to a number of important data and modelling caveats:

- The analysis only focuses on Amount A of Pillar One, leaving aside the potential effects of Amount B and of the improved tax certainty processes through innovative dispute prevention and dispute resolution mechanisms (Tax certainty component), which are difficult to assess due to limitations of the data available to the OECD Secretariat as well as methodological challenges.
    - More specifically, modelling Amount B would require a comprehensive cross-country dataset of entity level data combining information on (i) the nature of the activities of each entity (to identify entities performing baseline distribution and marketing functions that would be in scope of Amount B) and (ii) their financial information (to quantify the effect of applying Amount B). A qualitative assessment suggests that Amount B could reduce administration costs for governments and increase tax certainty for taxpayers, and may be of particular benefit to jurisdictions with low administrative capacity. Where the fixed return for baseline and marketing functions exceeds current returns taxable in market jurisdictions, Amount B would contribute to additional revenues in those jurisdictions. A number of jurisdictions with low administrative capacity assess that this is likely to be the case in their jurisdiction, as a result of the challenges they face applying the existing transfer pricing rules effectively. However, at the global level, the revenue effect of Amount B is likely to be modest, as it does not provide market jurisdictions

with a new taxing right, but is merely designed to simplify the administration of the current transfer pricing system.

- Modelling the tax revenue implications of the Tax certainty component in Pillar One (the scope of which remains subject to future decisions by the Inclusive Framework) poses methodological challenges, reflecting that this component is of a 'non-numerical' nature, in contrast with Amounts A and B, which means that it does not naturally lend itself to numerical quantification.

- The estimates do not assume that Pillar One would operate under a 'safe harbour' regime as was proposed by the United States in December 2019.
- The data underlying the analysis have limitations in terms of coverage, consistency and timeliness. Most prominently, data on MNEs' profit and its location relates to years 2016 and 2017. As a result, they pre-date significant recent developments, including the implementation of various measures under the OECD/G20 BEPS project,[1] the introduction of the US Tax Cuts and Jobs Act (TCJA) and, more recently, the COVID-19 crisis.
- The analysis relies on a number of simplifying assumptions about the design of Amount A, reflecting the challenges involved in modelling certain potential provisions of Amount A (e.g. foreign in-scope revenue threshold, business line segmentation, loss carry-forward mechanism, marketing and distribution profits safe harbour) with the available data. These simplifying assumptions on the design of Amount A could have an effect on the estimates. For example, the effect of a potential loss carry-forward mechanism is likely to be moderate in 'normal' times, but could be more significant in the aftermath of the COVID-19 crisis as some MNEs may experience substantial losses during the crisis.
- The analysis also relies on simplifications in the modelling of the effect of Pillar One, which is unavoidable given the lack of an exhaustive source of micro-level data covering MNE entities in all jurisdictions in the world. In particular, the reliance on aggregate data in certain parts of the analysis and for certain jurisdictions implies that some firm-level heterogeneities are overlooked, which could affect the results.
- The framework to assess the effect of Pillar One is 'static', in the sense that it does not take into account the effect of potential strategic reactions by MNEs and governments. This contrasts with the OECD Secretariat's revenue estimates for Pillar Two, where some behavioural reactions have been modelled in a stylised way (see Chapter 3). The reason for this difference is that behavioural reactions are likely to be more significant for Pillar Two than for Pillar One.
- The potential interaction between Pillar One and Pillar Two is not taken into account in the Pillar One estimates presented in this chapter. The interaction is modelled in the Pillar Two estimates presented in Chapter 3. The revenue effect of the interaction between Pillar One and Pillar Two is estimated to be relatively small as a share of the overall effect of the proposals.

57. Given these caveats, the estimates presented in this chapter should be interpreted as illustrating the broad order of magnitude of the impacts of Pillar One, rather than being precise point estimates. Consistent with this, revenue estimates are presented as ranges to reflect the data-related uncertainty around the estimates.

## 2.2. Overall approach to assess the revenue effects of Pillar One

58. The analysis of Pillar One in this chapter focuses exclusively on Amount A, as described in the Pillar One Blueprint report (OECD, 2020[1]). Amount A would give market jurisdictions a new taxing right over certain in-scope MNE groups with revenue above an agreed threshold. Although political decisions on the scope of Amount A have not yet been made, the analysis in this chapter has proceeded on the basis of the technical proposals to define the in-scope activities as Automated Digital Services (ADS) and Consumer Facing Businesses (CFB). Amount A would be calculated on an MNE group or segment basis

using a formula. This formula would determine a portion of the residual profit of a group or segment, defined as profit in excess of a profitability threshold that would then be apportioned between eligible market jurisdictions based on revenue. It is envisaged that this profitability threshold would be an agreed ratio of profit before tax (PBT) to turnover. Market jurisdictions would be eligible for Amount A where an MNE group meets the new nexus rules, rules that would not be dependent on the MNE group having a physical presence in a jurisdiction. Finally, to ensure that Amount A does not give rise to double taxation, it would involve a mechanism to effectively determine which jurisdiction or jurisdictions need to relieve the double taxation arising from Amount A.

59. The main steps of the approach to quantify the tax revenue effects of Pillar One are summarised in the simplified formula in Figure 2.1 and detailed in the following sections of this chapter. The approach first focuses on assessing the global residual profit of the MNE groups that would be in scope, based on an extensive dataset of consolidated financial accounts of MNE groups from the ORBIS database complemented with other sources, such as the Worldscope database (component A of the formula). This step is carried out using a variety of illustrative global revenue and profitability thresholds, focusing only on MNE groups with a primary activity in ADS or CFB. A certain percentage of residual profit (i.e. the reallocation percentage), to be defined by the Inclusive Framework, is then assumed to be reallocated to market jurisdictions (component B). Taken together, components A and B represent the total amount of global residual profit that would be reallocated to market jurisdictions under Amount A. These components are 'global' numbers focusing on all MNE groups worldwide, while the components inside the parentheses of the formula (components C to F) are jurisdiction-specific.

Figure 2.1. Simplified formula summarising the approach on Pillar One (Amount A)

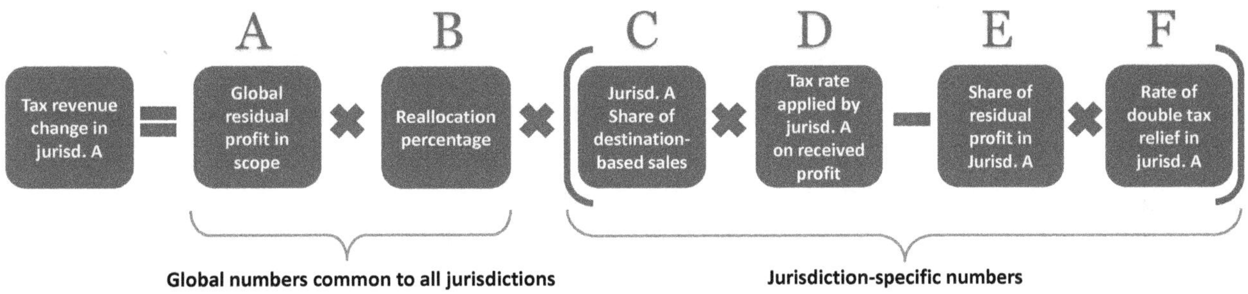


Source: OECD Secretariat.

60. Components C and D relate to the tax revenue a jurisdiction receives as a result of the reallocation of a percentage of the residual profit, and the components E and F relate to the tax revenue that it gives away in the reallocation. In both cases, the tax revenue impact is the product of a tax base effect (A*B*C and A*B*E) and the tax rate applied to it (D and F).

61. On the receiving side (components C and D), it is assumed that a jurisdiction is allocated residual profit in proportion to the share of the global sales of the MNE groups in scope that take place in its jurisdiction (as a share of global MNE sales). For internal consistency, all MNE groups in scope (including those that do not sell in the jurisdiction) are considered in the denominator (i.e. the global sales of MNEs) since all MNE groups in scope are also included in component A of the formula. The computation of component C is based on a proxy measure of MNE destination-based sales relying on (i) data from the OECD Analytical Activity of Multinational Enterprises (Analytical AMNE) database (for the location of CFB sales) and (ii) World Bank data on the number of internet users, and United Nations data on average consumption per person (for the location of ADS sales or users), as further described below. Component C takes into account the potential application of a revenue nexus test. Under such a test, no taxing rights

would be allocated to a jurisdiction under Amount A in respect of an MNE group if the revenues of this MNE group derived from that jurisdiction fall below a certain nexus threshold that would be defined by the Inclusive Framework. Several potential levels of the nexus revenue threshold are illustratively modelled, including a situation without a threshold. Finally, the tax rate applied to residual profit received as a result of any reallocation is assumed to be the statutory corporate income tax (CIT) rate (component D).

62. On the relieving side (components E and F), it is assumed that a jurisdiction would provide 'double tax relief' in proportion to the share of global residual profit currently booked in the jurisdiction. This is a simplifying assumption as the approach to identify the entities providing double tax relief has not yet been agreed by the Inclusive Framework and could potentially be more complex (e.g. by taking into account the nature of the activities of entities and the extent to which they have contributed to the generation of residual profit). The share of residual profit located in each jurisdiction (component E) is assessed based on the 'profit matrix', which combines in a consistent framework a range of data sources, including aggregated and anonymised data from Country-by-Country Reports (CbCRs), firm-level unconsolidated account data from the ORBIS database, and extrapolations based on macroeconomic data, including foreign direct investment (FDI) data. It also relies on a 'turnover matrix', which has been developed using the same approach. Both matrices are described in more detail in Chapter 5. For the ADS sector, data from the US Bureau of Economic Analysis (BEA) on the location of profit of US MNEs are also used. The tax rate on relieved profit (component F), i.e. the rate of double tax relief, which determines the gross tax revenue loss of a jurisdiction, is assumed to be in a range between the statutory CIT rate and a lower rate. As further discussed below, the use of a range reflects that the effective tax rate currently applicable to an MNE's income in a jurisdiction and/or the amount of tax relief to be provided by that jurisdiction may be lower than the statutory CIT rate.

63. The formula in Figure 2.1 is simplified, in the sense that it does not take into account certain firm-level heterogeneities in the estimation of revenue effects at the jurisdiction level. For example, if all MNE groups having sales (or users) in a given jurisdiction have relatively high levels of global profitability, this jurisdiction will be allocated more residual profit under Amount A than if these MNE groups are relatively less profitable. This is not taken into account in the formula in Figure 2.1, which allocates residual profit to jurisdictions based on their average share in global MNE sales, regardless of the profitability of the specific MNE groups selling in the jurisdiction. A more precise approach would require entity-level data on MNE sales (or users) across all jurisdictions, which are not available to the OECD Secretariat. This simplifying assumption may significantly affect estimated revenue effects at the level of individual jurisdictions, but is unlikely to have a large effect on results at the global level or for wide groups of jurisdictions, since the approximations involved are likely to offset each other at least to some extent (e.g. if highly-profitable MNE groups sell relatively more in a given jurisdiction, they will sell relatively less in other jurisdictions compared to the average MNE group).

## 2.3. Component A: Global residual profit in scope

64. The global residual profit of MNE groups is computed as profit in excess of a certain profitability threshold percentage. The measure of profitability considered is profit before tax (PBT) divided by turnover, as measured in the consolidated financial accounts of the MNE group. For example, if an MNE group has a consolidated PBT to turnover ratio of 15% and the profitability threshold percentage is 10%, then a third of the profit of the MNE group is deemed to be residual profit. While a share of this residual profit will be subject to reallocation to market jurisdictions, it is assumed that no reallocation takes place in situations where an MNE group's profitability is below the threshold.[2]

65. As further discussed below, the assessment of global residual profit in scope is based on an extensive dataset of MNE group consolidated financial accounts, and a detailed assessment of which MNE groups would be in scope, based on the level of their global revenues (above or below a potential global

revenue threshold) and the nature of their activities (ADS, CFB or out of scope). An important caveat is that this assessment classifies each MNE group based only on its primary business activity, and does not take into account the potential implications of business line segmentation, for example if some activities of an MNE group are in scope while others are out of scope. This leads at the same time to some underestimation of global residual profit (as some MNE groups are excluded while they have some secondary activities in scope) and some overestimation of it (as some MNE groups are fully included while they have some activities out of scope). While it is not possible to quantify the implications of these two sources of inaccuracy, they can be expected to offset each other at least to some extent.

### *2.3.1. The dataset of MNE consolidated financial accounts*

66. The starting point for the analysis on global residual profit is an extensive dataset of the consolidated financial accounts of MNE groups (see Annex 2.A for a detailed description of the dataset). This dataset builds primarily on consolidated accounts from the ORBIS database. Indeed, the coverage of consolidated account data in ORBIS is generally good across countries, in contrast with unconsolidated account data, for which certain countries have weak coverage (e.g. the United States) (Tørsløv, Wier and Zucman, 2018[2]). In particular, ORBIS contains data on both listed and non-listed firms.

67. To further enhance coverage, ORBIS data has been complemented with (i) data from the Worldscope database, which contains the financial accounts of (mainly listed) firms worldwide, (ii) data from the EU Industrial R&D Investment Scoreboard, which covers the 2,500 companies with the highest level of R&D spending worldwide (Hernández et al., 2017[3]), and (iii) data from the Fortune Global 500 list (i.e. 500 firms with the highest turnover globally).

68. Extensive checks have been performed on the dataset to ensure data reliability, building on the ORBIS data expertise accumulated by the OECD Secretariat over the course of a wide range of projects. In particular, financial accounts have been cleaned with procedures in the spirit of Gal (2013[4]) and Johansson et al. (2017[5]) to identify and remove implausible values. Ownership information has been cleaned with procedures following Bajgar et al. (2019[6]) to identify missing or incorrect ownership links.

69. The final dataset of consolidated MNE group accounts comprises more than 27,000 MNE groups (Table 2.1). This dataset focuses on the whole economy and is therefore much wider than the set of MNEs that would meet the conditions to be in the envisaged scope of Pillar One, which involve having a global turnover and profitability rate above certain thresholds and activities in ADS and CFB. A comparison of the total turnover of MNEs in the sample with macro-level estimates suggests that data coverage is extensive. The combined turnover of MNE groups in the dataset is USD 51.5 trillion, which is close to the estimate of the global production of MNEs in the OECD Analytical AMNE database (USD 52.9 trillion), suggesting that the universe of MNE groups of a significant size is very well covered.[3] In addition, extensive manual checks have been undertaken to ensure that large MNE groups are adequately covered, including major digital-oriented MNE groups.

Table 2.1. Dataset of MNE groups consolidated financial accounts (all sectors)

Number of MNE groups and aggregate financial variables (USD trillion)

| | Number of MNE groups | Turnover | Tangible fixed assets | Total assets | EBIT | PBT |
|---|---|---|---|---|---|---|
| **Total in the dataset** | **27 667** | **51.5** | **21.6** | **170.2** | **4.8** | **4.1** |
| **Of which data from:** | | | | | | |
| ORBIS | 26 704 | 41.5 | 20.1 | 87.2 | 3.5 | 3.0 |
| Worldscope | 888 | 6.6 | 1.4 | 79.7 | 1.1 | 0.9 |
| Other sources (EU R&D scoreboard, Fortune Global 500 and manual additions) | 75 | 3.5 | 0.05 | 3.3 | 0.2 | 0.2 |

Note: The sample presented in this table focuses on the whole economy (combining ADS, CFB and out of scope activities) and does not take into consideration the application of a potential global revenue threshold. The total assets of MNE groups from Worldscope tend to be relatively high compared to other sources, which relates to the fact that many MNE groups from Worldscope are large financial firms with extensive financial assets. EBIT stands for earnings before interest and taxes. PBT stands for profit before tax.
Source: OECD Secretariat.

### *2.3.2. Identifying MNE groups in scope of Pillar One*

70. Although political decisions on the scope of Pillar One have not yet been made, for present purposes the identification of whether a given MNE group would be in scope of Pillar One takes into account the application of a potential global revenue threshold, as well as the nature of the group's activities (ADS, CFB or out of scope). Regarding the global revenue threshold, a variety of potential thresholds are considered, and only MNE groups with global revenues above the considered threshold are assumed to be in scope. The lack of segmented data on both a business line and geographic basis means it has not be possible to model the impact of a potential threshold for in-scope revenues, nor of a potential 'domestic business exemption' (e.g. an exception for MNEs generating almost all their revenues from their domestic market).

71. The classification of MNE groups as ADS, CFB or out of scope is based on the proposed definitions of ADS and CFB outlined in the Pillar One Blueprint report (OECD, 2020[1]). ADS is defined by recognising that "certain MNEs generate revenue from the provision of automated digital services (including revenue from the monetisation of data) that are provided on an automated and standardised basis to a large and global customer or user base and can do so remotely to customers in markets with little or no local infrastructure". The general definition of ADS is "built on two elements: (i) automated, i.e. once the system is set up the provision of the service to a particular user requires minimal human involvement on the part of the service provider; and (ii) digital, i.e. provided over the Internet or an electronic network". In particular, ADS would cover activities in a non-exhaustive "positive list" including "online advertising services; sale or other alienation of user data; online search engines; social media platforms; online intermediation platforms; digital content services; online gaming; standardised online teaching services; and cloud computing services."

72. In turn, CFB is defined as covering "businesses that generate revenue from the sale of goods and services of a type commonly sold to consumers, including those selling indirectly through intermediaries and by way of franchising and licensing."

73. Though considerable technical work has been carried out on how ADS and CFB could be defined, as outlined in the Pillar One Blueprint report, no political agreement has been reached to date on the use of these categories and their exact boundaries. Reflecting this, the classification used in this chapter should only be considered as illustrative and not prejudging the final decisions to be made by the Inclusive Framework. In addition, as discussed below, the identification of ADS and CFB in this chapter relies on

existing classifications of activities (e.g. industrial classification of economic activities) which were not designed for the purpose of identifying ADS and CFB, which may lead to some approximations (e.g. because certain categories may contain a mix of ADS, CFB and out-of-scope activities).

74. The classification of MNE groups in this chapter, based on their primary business activity, is done in three steps:

- **Step 1: By using the UNCTAD list of the top digital and ICT MNEs** (UNCTAD, 2017[7]). The UNCTAD list classifies 200 digital oriented MNE groups into 14 categories (e.g. search engines, social networks, IT devices). The classification of these categories as ADS, CFB or out of scope, based on the Inclusive Framework proposed definition of ADS and CFB, is presented in Table 2.2, Panel A. The financial data from the MNE groups in the UNCTAD list is retrieved from the financial account dataset described in the previous section, in which these groups are identified manually based on their name.
- **Step 2: By applying a detailed industrial classification**. For MNE groups not included in the UNCTAD list (i.e. non digital oriented groups, as well as relatively small digital oriented groups), the classification relies on the NACE Rev. 2 nomenclature of economic activities, at the 4-digit level (Eurostat, 2008[8]). This nomenclature comprises 615 categories, which are classified as ADS, CFB or out of scope in the way presented in Table 2.2, Panel B. Information on the primary activity of the MNE groups in the dataset with respect to this nomenclature is sourced from the ORBIS database.
- **Step 3: By carrying out manual checks of the largest and most profitable MNE groups**. The aim of these manual checks is to ensure that the MNE groups with the highest levels of residual profit, and therefore the largest potential impact on the results, are properly classified. They also aim to address the issue arising from the fact that certain categories in the UNCTAD and NACE Rev. 2 classifications may contain a mix of in-scope and out-of-scope activities.[4] These manual checks are based on a variety of information sources including company websites, company annual reports, newspaper articles and other credible online sources. The extent of these checks has been extensive, including the top-500 largest MNE groups (by turnover), the top-100 MNE groups with the highest residual profit, the top-25 ADS MNE groups with the highest residual profit, and the top 3 MNE groups with highest residual profit in each industry (30 industries, based on the NACE Rev. 2 classification). Overall, these manual checks have confirmed the classification based on the two steps above for most MNE groups, and led to the reclassification of only a few MNE groups.

## Table 2.2. Identification of ADS and CFB activities

| **Panel A**: Classification based on the UNCTAD list | | | |
|---|---|---|---|
| | **ADS** | **CFB** | **Out of scope** |
| **Category in the UNCTAD list** | Search engines<br>Social networks<br>Other platforms<br>Other e-commerce<br>Games<br>IT software and services | Internet retailers<br>Digital media<br>IT devices<br>Telecom | Components<br>Electronic payments<br>Other digital solutions<br>Info and data |

| Panel B: Classification based on the industrial classification (NACE Rev. 2, at the 4-digit level) | | | |
|---|---|---|---|
| | **ADS** | **CFB** | **Out of scope** |
| **Category in the NACE Rev. 2 classification** | 58.2, 62.03, 62.09, 63.1 | 10.4, 10.5, 10.6, 10.7, 10.8, 10.92, 11, 12, 14, 15, 17.22, 18, 20.4, 21, 25.7, 26.2, 26.3, 26.4, 26.52, 26.7, 27.5, 27.9, 29.1, 30.9, 31, 32.12, 32.13, 32.2, 32.3, 32.4, 32.9, 35.13, 35.22, 35.3, 36, 37, 38.1, 45.1, 45.2, 45.32, 45.4, 47, 49.1, 49.3, 50.3, 53, 55, 56, 58.1, 59, 60, 61, 63.9, 77.11, 77.2, 79, P, Q, R, 95, 96, T | A, B, 10.1, 10.2, 10.3, 10.91, 13, 16, 17.1, 17.21, 17.23, 17.24, 17.29, 19, 20.1, 20.2, 20.3, 20.5, 20.6, 22, 23, 24, 25.1, 25.2, 25.3, 25.4, 25.5, 25.6, 25.9, 26.1, 26.51, 26.6, 26.8, 27.1, 27.2, 27.3, 27.4, 28, 29.2, 29.3, 30.1, 30.2, 30.3, 30.4, 32.11, 32.5, 33, 35.11, 35.12, 35.14, 35.21, 35.23, 38.2, 38.3, 39, F, 45.31, 46, 49.2, 49.4, 49.5, 50.1, 50.2, 50.4, 51, 52, 62.01, 62.02, K, L, M, 77.12, 77.3, 77.4, 78, 80, 81, 82, O, 94, U |

Note: The categories are identified as ADS, CFB or out of scope based on the proposed definition of ADS and CFB in the Pillar One Blueprint report (OECD, 2020[1]). This classification should be seen as nothing more than illustrative, given that no political agreement has been reached to date on the use of these categories and their exact boundaries. In addition, certain categories in the table may contain a mix of ADS, CFB and out of scope activities.The UNCTAD categories are taken from a classification of the top-100 digital and top-100 ICT MNEs (UNCTAD, 2017[7]). The industrial classification is NACE Rev. 2 at the 4 digit level (Eurostat, 2008[8]). This classification contains 615 categories (called 'classes'). The information in this table is presented at the level of classes, or at a higher level of aggregation ('divisions' or 'groups') when all classes in a division or a group are in the same category (ADS, CFB or out of scope).
Source: OECD Secretariat.

### *2.3.3. Estimates of global residual profit*

75. Based on the data presented in the previous sections, it is possible to compute the amount of global residual profit in scope of Amount A of Pillar One for a variety of global revenue and profitability thresholds. The results for an illustrative set of thresholds are presented in Table 2.3.

76. One insight from these results is that the amount of global residual profit declines only relatively slowly when higher global revenue thresholds are considered, reflecting that an important share of residual profit is concentrated among relatively large MNE groups (Panel A). In contrast, the amount of global residual profit in scope declines relatively rapidly when higher profitability thresholds are considered (Panel B).

### *2.3.4. Developments of global residual profit over time and impact of COVID-19 crisis*

77. The results in Table 2.3 are based on underlying data focusing on year 2016, reflecting the lack of availability of a more timely set of comprehensive firm-level data at the time of this analysis. As a result, the estimates in Table 2.3 do not take into account recent and ongoing developments that can affect the amount of residual profit in ADS and CFB activities, such as the trend towards digitalisation of the economy and the implications of the COVID-19 crisis. While the general conclusions above on the sensitivity of global residual profit to the Pillar One parameters considered can be expected to remain valid, the overall amount of global residual profit is likely to have evolved in recent years and to continue evolving in the future.

### Table 2.3. Global residual profit for a variety of thresholds

**Panel A:** Global residual profit for a range of global revenue thresholds

| Global revenue threshold | Global residual profit in scope (in USD billion) | | | | | |
|---|---|---|---|---|---|---|
| | ADS | | CFB | | **Total (ADS + CFB)** | |
| | 10% profitability threshold | 20% profitability threshold | 10% profitability threshold | 20% profitability threshold | **10% profitability threshold** | **20% profitability threshold** |
| **No threshold** | 83 | 38 | 433 | 145 | **516** | **183** |
| **EUR 100m** | 83 | 37 | 430 | 144 | **513** | **181** |
| **EUR 300m** | 82 | 37 | 424 | 142 | **506** | **179** |
| **EUR 500m** | 81 | 37 | 417 | 139 | **498** | **176** |
| **EUR 750m** | 81 | 37 | 413 | 138 | **493** | **174** |
| **EUR 1bn** | 80 | 36 | 407 | 135 | **487** | **171** |
| **EUR 2bn** | 78 | 36 | 388 | 129 | **466** | **165** |
| **EUR 5bn** | 74 | 35 | 341 | 112 | **415** | **147** |

**Panel B:** Global residual profit for a range of profitability thresholds

| Profitability threshold | **Global residual profit in scope (USD billion)**, assuming a EUR 750m global revenue threshold | | |
|---|---|---|---|
| | ADS | CFB | **Total** |
| **8%** | 90 | 513 | **604** |
| **10%** | 81 | 413 | **493** |
| **15%** | 58 | 230 | **288** |
| **20%** | 37 | 138 | **174** |
| **25%** | 18 | 85 | **103** |

Note: Panel A explores the implication of different global revenue thresholds for two potential profitability thresholds (10% and 20%). Panel B explores the implications of a wider variety of profitability thresholds while assuming a EUR 750 million global revenue threshold. Global revenue thresholds are defined in EUR (while most other data in the analysis are in USD) for comparability with the revenue threshold for country-by-country reporting, which is defined in EUR. The data underlying the estimates in both panels focus on year 2016. Residual profit is computed as profit in excess of a certain profitability threshold percentage, which is defined as profit before tax (PBT) to turnover, based on the consolidated financial accounts of the MNE group considered. In both panels, only MNE groups with a primary activity in ADS and CFB sectors are included. The fact that MNE groups may have different business lines or units operating in different sectors is not taken into account.
Source: OECD Secretariat.

78. In particular, the longstanding trend towards digitalisation of the economy is likely to lead to further rapid increases in demand for ADS. This could translate into higher levels of residual profit in ADS, especially given the fact that markets for certain digital activities (e.g. online advertising) are concentrated among a few global players with low marginal costs and relatively high profitability rates, due notably to

the winner-takes-most nature of certain digital activities involving strong network effects. In such markets, growth in consumer demand seems more likely to translate into higher residual profit than in markets with higher marginal costs and lower concentration. Reflecting these trends, a simple analysis focusing on the (manually retrieved) financial accounts of the top-10 MNEs with the highest levels of residual profit in 2016 among MNEs with a primary activity in the ADS sector suggests that their residual profit has increased by 30% on average between 2016 and 2019.

79. The impact of the COVID-19 crisis on global residual profit is more difficult to anticipate at this stage as the crisis is still unfolding and the data available for analysis is very limited. For many MNEs in the CFB sector, the crisis is likely to have a strong negative impact on profitability at least in the short to medium term, reflecting the negative impact of the crisis on consumer demand as well as potential difficulties with production (e.g. locked-down workers, supply chain disruptions, restrictions on travel). The longer term effect of the crisis on profitability among MNEs in the CFB sector will depend on the shape of the economic recovery, as well as potential structural changes to the economy that the crisis may bring or accelerate (e.g. changes in the sectoral structure of economies, the structure of global value chains and competition dynamics among firms). Among MNEs in the ADS sector, the impact of the COVID-19 crisis has been heterogeneous, but overall it seems at this stage to have been less negative than in CFB. While certain ADS activities have been hit hard by the crisis (e.g. ride hailing and accommodation sharing platforms) or at least moderately affected (e.g. online advertising), others have tended to benefit from increased demand (e.g. cloud computing, video streaming, video conferencing facilities, online marketplaces). Overall, notwithstanding the high degree of uncertainty about the impact of the COVID-19 crisis, the developments so far suggest that the crisis could further increase the relative share of ADS in the overall envisaged scope of Pillar One.

80. Another limitation of using data for a single year (namely 2016) is that the results do not take into account the potential effects of a loss carry-forward mechanism in Pillar One. The exact design of such a mechanism remains to be defined by the Inclusive Framework. The possibility for MNE groups to use past losses to offset some or all of their Amount A tax liability would reduce the amount of residual profit allocated under Pillar One. The reduction in residual profit would be larger if it were agreed that the loss carry-forward mechanism should account for profit shortfalls (i.e. prior periods where profitability falls below the agreed profitability threshold) rather than losses.

81. In 'normal' times, the effect of including a loss carry-forward mechanism in Pillar One is likely to be moderate, given that it is relatively rare that MNE groups switch rapidly from a loss position to a profitability rate above the potential profitability thresholds considered in this chapter. For example, among MNE groups with a profitability rate above 10% in 2016, only 9% of groups have made losses in at least one of the three preceding years.[5] Another 32% have made no loss but have had a profit shortfall (i.e. profitability rate below 10%) in at least one of the three preceding years. The remaining 59% have had a profitability rate consistently above 10% over the three preceding years.

82. However, the share of firms making losses tends to increase during economic recessions, especially severe ones. As a result, the number of MNE groups switching from making losses to having high profitability is likely to be higher in the years following recessions than after periods of economic growth. This is particularly relevant in the current situation, since many MNE groups are likely to suffer significant losses as a result of the COVID-19 crisis. As a result, the design of a loss carry-forward mechanism in Pillar One (which is still to be determined by the Inclusive Framework) could have significant implications for the revenue impacts of Pillar One, at least in the short and medium term, particularly if "pre-regime" losses incurred during the COVID-19 crisis were included in the mechanism.

### *2.3.5. Firm-level concentration of residual profit*

83. A closer analysis of the firm-level data reveals that global residual profit tends to be concentrated among a relatively small number of MNE groups. For example, assuming a EUR 750m global revenue

threshold and a 10% profitability threshold percentage, about 85% of global residual profit in ADS would be concentrated among 10 MNE groups and about 70% of global residual profit in CFB would be concentrated among 50 MNE groups.

## 2.4. Component B: Percentage of residual profit reallocated to market jurisdictions

84. The percentage of residual profit reallocated to market jurisdictions (i.e. the reallocation percentage) has not yet been determined by the Inclusive Framework. Figure 2.2 presents the amount of allocable residual profit for an illustrative set of reallocation percentages (10%, 20%, 30%) and across a variety of profitability thresholds. As such, the figure illustrates the combined effects of these two parameters. For example, it shows that the amount of global residual profit would be slightly higher under a scenario with a 10% profitability threshold and a 20% reallocation percentage than under a scenario with a 15% profitability threshold and a 30% reallocation percentage.

### Figure 2.2. Allocable global residual profit for different reallocation percentages

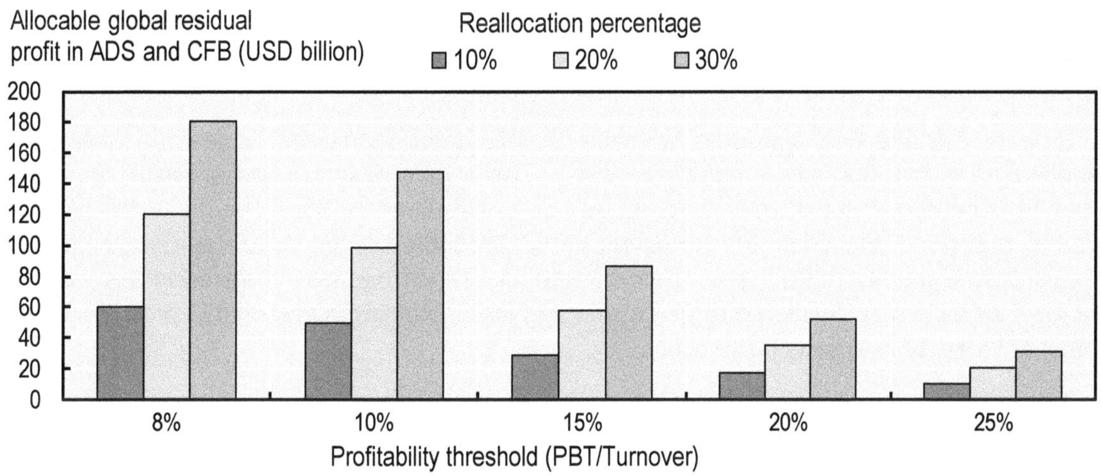


Note: These estimates are derived by multiplying the estimates of global residual profit in scope (Table 2.3, Panel B) by the allocation percentage considered. Consistent with Table 2.3, Panel B, the estimates assume a global revenue threshold of EUR 750 million and focus only on MNE groups with a primary activity in the ADS and CFB sectors.
Source: OECD Secretariat.

## 2.5. Component C: Share of jurisdiction in global MNE sales

85. According to the Pillar One Blueprint report, the right to tax profits allocated under Amount A of Pillar One would be distributed amongst eligible market jurisdictions according to an allocation key, which would be "based on locally sourced in-scope revenue determined by applying the rules on scope, nexus and revenue sourcing". A set of "revenue sourcing rules" is outlined in the Pillar One Blueprint report, taking into account the specificities of the different business models associated with the activities in the scope of Pillar One. For example, for certain ADS activities such as online advertising, sourcing rules will deem revenue to arise in the jurisdiction where the user is located (e.g. where the advertising is viewed rather than the jurisdiction where the advertising is purchased, which may be different). In the case of CFB goods

sold through independent distributors, sourcing rules will deem revenue to arise in the jurisdiction of the place of final delivery of the goods to the consumer.

86. The concept of "locally sourced in-scope revenues" broadly corresponds to the concept of "destination-based sales" that is commonly discussed in the economic literature. This latter expression is used in the remainder of this chapter and should be understood as being equivalent to the notion of "locally sourced in-scope revenues" (including regarding the location of users when relevant).

87. Identifying with precision the location of MNE destination-based sales according to the definition outlined in the Pillar One Blueprint report poses a number of conceptual and data challenges that are discussed in the next section. In light of these challenges, the approach in this chapter, which is further detailed below, is to compute proxy measures of the global distribution of MNE destination-based sales in ADS and CFB activities at a relatively aggregate level. In the case of CFB, the approach relies on data from the OECD Analytical AMNE database, which are available across more than 50 jurisdictions. For jurisdictions where Analytical AMNE data are not available, extrapolations based on widely available and relevant macroeconomic indicators (e.g. GDP, GDP per capita, trade openness) are used.

88. The data used to proxy for CFB sales are not well suited to assessing the location of remote digital sales. Reflecting this, a more targeted approach is used for ADS sales (the general approach employed for CFB sales being also tested as a robustness check). This approach is based on data on the number of regular internet users per jurisdiction, combined with data on the average consumption per person, as further described below. These indicators are widely available (more than 200 jurisdictions are covered). Extrapolations based on macroeconomic variables are employed to extend the coverage to the few non-covered jurisdictions.

89. Both in ADS and CFB, the proxy indicator of MNE destination-based sales in a jurisdiction is not used in absolute terms, but only in relative terms, i.e. as a percentage of global MNE sales, which are computed by summing the indicator used across all jurisdictions.[6] This is because the analysis only requires the use of an allocation key to distribute the allocable residual profit across jurisdictions (i.e. component C in Figure 2.1). This is an important consideration because measuring the exact *level* of relevant MNE sales in a jurisdiction is more challenging than obtaining a reasonable proxy measure of the *distribution* of these sales across jurisdictions.

### *2.5.1. Main challenges to defining and measuring MNE destination-based sales*

90. The stylised example in Figure 2.3 illustrates some of the challenges involved in defining and measuring MNE destination-based sales. In this example, the destination-based sales of MNE Group A in jurisdiction J may include, fully or in part, (i) sales from MNE Group A entities located in J to third-party entities in J (red arrow) and (ii) direct sales into J from MNE Group A entities located in other jurisdictions (red dotted arrow). These direct sales may include remote digital sales into J (related to ADS activities, e.g. subscription to an online streaming service). They may also include direct export of physical CFB products to consumers or third-party firms in J. The extent to which these remote physical sales would give rise to nexus and be considered in the allocation under Amount A will ultimately depend on decisions to be taken by the Inclusive Framework. The Pillar One Blueprint report suggests that remote physical sales would generally not be considered unless the MNE group has a sufficient degree of engagement with the relevant market jurisdiction. The exact criteria to assess this level of engagement will be the subject of future decisions by the Inclusive Framework. For both ADS and CFB sales, another factor to determine if remote sales give rise to nexus is the potential nexus revenue threshold, as discussed further in Section 2.5.4 below.

Figure 2.3. Stylised example on destination-based sales

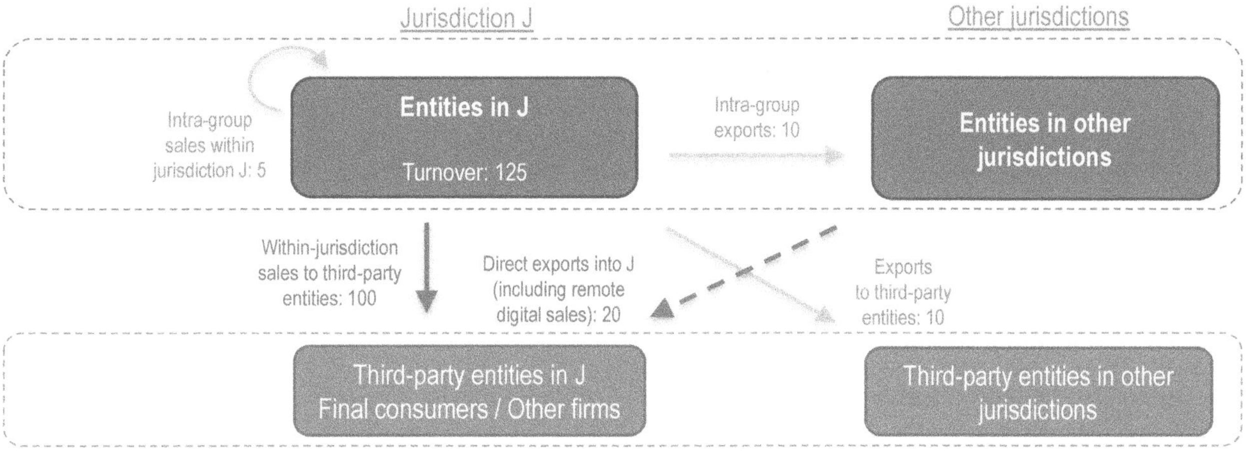


Note: This stylised example illustrates the different product flows between entities in a given MNE group (group A) and third party entities (final consumers or other firms), for the purpose of identifying destination-based sales into a certain jurisdiction (jurisdiction J). These destination-based sales may include both within-J sales (red arrow) and some (physical or digital) remote sales into J (red dotted arrow).
Source: OECD Secretariat.

91. Measuring MNE destination-based sales poses a number of data challenges. First, data available to the OECD Secretariat lacks sufficient granularity to identify the location of the sales of individual MNE groups, meaning that the analysis has to rely on relatively aggregated data. This comes at the cost of overlooking potential effects related to heterogeneities across MNE groups (e.g. if MNE groups with high residual profit would tend to sell their products in different jurisdictions than MNE groups with low or no residual profit). In addition, data on remote digital sales, or the location of users of digital services, are scarce and of uneven quality, as further discussed below. Even for physical goods, available data in most jurisdictions generally does not allow for exports to third parties to be distinguished from exports to related parties. Finally, the available data does not allow the location of final consumers of products sold by MNEs to be observed when sales go through intermediaries, such as retailers. Reflecting all these challenges, the approach in this chapter is to build proxy measures for the distribution of CFB and ADS sales based on relatively aggregated data.

### *2.5.2. The proxy measure of MNE destination-based sales in CFB*

#### *Proxy of CFB sales considered and limitations*

92. The proxy measure of the destination-based sales of CFB MNEs into a jurisdiction that is used in this chapter is the turnover of MNE entities in this jurisdiction, minus the exports by MNE entities from this jurisdiction (Figure 2.4). This proxy builds on the data available on CFB MNE turnover and exports in the OECD Analytical AMNE database, as further described below. In the example of Figure 2.3, this proxy would correspond, for the MNE Group A, to the turnover of Group A entities in jurisdiction J (125), minus their exports to related-party entities (10) and to third-party entities (10). The proxy would therefore equal 125-10-10=105.

Figure 2.4. Approach to proxy CFB destination-based sales

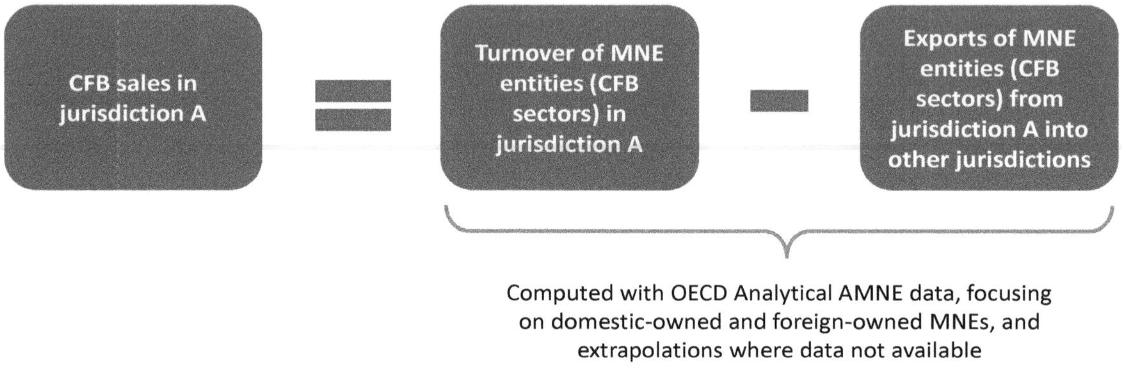


Note: CFB sectors are identified based on the NACE Rev. 2 classification and the assumptions presented in Table 2.2.
Source: OECD Secretariat

93. This measure is arguably a better proxy of CFB destination-based sales than measures based on data on origin-based sales (e.g. US BEA data on the sales of US MNEs) or more aggregated measures that do not distinguish MNE and non-MNE sales (e.g. household consumption in national accounts). Nevertheless, it suffers from several limitations:

- In theory, intra-group sales within jurisdiction J (equal to 5 in the stylised example above) should also be subtracted from the proxy measure. In practice, the available data makes this difficult since turnover data in the Analytical AMNE database is not net of intra-group sales. This issue is likely to be of limited significance: for example, within-country intra-group sales represent only about 9% of sales among US affiliates abroad according to data on the foreign activity of US multinationals published by the US BEA.[7] Robustness checks using alternative proxies not affected by this issue (e.g. subtracting intermediate consumption from the proxy) provide broadly similar results overall.[8]
- Remote sales (i.e. the red dotted arrow in Figure 2.3), both digital and physical, are not included in this proxy measure of CFB destination-based sales. More precisely, in the proxy measure used in this chapter, remote sales are not included at their point of origin, as they are counted in turnover but subtracted when subtracting exports, and they are not included either at their point of destination. As the focus of this section is on CFB, the omission of remote digital sales (which would mainly fall in the ADS sector) is unlikely to affect significantly the results (a different method is used to proxy ADS sales, as discussed below). Regarding remote physical sales, the significance of the omission will depend on design choices to be made by the Inclusive Framework, as discussed above, on the degree of market engagement that would be necessary to give rise to nexus. In any case, it is likely that the location of remote physical sales is broadly correlated with the location of non-remote MNE sales, in which case the impact of this omission on the measure of Component C would be small. This is because the aim of component C is to measure the *share* of each jurisdiction in global destination-based sales, rather than the absolute *level* of sales in each jurisdiction.

### *Computation of the proxy of CFB sales with Analytical AMNE data*

94. The OECD Analytical AMNE database contains data on the turnover and exports of foreign-owned MNE entities as well as domestic-owned entities (either belonging to an MNE group or not) across 59 jurisdictions (Cadestin et al., 2018[9]).[9] In addition, the database includes a split of these domestic-owned entities between MNE and non-MNE entities, which is based on 'hard' data for 16 jurisdictions and imputations for the other jurisdictions. Finally, the database offers a breakdown of these different data across 34 industries, based on the NACE Rev. 2 classification with an aggregation at the 1-or-2-digit level,

depending on the industry. CFB sectors are identified based on this industry classification, following the assumptions presented in Panel B of Table 2.2 regarding which sectors are considered CFB.[10]

95. The proxy measure of CFB destination-based sales (turnover of CFB MNEs minus exports of CFB MNEs) is computed directly from the Analytical AMNE database for these 16 jurisdictions where the split of domestic-owned entities between MNE and non-MNE entities is based on hard data (Figure 2.5). For the jurisdictions where the split is not based on hard data, the split is imputed based on the assumption that the share of domestically-owned MNEs in total CFB sales by domestically-owned firms corresponds to the average across those 16 jurisdictions (approximately 14%).[11] As an additional check, the sales based on this imputation are compared to the predictions of the regression used in the next section to extrapolate MNE destination-based sales to jurisdictions not covered in Analytical AMNE.[12]

Figure 2.5. Proxy measure of CFB destination-based sales

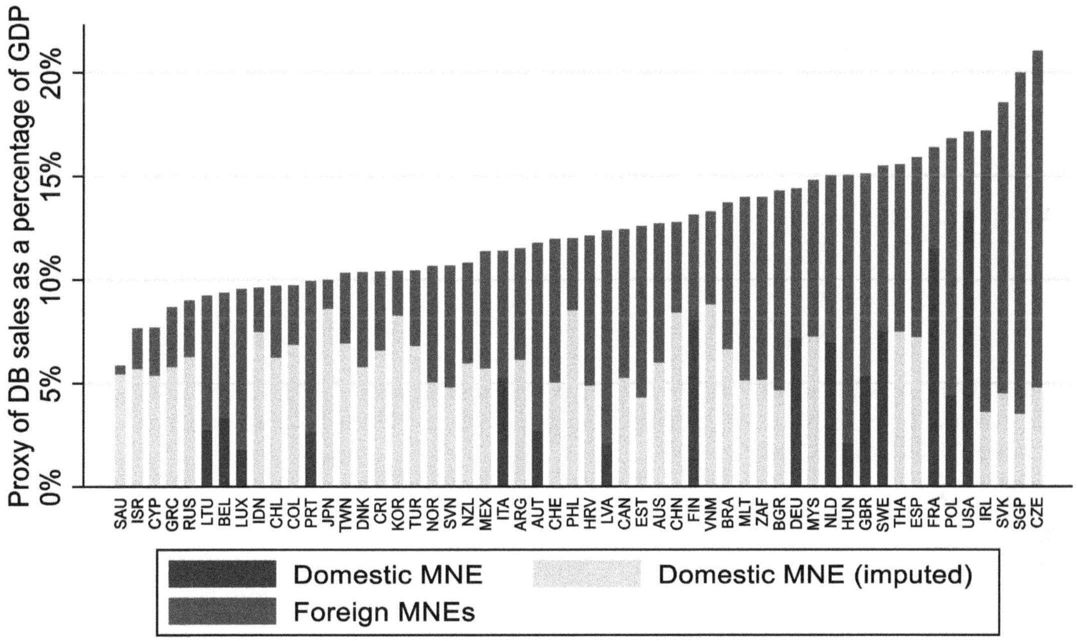


Note: This Figure presents the ratio of the proxy measure of CFB MNE destination-based sales (CFB MNE turnover minus CFB MNE exports) to GDP. The different shades of blue reflect whether the split between MNE and non-MNE entities among domestic-owned firms was based on hard data from the OECD Analytical AMNE database (dark blue bars) or was imputed (light blue bars). In the latter case, data for domestic-owned MNEs are imputed by assuming that their share in total sales by domestic firms is equal to the average among jurisdictions with hard data (i.e. jurisdictions with dark blue bars).
Source: OECD Secretariat calculations based on the OECD Analytical AMNE database.

### *Extrapolation of the proxy of CFB sales to jurisdictions not covered in Analytical AMNE*

96. The method to extrapolate the proxy measure of CFB destination-based sales of MNEs in jurisdictions where Analytical AMNE data are not available consists in regressing the proxy of destination-based sales constructed in the previous section (considering the total sales of domestic-owned plus foreign-owned MNEs) on a number of its potential macroeconomic drivers (e.g. GDP, trade openness). The regression is estimated over the jurisdictions where data are available in Analytical AMNE. The regression results are used to extrapolate destination-based sales to the other jurisdictions.

97. Regression results, which are presented in Table 2.4 suggest that CFB destination-based sales (as a share of GDP) are mainly driven by GDP, possibly because a larger market size may attract more sales from foreign-owned MNEs, and by trade openness (measured as the ratio of imports plus exports to GDP), reflecting the fact that MNE presence (both foreign and domestic) is correlated with the intensity of foreign trade. In contrast, GDP per capita and the trade balance (measured as exports less imports as a share of GDP) are not found to play a significant role once the effect of GDP and trade openness are taken into account. The specification retained for the extrapolation corresponds to the first column of the table.

## Table 2.4. Regression used for the extrapolation of CFB destination-based sales

| | Destination-based sales divided by GDP (log) | |
|---|---|---|
| **Log GDP** | 0.0874*** | 0.0840*** |
| | (3.30) | (2.88) |
| **Log GDP per capita** | -0.0314 | -0.0367 |
| | (-0.85) | (-0.97) |
| **Log Trade openness** | 0.315*** | 0.284*** |
| | (4.74) | (2.89) |
| **Trade balance (level)** | | 0.474 |
| | | (0.59) |
| **Constant** | -4.063*** | -3.937*** |
| | (-5.90) | (-5.07) |
| | | |
| **N** | 51 | 50 |
| **R-sq** | 0.33 | 0.36 |

Note: This table shows the regression results of the proxy for CFB destination-based sales presented above, as a share of GDP, on several macroeconomic variables. The results used for the extrapolation correspond to the first column. T-statistics are shown in parentheses. ***, **, *: denote significance at 1%, 5%, and 10% levels respectively.
Source: OECD Secretariat.

98. An additional adjustment is made for remittances and foreign aid. Indeed, for a given GDP level, these sources of income can increase the consumption potential (and therefore likely CFB MNE sales) in recipient countries. To take this effect into account, the ratio of destination-based sales to GDP obtained from the extrapolated regression results is multiplied by the following adjustment term: $\frac{GDP+Remittances+Foreign\ Aid}{GDP}$. Data on remittances and foreign aid are sourced from the World Bank and the OECD.[13]

### *Resulting proxy indicator of CFB destination-based sales*

99. The resulting proxy measure of CFB destination-based sales is presented in Figure 2.6. Consistent with results of the regression above, larger and more open economies tend to have relatively higher sales. It is also notable that economies with similar characteristics in terms of size, income levels and openness tend to have broadly similar levels of CFB sales (as a share of their GDP).[14]

Figure 2.6. Proxy measure of CFB destination-based sales, including extrapolation

% of GDP

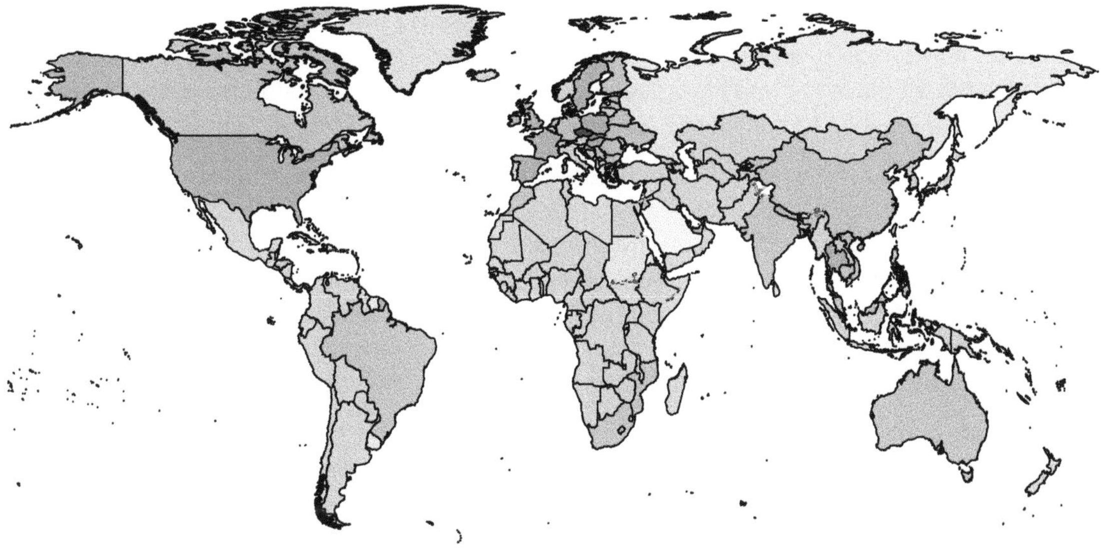


Note: Destination-based sales of CFB MNEs are proxied by CFB MNE turnover minus CFB MNE exports, using data from the OECD Analytical AMNE database. For jurisdictions not covered in the OECD Analytical AMNE database, destination-based sales are extrapolated based on a regression of CFB MNE sales on GDP, GDP per capita and trade openness. A correction is applied to take into account foreign aid and remittances, which can increase sales relative to GDP in low-income jurisdictions. CFB sales are presented as a share of GDP for comparability across jurisdictions. Grey areas correspond to missing data.
Source: OECD Secretariat.

100. To reflect the uncertainties around the proxy measure of CFB MNE destination-based sales, the results presented in the final section of this chapter integrate an uncertainty range around the share of CFB MNE destination-based sales in a jurisdiction in global CFB MNE sales. The range is defined as ±10% around the point estimate for jurisdictions covered in Analytical AMNE data, and ±20% around the point estimate for jurisdictions where the estimates are based on the extrapolation regression, reflecting that there is more uncertainty around the extrapolated values than around the values based on hard data.

### *2.5.3. The proxy measure of MNE destination-based sales in ADS*

101. The methodology employed above to assess the location of CFB sales is a priori not well suited to identifying the location of ADS consumers (or users). This is because, as discussed above, the proxy measure used (turnover of MNE entities, minus exports of MNE entities) does not capture remote sales, including remote digital sales, which represent a large share of sales in the ADS sector. One could still rely on the methodology used for CFB sales, as is done in a robustness check presented in Annex 2.D, by assuming that the distribution of remote digital sales across jurisdictions is relatively well correlated with the distribution of non-remote physical sales, but a more direct approach to measuring ADS sales seems preferable.

102. A potential approach would be to use the increasingly available data on the location of users of digital services (e.g. based on traffic on websites and mobile applications). However, the quality of these data remains uncertain and their direct use for the analysis would pose a number of methodological challenges, as discussed in Box 2.1. Overall, these data suggest that the number of users of the main digital services is relatively well correlated with internet penetration and income-per-capita levels (these two variables being strongly correlated with each other). The methodology described below is based on this insight.

## Box 2.1. Assessing the location of users of digital services

The OECD Secretariat has explored several data sources to assess the location of users of digital services, including data from Priori (on mobile application users), SEMrush (on website users) and Alexa (on both). Overall, while these data have informative value, they are still relatively untested for statistical analysis and their quality has not been judged sufficient to use them directly in the revenue estimates in this report.

Beyond data quality issues, there are other practical difficulties in assessing the location of users of MNE services and testing its effect as an allocation key for residual profit under Pillar One. One difficulty is that digital service firms can offer various services/apps simultaneously (e.g. Facebook, Instagram and WhatsApp all belong to the same MNE group) with users potentially in different locations and making varying contributions of "value". In addition, certain firms offer a combination of digital services and physical products (e.g. Apple). Finally, users can be located in multiple jurisdictions in the case of multi-sided markets (e.g. the location of the property owner and the tenant in the case of Airbnb or Booking.com).

Overall, preliminary analysis based on data from Priori, SEMrush and Alexa suggests that the location of users of large digital service providers is broadly correlated with internet penetration as well as income levels (see for example Figure 2.7 below on the correlation with income levels for two illustrative examples of services). The main exception appears to be China, where certain non-Chinese digital firms have no or limited operations and where certain Chinese digital firms operate predominantly. The "value" of users is more difficult to measure with these sources, but is also likely to depend on income levels.

### Figure 2.7. Example on the location of digital services users

Number of regular monthly users (access via iOS only) per 100 inhabitants (y-axis) and GDP per capita (x-axis)

Average over year 2018

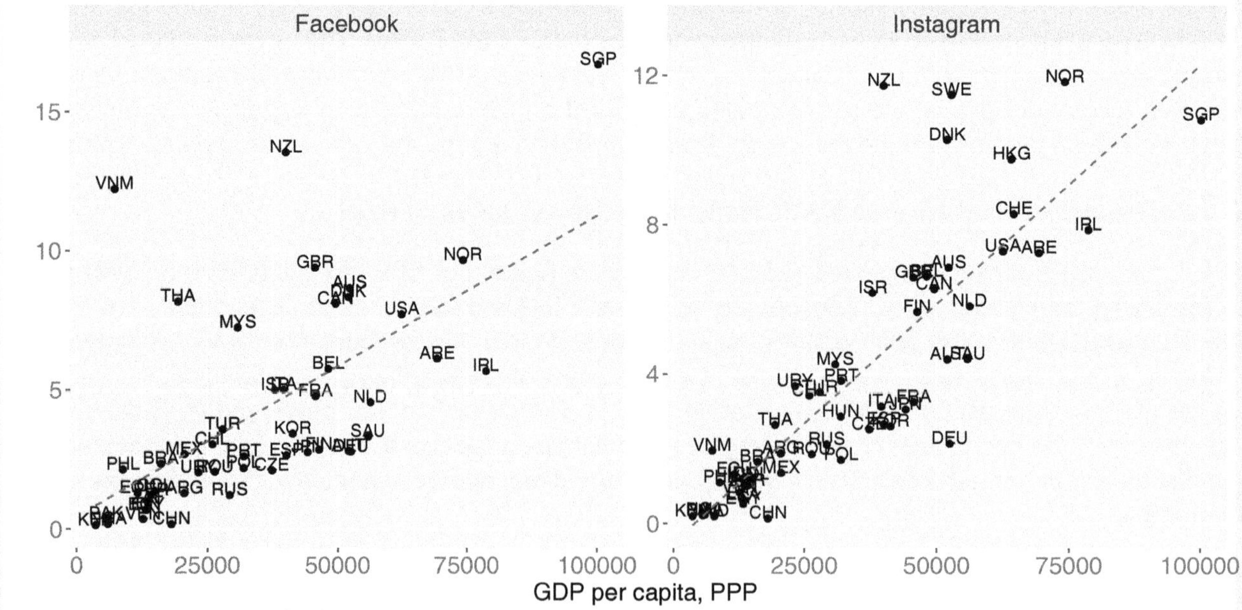


Note: Data only cover devices equipped with the iOS operating system. Therefore, they may not necessarily be representative of the frequency of use across all Internet users.

Source: OECD Secretariat calculations based on Priori data.

103. The proxy of ADS sales in a jurisdiction used as the baseline in the analysis is (i) the number of regular internet users in a jurisdiction, multiplied by (ii) the average consumption per person in the jurisdiction (as a proxy for the average consumption of an internet user), and by (iii) the weight of ADS in the average consumption basket of an internet user (Figure 2.8). The first two variables are sourced from the International Telecommunication Union and United Nations statistics respectively.[15] In the few jurisdictions where they are not available (representing less than 1.5% of world GDP for each variable), these variables are extrapolated based on GDP per capita.[16] The third variable, which is not directly observed due to lack of comprehensive cross-country data on ADS consumption, is assumed to be constant across jurisdictions. It is not necessary to make an assumption about the exact value of this constant, given that the aim of the exercise is only to measure the share of global ADS sales taking place in each jurisdiction, rather than their absolute level.

Figure 2.8. Approach to proxy ADS destination-based sales

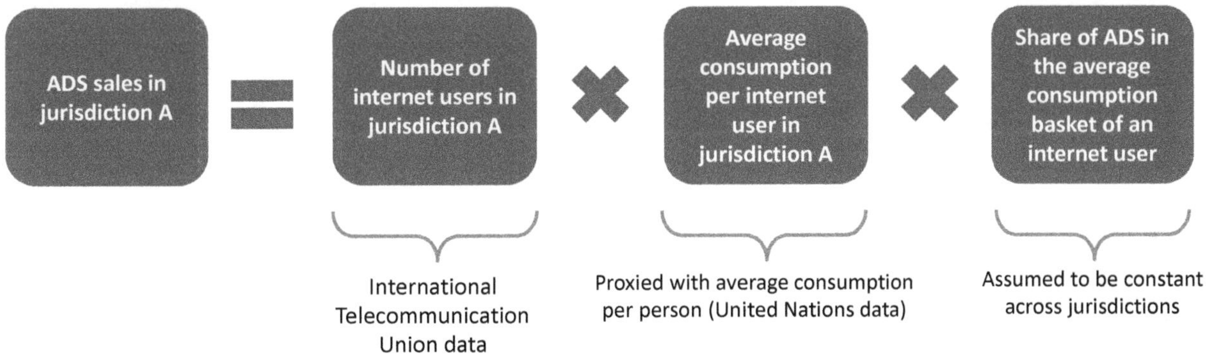


Source: OECD Secretariat

104. This proxy measure has two main limitations that are likely to partly offset each other. First, average consumption per person is measured across the whole population of the jurisdiction, rather than among the subset of its internet users. However, internet users are likely to have higher incomes and consumption levels than non-internet users. This difference may not be consequential in jurisdictions with very high internet penetration (e.g. most OECD economies), but it could lead to a significant underestimation of sales in lower-income economies where internet penetration is relatively low. The second limitation relates to the assumption that ADS represents a constant share of the consumption basket of internet users across countries. Indeed, it is likely that ADS represents a smaller fraction of the consumption basket in lower-income jurisdictions, where a number of non-service items (e.g. food, energy) tend to have a greater weight in the consumption basket than in higher-income jurisdictions. This would lead to an overestimation of sales in lower-income jurisdictions. Overall, the effects of these two limitations go in opposite directions, implying that it is difficult to assess if the proxy measure employed overstates or understates the share of ADS sales in lower-income vs. higher-income jurisdictions.

105. A sensitivity analysis presented in Annex 2.D suggests that overall Pillar One revenue estimates are not very sensitive to using an assumption resulting in lower ADS sales in lower income jurisdictions than the baseline assumption described above. Compared to the baseline, it is assumed in this sensitivity analysis that ADS sales in low income jurisdictions are divided by two, that ADS sales in middle income jurisdictions are divided by one and a half and that ADS sales in high income jurisdictions are unchanged.[17] The other sensitivity analysis presented in Annex 2.D suggests that using the methodology used for CFB sales instead of the baseline methodology presented in this section would also have relatively little effect on overall Pillar One revenue estimates.

106. The baseline proxy measure of ADS destination-based sales is presented in Figure 2.9. The overall distribution of ADS sales has similarities with that of CFB sales (Figure 2.6), but the distribution of ADS sales appears to be more strongly correlated to jurisdictions' income levels than CFB sales. Similar to CFB sales, uncertainty ranges are built around the estimates of ADS sales for the purpose of computing the Pillar One revenue effects presented in the final section of this chapter. These uncertainty ranges are defined as ±25% around the point estimate.

Figure 2.9. Proxy measure of ADS destination-based sales

ADS sales as a share of GDP, global average = 100

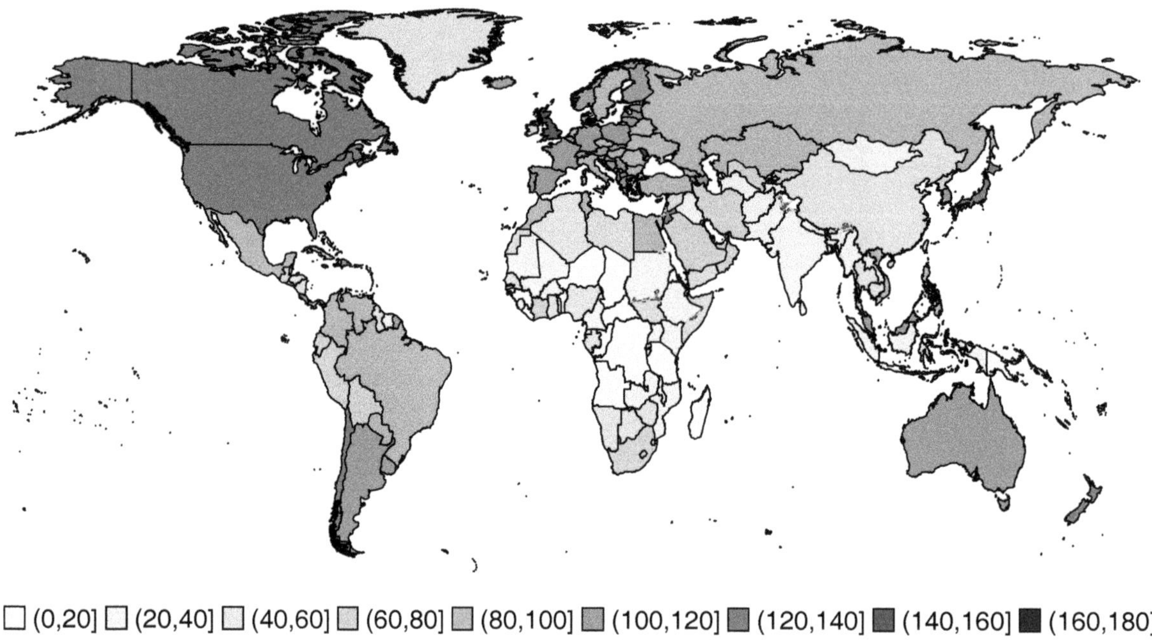


Note: Destination-based sales of ADS MNEs are proxied by (i) the number of regular internet users in a jurisdiction, multiplied by (ii) the average consumption per person in the jurisdiction (as a proxy for the average consumption of an internet user), multiplied by (iii) the weight of ADS in the average consumption basket of an internet user. ADS sales are presented as a share of GDP for comparability across jurisdictions. Their absolute level is not computed in the analysis (which focuses on the distribution across jurisdictions), which is why sales are presented relatively to the global average (GDP weighted) of the ADS sales to GDP ratio. Grey areas correspond to missing data. Data focus on year 2016.
Source: OECD Secretariat.

### *2.5.4. Modelling the effect of a potential nexus revenue threshold*

107. New nexus rules may involve a revenue threshold to define whether an MNE group has a taxable presence in a jurisdiction. Such a nexus revenue threshold would mean that the residual profit of a given MNE group would not be allocated to the jurisdictions where the total revenues of this group are below the threshold.

108. Assessing the impact of a potential nexus revenue threshold is challenging due to a lack of comprehensive entity level data on MNE sales. To overcome this challenge, a probabilistic modelling approach has been developed to approximate the effect of an illustrative range of potential nexus revenue thresholds across jurisdictions, based on repeated simulations under a set of assumptions that is described in this section. As this approach is inevitably assumption-dependent, results should be considered as illustrative of the orders of magnitude rather than precise estimates.

109. The intuition of the modelling is as follows. If all (ADS or CFB) MNE groups had sales in all jurisdictions in the world, a reasonable proxy of the sales of a given (ADS or CFB) MNE group in a given jurisdiction would be the global sales of this MNE group, multiplied by the average share of this jurisdiction in the global sales of all (ADS or CFB) MNEs. This proxy would overlook heterogeneities across MNEs, but it would nevertheless give a good indication of whether the sales of the group in a jurisdiction are likely to be above or below the nexus revenue threshold.

110. In reality, the situation is more complex, since not all MNE groups have sales in each jurisdiction. To reflect this, the approach (based on the Monte Carlo method) is to carry out many simulations assuming the presence of different MNEs in different jurisdictions and to apply the nexus revenue threshold in each simulation. Finally, the effect of the nexus revenue threshold is computed as the average effect obtained across these many simulations. A benefit of this simulation approach is that it yields estimates of the average effect of the threshold, but also estimated uncertainty ranges, which are in turn used to create the uncertainty ranges around the measure of post-nexus sales that underlie the Pillar One estimates presented in the final section of this chapter.

111. In practice, the global sales of each MNE are taken from the dataset of consolidated financial accounts (mainly based on ORBIS) used for component A of the analysis. The dataset is restricted to MNE groups with a primary activity in ADS or CFB and with global revenues above EUR 750 million. The average distribution of ADS and CFB sales across jurisdictions is taken from the estimates presented in Sections 2.5.2 and 2.5.3 above. Finally, the probability that a given (ADS or CFB) MNE group has sales in jurisdiction *j* is assumed to follow the following equation:

$$Pr(Sales\ Presence_j) = \lambda * Share\ of\ Sales_j$$

112. $Share\ of\ Sales_j$ is the share of the global sales of all (ADS or CFB) MNEs that take place in jurisdiction *j*, and $\lambda$ is a scaling parameter. The idea behind the equation is that MNE groups are more likely to be present in larger markets than in smaller ones. For example, in practice, some of the largest ADS and CFB MNEs appear to have sales (or users) in almost all jurisdictions in the world, while smaller MNEs may tend to be less present in smaller markets (e.g. developing economies). This implies that smaller markets will generally have a lower number of MNEs selling in their jurisdiction. The $\lambda$ parameter captures the strength of this propensity of MNEs to be more present in larger than smaller markets (a higher $\lambda$ would indicate a stronger propensity to favour larger markets).[18] This parameter is not directly observed, and its value has been calibrated based on observations on the subset of jurisdictions where entity-level data is available in Eurostat FATS database. The sensitivity of the results to different values of $\lambda$ has also been tested and results are broadly consistent with the baseline (see Annex 2.B).

113. In each simulation *s*, an (ADS or CFB) MNE *m* will either have some revenues in the jurisdiction *j* considered ($Sales\ Presence_{jms} = 1$), or no revenues in this jurisdiction ($Sales\ Presence_{jms} = 0$).[19] In turn, the amount of sales of this MNE in the jurisdiction *j* is proxied by multiplying the global sales of the MNE *m* by the share of jurisdiction *j* in global (ADS or CFB) sales:[20]

$$Sales_{jms} = Sales\ Presence_{jms} * MNE\ Global\ Sales_m * Share\ of\ Sales_j$$

114. If $Sales_{jms}$ is greater than the nexus revenue threshold considered, a share of the residual profit of *m* is allocated to *j*. The residual profit of *m* is computed based on the consolidated accounts of *m*, in the same way as in component A. In contrast, if $Sales_{jms}$ is below the nexus revenue threshold, no residual profit is assigned from MNE *m* to jurisdiction *j* in that simulation.

115. The simulations are repeated 200 times for each MNE-jurisdiction pair. Based on this, the average amount of allocated residual profit is computed for each MNE and jurisdiction across these 200 simulations.[21] Finally, these values are summed across all MNEs and compared to the baseline estimate of residual profit allocated to that jurisdiction in the absence of the nexus revenue threshold. The results for an illustrative set of potential nexus revenue thresholds are presented in Figure 2.10 for five broad jurisdiction groups based on economy size (see the composition of the groups in Table 2.5).

116. Overall, the effect of the revenue nexus thresholds on allocated residual profit is mainly significant in the first two groups (i.e. the smallest economies) and negligible in the last two groups (i.e. the largest economies). The magnitude of the effect among smaller economies depends significantly on the level of the threshold considered. Finally, for the thresholds considered in this chapter, the effect of the threshold on the amount of global residual profit allocated is small (reduction by less than 0.2%), implying that the threshold would not affect significantly the amount of double tax relief that would be provided by relieving jurisdictions (estimated in component E below).

### Figure 2.10. Estimated effect of a potential revenue nexus threshold on allocated profit

For revenue nexus thresholds of EUR 1m, EUR 3m and EUR 5m, compared to a situation with no threshold

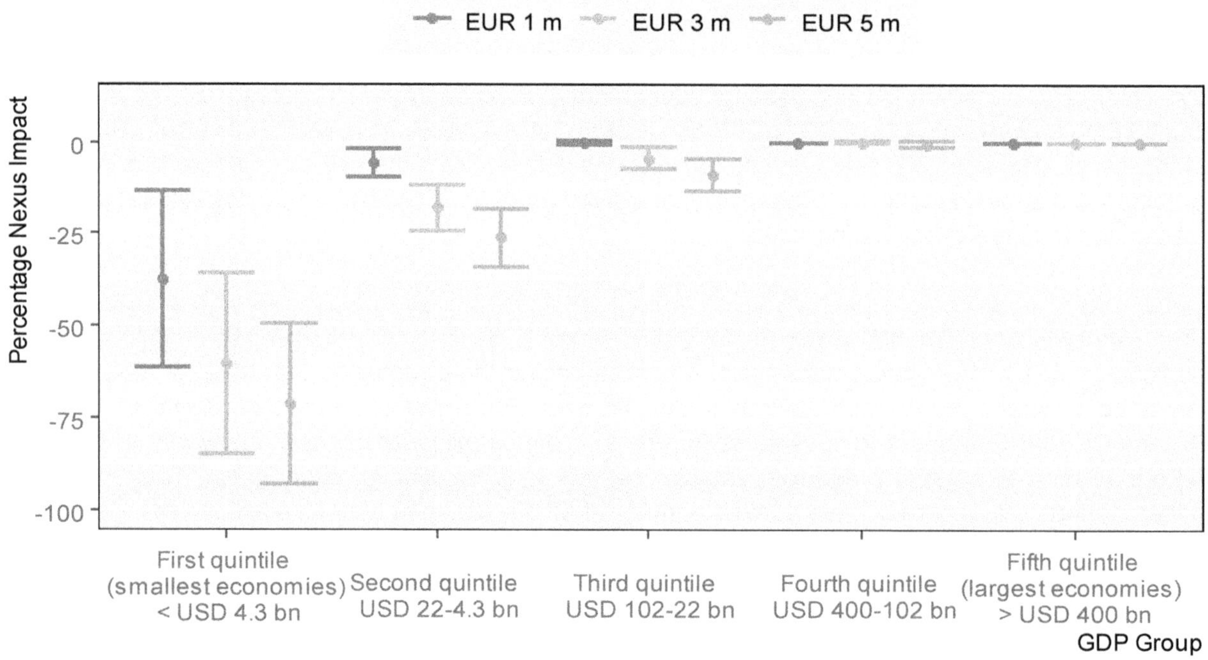


Note: For example, the application of a revenue nexus threshold of EUR 1 million is estimated to reduce the amount of allocated residual profit by 13.2% to 61.1% on average among the first group of jurisdictions (i.e. the smallest jurisdictions, which have a GDP below USD 4.3 bn, see Table 2.5) compared to a situation without revenue nexus threshold. The intervals are based on the standard deviation of results across the repeated simulations. The results presented in this Figure combine ADS and CFB results.
Source: OECD Secretariat

Table 2.5. Details of jurisdiction groupings for revenue nexus threshold results

| Jurisdiction Group by GDP Range (USD bn) | Jurisdictions in Group |
|---|---|
| First quintile (smallest economies) <4.3 bn (26 jurisdictions) | Andorra, Anguilla, Antigua and Barbuda, Aruba, Bailiwick of Guernsey, Belize, British Virgin Islands, Cabo Verde, Cayman Islands, Cook Islands, Curacao, Djibouti, Dominica, Faroe Islands, Greenland, Grenada, Liberia, Montserrat, Saint Kitts and Nevis, Saint Lucia, Saint Vincent and the Grenadines, San Marino, Seychelles, Sierra Leone, Turks and Caicos Islands |
| Second quintile 22-4.3 bn (26 jurisdictions) | Armenia, Bahamas, Barbados, Benin, Bermuda, Botswana, Brunei Darussalam, Burkina Faso, Congo, DPRK, Gabon, Georgia, Haiti, Iceland, Isle of Man, Jamaica, Jersey, Liechtenstein, Maldives, Malta, Mauritius, Monaco, Mongolia, Papua New Guinea, Senegal, Zambia |
| Third quintile 102-22 bn (26 jurisdictions) | Angola, Bahrain, Bulgaria, Cameroon, Costa Rica, Cote d'Ivoire, Croatia, Dominican Republic, DRC, Estonia, Kenya, Latvia, Lithuania, Luxembourg, Macau (China), Oman, Panama, Paraguay, Serbia, Slovak Republic, Slovenia, Sri Lanka, Trinidad and Tobago, Tunisia, Ukraine, Uruguay |
| Fourth quintile 400-102 bn (26 jurisdictions) | Austria, Chile, Colombia, Czech Republic, Denmark, Egypt, Finland, Greece, Hong Kong (China), Hungary, Ireland, Israel, Kazakhstan, Malaysia, Morocco, New Zealand, Norway, Pakistan, Peru, Portugal, Qatar, Romania, Singapore, South Africa, United Arab Emirates, Viet Nam |
| Fifth quintile (largest economies) >400 bn (25 jurisdictions) | Argentina, Australia, Belgium, Brazil, Canada, China, France, Germany, India, Indonesia, Italy, Japan, Mexico, Netherlands, Nigeria, Poland, Russia, Saudi Arabia, Spain, Sweden, Switzerland, Thailand, Turkey, United Kingdom, United States |

Note: GDP is based on 2016 GDP data.
Source: OECD Secretariat.

## 2.6. Component D: Tax rate on residual profit received

117. The assumption for the purpose of modelling in this chapter is that the residual profit allocated to a jurisdiction would be taxed at the statutory CIT rate of this jurisdiction.[22] In practice, the tax rate used in the estimates is the combined CIT rate (i.e. national plus subnational) sourced from the 2019 data from the OECD Corporate Tax Statistics database, which covers more than 90 jurisdictions (OECD, 2020[10]). For jurisdictions not covered in the OECD Corporate Tax Statistics database, other sources of data are used (namely, the International Bureau of Fiscal Documentation, KPMG, EY and the Tax Foundation).

## 2.7. Component E: Share of jurisdiction in global residual profit

118. Component E focuses on the 'relieving jurisdictions', i.e. jurisdictions from which residual profit would be taken for reallocation. In practice, it is envisaged that these jurisdictions would provide "double tax relief" to ensure that the profit allocated to other jurisdictions would not be subject to double taxation.

119. The exact design of double tax relief rules remains the subject of future decisions by the Inclusive Framework, both regarding the identification of the entities benefitting from double tax relief and whether double tax relief is provided by exempting the reallocated profits from tax or providing a tax credit for the foreign tax incurred, as discussed in the Pillar One Blueprint report. The estimates in this chapter are based on the illustrative assumption that double tax relief would be provided under the exemption method, and that jurisdictions would provide double tax relief in proportion to the share of the global residual profit of the MNE group considered that is located in their jurisdiction. As stated elsewhere in this chapter, this assumption should not be seen as prejudging any final decisions to be taken by the Inclusive Framework. Different rules on double tax relief would be difficult to model precisely with the data available to the OECD Secretariat, but they could yield different results from the estimates in this chapter.

### 2.7.1. Main challenges to assess the location of residual profit

120. Assessing the location of residual profit of ADS and CFB MNE groups across jurisdictions poses three main challenges:

- Entity-level data is only available to the OECD Secretariat for a subset of 24 jurisdictions, i.e. jurisdictions where the coverage of ORBIS unconsolidated account data is good. In other jurisdictions, only relatively aggregated data are available to the OECD Secretariat. However, trying to compute residual profit by applying a profitability threshold directly on data aggregated at the jurisdiction level would be misleading. For example, if a jurisdiction has two unrelated MNE entities of equal size, one having a 20% profitability rate and the other a 0% profitability rate, the profitability rate at the aggregate level would equal 10%. If residual profit is defined with a 10% profitability threshold, aggregate numbers taken at face value would suggest that there is no residual profit in this jurisdiction, while there is in fact residual profit in the first entity.
- Most of the data on profit location that is available to the OECD Secretariat (including anonymised and aggregated CbCR data) does not contain sectoral information, making it difficult to identify ADS and CFB MNEs from out-of-scope MNEs.
- Even once the amount of residual profit of an MNE group in each jurisdiction is identified, the share of this residual profit that would give rise to double tax relief depends on the amount of residual profit at the group-wide level, as computed based on the consolidated accounts of the group. Indeed, the sum of residual profit computed on a jurisdiction by jurisdiction basis (i.e. "bottom-up") could be different from the "top-down" measure of residual profit obtained on the consolidated accounts as described in component A above. In general, the "bottom-up" measure tends to be higher than the "top-down" measure. This is because of averaging effects, similar to those described in the first bullet point above. For example, an MNE group composed of two entities with profitability of 5% and 15% respectively could have an average profitability of 10% at the consolidated level. Using a 10% profitability threshold to define residual profit, it would have no residual profit with a "top-down" measure of profitability, but it would have some (in the second entity) using a "bottom-up" measure.[23]

### 2.7.2. Overall approach to assess the location of residual profit

121. To address these different challenges, the approach in this chapter follows a number of steps, which are summarised in Figure 2.11 and further detailed in the following sections. The ultimate goal is to build a 'residual profit matrix' mapping the amount of residual profit that would be subject to double tax relief in each jurisdiction (matrix rows) and for each jurisdiction of ultimate parent (matrix columns). For example, the France-United States cell would contain the total amount of profit of US MNEs in France that would be subject to double tax relief.

## Figure 2.11. Overview of the methodology to assess the location of residual profit

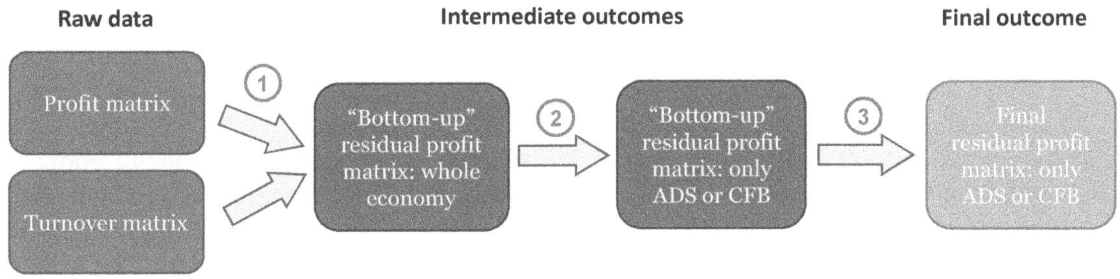


**Overview of the main steps of the methodology**

(1) For a given residual profit threshold:
- Where micro-data is available with good coverage (ORBIS), compute the share of profit that is residual directly on micro-data
- Elsewhere, compute the aggregate PBT/Turnover ratio in each matrix cell based on the profit and turnover matrices
- Based on the average relationship between this aggregate ratio and the share of profit that is residual (estimated on ORBIS data), compute residual profit in each cell

(2) Eliminate out-of-scope residual profit in each row of the residual profit matrix:
- Commodities: residual profit eliminated in proportion to the share of commodities in exports (UNCTAD data)
- Other out-of-scope sectors: residual profit eliminated in proportion to their share in value-added (Analytical AMNE data)
- Foreign profit of US ADS MNEs: use a more direct measure based on data from the US BEA

(3) 'Rescale' the residual profit matrix to ensure that the total in each column corresponds to firm-level estimates based on MNE consolidated accounts (ORBIS, Worldscope and other sources)
- This is necessary because computing residual profit jurisdiction by jurisdiction (i.e. "bottom-up", as done in the earlier steps) generally yields more residual profit than computing it at the consolidated level.
- The "bottom-up" measure of residual profit is used only as a key to distribute double tax relief across jurisdictions, while the total amount of double tax relief depends on the amount of residual profit computed from consolidated accounts

Source: OECD Secretariat

122. The main steps to build this residual profit matrix – for a given profitability threshold – are the following:

1. The first step is to compute a 'bottom-up' residual profit matrix (i.e. where residual profit is computed jurisdiction by jurisdiction, regardless of the total amount of residual profit at the consolidated level), focusing on the whole economy (i.e. without consideration of Pillar One scope) and without consideration of a potential global revenue threshold.[24] The starting point for this is to build a 'profit matrix', which combines several data sources in a consistent framework to map the location of profit across jurisdictions (see section 2.7.3 and Chapter 5 for more details). The share of profit in this matrix that is deemed residual – for the profitability threshold considered – is computed using entity-level data from ORBIS in jurisdictions with good ORBIS coverage (see list in Annex 5.A of Chapter 5). For matrix cells in other jurisdictions, the approach is to use the aggregate ratio of profit to turnover, as computed from the profit matrix and a turnover matrix built using the same approach (see section 2.7.4 and Chapter 5). Because of the 'averaging' challenge discussed above, the aggregate ratio in a jurisdiction cannot be used directly to assess the share of residual profit in that jurisdiction. Instead, this share of residual profit is projected based on the average relationship between the aggregate ratio and the share of residual profit in a jurisdiction. This relationship is estimated using ORBIS firm-level data in jurisdictions with good coverage, as further described in section 2.7.5 below.
2. The second step is to eliminate residual profit from out-of-scope sectors to obtain a residual profit matrix focusing only on ADS and CFB. As the share of different sectors in profit is not directly observed, this step relies on the following proxies: (i) to eliminate residual profit related to commodities, the share of commodities in exports (based on data from UNCTAD)[25], (ii) to eliminate residual profit from other out-of-scope sectors, the share of these sectors in value added (based on OECD Analytical AMNE data). One exception is the residual profit of US MNEs in the ADS sector, where a more direct method is employed, thanks to the greater level of detail offered by the data published by the US BEA (see details in section 2.7.6).
3. The third and final step is to 'rescale' the residual profit matrix based on the 'top-down' estimates of residual profit based on MNE consolidated accounts for each jurisdiction of ultimate parent, as computed in component A of the methodology, and taking into account the application of a potential

global revenue threshold. As such, the jurisdiction by jurisdiction (i.e. "bottom-up") measure of residual profit is only used as a key to determine the proportions in which this amount would be taken from relieving jurisdictions. For example, if the consolidated accounts of an MNE group indicate a top-down residual profit of 100, while the jurisdiction by jurisdiction approach indicates a bottom-up residual profit of 60 in one jurisdiction, 60 in a second and 30 in a third, then the total bottom-up residual profit is 60+60+30=150, which is greater than 100. In this case, it is assumed that 40 (i.e. 60*100/150) is subject to double tax relief in the first jurisdiction, 40 from the second and 20 (i.e. 30*100/150) from the third, so that the sum of residual profit relieved (40+40+20=100) corresponds to the top-down measure of residual profit.

123. These steps are presented in more detail, along with intermediate results, in the following sections.

### *2.7.3. Building a 'profit matrix' to map the location of MNE profits*

124. Identifying the location of profit across jurisdictions is challenging due to limitations of existing data sources. Indeed, there is no single data source currently available that provides a comprehensive coverage across all jurisdictions. Reflecting this, the approach adopted in this report to assess the location of MNE profit is to combine data from different sources in a 'profit matrix', in order to ensure wide geographic coverage, while using for each data point the most reliable data source available. The other advantage of this approach is that when several data sources are available for the same data point, these sources can be used to benchmark each other, ensure consistency and identify potentially outlying values.

125. In practice, the 'profit matrix' contains the total profit of MNE entities for each possible 'ultimate parent-affiliate' pair of jurisdictions (Figure 2.12). For example, the France-United States cell would contain the total profit of US MNEs in France. The profit matrix can be seen as a square table of more than 200 columns (each column corresponding to a jurisdiction of ultimate parent) by more than 200 rows (each row corresponding to a jurisdiction of affiliate).

Figure 2.12. Profit matrix: Stylised overview and underlying data sources

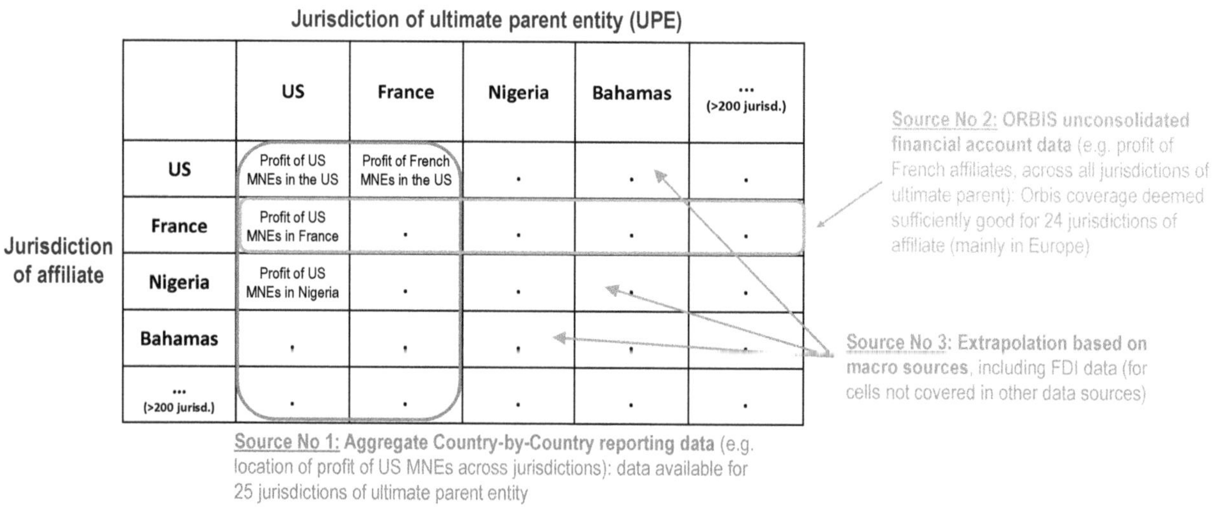


Note: Anonymised and aggregated CbCR data are used to fill *columns* of the profit matrix (e.g. profit of French MNEs across jurisdictions). ORBIS unconsolidated account data are used to fill *rows* of the profit matrix (i.e. MNE profit in France, split across ultimate parent jurisdictions). These two sources are used only where available, and in the case of ORBIS, where data coverage is sufficiently good. Other cells in the profit matrix are filled with extrapolations based on macroeconomic data, including FDI data.
Source: OECD Secretariat.

126. The profit matrix draws on three main sources of data, presented below in descending order of preference.

1) Anonymised and aggregated data from Country-by-Country Reports (CbCRs), across 25 jurisdictions of ultimate parent (see list in Annex 5.A of Chapter 5);
2) ORBIS unconsolidated account data in 24 jurisdictions of affiliate with good ORBIS coverage (see list in Annex 5.A of Chapter 5);
3) Extrapolations based on macroeconomic data (e.g. FDI data) in other cells.

127. Wherever possible, the data in the profit matrix (and in the turnover matrix described below) focus on MNE sub-groups with positive profits only (i.e. entities belonging to an MNE group that is reporting an overall profit in the jurisdiction considered), rather than all MNE sub-groups (i.e. profit-making *and* loss-making sub-groups). This focus on profit-making subgroups is adequate for the assessment of the location of residual profit, which is the aim of this section, since loss-making subgroups cannot be expected to have residual profit.

128. The profit matrix – at a relatively high level of aggregation – is displayed in Table 2.6. The full methodology underlying the construction of the profit matrix is presented in detail in Chapter 5. Chapter 5 also contains detailed information on the data sources used in the profit matrix, including a discussion of the caveats around their use. In addition, Chapter 5 displays a more disaggregated version of the profit matrix (i.e. with more jurisdiction groups than in Table 2.6), as well as information on the relative importance of the different data sources underlying the matrix. Finally, Chapter 5 contains the results of the extensive benchmarking that were undertaken to assess the quality of the data and its consistency across sources.

## Table 2.6. Profit matrix: Results aggregated by broad jurisdiction groups, whole economy

| | | **Jurisdiction of ultimate parent** | | | | |
|---|---|---|---|---|---|---|
| | (USD billion of 2016) | **High income** | **Middle income** | **Low income** | **Investment Hubs** | **Total** |
| **Jurisdiction of affiliate** | High income (64 jurisd.) | 3569.1 | 44.1 | 0.1 | 171.3 | **3784.5** |
| | Middle income (105) | 366.2 | 821.8 | 0.1 | 167.9 | **1356.0** |
| | Low income (29) | 1.3 | 1.3 | 3.1 | 0.2 | **5.8** |
| | Investment Hubs (24) | 650.9 | 69.5 | 0.0 | 314.3 | **1034.7** |
| | **Total** | **4587.4** | **936.7** | **3.3** | **653.7** | **6181.1** |

Note: Groups of jurisdictions (high, middle and low income) are based on the World Bank classification. The number of jurisdictions in each group is indicated in parentheses. Investment hubs are defined as jurisdictions with a total inward FDI position above 150% of GDP.
Source: OECD calculations based on a variety of sources including anonymised and aggregated CbCR data, ORBIS and macroeconomic data. See Chapter 5 for more details.

### *2.7.4. Building a turnover matrix*

129. To assess the share of profit that can be considered residual across the profit matrix, it is necessary to compute the ratio of profit to turnover across matrix cells. To this end, a turnover matrix has been built, using the same approach as the profit matrix. For the sake of internal consistency, the same data sources as in the profit matrix are used as much as possible, the same source preference order is applied and the data also focus on MNE sub-groups with positive profits. The detailed methodology and data sources are described in Chapter 5. An aggregated version of the turnover matrix is presented in Table 2.7.

Table 2.7. Turnover matrix: Results aggregated by broad jurisdiction groups, whole economy

| | | Jurisdiction of ultimate parent | | | | |
|---|---|---|---|---|---|---|
| | (USD billion of 2016) | High income | Middle income | Low income | Investment Hubs | Total |
| Jurisdiction of affiliate | High income (64 jurisd.) | 37034.1 | 943.4 | 19.0 | 2602.3 | **40598.7** |
| | Middle income (105) | 4392.3 | 11281.2 | 11.5 | 1895.1 | **17580.1** |
| | Low income (29) | 50.4 | 22.4 | 45.4 | 11.3 | **129.6** |
| | Investment Hubs (24) | 3398.3 | 176.9 | 3.6 | 1487.3 | **5066.2** |
| | **Total** | **44875.1** | **12423.9** | **79.6** | **5996.0** | **63374.6** |

Note: Groups of jurisdictions (high, middle and low income) are based on the World Bank classification. Investment hubs are defined as jurisdictions with a total inward FDI position above 150% of GDP.
Source: OECD Secretariat calculations based on a variety of sources including anonymised and aggregated CbCR data, ORBIS, Analytical AMNE data, AMNE data and macroeconomic variables. See Chapter 5 for more details.

### *2.7.5. Building a 'bottom-up' residual profit matrix*

130. The construction of a 'bottom-up' residual profit matrix requires assessing the share of profit that is considered residual across all cells of the profit matrix. This is done directly using ORBIS unconsolidated account data for the jurisdictions where ORBIS coverage is good for both domestic-owned and foreign-owned MNE entities (see list in Annex 5.A of Chapter 5).[26] In each of the jurisdictions considered, the total profit of each MNE sub-group is computed (by summing all MNE entities from the same MNE group that operate in this jurisdiction)[27] and divided by the total turnover of the MNE sub-group (computed in the same way). Profit above the considered residual profit threshold is then deemed residual. Finally, the total share of profit that is residual is computed by summing all residual profit across MNE sub-groups and dividing it by total profit of MNE sub-groups with positive profits within this jurisdiction.

131. For the matrix cells in other jurisdictions of affiliate, the share of profit that is residual is assessed based on the aggregate profit-to-turnover ratio (computed from the profit and turnover matrices) and the average relationship between the share of residual profit and this aggregate ratio across jurisdictions. This average relationship is estimated over the jurisdictions $j$ with good ORBIS coverage:

$$\left(\frac{Residual\,profit}{Total\,Profit}\right)_j = \alpha + \beta\left(\frac{Total\,profit}{Total\,turnover}\right)_j$$

132. This relationship, estimated for a 10% profitability threshold on profit-to-turnover, is presented in Figure 2.13, where each dot corresponds to one jurisdiction. There is no theoretical reason why this relationship should be linear, but in practice the number of observations is insufficient to consider more complex specifications. Also, it is not obvious that more complex specifications would significantly improve the quality of the fit compared to the linear specification presented in Figure 2.13.

133. The correlation for other potential profitability thresholds, not presented in this chapter, is broadly similar to the correlation observed with a 10% threshold, but the coefficients $\alpha$ and $\beta$ depend on the profitability threshold considered. In general, a higher threshold to define residual profit would lead to a lower $\alpha$ since it would reduce the amount of residual profit, while the potential differences in $\beta$ would depend on the shape of the distribution of profit across jurisdictions. The analysis makes use of the specific coefficients $\alpha$ and $\beta$ corresponding to the profitability threshold considered (e.g. results for a 20% profitability threshold are based on the $\alpha$ and $\beta$ estimated for that threshold).

Figure 2.13. Average relationship between the share of residual profit and the aggregate profit to turnover ratio

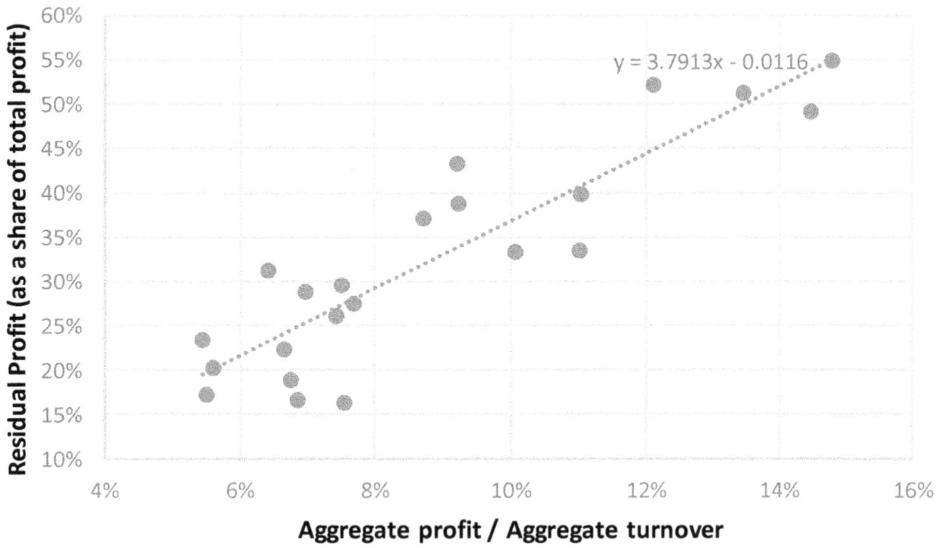


Note: Each dot corresponds to one jurisdiction. The sample consists of jurisdictions with relatively good coverage of unconsolidated accounts in ORBIS. Residual profit is computed for each MNE by applying a 10% threshold on the ratio of profit before tax (PBT) to turnover on the MNE accounts at the jurisdiction level (sum of all unconsolidated entities of the MNE in the jurisdiction considered). Loss-making MNEs in the jurisdiction are excluded from the sample. The ratio of total profit to turnover is computed from ORBIS using the same sample of firms to ensure consistency in the approach.
Source: OECD calculations based on ORBIS data.

134. Based on this method, 'bottom-up' residual profit matrices can be computed. Since the residual profit matrix depends on the profitability threshold considered, there is not a unique residual profit matrix. Instead, a different residual profit matrix can be computed for each profitability threshold. The results presented in this section focus illustratively on a 10% and a 20% profitability threshold. The resulting matrices are presented in Table 2.8. The matrices focus on the whole economy (rather than only ADS and CFB) and are based on a 'bottom-up' jurisdiction-by-jurisdiction computation of residual profit (rather than a 'top-down' computation based on consolidated group-level accounts), which explains why the total amount of residual profit is much higher than in the corresponding component A estimates above.

Table 2.8. 'Bottom-up' residual profit matrix, whole economy

**Panel A:** Assuming a 10% profitability threshold

| | | Jurisdiction of ultimate parent | | | | |
|---|---|---|---|---|---|---|
| | (USD billion of 2016) | **High income** | **Middle income** | **Low income** | **Investment Hubs** | **Total** |
| **Jurisdiction of affiliate** | High income (64 jurisd.) | 1394.1 | 20.0 | 0.0 | 65.9 | **1480.0** |
| | Middle income (105) | 165.8 | 254.7 | 0.1 | 76.2 | **496.8** |
| | Low income (29) | 0.8 | 1.0 | 0.8 | 0.1 | **2.7** |
| | Investment Hubs (24) | 503.8 | 66.4 | 0.0 | 260.4 | **830.6** |
| | **Total** | **2064.4** | **342.2** | **0.9** | **402.5** | **2810.0** |

| Panel B: Assuming a 20% profitability threshold | | | | | | |
|---|---|---|---|---|---|---|
| | | Jurisdiction of ultimate parent | | | | |
| | (USD billion of 2016) | High income | Middle income | Low income | Investment Hubs | Total |
| Jurisdiction of affiliate | High income (64 jurisd.) | 710.4 | 12.3 | 0.0 | 38.5 | **761.3** |
| | Middle income (105) | 94.0 | 113.5 | 0.1 | 50.2 | **257.8** |
| | Low income (29) | 0.5 | 0.8 | 0.3 | 0.1 | **1.7** |
| | Investment Hubs (24) | 402.4 | 64.1 | 0.0 | 224.7 | **691.3** |
| | **Total** | **1207.3** | **190.8** | **0.4** | **313.5** | **1712.0** |

Note: Groups of jurisdictions (high, middle and low income) are based on the World Bank classification. Investment hubs are defined as jurisdictions with a total inward FDI position above 150% of GDP. This 'bottom-up' residual profit matrix considers the amount of residual profit computed jurisdiction by jurisdiction, based on a 10% (Panel A), or 20% (Panel B) PBT to turnover profitability threshold including all sectors.
Source: OECD Secretariat.

### 2.7.6. Focusing the 'bottom-up' residual profit matrix on ADS and CFB sectors

135. The aim of this step of the methodology is to eliminate residual profit from out-of-scope sectors to obtain a residual profit matrix focusing only on ADS and CFB. This is not straightforward as the share of different sectors in profit (and even more so in residual profit) is generally not observed in the available data (e.g. anonymised and aggregated CbCR data). The only exception is data from the US BEA, which combines geographic and sectoral information on the location of MNE profit and sales, as further discussed below.

136. Against this background, the methodology is based on the following proxies and assumptions:

- The share of residual profit related to commodities in a jurisdiction is assumed to be proportional to the share of commodities in the merchandise exports of this jurisdiction. Data on the composition of exports by product category is taken from the merchandise trade matrix of UNCTAD.[28]
- Residual profit from other out-of-scope sectors is more difficult to identify and may be spread more evenly across jurisdictions than commodity-related residual profit, which is likely to be primarily concentrated among commodity-producing jurisdictions. The share of residual profit from these other out-of-scope sectors is assumed to be proportional to the share of these out-of-scope sectors in the value added of MNEs in the jurisdiction considered. These shares are computed from OECD Analytical AMNE data, which presents the advantage of combining the geographic and sectoral dimensions. Unfortunately, Analytical AMNE data does not cover profit, and the distribution of value added is the closest available proxy of the distribution of profit. ADS and CFB sectors in Analytical AMNE are identified in the same way as in the section 2.5 above.

137. One exception to this methodology is made for the residual profit of US MNEs in the ADS sector, where a more direct method is employed based on detailed data from the US BEA. For these MNEs, the distribution of residual profit outside of the United States is computed based on the location of profit (using 'profit-type return' as the measure of profit) and sales of MNEs in the 'information sector'. While this sector does not exactly overlap with ADS, it seems sufficiently close to be used as a proxy.[29] This approach is possible only for US MNEs, since other jurisdictions do not publish data with the same level of detail, i.e. combining geographic and sectoral information on the location of MNE profits and sales. The approach based on BEA data is preferred to the methodology described above that is used in other jurisdictions, since it offers more direct information on the location of profit and sales in the ADS sector. The measure of profit used ('profit-type return') is not subject to the double counting issue pointed out by Blouin and Robinson (2019[11]) (see also the discussion in Clausing (2020[12])). For consistency with the rest of the methodology, the share of profit of US ADS MNEs that is residual in each foreign jurisdiction is computed based on the aggregate ratio of profit to sales (from the BEA data) and the relationship presented in

Figure 2.13. In contrast to ADS, the BEA data is not used for CFB, as CFB activities would be much more difficult to isolate in the BEA data (most sectors in the BEA data containing a mix of CFB and non-CFB activities).

138. The resulting 'bottom-up' residual profit matrices focusing on ADS and CFB, for a 10% and 20% profitability threshold, are presented in Table 2.9. The amounts of global residual profit are much lower than in Table 2.8, reflecting that the scope has been narrowed compared to that table. Indeed, estimates in Table 2.8 cover the whole economy, including out-of-scope activities. Still, the amount of global residual profit remains significantly higher than computed in component A above (see Table 2.3), confirming the need for the 'rescaling' undertaken in the next section.

Table 2.9. 'Bottom-up' residual profit matrix, ADS and CFB only

**Panel A:** Assuming a 10% profitability threshold

| | | Jurisdiction of ultimate parent | | | | |
|---|---|---|---|---|---|---|
| | (USD billion of 2016) | **High income** | **Middle income** | **Low income** | **Investment Hubs** | **Total** |
| **Jurisdiction of affiliate** | High income (64 jurisd.) | 531.4 | 6.4 | 0.0 | 24.0 | **561.8** |
| | Middle income (105) | 57.2 | 87.9 | 0.0 | 24.5 | **169.5** |
| | Low income (29) | 0.2 | 0.2 | 0.2 | 0.0 | **0.7** |
| | Investment Hubs (24) | 192.4 | 26.5 | 0.0 | 104.4 | **323.4** |
| | **Total** | **781.2** | **121.0** | **0.3** | **152.9** | **1055.3** |

**Panel B:** Assuming a 20% profitability threshold

| | | Jurisdiction of ultimate parent | | | | |
|---|---|---|---|---|---|---|
| | (USD billion of 2016) | **High income** | **Middle income** | **Low income** | **Investment Hubs** | **Total** |
| **Jurisdiction of affiliate** | High income (64 jurisd.) | 268.8 | 3.9 | 0.0 | 13.6 | **286.2** |
| | Middle income (105) | 30.7 | 39.5 | 0.0 | 16.8 | **87.0** |
| | Low income (29) | 0.1 | 0.2 | 0.1 | 0.0 | **0.4** |
| | Investment Hubs (24) | 152.1 | 25.7 | 0.0 | 90.4 | **268.1** |
| | **Total** | **451.8** | **69.1** | **0.1** | **120.7** | **641.8** |

Note: Groups of jurisdictions (high, middle and low income) are based on the World Bank classification. Investment hubs are defined as jurisdictions with a total inward FDI position above 150% of GDP. This 'bottom-up' residual profit matrix considers the amount of residual profit computed jurisdiction by jurisdiction, based on a 10% (Panel A) or 20% (Panel B) PBT to turnover profitability threshold, including only ADS and CFB MNEs.
Source: OECD Secretariat.

## *2.7.7. Residual profit matrix: Rescaling to ensure consistency with 'top-down' measure of residual profit*

139. The last step to obtain the final 'top-down' residual profit matrix that is used to compute the amount of profit subject to double tax relief across jurisdictions is to rescale the 'bottom-up' matrix presented in Table 2.9 to ensure that it matches with 'top-down' estimates of residual profit. As discussed above, this rescaling is required to take into account the fact that the 'bottom-up' measure of residual profit would only serve as a key to identify where double tax relief should occur, while the total amount of double tax relief to provide would depend on the amount of residual profit as computed based on MNE consolidated accounts. For example, certain MNE groups may have a profitability above the profitability threshold in

some jurisdictions, but low profitability in some other jurisdictions, allowing them to offset partly or fully this residual profit.[30]

140. This rescaling is done by adjusting residual profit proportionally within each column of the 'bottom-up' matrix, to ensure that the total residual profit in each column equals the total residual profit of the MNEs with an ultimate parent in the jurisdiction considered, as computed from the database of consolidated MNE group accounts used in the analysis of component A, focusing only on ADS and CFB MNEs. For example, if US MNEs have a total residual profit of 100 in the 'bottom-up' matrix (i.e. total residual profit in the US column) and if the consolidated financial accounts of US MNEs indicate a total residual profit of 60, then the rescaling consists in reducing by 40% the amount in each cell of the US column of the 'bottom-up' residual profit matrix to obtain the final 'top-down' matrix.

141. This rescaling ensures consistency between the final residual profit matrix and the estimates of global residual profit presented in component A above, and therefore ensures that the amount of residual profit allocated under Pillar One equals the amount of residual profit on which double tax relief is provided. The rescaling also takes into account the potential implications of applying a global revenue threshold under Pillar One. This is because the estimates of residual profit used as column totals take into account the application of this revenue threshold. For example, if under the revenue threshold considered, a jurisdiction of ultimate parent sees some of its MNE groups being excluded from scope, and that these MNE groups were representing 30% of the total residual profit of all MNE groups from this jurisdiction, then the amount of residual profit in the column corresponding to this jurisdiction will be reduced by 30% compared to the situation without revenue threshold. This methodology ultimately ensures that global residual profit in each column of the final matrix is consistent with the estimate from component A after application of the revenue threshold.[31]

142. The final residual profit matrices, for a 10% and 20% profitability threshold and a EUR 750 million global revenue threshold, are presented in Table 2.10. The total residual profit is close to USD 500 billion in the first case, and about USD 170 billion in the second. By construction, these totals correspond exactly to the estimates in component A for the same assumptions (presented in Table 2.3). Based on these assumptions, the results indicate that the residual profit of ADS and CFB MNEs is primarily located in high income jurisdictions and investment hubs, suggesting that they would be the main jurisdictions providing double tax relief, while there is very little residual profit in low income jurisdictions.

### Table 2.10. Final 'top-down' residual profit matrix used to compute double tax relief, ADS and CFB

**Panel A:** Assuming a 10% profitability threshold and a EUR 750 million global revenue threshold

| | | Jurisdiction of ultimate parent | | | | |
|---|---|---|---|---|---|---|
| | (USD billion of 2016) | **High income** | **Middle income** | **Low income** | **Investment Hubs** | **Total** |
| **Jurisdiction of affiliate** | High income (64 jurisd.) | 275.3 | 1.2 | 0.0 | 11.8 | **288.3** |
| | Middle income (105) | 26.7 | 26.1 | 0.0 | 5.7 | **58.5** |
| | Low income (29) | 0.1 | 0.1 | 0.0 | 0.0 | **0.1** |
| | Investment Hubs (24) | 111.6 | 7.0 | 0.0 | 27.9 | **146.4** |
| | **Total** | **413.6** | **34.3** | **0.0** | **45.4** | **493.4** |

**Panel B:** Assuming a 20% profitability threshold and a EUR 750 million global revenue threshold

| | | Jurisdiction of ultimate parent | | | | |
|---|---|---|---|---|---|---|
| | (USD billion of 2016) | High income | Middle income | Low income | Investment Hubs | Total |
| Jurisdiction of affiliate | High income (64 jurisd.) | 86.0 | 0.4 | 0.0 | 3.1 | **89.5** |
| | Middle income (105) | 7.6 | 5.8 | 0.0 | 1.4 | **14.8** |
| | Low income (29) | 0.0 | 0.0 | 0.0 | 0.0 | **0.0** |
| | Investment Hubs (24) | 55.6 | 3.4 | 0.0 | 10.9 | **69.8** |
| | **Total** | **149.2** | **9.6** | **0.0** | **15.4** | **174.2** |

Note: Groups of jurisdictions (high, middle and low income) are based on the World Bank classification. Investment hubs are defined as jurisdictions with a total inward FDI position above 150% of GDP. This 'top-down' residual profit matrix is computed by 'rescaling' the matrix in Table 2.9 to ensure that the total amount of residual profit in each column equals the total amount of residual profit as computed based on MNE consolidated accounts in component A. This matrix assumes illustratively a 10% (Panel A) or 20% (Panel B) profitability threshold (based on PBT to turnover) and a EUR 750 million global revenue threshold. It focuses on ADS and CFB.
Source: OECD Secretariat.

### *2.7.8. Resulting estimate of a jurisdiction's share of residual profit*

143. Ultimately, a jurisdiction's share in global residual profit, which corresponds to component E of the formula in Figure 2.1, is computed as the total of this jurisdiction's row in the final 'top-down' residual profit matrix (Table 2.10) divided by the total residual profit in this matrix.

144. To reflect the uncertainty around the data used, as in the case of destination-based sales (component C), the results presented in the final section of this chapter integrate an uncertainty range around the share of residual profit in each jurisdiction (i.e. component E). The width of this range depends on the extent to which data in the profit matrix for the jurisdiction considered (as a jurisdiction of affiliate, i.e. in the row of the profit matrix corresponding to its jurisdiction) is based on 'hard' data on MNE profit (anonymised and aggregated CbCR or ORBIS data) vs. extrapolations based on macroeconomic data (e.g. FDI). For a jurisdiction where the profit matrix is based exclusively on hard data, the range for component E is constructed as ±10% around the point estimate. For a jurisdiction where the profit matrix is based exclusively on extrapolations, the range is ±20%. For jurisdictions with a mix of sources, the width of the range is in-between.[32]

## 2.8. Component F: Tax rate on double tax relief

145. Once the amount of profit subject to double tax relief has been identified, the final step in the analysis is to assess the rate at which double tax relief would be provided, which relates to the rate at which relieved profit was taxed before the application of Pillar One. While this is an important component of the assessment, its modelling comes with significant uncertainty, due to data challenges related to the measurement of the effective tax rate (ETR) faced by MNEs across jurisdictions, and also because the tax rate on double tax relief will depend on considerations about Pillar One design and its interactions with other tax rules that will ultimately be decided by the Inclusive Framework.

146. As a starting point, one could assume that double tax relief would take place at the statutory CIT rate of the jurisdiction providing double tax relief. This would correspond to a case where, before the application of Pillar One, an MNE was paying a tax rate on its profit that was computed based on the statutory CIT rate of the jurisdiction considered. This MNE may have benefitted from tax provisions related to its economic activity, such as accelerated depreciation rules or tax incentives for R&D, resulting in an ETR (as computed for example with financial account data) below the statutory rate. This situation could

still be consistent with providing double tax relief at the statutory CIT rate, to the extent that these other provisions would not interfere with Pillar One.

147. However, it is also possible to envisage cases where the tax rate on double tax relief may be lower than the statutory rate. For example, this could happen in a case where MNE income benefits from a preferential tax rate lower than the statutory rate (e.g. patent box rate, special economic zone) under the assumption that double tax relief would be provided at this preferential rate. It could also correspond to a situation where double tax relief would be provided in the form of a tax credit (as opposed to a tax exemption) where a tax credit would be provided by the domestic jurisdiction against taxes paid in the market jurisdiction where residual profit is allocated. In this case, the tax rate on double tax relief could take place at a lower rate than the domestic CIT rate if the tax rate in the market jurisdiction is lower.

148. To reflect this uncertainty, the results presented in the final section of this chapter assume that the tax rate on double tax relief falls within a range between a high estimate, which corresponds to the statutory CIT rate (using the same sources as in component D above), and a lower estimate. This lower estimate is set arbitrarily at five percentage points below the statutory CIT rate, except in the case of investment hubs where it is based on the minimum effective tax rate on MNE income observed across a range of sources (US BEA data on taxes paid and profit-type returns, data from Tørsløv et al. (2018[2]), and anonymised and aggregated CbCR data) also used in the analysis of Pillar Two (see Chapter 3 for more detail on these sources).

## 2.9. Overview of the results

149. The estimated effect of Amount A of Pillar One on tax bases and tax revenues across jurisdictions has been computed by the OECD Secretariat based on the methodology presented in this chapter. As discussed in the Chapter 1, these jurisdiction-level results have been shared on a confidential and bilateral basis with most Inclusive Framework members. The OECD Secretariat has provided estimates to more than 115 jurisdictions at their request. Jurisdiction-specific results were shared in the form of revenue estimation 'tools'. These tools provide jurisdictions with the ability to consider the estimated impact on tax revenues in their jurisdiction of a range of potential Pillar One parameters (e.g. global revenue threshold, profitability threshold percentage, reallocation percentage and nexus threshold) and to distinguish the contribution of ADS and CFB activities to the estimated outcomes. Estimates in the tools are presented as ranges to reflect the data uncertainty.

150. After extensive consultation with members of the Inclusive Framework, there was no consensus over whether or not jurisdiction-specific estimates should be publicly released as part of the economic impact assessment. In view of this lack of consensus, no jurisdiction-specific estimates are included in this chapter.

151. This chapter presents results for jurisdiction groups, at a relatively high level of aggregation. Two groupings are considered:

- **By income levels**: Jurisdictions are distributed in four groups: (i) high, (ii) middle, and (iii) low income jurisdictions, based on a classification by the World Bank, and (iv) 'investment hubs', defined as jurisdictions having a ratio of inward FDI positions to GDP above 150%;
- **By statutory CIT rate**: Jurisdictions are distributed in four groups based on their statutory CIT rate in 2019: (i) below or equal to 10%, (ii) 10-20%, (iii) 20-30%, and (iv) above 30%.[33]

152. Results are presented for an illustrative set of Pillar One parameters, including a EUR 750 million global revenue threshold, a profitability threshold percentage (based on PBT to turnover) of 10% or 20%, a reallocation percentage of 10%, 20% or 30%, a EUR 1 million revenue nexus threshold for ADS and a EUR 3 million revenue nexus threshold for CFB. Results are subject to the caveats listed in the first section of this chapter. They are presented as ranges to reflect the data uncertainty around the estimates. The

assumptions used to build these ranges are presented in the different relevant components of the analysis (i.e. location of MNE destination-based sales, estimated effect of revenue nexus threshold, location of MNE residual profit, tax rate on double tax relief).[34]

### *2.9.1. Effect of Pillar One on tax bases*

153. The effect of Amount A of Pillar One on the global tax base equals zero. This is because Amount A reallocates tax base across jurisdictions without changing the global tax base. The jurisdiction groups benefitting most from this tax base reallocation (as a share of their GDP) are middle and low income jurisdictions, while tax base gains tend to be more modest among high income jurisdictions (see result Figures in Annex 2.C). In contrast, investment hubs would lose tax base in the reallocation, reflecting that a significant share of residual profit is currently located in investment hubs. Results by statutory CIT rate groups offer a consistent picture. Tax base gains are largest among jurisdictions with higher rates (20-30%, and even more above 30%), while jurisdictions with lower rates (10-20%, and even more 0-10%) tend to lose tax base.

### *2.9.2. Effect of Pillar One on tax revenues*

154. At the global level, Amount A of Pillar One involves a tax revenue gain (Figure 2.14). This is because, on average, tax base is reallocated from jurisdictions with relatively low tax rates towards jurisdictions with relatively higher tax rates. However, the magnitude of this global revenue gain is modest – less than 1% of global CIT revenues – across the set of assumptions underlying Figure 2.14. On average, high, middle and low income jurisdiction groups would all benefit from small tax revenue gains. Revenue gains tend to be larger (as a share of current CIT revenues) among low income jurisdictions, where little residual profit is currently located. Revenue gains also tend to be larger among jurisdictions with relatively high statutory CIT rates. In contrast, jurisdictions with statutory CIT rates below 10% and between 10% and 20% would lose revenue on average, the loss being relatively smaller in the former group (despite a greater loss of tax base in this group) since the low tax rate of jurisdictions in this group implies that they would have little double tax relief to provide (or even no double tax relief to provide for zero-tax jurisdictions).

Figure 2.14. Estimated effect of Pillar One on tax revenues, by jurisdiction groups

**Panel A:** 10% reallocation to market

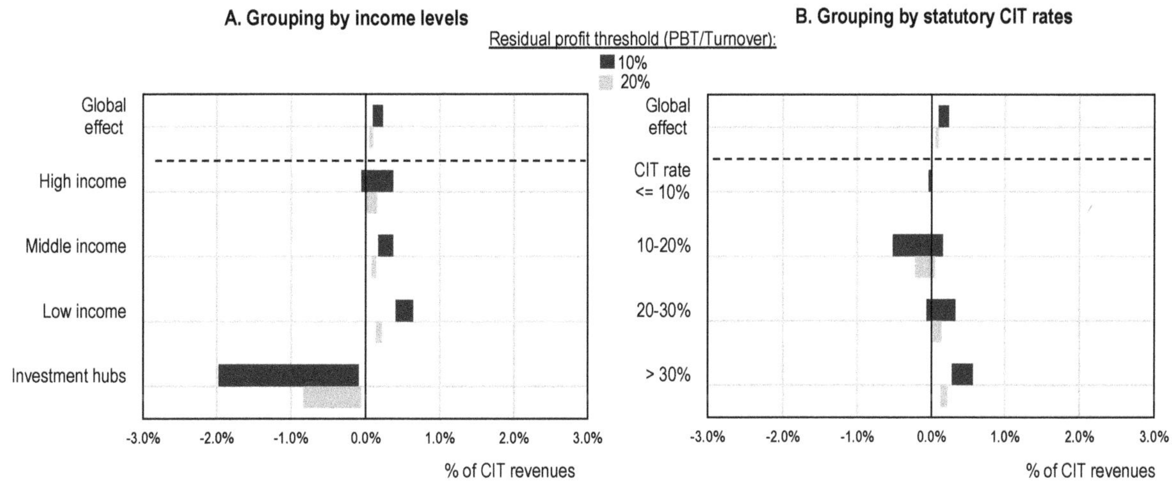

**Panel B:** 20% reallocation to market

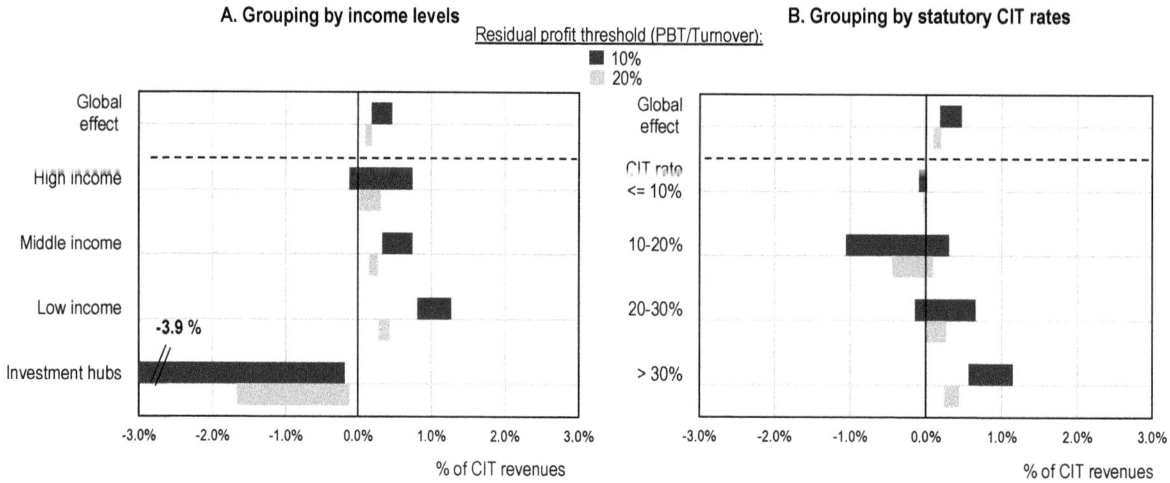


**Panel C:** 30% reallocation to market

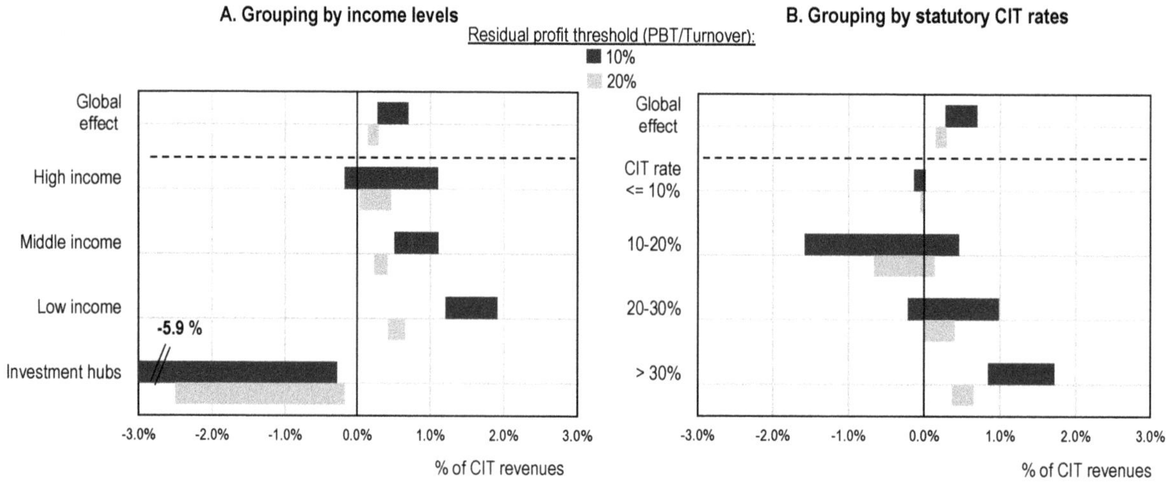


Note: All estimates are based on the methodology presented in this chapter and subject to the caveats listed in the first section of this chapter. Estimates are presented as ranges to reflect data uncertainty. The ranges measure the uncertainty around the estimate of each jurisdiction group, without necessarily implying that all jurisdictions in the group fall within the range. Results assume illustratively a EUR 750 million global revenue threshold, a profitability threshold (based on PBT to turnover) of 10% or 20%, a reallocation of 10% (Panel A), 20% (Panel B) or 30% (Panel C) of residual profit to market jurisdictions, a EUR 1 million nexus revenue threshold for ADS and a EUR 3 million nexus revenue threshold for CFB. Groups of jurisdictions (high, middle and low income) are based on the World Bank classification. Investment hubs are defined as jurisdictions with a total inward FDI position above 150% of GDP.
Source: OECD Secretariat.

## 2.10. Conclusion

155. This chapter describes the methodology and data sources used by the OECD Secretariat to estimate the order of magnitude of potential tax revenue implications of Amount A of Pillar One, across a range of parameter options, and presents illustrative results for broad jurisdiction groups.

156. The data underlying the analysis in this chapter inevitably predates the COVID-19 crisis, as well as other important developments such as the implementation of various measures under the OECD/G20 BEPS project and the introduction of the US Tax Cuts and Jobs Act (TCJA). Many key results in this chapter can be expected to remain valid in the post-COVID-19 environment (e.g. on the sensitivity of the outcomes to the various Pillar One parameter choices). However, the amount of global residual profit and

the exact magnitude of tax revenue effects are likely to be substantially affected by the crisis. In particular, as discussed in this chapter, it is likely that ADS becomes relatively more important in the future (as a share of the economy, and also as a share of the combined global residual profit in ADS and CFB) than suggested by the estimates in this chapter, reflecting the accelerated digitalisation of economies.

## References

Bailin, A. et al. (2019), "Like it or not? The impact of online platforms on the productivity of service providers", *OECD Economics Department Working Papers*, No. 1548, OECD, http://dx.doi.org/10.1787/080a17ce-en. [13]

Bajgar, M. et al. (2019), "Industry Concentration in Europe and North America", *OECD Productivity Working Papers*, No. 19, OECD, https://www.oecd-ilibrary.org/economics/industry-concentration-in-europe-and-north-america_2ff98246-en. [6]

Blouin, J. and L. Robinson (2019), "Double Counting Accounting: How Much Profit of Multinational Enterprises Is Really in Tax Havens?", *SSRN Electronic Journal*, http://dx.doi.org/10.2139/ssrn.3491451. [11]

Cadestin, C. et al. (2018), "Multinational enterprises and global value chains: the OECD analytical AMNE database", *OECD Trade Policy Papers*, No. 211, OECD Publishing, Paris, https://dx.doi.org/10.1787/d9de288d-en. [9]

Clausing, K. (2020), "Profit Shifting Before and After the Tax Cuts and Jobs Act", *SSRN Electronic Journal*, http://dx.doi.org/10.2139/ssrn.3274827. [12]

Eurostat (2008), "NACE Rev. 2 - Statistical classification of economic activities in the European Community", *Eurostat Methodologies and Working papers*, Eurostat, Luxembourg, https://ec.europa.eu/eurostat/documents/3859598/5902521/KS-RA-07-015-EN.PDF. [8]

Gal, P. (2013), "Measuring Total Factor Productivity at the Firm Level using OECD-ORBIS", *OECD Economics Department Working Papers*, No. 1049, OECD Publishing, Paris, https://dx.doi.org/10.1787/5k46dsb25ls6-en. [4]

Hernández, H. et al. (2017), *The 2017 EU Industrial R&D Investment Scoreboard*, European Commission, https://ec.europa.eu/jrc/en/publication/eur-scientific-and-technical-research-reports/2017-eu-industrial-rd-investment-scoreboard. [3]

Johansson, Å. et al. (2017), "Tax planning by multinational firms: Firm-level evidence from a cross-country database", *OECD Economics Department Working Papers*, No. 1355, OECD Publishing, Paris, https://dx.doi.org/10.1787/9ea89b4d-en. [5]

OECD (2020), "Corporate Tax Statistics - Second Edition", OECD Publishing, https://www.oecd.org/tax/tax-policy/corporate-tax-statistics-second-edition.pdf. [10]

OECD (2020), *Tax Challenges Arising from Digitalisation – Report on Pillar One Blueprint: Inclusive Framework on BEPS*, OECD/G20 Base Erosion and Profit Shifting Project, OECD Publishing, Paris, https://dx.doi.org/10.1787/beba0634-en. [1]

Tørsløv, T., L. Wier and G. Zucman (2018), "The Missing Profits of Nations", *NBER Working Paper*, No. 24701, http://www.nber.org/papers/w24701.pdf. [2]

UNCTAD (2017), "The Top 100 Digital MNEs", in *World Investment Report 2017 - Investment and the Digital Economy*, https://unctad.org/en/PublicationChapters/wir2017ch4_Annex_en.pdf. [7]

# Annex 2.A. Main steps of the construction of the MNE consolidated financial account dataset

157. The dataset of MNE consolidated financial accounts relies primarily on data from ORBIS, provided by Bureau van Dijk (BvD). The ORBIS database is the largest cross-country database on ownership and financial accounts of firms worldwide. It relies on information from various underlying sources, including credit rating agencies (e.g. Cerved in Italy) and national banks (e.g. National Bank of Belgium). ORBIS contains data for both publicly listed and privately owned companies.

158. Given that ORBIS data is not primarily collected for statistical analysis, important processing and cleaning work is required to enhance data reliability (e.g. eliminating duplicates and reporting errors). This concerns ownership data and financial data. The main data cleaning steps in each area build on OECD expertise with ORBIS and follow as much as possible procedures used in previous OECD studies, while adapting them when necessary to the needs of the current exercise. These main cleaning steps are detailed in the sections below.

159. To ensure as exhaustive coverage as possible, ORBIS data are complemented with other firm-level data sources, namely Thomson Reuters Worldscope database, the EU Industrial R&D Investment Scoreboard, Fortune Global 500, as well as manual checks and additions from firms' annual reports.

## ORBIS Ownership data

160. The ORBIS historical ownership database contains extensive information on ownership links between firms, which can be used to identify entities belonging to the same corporate group. Following Bajgar et al. (2019[6]), entities in ORBIS are assigned to corporate groups based on their Global Ultimate Owner (GUO), using a 50% ownership threshold, and considering GUOs of corporate nature (i.e. Industrial companies, Banks, Financial companies, Insurance companies, or Financial companies) to avoid for example assigning to the same group two independent firms owned by the same individual or government entity.

161. In turn, MNE groups are defined as corporate groups having entities in at least two jurisdictions. For each MNE group, only the consolidated account of the GUO is kept in the sample, to avoid potential double counting.

162. The procedure to clean and extend ownership links in ORBIS has been implemented by the OECD Directorate for Science, Technology and Innovation, following Bajgar et al. (2019[6]) and updating it for year 2016. The procedure focuses on all entities with a turnover of at least EUR 10 million, and focuses on ownership links above a 50% threshold. Missing links are identified, or (in a smaller number of cases) existing links are corrected, using the following steps:

- Using the BvD Zephyr database on Mergers and Acquisitions (M&A) to identify changes in immediate (rather than global ultimate) owners not available from ORBIS.
- Using ORBIS historic ownership linkages to identify changes in immediate owners not available from ORBIS.
- Translating the changes in immediate owners (from the first two steps above) to changes in ultimate ownership.

- Imputing missing ownership information by using data on M&A or changes in ownership in earlier or later years.
- Correcting ultimate owners that are in fact majority owned by another firm, since by definition they cannot be an ultimate owner.
- Removing temporary (one or two year) changes in ultimate owner that reverse themselves – as such cases seem highly unlikely to occur in reality and probably reflect gaps in the ownership data.
- Detecting missing linkages for large firms that change from having no subsidiaries to having a large number of subsidiaries one year to the next.
- Identifying missing links for large firms that never have any subsidiaries, and for large groups of subsidiaries that never have a parent with financials.
- Using name-matching algorithms to identify potential links, in combination with detailed manual inspection (e.g. against firms' annual reports) to check if these potential links are correct or not.
- Manually checking the 300 largest firms, using the subsidiary structure in their financial statements to cross-check the ownership data.

163. Overall, this procedure identified the GUO of about 50,000 entities for which it was not reported in the raw ORBIS data, and corrected the GUO of about 4,000 entities. Overall, these entities (added and corrected GUOs) represent about 4% of turnover in the final sample of consolidated MNE group accounts.

## ORBIS Consolidated financial account data

164. The sample of consolidated account data comprises only entities that are the GUO of their corporate group. The sample is restricted to MNE groups, i.e. corporate groups that have entities in at least two jurisdictions.

165. In the raw ORBIS dataset, consolidated account data tend to be of better quality than unconsolidated data, reflecting that the financial amounts involved are larger on average, which tends to imply that they face stricter reporting and auditing requirements. Still, consolidated ORBIS data requires some cleaning to eliminate suspect values that could result from reporting errors.

166. The procedure for cleaning consolidated account data comprises the following steps, inspired by the cleaning steps in Gal (2013[4]), Johansson et al. (2017[5]) and Bailin et al. (2019[13]) that are relevant for this exercise:

- Selecting full-year accounts with closing date around December 2016 (from July 2016 to June 2017);
- Filtering duplicate firm-year observations, favouring those with non-missing key financial variables and with closing date equal to or closest to 31st of December;
- Eliminating implausible values: negative assets or turnover, implausibly high profit or turnover;
- Dropping observations with implausible profit margin (e.g. pre-tax profit or EBIT on turnover either below -100% or above 100%);
- Manually dropping apparent remaining duplicates, i.e. firms with different BvD identifiers but relating to the same group.

## Other firm-level data sources and manual checks

167. While the coverage of ORBIS at the consolidated account level is very good (unlike at the unconsolidated level), it is not entirely exhaustive, especially in certain sectors (banks, insurance), which

are covered in separate ORBIS databases that do not contain all the variables of interest. In order to improve coverage, the database is complemented with firm-level data from other sources.

168. The first complementary firm-level dataset used is Worldscope, edited by Thomson Reuters, which reports mandatory data for listed companies worldwide. The merger between ORBIS and Worldscope was done in two steps. The first step consisted of matching MNE GUOs in ORBIS with Worldscope data based on the International Securities Identification Number (ISIN) available in Worldscope, and keeping Worldscope financial information for the GUOs that had no financial information at the consolidated level in ORBIS. The second step consisted of considering the biggest Worldscope companies that could not be matched with any GUO in ORBIS based on the ISIN number and adding those that were actually MNEs and absent in the ORBIS database, based on manual checks.

169. The database was furthermore complemented with data from the 2017 EU Industrial R&D Investment Scoreboard and the 2016 Fortune Global 500 list, following the same approach as for the second step of the Worldscope additions (manual checks). The EU Industrial R&D Investment Scoreboard, which also relies on BvD data, contains limited financial information on 2,500 companies with the highest R&D expenditure worldwide. The Fortune Global 500 list, issued by the Fortune magazine, contains financial information on the 500 largest corporations worldwide as measured by total revenue. A few large missing MNE groups were also added manually based on information from their annual report.

170. Overall, data sources complementary to ORBIS and manual additions permitted the addition of 963 MNE groups to the dataset, representing nearly 20% of the turnover of the total sample.

171. Detailed manual checks were performed on the final dataset, with a specific focus on the top-500 largest MNE groups (by turnover), the top-100 MNE groups with the highest levels of residual profit, the top-400 MNE groups with highest pre-tax profit classified in financial sectors (including activities of holding companies), the top-25 ADS MNE groups with the highest levels of residual profit, and the top-3 MNE groups with highest residual profit in each industry (30 industries, based on the NACE Rev. 2 classification).

# Annex 2.B. Revenue nexus threshold modelling: Robustness check

Annex Figure 2.B.1. Estimated effect of a revenue nexus threshold on allocated profit for alternative values of the lambda parameter

Revenue nexus thresholds of EUR 1m, 3m and 5m, compared to a no-threshold situation

**Panel A: Assuming lambda = 3**

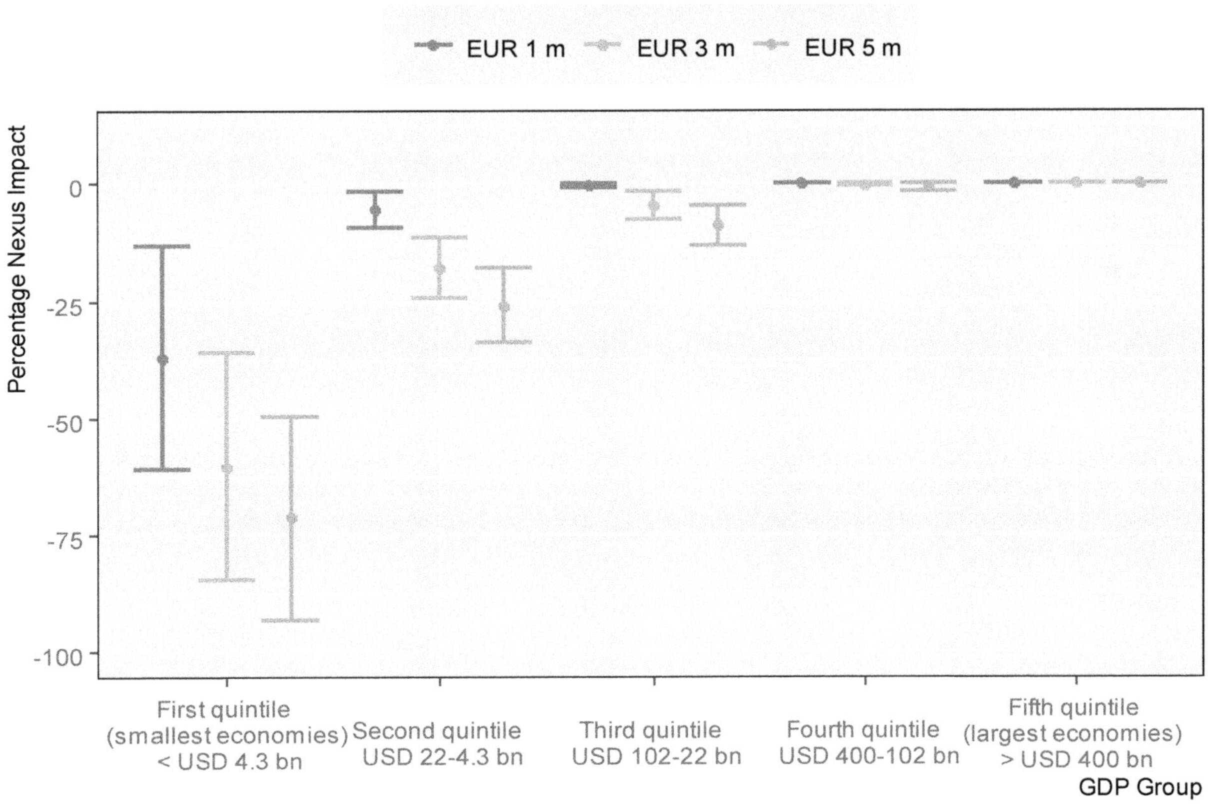

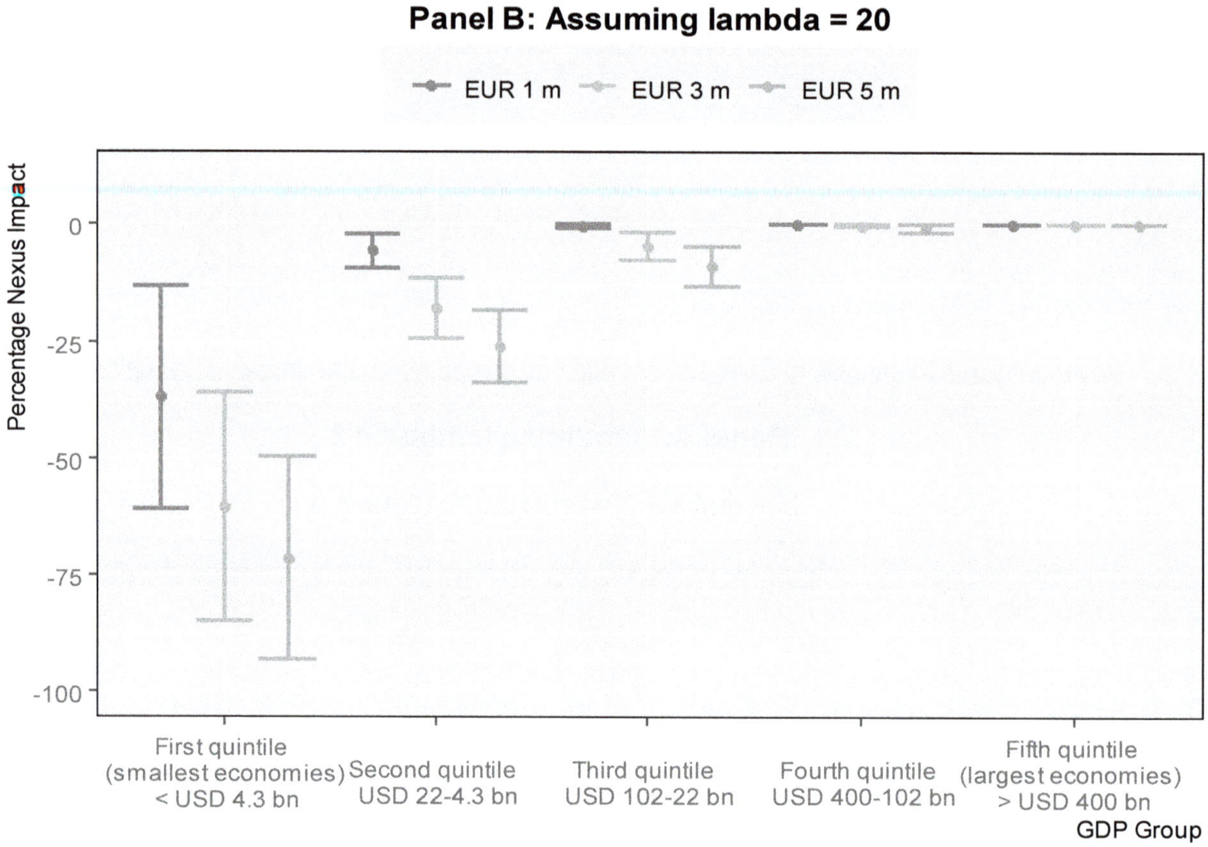


Note: These figures are alternative versions of Figure 2.10 for alternative values of the lambda parameter, which measures the propensity of MNEs to be more present in larger than smaller markets. Estimated differences are less than 1% on average for all jurisdiction groups and all nexus thresholds for values of lambda between 2 and 50. A value of 7 is used for lambda in the baseline estimate.
Source: OECD Secretariat.

# Annex 2.C. Estimated effect of Pillar One on tax bases

## Annex Figure 2.C.1. Estimated effect of Pillar One on tax bases, by jurisdiction groups

**Panel A:** 10% reallocation to market

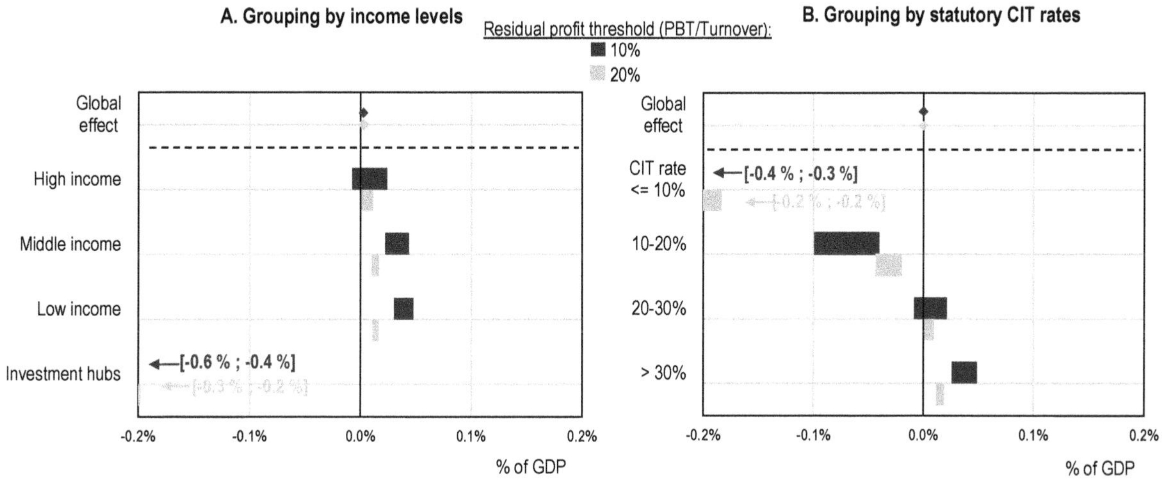


**Panel B:** 20% reallocation to market

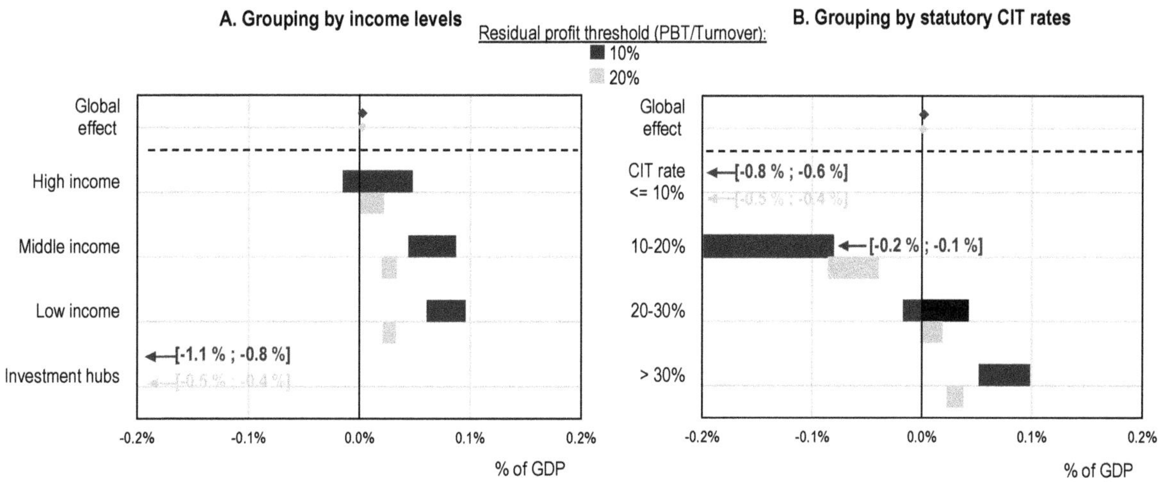

**Panel C:** 30% reallocation to market

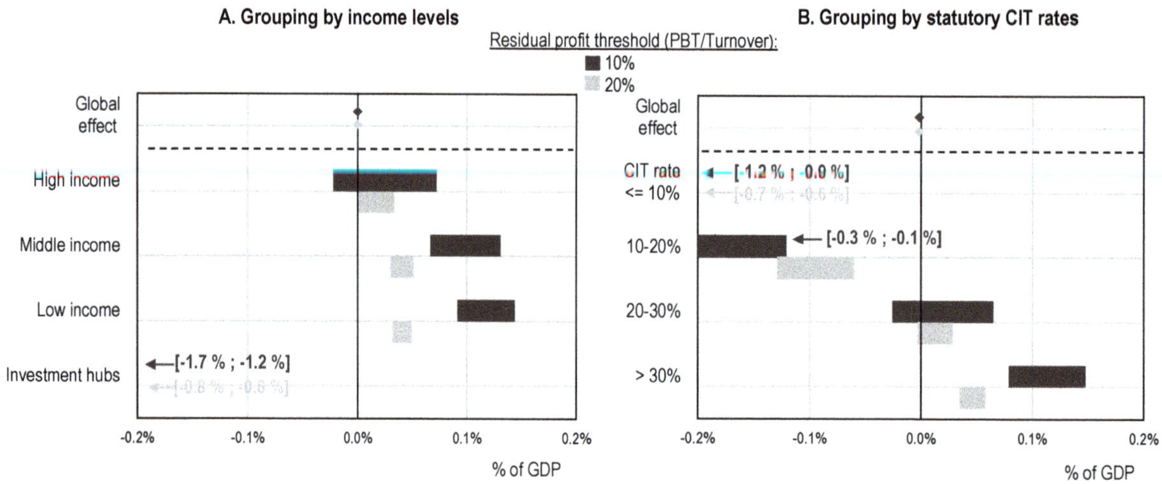


Note: All estimates are based on the methodology presented in this chapter and subject to the caveats listed in the first section of this chapter. Estimates are presented as ranges to reflect data uncertainty. The ranges measure the uncertainty around the estimate of each jurisdiction group, without necessarily implying that all jurisdictions in the group fall within the range. Results assume illustratively a EUR 750 million global revenue threshold, a profitability threshold (based on PBT to turnover) of 10% or 20%, a reallocation of 10% (Panel A), 20% (Panel B) or 30% (Panel C) of residual profit to market jurisdictions, a EUR 1 million nexus revenue threshold for ADS and a EUR 3 million nexus revenue threshold for CFB. Groups of jurisdictions (high, middle and low income) are based on the World Bank classification. Investment hubs are defined as jurisdictions with a total inward FDI position above 150% of GDP.
Source: OECD Secretariat.

# Annex 2.D. Robustness of results to alternative modelling of the location of ADS sales

172. As discussed in section 2.5.3, identifying the location of ADS destination-based sales poses data challenges. This annex contains a robustness check to assess the sensitivity of Pillar One revenue estimates to the assumptions used in modelling the location of ADS sales. The baseline results presented in Figure 2.14 are compared to results obtained with:

(i) An alternative distribution of ADS sales assuming lower sales in lower income jurisdictions. Compared to the baseline assumptions, ADS sales in low income jurisdictions are divided by 2, ADS sales in middle income jurisdictions are divided by 1.5 and ADS sales in high income jurisdictions are left unchanged. This alternative distribution can be interpreted as assuming that ADS represent a smaller share of the average consumption basket of internet users in lower income jurisdictions than in higher income jurisdictions. Ultimately, it is the *distribution* of global sales that is relevant for the revenue estimates in this chapter, and not the absolute *level* of sales.

(ii) An alternative distribution of ADS sales computed with the same method and the same data as the distribution of CFB sales (described in section 2.5.2).

173. Overall, results are not very sensitive to these different modelling assumptions.

## Annex Figure 2.D.1. Estimated effect of Pillar One on tax revenues, by jurisdiction groups, for alternative modelling assumptions on the location of ADS sales

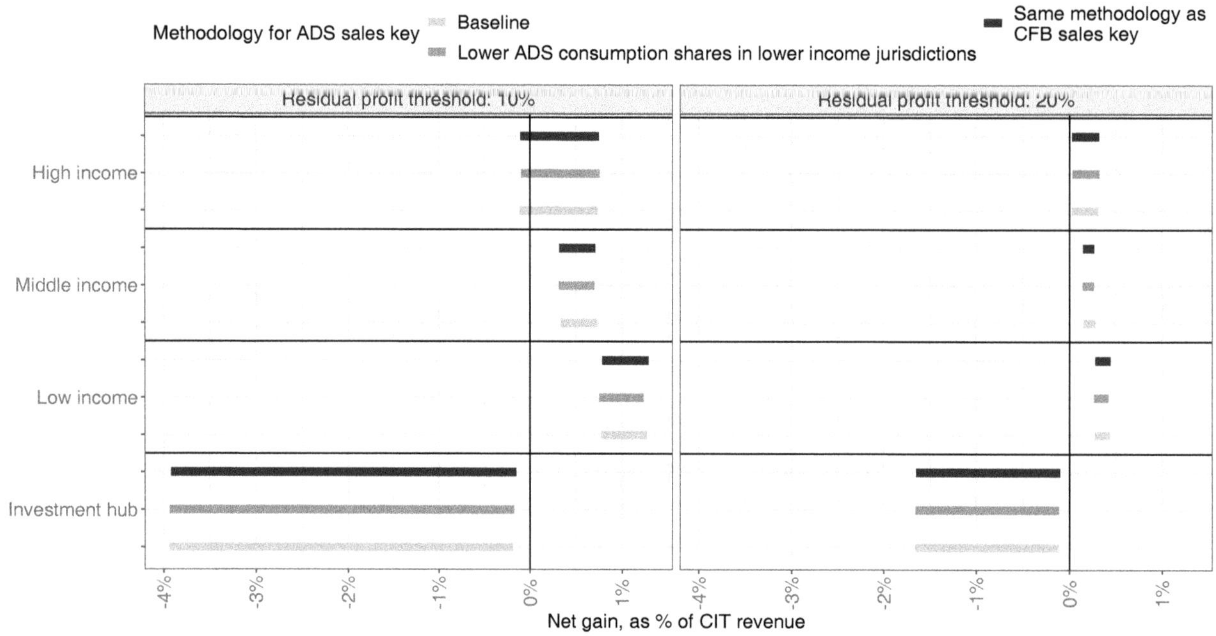


Note: This figure presents Pillar One revenue estimates by jurisdiction groups, illustrating the implications of using different assumptions to model the location of ADS sales. The baseline estimates in light blue correspond to those presented in Figure 2.14. The alternative estimates in darker shades of blue assume (i) that ADS represent a smaller share of the consumption basket of an internet user in lower income jurisdictions than in higher income jurisdictions, or (ii) computes ADS sales using the same methodology as the one used to estimate CFB sales. See section 2.5.3 for more details. Results assume illustratively a EUR 750 million global revenue threshold, a profitability threshold (based on the ratio of PBT to turnover) of 10%, a reallocation of 20% of residual profit to market jurisdictions, a EUR 1 million nexus threshold for ADS and a EUR 3 million nexus threshold for CFB. Groups of jurisdictions (high, middle and low income) are based on the World Bank classification. Investment hubs are defined as jurisdictions with a total inward FDI position above 150% of GDP.
Source: OECD Secretariat.

## Notes

[1] The OECD/G20 BEPS Package was released in October 2015 and various measures outlined in the package have been implemented in the years that have followed. A range of measures agreed to be implemented by members of the Inclusive Framework continue to be implemented by jurisdictions and, therefore, the full effect of these measures is not captured in the data available at the time of this analysis.

[2] This implies that, contrary to some other approaches in the literature, but in line with the Pillar One Blueprint report, the possibility to define (and potentially reallocate) 'negative residual profit' is not considered in this chapter.

[3] Total turnover of MNE groups in ORBIS and production of MNEs in Analytical AMNE are not fully comparable for two reasons, having effects going in opposite directions and broadly cancelling each other out: (i) turnover in Analytical AMNE includes intra-group transactions (which represent about a quarter of total MNE transactions according to aggregated CbCR data), while they are netted out in ORBIS consolidated account data; (ii) Analytical AMNE data focus on production, which is about a quarter smaller than turnover (the trade sector is where the difference is largest).

[4] For example, the 'IT software and services' category in the UNCTAD classification contains both producers of automated 'on-demand' software, which have been considered as ADS in the analysis in this chapter, and producers of more customised software involving heavier human intervention, which have been assumed to be out of scope. The main software producers have been classified manually to make this distinction. Another example is the NACE Rev. 2 category for the "activities of holding company", which contains some MNE groups with economic activities in different sectors. These MNE groups have been reclassified manually to the category corresponding to their economic activity.

[5] This estimate is based on MNE groups with financial data available in ORBIS for all the years from 2013 to 2016, with a global turnover above EUR 750 million in 2016, and with primary activities in all sectors excluding finance and insurance.

[6] The global MNE sales used in the denominator include sales of all MNE groups in scope, including MNE groups that do not sell in the jurisdiction considered, for consistency with component A, which focuses on the residual profit of all MNE groups in scope.

[7] Data from the BEA annual survey of the foreign activity of US multinationals are available on the BEA website (https://www.bea.gov/international/di1usdop). The yearly data includes specific statistics on majority-owned affiliates, which are the ones of interest here. In particular, several tables in Table II.E provide information on the industrial and geographical breakdown of goods and services supplied by US affiliates abroad. Table II.E.2 shows goods and services supplied by affiliates with a breakdown by jurisdiction. In 2015, foreign affiliates of US MNEs supplied USD 3.3 trillion of goods and services to their host countries including USD 3.1 trillion to unaffiliated entities.

[8] Using unpublished data underlying the OECD Analytical AMNE database, it is possible to subtract intermediate consumption sourced from (domestic or foreign-owned) MNE entities located in the same jurisdiction as the MNE entities considered. This corrects the issue posed by within-country intra-group sales (i.e. the arrow equal to 5 in Figure 2.3) but with the downside that within-country intermediate consumption from third-party entities is also subtracted, while it should not be.

[9] Entities are defined in the same way in Analytical AMNE as in the National Accounts, which means among other things that permanent establishments are treated in the same way as subsidiaries. Therefore, MNE sales going through a permanent establishment are counted at their destination in the proxy measure of destination-based sales.

[10] The classification in Table 2.2, Panel B implies that certain industries in Analytical AMNE contain subcategories that are CFB and others subcategories that are either ADS or out of scope. In this case, the sector has been included in proportion to the share of its activities that are CFB, based on data at the 4-digit level from the ORBIS database. For example, if a sector A contains two subcategories A1 (CFB) and A2 (out of scope), ORBIS consolidated account data is used to assess the relative importance of A1 and A2 in A, based on the global turnover of MNE groups in A1 and A2 (e.g. 70% in A1 and 30% in A2). Finally, the sector A is included in the computation of the proxy measure of destination-based sales in proportion to its share that is CFB (70% in this example), i.e. instead of adding to the proxy measure its turnover minus its exports, the approach is to add only 70% of its turnover minus 70% of its exports.

[11] This imputation is different from the imputation made in the online version of the Analytical AMNE database, which does not focus specifically on destination-based sales and therefore uses imputations based on another methodology, which is less relevant for the purpose of the present analysis.

[12] Ultimately, five jurisdictions (Hong Kong (China), India, Iceland, Morocco, and Romania) are deemed outliers in this regression, based on the Cook's distance – a statistical measure for outliers. For these five

jurisdictions, sales are based on the regression prediction rather than the imputation described above. These jurisdictions are also subsequently excluded from the final version of the extrapolation regression.

[13] Remittances received (https://data.worldbank.org/indicator/BX.TRF.PWKR.CD.DT) and paid (https://data.worldbank.org/indicator/BM.TRF.PWKR.CD.DT) consist of World Bank estimates based on balance of payments data from the IMF. Foreign aid is taken from the OECD Net Official Development Assistance database (https://data.oecd.org/oda/net-oda.htm).

[14] An analysis of more disaggregated data (not presented in this chapter) also suggests that the sectoral composition of MNE destination-based sales appears not to vary widely across jurisdictions. This may reflect the fact that sectoral specialisation is less pronounced in consumption patterns than in production patterns. While certain jurisdictions specialise in the production of certain goods or services, all jurisdictions generally consume a wide range of goods and services. Even the goods and services that are produced within a jurisdiction rather than imported (e.g. due to specialisation in production) may be produced by MNE entities and therefore included in MNE destination-based sales.

[15] Data on household consumption per capita is taken from the United Nations Statistics Division which provides consistent estimates of various national accounts aggregates in USD with a broad geographical coverage. Data on the share of internet users from the International Telecommunication Union was accessed through the World Bank data portal (https://databank.worldbank.org/reports.aspx?source=2&series=IT.NET.USER.ZS&country=) which shows the number of individuals who have used the internet in the last 3 months before the survey.

[16] The extrapolation regression of household consumption expenditure on GDP per capita presents outlying values for 9 jurisdictions (Brunei Darussalam, Kiribati, Macau (China), Nauru, Qatar, Sierra Leone, Turkmenistan, Venezuela, and Yemen), which have been identified based on a high Cook's distance. This suggests potential noise in the underlying data in these jurisdictions. To address this issue, the extrapolated values based on GDP-per-capita (which are likely to be generally less noisy) have been used for these jurisdictions.

[17] It is the distribution (rather than the level) of sales that matters in the estimation of Pillar One revenue effects in this chapter, and those assumptions should therefore be considered in terms of how they affect the distribution of sales rather than their level.

[18] A potential refinement to the approach would be to vary the $\lambda$ coefficient according to MNE size, reflecting that the propensity to focus only on larger markets is likely to be higher among smaller MNEs than among larger ones.

[19] For some very small jurisdictions this approach leads to very few MNEs being assigned presence, so a minimum probability of presence is assumed for very small jurisdictions so that there are always some MNEs present in each jurisdiction. In the baseline simulation, a minimum of 50 CFB MNEs and 15 ADS MNEs are assumed present.

[20] Using the share of jurisdiction *j* in global (ADS or CFB) sales is a conservative assumption, since the MNE considered may not have sales in all jurisdictions. A less conservative assumption would be to use the share of jurisdiction *j* in total (ADS or CFB) sales across the jurisdictions where the MNE is assumed to have sales.

[21] The number of simulations (200) is set sufficiently high to ensure that results would look similar if an even higher number of simulations were applied.

[22] Implicitly, this amounts to assuming that if residual profit is allocated to a jurisdiction where an MNE group is in a loss position, this MNE group is not allowed to offset residual profit against this loss.

[23] In contrast, consolidation effects can lead the "top-down" measure to be higher than the "bottom-up" one. This is the case if the denominator of the profitability ratio considered (e.g. turnover) includes intra-group transactions. For example, an MNE group may have a high profit-to-turnover ratio at the consolidated level (where intra-group transactions are consolidated and therefore not included in turnover), but relatively low profit-to-turnover ratios at the entity level, where turnover includes intra-group transactions.

[24] In practice, the residual profit matrix draws on a range of data sources, as further discussed below, including anonymised and aggregated CbCR data, which applies by construction a EUR 750m global revenue threshold, and other sources (e.g. ORBIS) where no such threshold is applied. This issue is discussed further in Chapter 5.

[25] UNCTAD produces a merchandise trade matrix which provides data on merchandise exports by country of origin, trading partner, and product group based on the Standard International Trade Classification.

[26] ORBIS unconsolidated account data has been cleaned and checked extensively, building on the OECD expertise from several earlier projects. The cleaning steps follow those applied to consolidated account data (described in Annex 2.A) but also include additional steps specific to unconsolidated level data (see details in Chapter 5)

[27] Ideally, it would be preferable to consolidate rather than sum the profit and turnover of entities from the same MNE group (i.e. to net out internal transactions) but this is not possible with the available data from ORBIS.

[28] Only fuels and metals are considered for this adjustment since the analysis of consolidated financial accounts of MNEs suggests that total residual profit in agriculture is very low compared to the fuels and metals sectors.

[29] The BEA data is taken from Table II.F.3 of the US Activities of US MNEs data. The 'information' sector in the BEA data regroups the following subcategories: publishing industries; motion picture and sound recording industries; broadcasting and telecommunications; data processing, hosting, and related services; other information services.

[30] This situation is more likely to occur for relatively high profitability thresholds than for lower thresholds. This explains why the "rescaling" is reducing the global amount of residual profit relatively more when assuming a 20% threshold than a 10% threshold (see Table 2.9 and Table 2.10).

[31] Ideally, the impact of revenue thresholds should also be taken into account in the computing of the 'bottom-up' residual profit matrix. However, limitations of the data underlying the profit and turnover matrices make this impossible to do.

[32] More precisely, the range is constructed as ±[10%+s*10%], with the variable 's' being the total residual profit that is based on extrapolations in the row of the residual profit matrix corresponding to the jurisdiction considered, divided by the total residual profit (extrapolated or not) in that row. Residual profit is considered to be based on extrapolations in cells of the residual profit matrix where the profit matrix upon which it builds is filled with extrapolations rather than with aggregated CbCR or ORBIS data.

[33] Jurisdictions with a CIT rate of exactly 20% are included in the second group (10-20%) and 30% in the third group (20-30%).

[34] The assumptions presented in the different sections of the chapter focus on building ranges for individual jurisdiction results. Ranges for jurisdiction groups are built with consistent assumptions by treating the group as a (fictitious) single jurisdiction. For example, for CFB sales in component C (i.e. CFB MNE sales into a jurisdiction, as a share of global CFB MNE sales), the methodology is to build a range of ±10% around the point estimate for a jurisdiction when the estimate is based on hard data, and ±20% when it is based on extrapolations. For a group of jurisdictions, the range would be ±[10%+s*10%] around the point estimate (which would be the total MNE sales into the group of jurisdiction, as a share of global MNE sales), with s representing the share of MNE sales that are based on extrapolation in the jurisdiction group considered.

# 3 Tax revenue effects of Pillar Two

## 3.1. Introduction

174. This chapter presents the analytical framework and data sources used by the OECD Secretariat to assess the effect on corporate tax revenues of Pillar Two. It also contains high-level estimates of the impact of Pillar Two at the global level and at the level of broad groups of jurisdictions. Pillar Two addresses remaining BEPS challenges and is designed to ensure that large internationally operating businesses pay a minimum level of tax regardless of where they are headquartered or the jurisdictions they operate in (OECD, 2020[1]).

175. The analytical framework presented in this chapter explores the implications of (i) several illustrative design and parameter options under Pillar Two, (ii) the interaction between Pillar One and Pillar Two and how this interaction can affect the revenue effects of Pillar Two, and (iii) potential behavioural reactions by multinational enterprises (MNEs) and governments to the introduction of Pillar Two. A number of design elements and parameters of Pillar One and Pillar Two will be the subject of future decisions by the Inclusive Framework. The Pillar One and Pillar Two design and parameter options considered in this chapter are only illustrative examples and should not be seen as prejudging any final decisions to be taken by the Inclusive Framework.

176. Similar to the framework used to assess the effect of Pillar One (see Chapter 2), the framework presented in this chapter spans more than 200 jurisdictions and combines a variety of micro- and macro-level data sources into a consistent structure. One central element of this structure is the set of data matrices described in detail in Chapter 5.

177. The framework is building on the best data sources available to the OECD Secretariat, and the underlying data has been subject to extensive checks and comparisons across data sources. The resulting estimates are nevertheless subject to a number of important caveats:

- The assessment of Pillar Two revenue effects in this chapter is based on a number of simplifying assumptions on the design and implementation of Pillar Two, reflecting the challenges involved in modelling certain potential provisions of Pillar Two with the available data. In particular, the switch-over rule and the subject to tax rule have not been modelled, while the income inclusion rule and the undertaxed payments rule have been modelled only in a relatively stylised way. The potential effect of temporary or permanent differences between financial accounting profit and the Pillar Two tax base, and the effect of a loss carry-forward mechanism under Pillar Two (or any other profit smoothing mechanism) have not been taken into account. The modelling of a potential formulaic substance-based carve-out is based on a number of simplifying assumptions, as discussed further in this chapter.
- The approach to estimating the effect of Pillar Two focuses on low-taxed profits in generally low-tax jurisdictions,[1] but leaves aside potential "pockets" of low-taxed profit in generally higher-tax jurisdictions, due to limitations in the available data. The upper bound of the uncertainty ranges surrounding the estimates in this chapter has been increased to account for this uncertainty, as described further in this chapter.

- Due to data limitations, the effect of certain provisions that may already allow jurisdictions to levy taxes on profit that would otherwise be subject to low levels of effective taxation (e.g. withholding taxes, CFC rules) is not taken into account in the modelling in this chapter, which could lead to overestimating potential revenue gains.
- The data underlying the analysis have limitations in terms of coverage, consistency and timeliness. In particular, the reliance on aggregate data in certain parts of the analysis and for certain jurisdictions implies that some firm-level heterogeneities are overlooked, which could affect the results. Data on MNEs' profit relates primarily to years 2016 and 2017. It therefore pre-dates some significant recent developments, including the implementation of various measures under the OECD/G20 Base Erosion and Profit Shifting project,[2] the US Tax Cuts and Jobs Act (TCJA) and, more recently, the impact of the COVID-19 crisis. More specifically:
  - The implementation of the BEPS Action Plan is expected to reduce the amount of global low-taxed profit by reducing opportunities for MNEs to shift profit to low-tax jurisdictions. This reduces the potential revenue gains from Pillar Two.
  - Regarding the US TCJA, while no decision has been taken by the Inclusive Framework yet, the analysis assumes illustratively that the US Global Intangible Low Tax Income (GILTI) regime that has been in place since 2018 and results in a form of minimum tax on the foreign profit of US MNEs would "co-exist" with Pillar Two. Potential gains from Pillar Two presented in this chapter exclude US MNEs on the basis of the assumption that they would remain subject to GILTI and not be subject to the Pillar Two rules. Revenue gains from GILTI are discussed in section 3.8 of this chapter, based on ex ante estimates by the US Joint Committee on Taxation (US Joint Committee on Taxation, 2017[2]).
  - The COVID-19 crisis is likely to reduce the profitability of many MNEs – and, in turn, the amount of profit subject to Pillar Two – in the short and medium run, due to lower consumer demand, as well as potential difficulties with production (e.g. locked-down workers, supply chain disruptions, restrictions on travel). The longer term effect of the crisis on MNE profitability remains highly uncertain and will depend on the shape and speed of the economic recovery, as well as potential structural changes to the economy that the crisis may bring or accelerate (e.g. changes in the sectoral structure of economies, including faster-than-expected digitalisation of certain activities, as well as potential changes in the structure of global value chains and competition dynamics among firms).
- The methodology takes into account, in a stylised way, potential strategic reactions by MNEs and governments to the introduction of Pillar Two. More specifically, the analysis focuses on (i) potential changes in MNEs' profit shifting intensity, and (ii) potential tax rate increases in jurisdictions with an average effective tax rate (ETR) below the Pillar Two minimum rate. However, the exact nature and intensity of these reactions is difficult to anticipate with certainty, especially in the context of a coordinated multilateral tax reform, while existing studies are mainly based on jurisdiction-specific reforms. In particular, the exact location of MNE profits in a post-Pillar Two world is difficult to anticipate because MNE profit shifting schemes are often complex and could be modified in ways that are complex and difficult to anticipate following the introduction of Pillar Two.
- The analysis in this chapter does not try to model other potential reactions by MNEs and governments, including potential changes in MNEs' real investment decisions and policy reactions by other jurisdictions. The implications of Pillar One and Pillar Two on MNEs' real investment decisions and on tax competition between jurisdictions are discussed in detail in Chapter 4. Overall, the assessment in Chapter 4 is that Pillar One and Pillar Two would have a small negative direct effect on global MNE investment that could be partly or even fully offset by positive indirect effects. In addition, a consensus-based multilateral solution involving Pillar One and Pillar Two would lead to a more favourable environment for investment and growth than would likely be the case in absence of an agreement by the Inclusive Framework (see Chapter 4). Still, Pillar Two could lead

to significant increases in investment costs in jurisdictions where the ETR is currently below the potential level of the minimum rate under Pillar Two. This could significantly affect MNE investment in these jurisdictions and, in turn, affect CIT revenues, as well as revenues from other tax bases (e.g. personal income tax, value added tax) in these jurisdictions.

178. Given these caveats, the estimates based on the framework presented in this chapter should be interpreted as illustrating the broad order of magnitude of the impacts of Pillar Two, rather than precise point estimates. Actual gains from Pillar Two may differ from these ex ante estimates as these gains will ultimately depend on the final design and parameter decisions to be taken by the Inclusive Framework, the actual responses of MNEs and governments to the introduction of Pillar Two and the economic situation at the time of implementation. In light of this, the estimates presented in this chapter are expressed as ranges to reflect the uncertainty surrounding them. For simplicity, some intermediate results in this chapter are presented as point estimates, but the overall results in the final section are presented as ranges.

## 3.2. Assumptions on Pillar Two design underlying the estimates

179. As described in the Pillar Two Blueprint report (OECD, 2020[1]), Pillar Two comprises a number of interlocking rules that seek to (i) ensure minimum taxation while avoiding double taxation or taxation where there is no economic profit, (ii) cope with different tax system designs by jurisdictions as well as different operating models by businesses, (iii) ensure transparency and a level playing field, and (iv) minimise administrative and compliance costs.

- The principal mechanism to achieve this outcome is the **income inclusion rule** (IIR) together with the **undertaxed payments rule** (UTPR) acting as a backstop (the "GloBE rules"). The operation of the IIR is, in some respects, based on traditional controlled foreign company (CFC) rule principles and triggers an inclusion at the level of the shareholder where the income of a controlled foreign entity is taxed at below the effective minimum tax rate. It is complemented by a **switch-over rule** (SOR) that removes treaty obstacles from its application to certain branch structures and applies where an income tax treaty otherwise obligates a contracting state to use the exemption method. The UTPR is a secondary rule and only applies where a Constituent Entity is not already subject to an IIR. The UTPR is nevertheless a key part of the rule set as it serves as back-stop to the IIR, ensures a level playing field and addresses inversion risks that might otherwise arise.
- The **subject to tax rule** (STTR) complements these rules. It is a treaty-based rule that targets risks to source countries posed by BEPS structures relating to intragroup payments that take advantage of low nominal rates of taxation in the other contracting jurisdiction (that is the jurisdiction of the payee).

180. In this chapter, the revenue effects of Pillar Two are assessed by identifying low-taxed profits of MNEs (i.e. profits that are taxed below a potential minimum rate) and assuming that a top-up tax would apply to bring the ETR on these profits (after application of a potential formulaic substance-based carve-out) up to the level of the minimum rate (Figure 3.1). The four components listed above (IIR, UTPR, SOR and STTR) would all contribute to this outcome. In practice, as further discussed in the next paragraphs, it is difficult to disentangle with precision the contribution of each of these components, due to data limitations and uncertainties about the exact design of the Pillar Two components and their interactions, which will ultimately be defined by the Inclusive Framework.

Figure 3.1. Simplified formula summarising the approach on Pillar Two

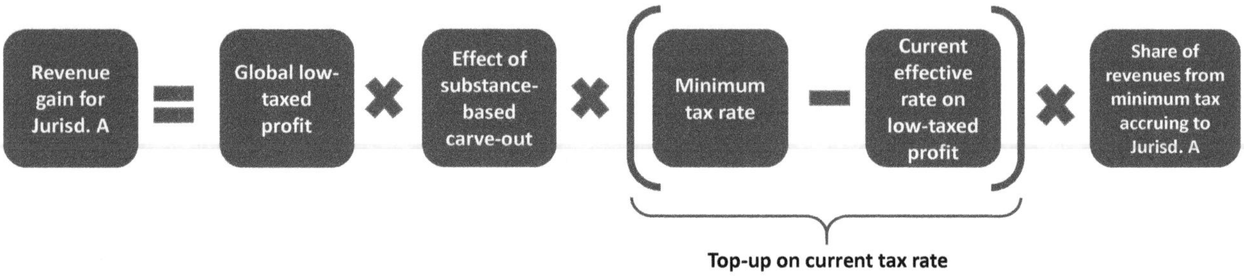


Note: The starting point to compute the revenue effects of Pillar Two is to assess the amount of low-taxed profit of MNEs (i.e. profit taxed at a rate below the potential minimum rate level). The effect of a potential formulaic substance-based carve-out is to exclude a fraction of these low-taxed profits from the scope of Pillar Two. Then, Pillar Two operates as a 'top-up' to bring the effective tax rate on the low-taxed profits in scope up to the level of the minimum rate (parenthesis of the formula). Finally, the share of Pillar Two revenue gains accruing to each jurisdiction is determined based on assumptions on the functioning of Pillar Two that are described in this chapter.
Source: OECD Secretariat

181. Consistent with the Pillar Two Blueprint report, the approach in this chapter is to assume that MNEs' low-taxed profits would generally be subject to a top-up tax in the jurisdiction of the ultimate parent entity of the MNE group under the **income inclusion rule**. The **switch-over rule** is not explicitly modelled in this chapter, but would implicitly contribute to the application of the income inclusion rule. Similarly, it is challenging to determine, based on the design of the **subject to tax rule** and the available data, what impact that rule would have on a jurisdiction's tax base. Given these challenges, the impact of the subject to tax rule has not been modelled in this chapter.

182. In the stylised scenarios considered for the purpose of modelling in this chapter, certain ultimate parent jurisdictions would not necessarily introduce an income inclusion rule (e.g. jurisdictions that do not have a corporate tax system today). The low-taxed profits of MNEs with an ultimate parent in these jurisdictions are assumed to face the top-up tax in other jurisdictions, in proportion to the distribution of their economic activity across these other jurisdictions. This assumption is a proxy for the transaction-based approach envisaged under the **undertaxed payments rule**, with the idea that transactions subject to this rule are likely to originate in jurisdictions where the MNE group considered engages in economic activity. This assumption can also be seen as a possible proxy for situations where the jurisdiction of an intermediate parent would apply the income inclusion rule, as envisaged in the Pillar Two Blueprint report, assuming that the location of these intermediate parents (on which no data are available in most jurisdictions) is broadly aligned with the location of economic activity.

183. Another important Pillar Two design question is the degree of "blending" (i.e. the level of aggregation at which the effective tax rate would be computed and the minimum rate applied). While no decision has been taken by the Inclusive Framework yet, it is assumed in this chapter that Pillar Two would entail jurisdictional blending in line with the Pillar Two Blueprint report. This would imply that the ETR of an MNE would be computed by aggregating taxes paid and profits at the jurisdiction level. This ETR would then be compared to the minimum tax rate.

184. Other Pillar Two design and parameter choices will also influence the revenue effects of Pillar Two. A key parameter is the potential minimum tax rate – in this area, several possibilities are illustratively explored in this chapter. Other questions include the definition of the tax base (including questions related to adjustments for permanent and temporary book-tax differences), the definition of taxes covered in the computation of the ETR, the existence and design of a potential loss carry-forward mechanism, and the existence and scope of potential 'carve-outs' based on substantive activities and/or for certain sectors or in relation to MNE size. Consistent with the Pillar Two Blueprint report, MNEs with a global turnover below EUR 750 million (i.e. the Country-by-Country Reporting threshold) are assumed not to be in the scope of

Pillar Two in the estimates in this chapter. The implications of a potential formulaic substance-based carve-out are illustratively modelled in this chapter, while no sectoral carve-outs are considered in the estimates due to data limitations. Finally, the effect of a potential loss carry-forward mechanism is not taken into account, due to lack of time series data on MNE profit across jurisdictions,[3] while the inclusion of such a mechanism could reduce potential revenue gains from Pillar Two.

185. While no decision has been taken by the Inclusive Framework yet, the estimates in this chapter are based on the illustrative assumption that the US GILTI regime would "co-exist" with Pillar Two. Reflecting this, the estimates presented in this chapter generally exclude the potential revenue gains related to US MNEs on the basis that they would remain subject to GILTI and not subject to Pillar Two rules. This means that in the tables and figures presenting estimates of Pillar Two revenue gains in this chapter, gains related to US MNEs (including both direct gains from the minimum tax and indirect gains from reduced profit shifting or ETR increases) are generally excluded. This is indicated in the subtitles and reading notes of these tables or figures. Other tables containing intermediate data or results not directly representing Pillar Two gains (e.g. profit matrix at an aggregated level) generally include data relative to US MNEs, as indicated in the notes of these tables. Revenue gains related to US MNEs are discussed in Section 3.8, based on the ex ante estimates of GILTI revenue gains from the US Joint Committee on Taxation (JCT).

## 3.3. Scenarios considered in terms of behavioural reactions

186. In considering potential behavioural reactions, a series of four stylised scenarios are modelled. These scenarios are summarised in Figure 3.2. These scenarios and the strategy to quantify their revenue implications are described in more detail in the following sections.

- **Scenario 1**, which is the starting point for the estimates, is a "static" scenario. In this scenario, potential behavioural reactions of MNEs and governments to the introduction of Pillar Two are not taken into account, and Pillar Two is modelled in isolation, in the sense that its potential interaction with Pillar One is not taken into account.
- **Scenario 2** takes into account the interaction between Pillar One and Pillar Two. In this scenario, Pillar Two is assumed to apply on profit after the reallocation implied by Amount A of Pillar One, as modelled in Chapter 2, based on illustrative assumptions on Pillar One design and parameters. Alternative results ignoring this interaction but accounting for the reactions of MNEs and governments modelled in Scenarios 3 and 4 are presented in Annex 3.B.
- **Scenario 3** builds on Scenario 2 by adding the assumption that MNEs' profit shifting intensity would be reduced by Pillar Two. This is because Pillar Two would reduce tax rate differentials between jurisdictions, which are a primary driver of profit shifting. This reduction in profit shifting is assessed based on stylised modelling assumptions that are discussed further in Section 3.6.
- **Scenario 4** builds on Scenario 3 by adding the assumption that certain jurisdictions would change certain tax rules/rates to increase the ETR on MNE profit that is currently taxed below the minimum rate in their jurisdiction. The rationale for this reaction is that it could allow the jurisdictions increasing their ETR to collect a greater share of global tax revenues, while having only a generally limited effect on the overall tax payments of MNE groups (as discussed below, this effect would depend on the design of Pillar Two and notably on the potential inclusion of a formulaic substance-based carve-out, as well as the potential co-existence of the US GILTI regime with Pillar Two).

Figure 3.2. Scenarios considered in the Pillar Two estimates

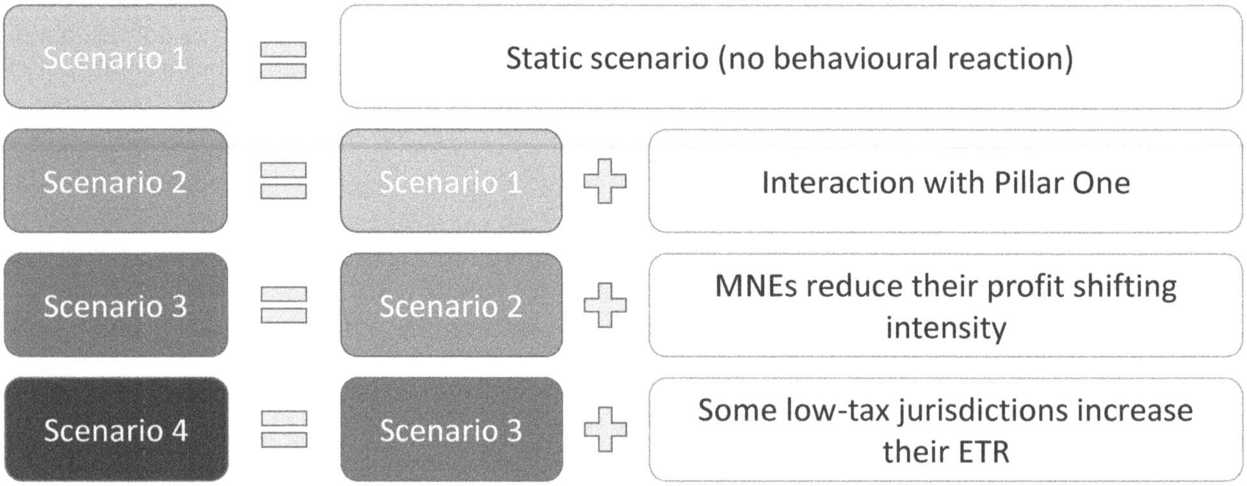


Note: Other behavioural reactions to Pillar Two are also possible, but they are not modelled in this chapter. These non-modelled reactions include for example changes in MNE 'real' investment location (with potential implications for CIT revenues but also for revenues from other tax bases) as well as policy changes in jurisdictions with an average ETR above the minimum rate. These potential reactions are discussed in Chapter 4.
Source: OECD Secretariat.

187. The timing of MNEs' and governments' reactions considered in Scenarios 3 and 4 is uncertain, raising the question of the order in which they should be considered in the analysis. It is possible that MNEs' profit shifting strategies would be adjusted faster and with more precision than governments' corporate tax systems. Indeed, the latter may involve a multiplicity of interconnected statutory provisions, all having different effects on the tax position of different firms, and any adjustments could require lengthy law-making processes to take place. This justifies considering MNE reactions first (in Scenario 3) and government reactions second (in Scenario 4). However, given the scenarios and assumptions considered in this chapter, reversing this order (i.e. considering government reactions first and MNE reactions second) would have virtually no (or at most a quantitatively very small) effect on the final results. The reason is that the government reactions considered in this chapter do not significantly affect the profit shifting incentives of MNEs, since they do not change significantly the overall amount of taxes paid by MNEs (they only change where taxes are paid).[4] As a result, MNEs' reactions are not expected to depend substantially on whether they are considered before or after government reactions, at least under the stylised scenarios considered in this chapter.

188. The four stylised scenarios presented in this chapter do not aim to cover the full universe of possible reactions, but to illustrate the implications of some of the most widely expected reactions to Pillar Two. The reactions considered have been selected based on earlier discussions with jurisdiction representatives, academics, private sector representatives and other international organisations. Other potential reactions are not modelled in this chapter, including MNEs modifying their 'real' investment behaviour (as opposed to profit shifting intensity), MNEs modifying their profit shifting strategies in more complex ways than envisaged in this chapter, and governments from higher-tax jurisdictions (i.e. with average ETRs above the potential minimum rate under Pillar Two) reacting to the introduction of Pillar Two by changing their tax rules or rates:

- **On MNEs' real investment behaviour**, the OECD Secretariat estimates suggest that Pillar Two would only result in limited effects on forward-looking average ETRs at the global level and across most jurisdictions (Chapter 4). This would indicate that the scale of investment effects would generally be limited (in addition, these effects could be offset, partly or fully, by the indirect effects discussed in Chapter 4), providing justification for the assumption not to take these effects into account in this chapter. An important exception is that jurisdictions that currently have an ETR below the potential minimum rate could face significant ETR increases. This would affect MNE investment into these low-tax jurisdictions, while possibly benefitting higher-tax jurisdictions where some investment may be redirected. In turn, this would reduce corporate tax revenues in these low-tax jurisdictions, as well as revenues from other tax bases (e.g. personal income tax, value added tax). These effects are not modelled in this chapter.

- **On MNE profit shifting strategies**, the modelling in this chapter is based on simplified assumptions described below relating to profit shifting intensity to tax rate differentials between jurisdictions. In practice, MNE profit shifting schemes are often complex and largely firm-specific. The exact way in which these schemes could be modified in reaction to Pillar Two may differ from these simplified assumptions, which would influence final outcomes, but this is impossible to model with precision, as further discussed below.
- **On the policy reaction of "higher-tax" jurisdictions** (i.e. jurisdictions with an average ETR above the potential minimum rate), the expected reaction is ambiguous and therefore difficult to anticipate with certainty, as further discussed in Chapter 4. In theory, the introduction of a minimum rate could strengthen or weaken tax competition depending on the assumptions considered (Keen and Konrad, 2013[3]).[5] An empirical study on the 2004 introduction of a minimum tax rate at the municipal level in Germany suggests that, on average, it led to municipalities with rates above the minimum significantly increasing their rates (von Schwerin and Buettner, 2016[4]), However, it is not clear to what extent these results can be generalised from a national to a global context.

## 3.4. Scenario 1: Static estimates of Pillar Two revenue effects

189. The simplified approach followed in this chapter is to identify jurisdictions where the average (backward-looking) ETR on MNE profit is below the potential minimum tax rate. All MNE profit in these jurisdictions is assumed to be taxed at this average ETR (due to lack of available firm-level data on ETRs in most jurisdictions), and therefore – after application of a potential formulaic substance-based carve-out – to face a top-up tax up to the level of the minimum tax.

190. This is a simplification in the sense that it does not take into account that (i) some MNE profit may be subject to a higher ETR than the minimum rate in low-tax jurisdictions (pockets of high-taxed profits) and (ii) some MNE profit may be subject to a lower ETR than the minimum rate in higher-tax jurisdictions (pockets of low-taxed profits). Pockets of low-taxed profit are further discussed in Box 3.1 below and are taken into account in the uncertainty ranges around the results. Pockets of high-taxed profit seem likely to be less common than pockets of low-taxed profit and the effect of their omission is a priori ambiguous (because taking pockets of high-taxed profit into account would reduce the estimated amount of profit subject to Pillar Two in low-tax jurisdictions, but also reduce the average ETR on profit subject to Pillar Two in these jurisdictions). Due to data limitations, the approach also overlooks the fact that some foreign profit may already be taxed at the parent level via controlled foreign company (CFC) rules and withholding taxes. This would reduce Pillar Two gains.

191. This modelling approach requires data on the location of profit as well as data on ETRs. The source of data on profit is described in the next section, while data on ETRs are presented in the following one. The modelling of the implications of a potential formulaic substance-based carve-out is described afterwards.

### 3.4.1. Data source on profit location: The "profit matrix"

192. As in Chapter 2, the analysis in this chapter relies on the "profit matrix", which combines data from different sources on the location of MNE profit (see stylised illustration in Figure 3.3 and detailed description in Chapter 5).

Figure 3.3. Profit matrix: Stylised overview and underlying data sources

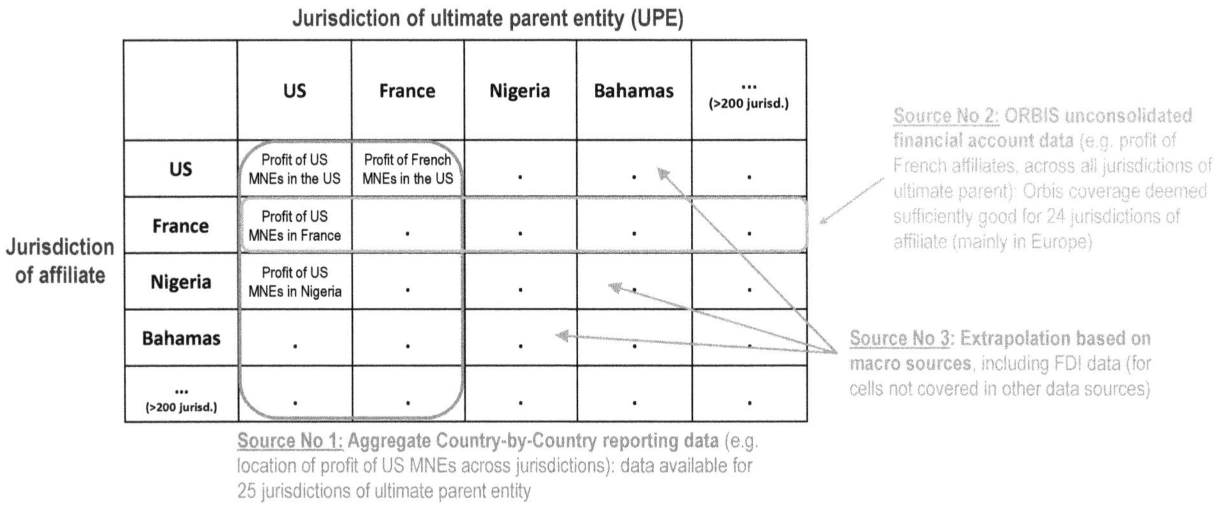


Note: Aggregate CbCR data are used to fill *columns* of the profit matrix (e.g. profit of French MNEs across jurisdictions). ORBIS unconsolidated account data are used to fill *rows* of the profit matrix (i.e. MNE profit in France, split across ultimate parent jurisdictions). These two sources are used only where available, and in the case of ORBIS, where data coverage is sufficiently good. Other cells in the profit matrix are filled with extrapolations based on macroeconomic data, including FDI data.
Source: OECD Secretariat.

193. The profit matrix draws on three main sources of data, presented below in descending order of preference:

1) Anonymised and aggregated data from Country-by-Country Reports (CbCRs), across 25 jurisdictions of ultimate parent (see list in Annex 5.A of Chapter 5);[6]
2) ORBIS unconsolidated account data in 24 jurisdictions of affiliate with good ORBIS coverage (see list in Annex 5.A of Chapter 5);
3) Extrapolations based on macroeconomic data (e.g. FDI data) in other cells.

194. Wherever possible, the data in the profit matrix (and in the tangible assets and payroll matrices described below) focus on MNE sub-groups with positive profits (i.e. entities belonging to an MNE group that is reporting an overall profit in the jurisdiction considered), rather than all MNE sub-groups (i.e. profit-making *and* loss-making sub-groups). Indeed, only MNE sub-groups with positive profits potentially face additional taxes under Pillar Two, while loss-making sub-groups generally do not pay corporate income tax. Subtracting the losses of loss-making MNE sub-groups when computing total profit in a jurisdiction could therefore lead to an underestimation of the amount of profit that could be subject to Pillar Two.

195. Still, a limitation of the approach is that the effect of a loss carry-forward mechanism under Pillar Two is not taken into account in the estimates. Such a mechanism could reduce revenue gains from Pillar Two in situations where an MNE sub-group in a low-tax jurisdiction makes a (low-taxed) profit and can use its past losses in that jurisdiction to offset it partly or fully. Estimating with precision the effect of the loss carry-forward mechanism would require firm-level information on the profitability of MNE sub-groups over several successive years. This information is not available to the OECD Secretariat in most jurisdictions.[7]

In practice, the effect of the loss-carry forward mechanism on Pillar Two revenue gains will depend on how frequently MNE sub-groups in low-tax jurisdictions switch from being loss-making to being profitable. This may depend on the economic situation – for example, the COVID-19 crisis is likely to make losses more frequent – but also on profit shifting and loss shifting behaviour by MNEs. For example, even taking into account a carry-forward mechanism under Pillar Two, it may still be more beneficial for MNEs to incur losses in higher-tax than in low-tax jurisdictions, as these losses can be used to offset future profits at a higher rate in higher-tax jurisdictions.

196. The profit matrix – at a relatively high level of aggregation – is displayed in Table 3.1. The full methodology underlying the construction of the profit matrix is presented in detail in Chapter 5. Chapter 5 also contains detailed information on the data sources used in the profit matrix, including a discussion of the caveats around their use. In addition, Chapter 5 displays a more disaggregated version of the profit matrix (i.e. with more detailed jurisdiction groups than in Table 3.1), as well as information on the relative importance of the different data sources underlying the matrix. Finally, Chapter 5 contains the results of the extensive benchmarking that was undertaken to assess the quality of the data and its consistency across sources.

Table 3.1. Profit matrix: Results aggregated by broad jurisdiction groups

| | | Jurisdiction of ultimate parent | | | | |
|---|---|---|---|---|---|---|
| | (USD billion of 2016) | High income | Middle income | Low income | Investment Hubs | Total |
| Jurisdiction of affiliate | High income (64 jurisd.) | 3569.1 | 44.1 | 0.1 | 171.3 | **3784.5** |
| | Middle income (105) | 366.2 | 821.8 | 0.1 | 167.9 | **1356.0** |
| | Low income (29) | 1.3 | 1.3 | 3.1 | 0.2 | **5.8** |
| | Investment Hubs (24) | 650.9 | 69.5 | 0.0 | 314.3 | **1034.7** |
| | **Total** | **4587.4** | **936.7** | **3.3** | **653.7** | **6181.1** |

Note: Groups of jurisdictions (high, middle and low income) are based on the World Bank classification. The number of jurisdictions in each group is indicated in parentheses. Investment hubs are defined as jurisdictions with a total inward FDI position above 150% of GDP. MNEs with an ultimate parent in the United States are included in this table.
Source: OECD calculations based on a variety of sources including aggregated CbCR data, ORBIS and macroeconomic data. See Chapter 5 for more details.

### *3.4.2. Data sources on effective tax rates (ETRs)*

197. The relevant ETR to assess if an MNE has low-taxed profit in a jurisdiction and would be subject to Pillar Two will be computed at the level of each MNE sub-group in each jurisdiction (assuming that Pillar Two would involve jurisdictional blending). Estimating with precision the effect of Pillar Two would therefore require data on ETRs at that level. However, the data are not available to the OECD Secretariat in most jurisdictions, and the approach therefore relies on average ETRs computed from aggregated data.

198. The average ETR on MNE profit in a jurisdiction is measured as the median estimate obtained across the three following data sources:

- **Data from Tørsløv et al.** (2018[5]). These data, themselves based on a combination of sources and assumptions, focus on the ETR on the profit of foreign-owned MNEs across a range of jurisdictions in 2015. The underlying data generally does not distinguish between profit-making and loss-making MNE sub-groups and can thus lead to higher measures of ETR than data that would focus only on profit-making sub-groups.[8]
- **Data from the US Bureau of Economic Analysis (BEA) on US MNEs.** In an annual report on the global activity of US MNEs, the BEA provides information on foreign taxes paid by affiliates of

US MNEs across a set of jurisdictions. In each of these jurisdictions, the average ETR of US MNEs is computed by dividing foreign taxes paid by "profit-type return", which is a measure of profit included in the BEA data that aims to approximate profit before tax and excludes various sources of financial income. To reduce the impact of potential volatility in the data, the ETR used in this chapter is computed as the average ETR over several years (2013-16), i.e. the sum of taxes paid in a jurisdiction over the period divided by the sum of profit-type returns in this jurisdiction over the same period.[9] As with the data from Tørsløv et al. (2018[5]), the BEA data aggregates data relative to profit-making and loss-making MNE sub-groups, which leads to higher ETRs than when focusing only on profit-making sub-groups.

- **Data from anonymised and aggregated CbCR reports.** The anonymised and aggregated CbCRs from 25 jurisdictions of ultimate parent (see list in Annex 5.A of Chapter 5) have been used to compute average ETRs by jurisdiction of affiliate. The ETR in a given jurisdiction of affiliate is computed as the total taxes paid by foreign-owned MNEs (on an accrual basis) over total profit of foreign-owned MNEs, focusing only on profit-making sub-groups (contrary to the other two sources). Extreme outliers are eliminated (e.g. ETRs above 100%) and jurisdictions covered in the data of fewer than three ultimate parent jurisdictions are excluded. An important caveat is that due to potential inclusion of intracompany dividends in profit reported in CbCRs, ETRs may be underestimated, especially in jurisdictions with a large presence of parent companies (OECD, 2020[6]).

199. None of these three measures of ETRs is subject to the issue of profit double counting pointed out by Blouin and Robinson (2019[7]) (see also discussion in Clausing (2020[8])). In addition, using the median value across the three measures reduces the potential impact of limitations of individual data sources on the final revenue estimates (e.g. limitations related to the potential inclusion of dividends in CbCR data, which could lead to overestimating Pillar Two gains, or to the fact that data from Tørsløv et al. (2018[5]) and BEA data include loss-making sub-groups, which could lead to underestimating Pillar Two gains). A robustness analysis excluding CbCR data from the calculation and relying only on the average of the other two sources suggests that it could lead to lower estimates of Pillar Two gains, but without changing the broad order of magnitude of the results (see Annex 3.D).

200. All three data sources are available jointly for 42 jurisdictions representing 86% of world GDP (Table 3.2). At least one of the three data sources is available for another 99 jurisdictions, representing another 12% of world GDP. For the other 81 jurisdictions considered in the analysis, which are mainly lower income jurisdictions that together represent only 1% of world GDP, none of these three sources are available and the ETR is assumed to correspond to the statutory CIT rate, sourced from the OECD Corporate Tax Statistics (OECD, 2020[9]), complemented with other sources.[10] This is a conservative assumption since ETRs are generally lower than statutory rates. However, the impact of this assumption on the global estimates is likely to be marginal as less than 1% of total MNE profit is found to be located in these jurisdictions.

Table 3.2. Coverage of the three data sources on effective tax rates (ETRs)

| Number of ETR data sources available | Number of jurisdictions | Share of world GDP | Share of global MNE profit |
|---|---|---|---|
| All 3 sources available | 42 | 86% | 90% |
| 1 or 2 sources available | 99 | 12% | 10% |
| No source available | 81 | 1% | 0% |
| **Total** | **222** | **100%** | **100%** |

Note: Three data sources are used to measure ETRs on MNE profits across jurisdictions: (i) data from Tørsløv et al. (2018[5]), (ii) data from the US Bureau of Economic Analysis, and (iii) data from aggregated and anonymised CbCR reports. Not all sources are available for all jurisdictions. For example, the three sources are available simultaneously for 42 jurisdictions representing 86% of world GDP and 90% of global MNE profit. Profit location is computed based on the profit matrix presented in detail in Chapter 5. In jurisdictions where no ETR source is available, the statutory CIT rate is used as a proxy.
Source: OECD Secretariat.

### *3.4.3. Global low-taxed profit and global revenue gains (before carve-out)*

201. Based on the profit matrix and the ETR data described above, the global amount of low-taxed profit (i.e. profit taxed below a potential minimum rate) is presented in Table 3.3 for an illustrative range of potential minimum rates. Estimated global gains from Pillar Two are then obtained by topping up the tax rate on the low-taxed profits up to the level of the minimum rate.[11] A ±10% uncertainty range around the point estimates is applied to take into account data uncertainty. The results, which are presented in Table 3.3, correspond to the revenue gains in Scenario 1 (i.e. in a static scenario that does not take into account the interaction with Pillar One, nor behavioural reactions by MNEs and governments) with no formulaic substance-based carve-out. Consistent with the assumptions on GILTI discussed above, the table excludes the low-taxed profit of US MNEs and the corresponding revenue gains (revenue gains from GILTI are discussed in Section 3.8).

202. These estimates do not take into account potential gains related to pockets of low-taxed profit in higher-tax jurisdictions (i.e. jurisdictions with an average ETR above the minimum rate). These pockets, while difficult to assess with the available data, may be substantial, as discussed in Box 3.1. Not taking them into account could lead to significantly underestimating the revenue gains from Pillar Two. In light of this, the upper bound of the uncertainty ranges surrounding the estimates of the direct gains from Pillar Two in Scenario 1 is increased by 50% (last row in Table 3.3). Such an increase in revenue gains would correspond to a situation where pockets of low-taxed profit would represent close to 10% of total profit in higher-tax jurisdictions (Box 3.1). The lower bound of the uncertainty ranges is not changed and therefore assumes conservatively no revenue gains from these pockets. In scenarios with a formulaic substance-based carve-out (discussed below), the uncertainty around these pockets is reduced in proportion to the share of carved-out profit in higher-tax jurisdictions.[12]

### Table 3.3. Global low-taxed profit and Pillar Two revenue gains (Scenario 1, no carve-out)

Excluding MNEs with an ultimate parent in the United States

| Minimum tax rate | | 7.5% | 10% | 12.5% | 15% | 17.5% |
|---|---|---|---|---|---|---|
| Global low-taxed profit (in low-tax jurisdictions) subject to Pillar Two (USD bn) | | 329 | 478 | 604 | 639 | 1043 |
| Global Pillar Two revenue gains (Scenario 1) | In USD bn | 10-12 | 18-22 | 28-34 | 40-48 | 52-64 |
| | In % of global CIT revenues | 0.5%-0.6% | 0.8%-1.0% | 1.3%-1.6% | 1.8%-2.2% | 2.4%-2.9% |
| | Range also taking into account uncertainty on pockets of low-taxed profit in higher-tax jurisdictions (in % of global CIT revenues) | 0.5%-0.8% | 0.8%-1.5% | 1.3%-2.3% | 1.8%-3.2% | 2.4%-4.2% |

Note: The minimum tax rates considered are illustrative. For each rate, the amount of low-taxed profit (i.e. profit that is taxed below the minimum rate) is computed based on the profit matrix and the median between three data sources on ETRs. The global gains from Pillar Two are computed by topping up the tax rate on low-taxed profits to the level of the minimum rate, and applying a ±10% uncertainty range to account for data uncertainty. These estimates correspond to an assumption that Pillar Two is applied with jurisdictional blending and no carve-outs (the implications of a formulaic substance-based carve-out are considered in the next section) based on the jurisdiction-specific assumptions on Pillar Two implementation described in section 3.4.5. The estimates correspond to a static scenario without behavioural reactions by MNEs and governments. Consistent with the assumption that GILTI would coexist with Pillar Two, the estimates exclude low-taxed profit from MNEs with an ultimate parent in the United States and the associated revenue gains. To take into account uncertainty related to pockets of low-taxed profit in higher-tax jurisdictions (see Box 3.1), the upper bound of the uncertainty ranges is increased by 50% (last row of the table).
Source: OECD Secretariat.

203. The estimates in Table 3.3 are broadly consistent with recent estimates by the Oxford University Centre for Business Taxation (Devereux et al., 2020[10]). Assuming a 10% minimum tax rate, no formulaic substance-based carve-out, and including MNEs with an ultimate parent in the United States, they assess that global Pillar 2 revenue gains in a static scenario could reach USD 20 billion (1.1% of global CIT revenues) in an approach excluding pockets of low-taxed profit in higher-tax jurisdictions, or USD 32 billion (1.8% of global CIT revenues) in an approach including them.[13] This is higher than the estimates with corresponding assumptions in Table 3.3 (i.e. estimated gains of 0.8%-1.0% of CIT revenues excluding pockets of low-taxed profit, and 0.8%-1.5% of CIT revenues including them) but the difference is likely explained in large part by the fact that the estimates in Table 3.3 exclude MNEs with an ultimate parent in the United States, while the estimates by Devereux et al. (2020[10]) include them.

**Box 3.1. Pockets of low-taxed profit in higher-tax jurisdictions**

The methodological approach in this chapter focuses on low-taxed profit in low-tax jurisdictions (i.e. jurisdictions with an average ETR below the minimum rate) and overlooks potential "pockets" of low-taxed profit in higher-tax jurisdictions. It is impossible with the available data to assess with precision the size of these pockets. Indeed, this would require detailed data on profit and taxes paid at the firm level. The limited sources available to the OECD Secretariat (i.e. ORBIS database in jurisdictions with good data coverage, and confidential information from national sources collected via jurisdiction delegates to the OECD Working Party No. 2 on Tax Policy Analysis and Tax Statistics) suggest that the shape of the distribution of MNE ETRs varies widely across the jurisdictions covered. In addition, while these sources suggest that these pockets can be substantial, they give inconsistent signals on the shape of the ETR distribution in certain jurisdictions, suggesting potential differences in the definition of ETR considered (e.g. due to different accounting methods) or data quality issues. In particular, the available data may not necessarily allow for the measurement of ETRs in a way that would be consistent with the approach used in the context of Pillar Two.

An estimate based on stylised and illustrative assumptions on the distribution of ETRs across firms suggest that low-taxed profit (i.e. profit taxed at an ETR below the minimum rate) could represent about 8% of total profit in higher-tax jurisdictions, assuming a 12.5% minimum tax rate. This estimate is based on a methodology developed by the European Commission and applied to the data underlying this chapter.[14] Given the uncertainty around the actual distribution of ETRs, this estimate should be seen as an illustrative order of magnitude rather than a precise point estimate.

The total amount of profit in higher-tax jurisdictions (i.e. jurisdictions with an average ETR above the minimum rate) is about USD 3 400 billion, if one assumes illustratively a 12.5% minimum rate (for comparability with other results in this chapter, this excludes US MNEs). If, out of this total, one would assume – for the purpose of illustration – that 5-10% of profit is taxed below the minimum rate (consistent with the 8% estimate above), this would represent USD 170-340 billion of additional low-taxed profit globally, which would come on top of the USD 604 billion of profit in low-tax jurisdictions already considered in the analysis (see Table 3.3). This could imply an increase in estimated revenue gains (in a static scenario) by about 30-60%.[15]

As further discussed below, a formulaic substance-based carve-out could reduce the size of these pockets. Indeed, under the range of carve-out design and parameter options considered in this chapter, about 10-35% of profit in higher-tax jurisdictions could be carved out (Table 3.5), potentially reducing the size of these pockets by that amount.

### *3.4.4. Modelling the implications of a formulaic substance-based carve-out*

*General approach to model a formulaic substance-based carve-out*

204. The Pillar Two Blueprint report envisages that the GloBE rules (IIR and UTPR) could include a formulaic substance-based carve-out based on a fixed percentage of payroll plus a fixed percentage of depreciation expenses on a broad range of tangible assets (OECD, 2020[1]). These two percentages could be identical or different. The illustrative results presented in this chapter assume identical percentages.

205. For example, if one assumes illustratively a 10% carve-out percentage (or "mark-up") for both payroll and depreciation expenses, the GloBE rules would only apply to a given MNE sub-group in a given jurisdiction on the profits that exceed 10% of the sum of payroll plus depreciation expenses of that MNE sub-group in that jurisdiction. For example, if the profit of the sub-group is 100, its payroll 150 and its depreciation expenses 50, the profit on which Pillar Two applies would be 100-10%*(150+50)=80.

206. On this profit, Pillar Two would apply, as before, by topping-up the average ETR paid by the MNE sub-group in that jurisdiction up to the level of the agreed minimum tax rate. The Inclusive Framework will define at a later stage the exact rules to calculate this ETR in the presence of a carve-out, and in particular whether an MNE group that claims the benefit of the carve-out should be required to make a corresponding and proportional adjustment to the covered taxes. For example, if before the application of the carve-out a taxpayer has EUR 100 of profit and EUR 20 of covered taxes, the ETR in absence of carve-out is 20% (EUR 20 divided by EUR 100). If the carve-out reduces the taxpayer's profit to EUR 80, then the ETR for the purposes of the GloBE rules could be either (i) EUR 20 of covered taxes divided by EUR 80 of profit (i.e. 25%) if the MNE is not required to make an adjustment to the covered taxes, or (ii) EUR 16 of covered taxes divided by EUR 80 of profit (i.e. 20%) if the MNE is required to make an adjustment to the covered taxes that would be corresponding and proportional to the effect of the carve-out on profit. The approach modelled in this chapter is the second, since the modelling relies on the same ETRs in the scenarios with and without the carve-out. This reflects that modelling the situation without adjustment would be difficult with the available data, and does not prejudge future decisions by the Inclusive Framework on this question. Since the first approach (i.e. without adjustment) would result in higher ETRs than the second approach, it would lead to lower revenue gains (for a given level of the minimum rate and the carve-out percentage).

207. Modelling with precision the impact of a carve-out would require firm-level information on tangible assets depreciation and payroll across all jurisdictions. Sufficiently detailed firm-level data at the unconsolidated level is available in the ORBIS database with good coverage for only 18 to 24 jurisdictions depending on the variable considered (see list in Annex 5.A of Chapter 5).[16] In these jurisdictions, the share of carved-out profit is computed directly with ORBIS data, at the level of each MNE sub-group, as discussed below. In the other jurisdictions, the approach relies on more aggregate data, in combination with an analysis based on ORBIS data on the average relationship between firm-level and aggregate data, which is also described below.

208. The approach in this chapter is to estimate the share of carved-out profit in all jurisdictions, even those with average ETRs above the minimum rate. This offers the benefit of helping to gauge the effect of the carve-out on potential pockets of low-taxed profit in these jurisdictions. For practical reasons, the payroll carve-out and the depreciation carve-out are modelled separately, and their effects are summed to obtain the effect of a combined carve-out.[17] This represents an approximation compared to the actual effect of a combined carve-out, because it could lead to some 'double counting' of carve-out effects in cases where the sum of the amounts carved out under each carve-out taken individually would exceed the total profit of the MNE sub-group considered.[18] Computations based on ORBIS firm-level data suggest that this double counting is not quantitatively significant under the carve-out percentages considered in this chapter, as it leads to an overestimation of the effect of the carve-out by less than 4% on average across jurisdictions.

209. The coverage of depreciation expenses in ORBIS is less extensive than the coverage of tangible assets. In addition, depreciation is generally aggregated with amortisation of intangible assets. In aggregate data as well, the level of tangible assets is generally better covered than depreciation expenses. Against this background, the approach to approximate depreciation expenses is to use data on tangible assets combined with an assumption on the average depreciation rate. Evidence from the available data from the US BEA and the ORBIS database suggests that the average depreciation rate of tangible assets (i.e. property, plant and equipment) is about 5-10%,[19] and this percentage is conservatively assumed to be 10% in the estimates of this chapter.

### *The aggregate data in the tangible assets and payroll matrices*

210. Aggregate data on the location of MNE tangible assets and payroll across jurisdictions are based on a 'tangible assets matrix' and a 'payroll matrix' that combine various data sources and extrapolations, in the same spirit as the profit matrix. These data sources and methodology underlying these two matrices,

as well as extensive benchmarking and checks to assess their quality are presented in Chapter 5. These matrices are presented at an aggregate level in Table 3.4.

Table 3.4. The tangible assets and payroll matrices: Results aggregated by broad jurisdiction groups

**Panel A**: The tangible assets matrix

| | | Jurisdiction of ultimate parent | | | | |
|---|---|---|---|---|---|---|
| | (USD billion of 2016) | High income | Middle income | Low income | Investment Hubs | Total |
| Jurisdiction of affiliate | High income (64 jurisd.) | 11463.1 | 314.5 | 6.2 | 614.8 | 12398.7 |
| | Middle income (105) | 1320.4 | 4357.9 | 5.0 | 757.4 | 6440.7 |
| | Low income (29) | 20.5 | 11.2 | 17.1 | 4.2 | 53.1 |
| | Investment Hubs (24) | 437.8 | 69.5 | 0.9 | 422.1 | 930.3 |
| | **Total** | **13241.8** | **4753.2** | **29.2** | **1798.5** | **19822.8** |

**Panel B**: The payroll matrix

| | | Jurisdiction of ultimate parent | | | | |
|---|---|---|---|---|---|---|
| | (USD billion of 2016) | High income | Middle income | Low income | Investment Hubs | Total |
| Jurisdiction of affiliate | High income (64 jurisd.) | 6967.3 | 153.6 | 3.0 | 472.2 | **7596.2** |
| | Middle income (105) | 497.8 | 1495.6 | 1.5 | 186.5 | **2181.4** |
| | Low income (29) | 7.0 | 3.1 | 6.8 | 1.8 | **18.7** |
| | Investment Hubs (24) | 225.3 | 18.2 | 0.4 | 170.3 | **414.2** |
| | **Total** | **7697.5** | **1670.5** | **11.8** | **830.7** | **10210.5** |

Note: Groups of jurisdictions (high, middle and low income) are based on the World Bank classification. The number of jurisdictions in each group is indicated in parentheses. Investment hubs are defined as jurisdictions with a total inward FDI position above 150% of GDP. MNEs with an ultimate parent in the United States are included in these tables.
Source: OECD Secretariat (see details in Chapter 5).

211. An important caveat to the analysis of carve-outs is that the definition of tangible assets and payroll in the data underlying the matrices may not necessarily match the exact definitions of the variables considered for a formulaic substance-based carve-out. The tangible assets matrix focuses on property, plant and equipment, net of accumulated depreciation, while the payroll matrix focuses on expenditures for salaries and wages, including bonuses, social contributions and other employee benefits (see Chapter 5). While this is broadly consistent with the variables considered for a carve-out, which are described in the Pillar Two Blueprint report, there may be differences related, for example, to the treatment of land or subcontracted labour expenses, which, depending on the exact definition of the carve-out, could affect the accuracy of the estimates.

## Figure 3.4. Share of carved-out profit, as estimated with firm-level data, and relationship with aggregate profitability

**Panel A:** Carve-out of 10% of depreciation of tangible assets (modelled as 1% of tangible assets)

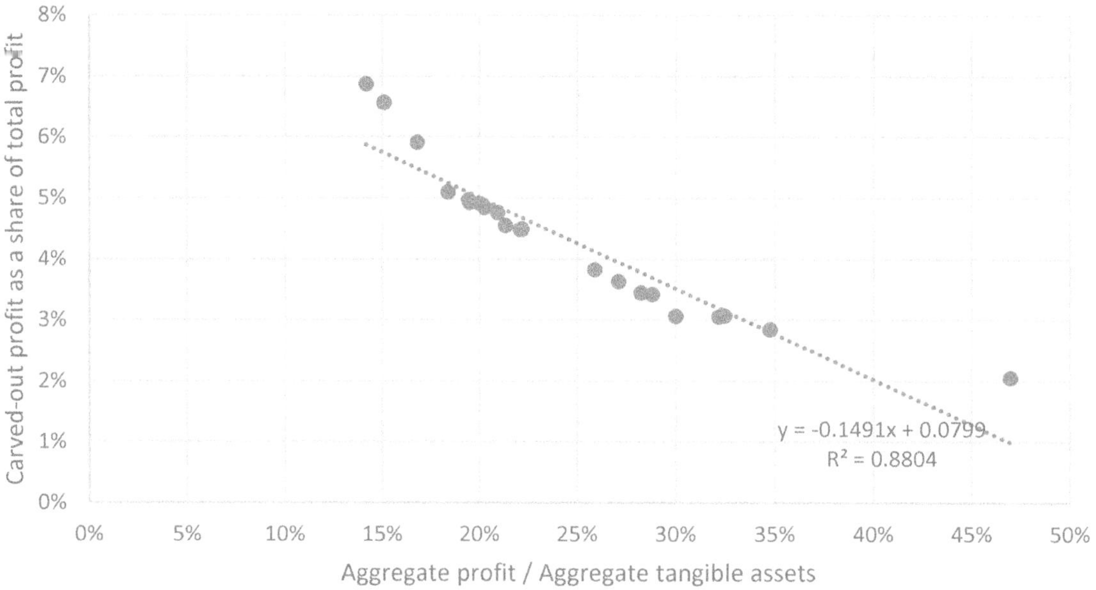


**Panel B:** Carve-out of 10% of payroll

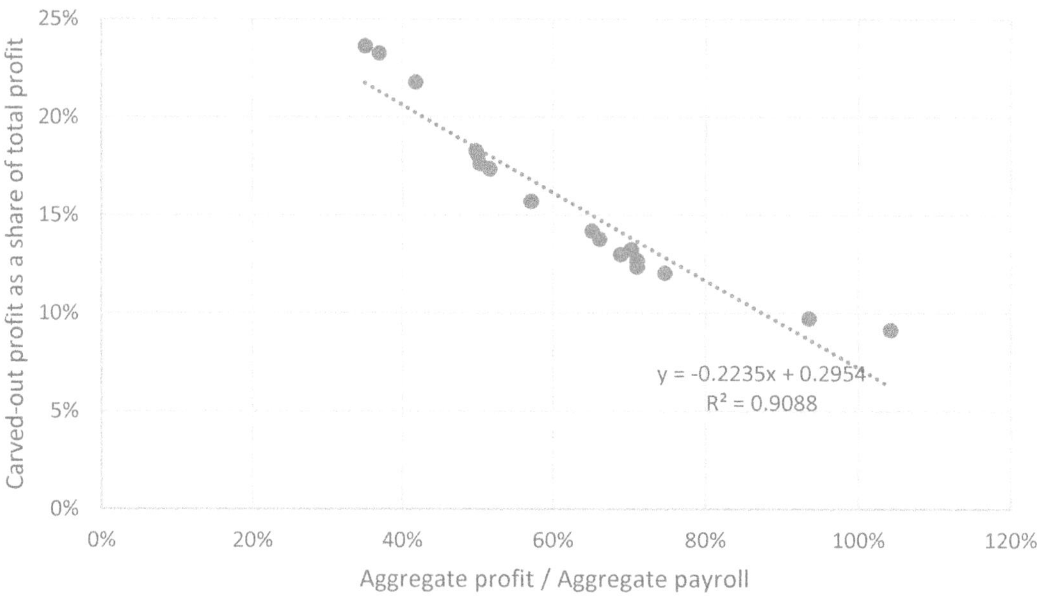


Note: Each dot corresponds to one jurisdiction. Non-carved-out profit is computed for each MNE sub-group as profit before tax in excess of 1% of tangible assets (panel A) or 10% of payroll (Panel B). These figures focus on all profit-making MNE sub-groups in the jurisdictions considered, regardless of their ETR. Loss-making MNE sub-groups in the jurisdiction are not included. The sample consists of jurisdictions with relatively good coverage of unconsolidated accounts in ORBIS on both foreign and domestic MNE entities for the variables considered (tangible assets in Panel A, payroll in Panel B), see list in Annex 5.A of Chapter 5.
Source: OECD Secretariat calculations based on ORBIS data.

### *Average relationship between firm-level estimates of carved-out profit and aggregate data on profitability*

212. The share of profit that would be carved out for a range of illustrative carve-out percentages is computed with precision, at the level of each MNE sub-group, with ORBIS unconsolidated firm-level data across the jurisdictions with good ORBIS coverage on both foreign and domestic MNE entities (see list in Annex 5.A of Chapter 5). ORBIS financial and ownership data used for this analysis have been cleaned extensively using OECD Secretariat expertise from past projects, as described in Annex 5.B of Chapter 5.

213. As discussed above, the effect of the payroll and depreciation components of the carve-out are computed separately, and then summed. The results on the share of carved-out profit for each component are presented in Figure 3.4 for an illustrative value of the carve-out percentage (10%) across the jurisdictions with good ORBIS coverage (each dot corresponding to one jurisdiction).

214. The results in Figure 3.4 suggest that the share of carved-out profit in a jurisdiction is relatively well correlated with the aggregate profitability ratio at the jurisdiction level (profit to tangible assets or profit to payroll, depending on the panel considered). For example, results in Panel A suggest that the share of carved-out profit with a 10% carve-out on tangible assets depreciation is well correlated with the ratio of aggregate profit to aggregate tangible assets at the jurisdiction level. This average relationship is used to extrapolate the share of carved-out profit in jurisdictions with poor ORBIS coverage, based on aggregate data from the profit, tangible assets and payroll matrices. The approach is very similar to the one employed on the assessment of Pillar One to assess the share of profit that is residual based on aggregate profit and turnover (see Chapter 2). For example, in the case of tangible assets, the relationship, which is estimated over the jurisdictions $j$ with good ORBIS coverage, is the following:

$$\left(\frac{Carved\ out\ profit}{Total\ Profit}\right)_j = \alpha + \beta\left(\frac{Total\ profit}{Total\ tangible\ assets}\right)_j$$

215. This relationship is estimated for each carve-out percentage considered in the analysis (5%, 10%, 15% and 20%). There is no theoretical reason why this relationship should be linear, but in practice a linear relationship seems to offer a reasonably good fit and the number of observations is insufficient to consider more complex specifications.[20]

216. The estimation for a 10% carve-out percentage is presented in Figure 3.4 for depreciation (Panel A) and payroll (Panel B). The correlation for the other percentages considered in the analysis is broadly similar to the correlation observed with a 10% percentage, but the coefficients $\alpha$ and $\beta$ differ. In general, a higher carve-out percentage would lead to a higher $\alpha$ since it would increase the share of carved-out profit, while the differences in $\beta$ depend on the shape of the distribution of profit, tangible assets, and payroll across jurisdictions. The results presented in the following sections are based on the specific coefficients $\alpha$ and $\beta$ corresponding to the carve-out percentage considered (e.g. results for a 5% carve-out percentage are based on the $\alpha$ and $\beta$ estimated for that percentage).

### *Share of carved-out profit across jurisdiction groups*

217. Based on this methodology, the share of carved-out profit in each cell of the profit matrix is computed for a range of carve-out percentages. The results are presented (at a high level of aggregation) in Table 3.5. For example, assuming a 10% carve-out percentage, 15% of global profit would be carved out. This share is much lower in investment hubs (2%) than in other jurisdictions groups (16-19%) reflecting that a relatively high share of MNE profit is located in investments hubs compared to their share of tangible assets and payroll. Among investment hubs, the share of carved-out profit tends to be even lower among zero-tax jurisdictions (less than 1%) than non-zero-tax jurisdictions (2%).

**Table 3.5. Share of carved-out profit by jurisdiction groups**

| Carve out percentage | 5% | 10% | 15% | 20% |
|---|---|---|---|---|
| High income | 10% | 19% | 27% | 34% |
| Middle income | 8% | 16% | 23% | 29% |
| Low income | 9% | 16% | 23% | 29% |
| Investment hubs | 1% | 2% | 3% | 4% |
| *Of which non-zero tax* | *1%* | *2%* | *4%* | *4%* |
| *Of which zero-tax* | *0%* | *0%* | *0%* | *0%* |
| **Global average** | **8%** | **15%** | **22%** | **28%** |

Note: For example, assuming a 10% carve-out on payroll plus depreciation expenses, the share of profit that would be carved out in high income jurisdictions would be on average 19%. The results in this table focus on all profit, regardless of whether it is low-taxed (and therefore would be subject to Pillar Two) or not. As Pillar Two operates by allowing jurisdictions to 'tax back' profit that is located in other jurisdictions, the share of carved-out profit in a jurisdiction influences Pillar Two gains in other jurisdictions. Groups of jurisdictions (high, middle and low income) are based on the World Bank classification. Investment hubs are defined as jurisdictions with a total inward FDI position above 150% of GDP. Zero-tax jurisdictions are those with no CIT system or a zero statutory CIT rate.
Source: OECD Secretariat.

218. As Pillar Two operates by allowing jurisdictions to 'tax back' low-taxed profit that is located in other jurisdictions, the share of carved-out profit in a jurisdiction influences Pillar Two gains in other jurisdictions. In particular, the fact that the share of carved-out profit in investment hubs is relatively small (while an important share of global low-taxed profit is located in investment hubs) implies that the effect of the formulaic substance-based carve-out considered in this chapter on Pillar Two revenue gains across jurisdictions is limited, as can be seen in the next section.

### *Effect of formulaic substance-based carve-out on Pillar Two gains under Scenario 1*

219. The effect of Pillar Two in a static scenario (i.e. Scenario 1) with a formulaic substance-based carve-out is computed in the same way as before the carve-out, with the difference that the amount of profit on which Pillar Two is applied is non-carved-out profit, instead of total profit. The data on ETRs are the same as in the no-carve-out case, which, as discussed above, is consistent with the assumption that MNEs would be required to make an adjustment to the covered taxes that would be corresponding and proportional to the effect of the carve-out on profit.

220. The results, which are presented in Table 3.6, suggest that the effect of a formulaic substance-based carve-out on Pillar Two revenue gains is relatively small, especially when pockets of low-tax profit in higher-tax jurisdictions are not considered. For example, in the case of a 10% carve-out, the estimated Pillar Two gains would be reduced by about 3%. When taking into account the potential effect of the carve-out on pockets of low-taxed profit in the uncertainty ranges (last row in Table 3.6), the upper bound of the ranges is reduced significantly by the carve-outs. This reflects that profit in these pockets is likely to benefit more from a formulaic substance-based carve-out than profits in jurisdictions with low average ETRs, where less economic activity may generally be located.[21]

Table 3.6. Global low-taxed profit and Pillar Two gains (Scenario 1), with formulaic substance-based carve-out

Assuming illustratively a 12.5% minimum tax rate, excluding MNEs with an ultimate parent in the United States

| Carve out percentage | | No carve-out | 5% | 10% | 15% | 20% |
|---|---|---|---|---|---|---|
| Global low-taxed profit subject to Pillar Two (USD bn) | | 604 | 588 | 574 | 560 | 548 |
| Global Pillar Two revenue gains (Scenario 1) | In USD bn | 28-34 | 28-34 | 27-33 | 27-33 | 26-32 |
| | In % of CIT revenues | 1.3%-1.6% | 1.3%-1.5% | 1.2%-1.5% | 1.2%-1.5% | 1.2%-1.5% |
| | In % of CIT revenues, taking into account uncertainty on pockets of low-taxed profit | 1.3%-2.3% | 1.3%-2.2% | 1.2%-2.1% | 1.2%-2.0% | 1.2%-1.9% |

Note: The estimates in the no-carve-out situation correspond to those presented in Table 3.3, assuming illustratively a 12.5% minimum tax rate. The carve-out percentages considered are illustrative. Consistent with the assumption that GILTI would coexist with Pillar Two, the estimates exclude low-taxed profit from MNEs with an ultimate parent in the United States and the associated revenue gains. Uncertainty ranges taking into account pockets of low-taxed profit in higher-tax jurisdictions are computed by increasing the upper-bound estimate by 50% in the no-carve-out case, and by a lower percentage in the presence of a carve-out, depending on the share of carved-out profit in higher-tax jurisdictions (e.g. if about 20% of profit in higher-tax jurisdictions is carved-out, the increase in the upper bound is 40% instead of 50%).
Source: OECD Secretariat.

### *3.4.5. Methodology to estimate jurisdiction-level revenue gains*

221. Revenue gains at the jurisdiction level and, in turn, for jurisdiction groups are derived using the following stylised modelling assumptions, also summarised in Figure 3.5, which do not pre-judge jurisdictions' actual implementation decisions:

- **Group 1: Jurisdictions with an average ETR above the minimum rate.** These jurisdictions are assumed to implement an income inclusion rule (IIR), in the sense that they would apply a top-up tax to ensure that the profit of MNE entities (blended at the jurisdictional level) with an ultimate parent in their jurisdiction is taxed at least at the minimum rate.[22] They are also assumed to implement an undertaxed payments rule (UTPR). Consistent with the Pillar Two Blueprint report, the IIR is assumed to apply in priority to the UTPR.[23]
- **Group 2: Jurisdictions with a zero corporate tax rate.** For the purposes of modelling, these jurisdictions are assumed not to introduce an IIR nor a UTPR, as it would also require introducing a corporate income tax (CIT) system, which many of these jurisdictions do not have. As a result, the low-taxed profit of MNE entities with an ultimate parent in these jurisdictions would not be taxed by these jurisdictions (since they would not introduce an IIR). If an intermediate-level parent (i.e. a parent entity that is not the ultimate parent) in the MNE group is located in a jurisdiction introducing an IIR, this low-taxed profit would be taxed by the jurisdiction of this intermediate parent (if there are several intermediate parents in this case, the highest one in the ownership chain would have priority according to the top-down principle described in the Pillar Two Blueprint report). If the low-taxed profit is not in scope of an applicable IIR (e.g. if there is no intermediate-level parent, or if intermediate parent jurisdictions are not introducing an IIR, or if the ultimate parent jurisdiction is low tax), the low-taxed profit could be taxed under the UTPR of a jurisdiction introducing a UTPR and from which intra-group payments originate.
  - In practice, it is difficult with the available data to model these rules with precision, as little information is available on the location of intermediate parents and transaction origins. Reflecting this, it is assumed for the purposes of modelling in this chapter that the profits of MNEs with an ultimate parent in Group 2 would be subject to a top-up tax imposed by other

jurisdictions, in proportion to the amount of economic activity located in these jurisdictions (as a proxy for the location of intermediate parents in the case of IIR, and of the transactions-based nature of the UTPR).

- Economic activity is proxied by MNE turnover, sourced from the "turnover matrix" described in Chapter 5.[24,25] Results are broadly robust to using tangible assets or payroll instead of turnover as a proxy (see Annex 3.C). When economic activity is located in a jurisdiction that does not implement an IIR nor a UTPR (e.g. a jurisdiction in Group 2), the corresponding low-taxed profit is assumed not to be subject to the top-up tax. However, this represents a relatively small fraction of total low-taxed profit under the assumptions considered in this chapter.

- **Group 3: Jurisdictions with an average ETR below the minimum rate, but greater than zero.** Among jurisdictions in Group 3, for the purposes of this modelling scenario, half are assumed to implement an IIR and a UTPR (as jurisdictions in Group 1), and the other half are assumed not to implement them (as jurisdictions in Group 2). One reason why it is likely that not all jurisdictions in this group would implement an IIR and a UTPR is that some of these jurisdictions may decide that imposing a minimum tax rate on foreign profits could seem inconsistent with maintaining an average ETR below this minimum rate on local profit. As a result, this choice may be linked to choices relative to other tax policy parameters, and more specifically whether the ETR on local profit is increased, which not all jurisdictions in this group may be willing to do (see assumptions underlying Scenario 4 in section 3.7.1 below, with which these assumptions aim to be consistent). In practice, identifying the jurisdictions in this group that would implement an IIR and a UTPR is not straightforward. Instead of arbitrarily selecting half of the jurisdictions in the group, a simplifying assumption is made that all jurisdictions in this group apply an IIR and a UTPR on half of the low-taxed profit on which they could apply them. This is by no means realistic in itself, but it aims to be a representative and neutral proxy for a situation where half of the jurisdictions in this group would implement and the other half would not.

## 3.5. Scenario 2: Taking into account the interaction of Pillar One with Pillar Two

### *3.5.1. Rationale for taking the interaction between both pillars into account*

222. Scenario 1 considers Pillar Two in isolation, without taking into account its potential interaction with Pillar One. Scenario 2 aims to take this interaction into account, by assuming illustratively that both pillars would be introduced together and that Pillar Two would apply after the reallocation of profit induced by Pillar One.

223. For example, in an extreme case where an MNE group would have all its profit in a jurisdiction where it is taxed at a rate below the Pillar Two minimum rate, all its profit (after potential application of a formulaic substance-based carve-out) would be subject to Pillar Two if Pillar Two was introduced in isolation (Figure 3.6). However, if the reallocation of profit induced by Pillar One was applied first, a portion of these profits (or, more precisely, the taxing rights corresponding to these profits) would be reallocated to market jurisdictions (assuming that the MNE group is in scope of Pillar One and above the residual profit threshold). If the tax rate in these market jurisdictions is above the minimum rate under Pillar Two, these reallocated profits would not be subject to Pillar Two, reducing the overall revenue gains from Pillar Two.

Figure 3.5. Stylised modelling assumptions on Income Inclusion Rule (IIR) and Undertaxed Payments Rule (UTPR)

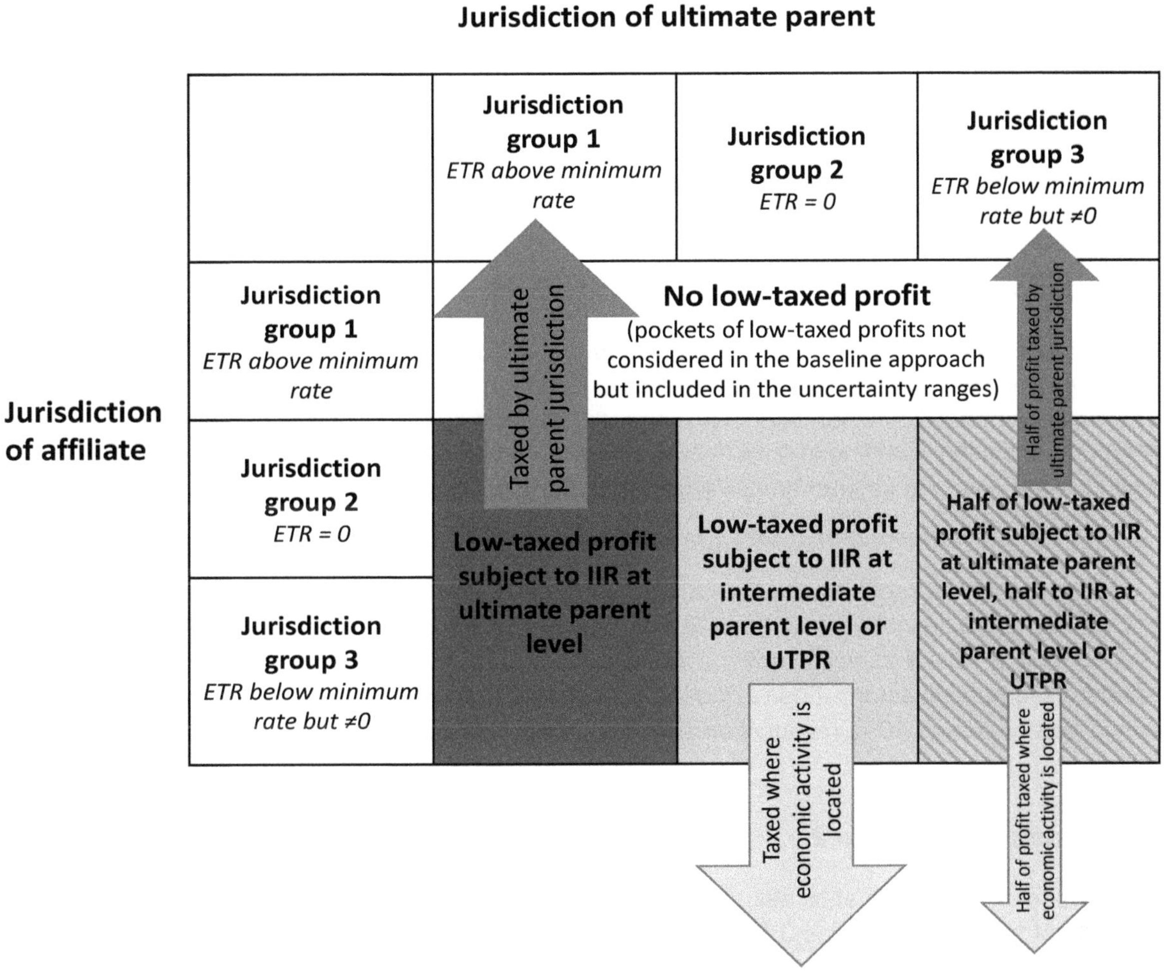


Note: These assumptions are stylised modelling assumptions and do not pre-judge actual implementation of IIR and UTPR. The United States (which is in group 1) is assumed to apply GILTI instead of an income inclusion rule.
Source: OECD Secretariat.

Figure 3.6. Stylised example on Pillar Two interaction with Pillar One

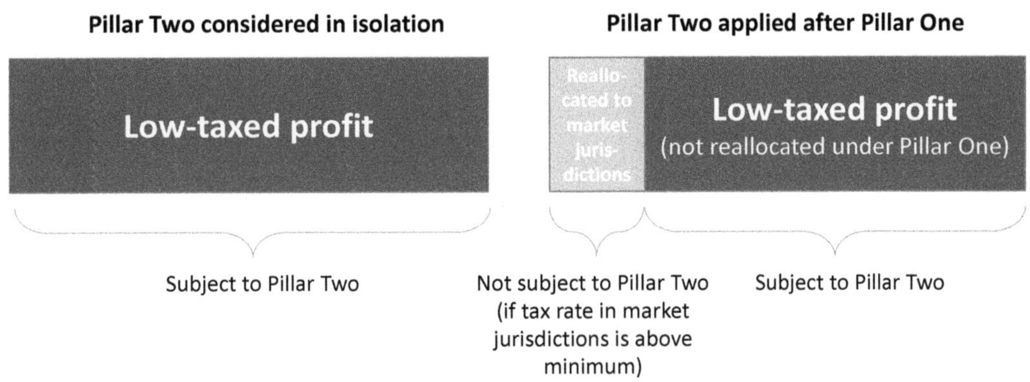


Source: OECD Secretariat.

224. In this example, computing the revenue gains from Pillar One and Pillar Two independently of each other would overstate the overall gains compared to computing the joint effect of both pillars in a way that takes into account the interaction between them. It is possible to consider an opposite example, where the reallocation taking place under Pillar One would increase the amount of low-taxed profits and therefore increase the revenue gains from Pillar Two. This would be the case for example if an MNE group had most of its profit located in higher-tax jurisdictions and most of its sales in low-tax jurisdictions. However, in practice, MNE profit tends to be more concentrated in low-tax jurisdictions than MNE final sales, which is why the reallocation taking place under Pillar One is expected to reduce the global amount of low-taxed profit. Therefore, taking into account the interaction with Pillar One is expected to reduce the estimated revenue gains from Pillar Two.

### *3.5.2. Methodology on the interaction between both pillars*

225. To take the interaction between both pillars into account, Scenario 2 applies Pillar Two in exactly the same way and with the same assumptions as in Scenario 1, but after adjusting the location of profit for the reallocation induced by Pillar One. In practice, this is done by computing an adjusted profit matrix post Pillar One reallocation. Each matrix cell $Profit_{ij}$ (corresponding to the profit in jurisdiction *i* of MNE groups with an ultimate parent in jurisdiction *j*) is adjusted in the following way:

$$ProfitAdjustedForPillar1_{ij} = Profit_{ij} + ProfitReceived_{ij} - ProfitRelieved_{ij}$$

226. The amount of profit received and relieved under Pillar One in each matrix cell is based on the Pillar One estimates described in Chapter 2.[26] In theory, this adjustment can be done for any combination of Pillar One parameter and design options. For simplicity, only one illustrative set of Pillar One design and parameter assumptions among those explored in Chapter 2 is considered in this chapter (i.e. residual profit threshold percentage of 10%, reallocation percentage of 20% and global revenue threshold of EUR 750 million).

### *3.5.3. Results on Scenario 2*

227. The resulting profit matrix, adjusted for Pillar One reallocation is presented in Table 3.7. Compared to the original profit matrix (Table 3.1), the total in each column is the same (by construction), but there has been some reallocation across rows, away from investment hubs and into other jurisdiction groups. The scale of this reallocation is limited, which implies that the global amount of low-taxed profit and the estimated revenue gains from Pillar Two are reduced only slightly by taking into account the interaction with Pillar One (Table 3.8). To the extent that the interaction with Pillar One has only a modest effect on Pillar Two results, considering different assumptions regarding Pillar One would likely affect the Pillar Two estimates only at the margin.

### Table 3.7. Profit matrix adjusted for Pillar One profit reallocation

| | | Jurisdiction of ultimate parent | | | | |
|---|---|---|---|---|---|---|
| | (USD billion of 2016) | High income | Middle income | Low income | Investment Hubs | Total |
| **Jurisdiction of affiliate** | High income (64 jurisd.) | 3567.4 | 48.4 | 0.1 | 175.1 | **3790.9** |
| | Middle income (105) | 385.5 | 818.7 | 0.1 | 169.1 | **1373.4** |
| | Low income (29) | 1.6 | 1.3 | 3.1 | 0.2 | **6.2** |
| | Investment Hubs (24) | 632.9 | 68.3 | 0.0 | 309.3 | **1010.5** |
| | **Total** | **4587.4** | **936.7** | **3.3** | **653.7** | **6181.1** |

Note: Groups of jurisdictions (high, middle and low income) are based on the World Bank classification. Investment hubs are defined as jurisdictions with a total inward FDI position above 150% of GDP. The assumptions on Pillar One (residual profit threshold percentage of 10%, reallocation percentage of 20% and global revenue threshold of EUR 750 million) are illustrative. MNEs with an ultimate parent in the United States are included in this table.
Source: OECD calculations.

### Table 3.8. Global low-taxed profit and global Pillar Two revenue gains (Scenarios 1 and 2)

Estimates in these tables exclude MNEs with an ultimate parent in the United States

| | Minimum tax rate | 7.5% | 10% | 12.5% | 15% | 17.5% |
|---|---|---|---|---|---|---|
| **Scenario 1** (i.e. before interaction with Pillar One) | Global low-taxed profit (USD bn) | 318 | 457 | 574 | 602 | 953 |
| | Global Pillar Two gains (% of CIT revenues) | 0.4%-0.5% | 0.8%-1.0% | 1.2%-1.5% | 1.8%-2.1% | 2.3%-2.8% |
| | Global Pillar Two gains, taking into account uncertainty on pockets of low-taxed profit (% of CIT revenues) | 0.4%-0.7% | 0.8%-1.3% | 1.2%-2.1% | 1.8%-2.9% | 2.3%-3.8% |
| **Scenario 2** (i.e. after interaction with Pillar One) | Global low-taxed profit (USD bn) | 313 | 451 | 566 | 595 | 943 |
| | Global Pillar Two gains (% of CIT revenues) | 0.4%-0.5% | 0.8%-1.0% | 1.2%-1.5% | 1.7%-2.1% | 2.2%-2.7% |
| | Global Pillar Two gains, taking into account uncertainty on pockets of low-taxed profit (% of CIT revenues) | 0.4%-0.7% | 0.8%-1.3% | 1.2%-2.0% | 1.7%-2.9% | 2.2%-3.7% |

Note: The minimum tax rates considered are illustrative. For each rate, the amount of low-taxed profit (i.e. profit that is taxed below the minimum rate) is computed based on the profit matrix and the median between three data sources on ETRs. The global gains from Pillar Two are computed by topping up the tax rate on low-taxed profits up to the level of the minimum rate. These estimates correspond to an assumption that Pillar Two is applied with jurisdictional blending and a formulaic substance-based carve-out based on 10% of payroll and tangible asset depreciation. Scenarios 1 and 2 correspond to static scenarios without behavioural reactions by MNEs and governments. Scenario 2 takes into account the interaction between Pillar One and Pillar Two, while Scenario 1 does not take any interaction into account. The revenue gains from Pillar One are not included in this table. Consistent with the assumption that GILTI would coexist with Pillar Two, the estimates exclude low-taxed profit from MNEs with an ultimate parent in the United States and the associated revenue gains.
Source: OECD Secretariat.

## 3.6. Scenario 3: Reduced MNE profit shifting intensity

228. Scenario 3 is based on the assumption that MNE profit shifting intensity would be reduced by the introduction of Pillar Two. This is because Pillar Two would reduce tax rate differentials between jurisdictions, which are a primary driver of profit shifting. The effect of this reduced profit shifting intensity

on tax revenues is estimated based on the assumption that profit shifting generally depends on tax rate differentials, and by comparing tax rate differentials *before* and *after* Pillar Two implementation. An adjusted profit matrix incorporating the reduced profit shifting intensity is derived from this comparison, as further described below.

229. Based on this adjusted profit matrix, revenue gains from Pillar Two in Scenario 3 are computed as the sum of two components: (i) a revenue effect of the reduction in profit shifting intensity, reflecting that profits that are no longer shifted are now taxed in the jurisdiction where they were generated, rather than in the jurisdiction where they used to be shifted, and (ii) revenues collected via the IIR and UTPR on remaining low-taxed profits, including profits that are still shifted to low-tax jurisdictions. This second component is expected to be smaller than the amount of revenues collected in Scenario 2, since the reduction in profit shifting should reduce the global amount of low-taxed profit. However, the sum of the two components is expected to be greater than the overall revenue gains in Scenario 2, since some profit that is no longer shifted to low-tax jurisdictions may ultimately be taxed at a higher rate than the minimum rate in the jurisdictions where it has been generated.

### *3.6.1. Assessing current profit shifting patterns*

230. To evaluate the effect of Pillar Two introduction on MNE profit shifting patterns, the first step is to assess *current* profit shifting patterns. For consistency with the methodology applied to quantify the revenue effects of Pillar Two in this chapter, profit shifting needs to be assessed on a "trilateral" basis, i.e. for each combination of (i) jurisdiction where profit was located before shifting ("profit origin"), (ii) jurisdiction where profit has been shifted ("profit destination"), and (iii) jurisdiction of ultimate parent of the profit shifting entity ("ultimate parent").[27] This third jurisdiction may or may not be the same as the "profit origin" jurisdiction. This level of granularity is necessary to create an adjusted profit matrix taking into account the effect of Pillar Two on profit shifting intensity, so that Pillar Two can then be applied to this adjusted profit matrix (with assumptions consistent with those used in Scenarios 1 and 2). This requires going beyond most studies on profit shifting, which often focus on measuring an average profit shifting semi-elasticity across a range of destination jurisdictions – for recent reviews of these studies, see for example Bradbury et al. (2018[11]) and Beer et al. (2019[12]).

#### *Profit shifting: Overview of the approach*

231. To obtain this "trilateral" profit shifting intensity, the approach in this chapter is based on the following steps, which are further detailed in the following sections and presented in a stylised way in Figure 3.7:

(i) **Identifying "profit destination" jurisdictions**, i.e. jurisdictions where profit may have been shifted to, based on foreign direct investment (FDI) and ETR data;

(ii) **Computing the amount of deemed shifted profit in these jurisdictions**, assuming that profit up to a certain "normal" profitability rate may not have been shifted, but may instead reflect real economic activity in these jurisdictions. The share of shifted profit is measured on a "bilateral" basis, i.e. for each pair of "profit destination"-"ultimate parent" jurisdictions;

(iii) **Identifying where the shifted profit originates from**. For each "profit destination"-"ultimate parent" pair of jurisdictions, shifted profits need to be reattributed to "profit origin" jurisdictions. This is done based on tax rate differentials vis-à-vis the "profit destination" jurisdiction (assuming that a higher tax rate differential leads to more profit shifting, all else equal) and on the geographic distribution of economic activity of MNEs from the "ultimate parent" jurisdiction considered (with the idea that profit is more likely to originate from jurisdictions where these MNEs have more economic activity).

Figure 3.7. Stylised illustration on the methodology to assess profit shifting

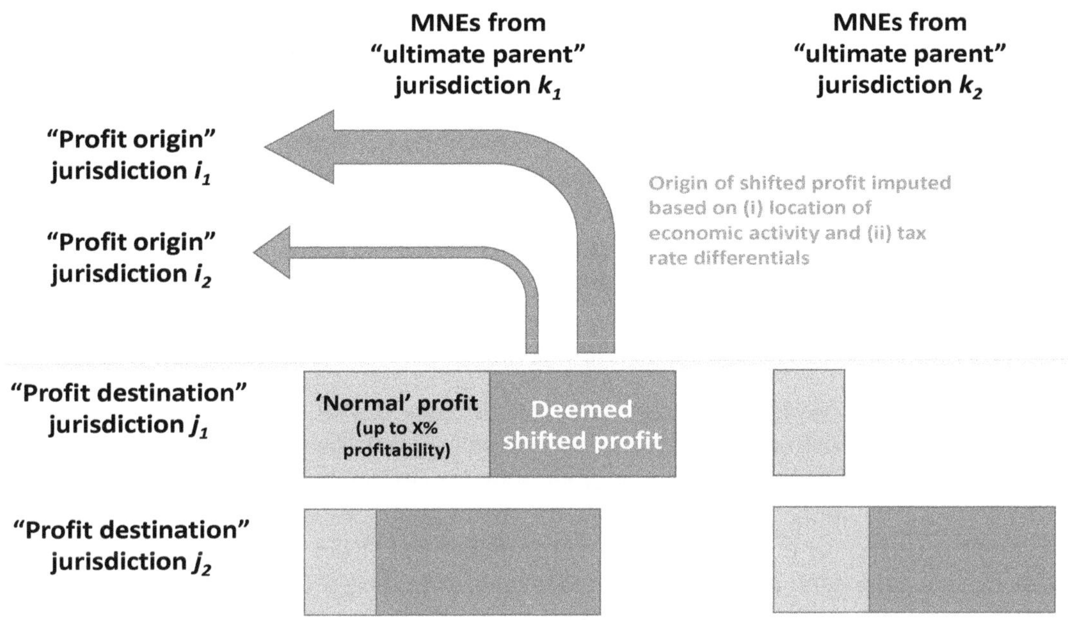


Note: In this stylised example, only two "ultimate parent" jurisdictions, two "profit origin" jurisdictions and two "profit destination" jurisdictions are represented. In reality, all jurisdictions in the profit matrix (more than 200 jurisdictions) are considered as "ultimate parent" jurisdictions, and all jurisdictions in the profit matrix are either "profit origin" or "profit destination", based on the criteria described in the next section (using FDI and ETR data). For each pair of "ultimate parent"-"profit destination" jurisdictions, profit up to a certain profitability rate is deemed 'normal' (orange bars), and the rest, if any, is deemed shifted (blue bars). In this example, some profit in the $k_1$-$j_1$, $k_1$-$j_2$ and $k_2$-$j_2$ pairs is deemed shifted, but not in the $k_2$-$j_1$ pair. Deemed shifted profit is assumed to originate from "profit origin" jurisdictions in a way that depends on the location of the MNEs' economic activity and tax rate differentials, as further described below. This is materialised by the blue arrows in the figure – in this example, profit in the $k_1$-$j_1$ pair is found to come predominantly from jurisdiction $i_1$ (thick arrow) and to a lesser extent from jurisdiction $i_2$ (thin arrow). The corresponding arrows identifying the origin of profit deemed shifted in jurisdiction pairs $k_1$-$j_2$ and $k_2$-$j_2$ are not represented to avoid overburdening the figure.
Source: OECD Secretariat.

232. This approach to measuring profit shifting is new, although it shares some common features with Tørsløv et al. (2018[5]), Cobham et al. (2019[13]) and Clausing (2020[8]). The approach is enabled by the level of detail offered by the profit matrix and the underlying data sources, including anonymised and aggregated CbCR data, which give a detailed account of the amount of profit located across low-tax jurisdictions for each ultimate parent jurisdiction. To benchmark the results against the vast existing literature on profit shifting, an average aggregate profit shifting semi-elasticity is computed based on the results and compared with existing estimates of this semi-elasticity.

### *Profit shifting: Identifying "profit destination" jurisdictions*

233. Potential "profit destination" jurisdictions are assumed to be those meeting at the same time both of the following two criteria:

- **Having an inward FDI-to-GDP ratio above 100%**, as computed based on hard or extrapolated FDI data (see Annex 5.C of Chapter 5 on the FDI extrapolation methodology);[28]
- **Having an average ETR on MNE profit below 17.5%**, based on the median of the three data sources considered in Section 3.4.2 above. This rate of 17.5% is not meant to represent an ETR ceiling above which profit shifting would not occur. Indeed, there may be profit shifting taking place between jurisdictions with higher rates than 17.5%. Instead, this rate is the highest rate in the range of potential minimum rates illustratively considered in this chapter. Since the incentive to shift profit

into jurisdictions with an average ETR above the minimum rate would not be directly affected by Pillar Two as modelled in this chapter,[29] the focus in this chapter is exclusively on profit shifting into jurisdictions with an average ETR below the minimum rate. For example, when the minimum rate is assumed to be 12.5%, only profit shifting to jurisdictions with an average ETR below 12.5% is assumed to be modified by Pillar Two.[30]

234. Based on these criteria, 39 jurisdictions are identified as potential "profit destinations". However, not all of them host deemed shifted profit, as this also depends on the profitability rate of MNEs in the jurisdiction (see next section). Overall, the list of jurisdictions with substantial amounts of deemed shifted profit overlaps widely with other lists in the literature, such as Tørsløv et al. (2018[5]), which often relate to the early list developed by Hines and Rice (1994[14]).

### *Profit shifting: Separating deemed shifted profit from "normal" profit*

235. In these potential "profit destination" jurisdictions, only a share of reported profits are deemed shifted. This is because MNEs can have local economic activity in these jurisdictions, which generate local (non-shifted) profits. To account for this, only profit above a certain "normal" profitability rate is deemed shifted. This normal profitability rate is set at 7.9% (on the ratio of pre-tax profit to turnover) in the baseline estimates, which corresponds to the average global profitability of MNEs observed in the ORBIS sample.[31] Robustness checks have been performed with other rates, including 5% and 10%. They give results that are qualitatively similar to the baseline (Table 3.9).

236. Based on data in the profit matrix and data on ETRs from Section 3.4.2, estimates of shifted profit are derived for each "profit destination"-"ultimate parent" jurisdiction pair. At the aggregate level, the amount of deemed shifted profit is estimated to be about USD 650-850 billion, or about 10-14% of global MNE profit (Table 3.9).[32] This is broadly consistent with the estimates of USD 741 billion and USD 667 billion obtained by Tørsløv et al. (2019[15]; 2019[16]), which are updates, for 2017 and 2016 respectively, of their earlier USD 616 billion figure for 2015 (Tørsløv, Wier and Zucman, 2018[5]). The share of deemed shifted profit in total profit tends to be higher among zero tax jurisdictions (88-94%) than in other "profit destination" jurisdictions (55-74%), which is in line with the intuition that there is less economic substance (and therefore a greater share of shifted profits) in zero-tax jurisdictions than in other "profit destination" jurisdictions.

### *Profit shifting: Identifying "profit origin"*

237. Once shifted profit has been identified, further assumptions are required to identify where profit originates from, i.e. the jurisdiction where it was generated before being shifted. This is done at the level of each "profit destination"-"ultimate parent" pair, using the following formula:

$$ProfitShifted_{i,j,k} = \lambda_{j,k}.Y_{i,k}.f(\tau_i - \tau_j)$$

238. In this formula, $ProfitShifted_{i,j,k}$ is the amount of profit shifted from jurisdiction *i* to jurisdiction *j* by MNEs with an ultimate parent in jurisdiction *k*. The intuition is that this profit is proportional to the economic activity in *i* of MNEs with an ultimate parent in *k*. For example, an MNE with very little economic activity in a jurisdiction is unlikely to have profit shifted away from this jurisdiction, whatever the tax rate differential with this jurisdiction. This economic activity is proxied by the turnover in *i* of MNEs with an ultimate parent in jurisdiction *k* (denoted $Y_{i,k}$) sourced from the turnover matrix.[33] Results are broadly robust to using tangible assets or payroll instead of turnover (Annex 3.C).

Table 3.9. Estimated global profit shifted to low-tax jurisdictions

| | | Baseline estimate ('normal' profitability: 7.9%) | Robustness check ('normal' profitability: 5%) | Robustness check ('normal' profitability: 10%) |
|---|---|---|---|---|
| Estimated amount of shifted MNE profit at the global level | In USD bn | 727 | 837 | 662 |
| | In % of global MNE profit | 11.3% | 13.5% | 10.7% |
| Share of shifted profits in total observed profit | In zero-tax "profit destination" jurisdictions | 90.8% | 94.1% | 88.5% |
| | In other "profit destination" jurisdictions | 61.7% | 73.7% | 54.7% |

Note: The amount of profit shifted is estimated based on a "profit matrix" combining a range of data sources to map the location of profit (see Chapter 5), and the median of three different data sources on ETRs on MNE profit across jurisdictions, following a methodology described in this chapter. "Profit destination" jurisdictions are identified based on FDI and ETR data. Only profit in excess of 'normal' profitability in "profit destination" jurisdiction is deemed shifted. For example, assuming that 'normal' profitability is 7.9%, i.e. the global average profitability in ORBIS data (first column), the estimates suggest that USD 727 billion of profit is shifted, which represents 11.3% of global MNE profit. In "profit destination jurisdictions", the share of observed profit that is shifted is 90.8% on average across zero-tax "profit destination" jurisdictions and 61.7% on average across other "profit destination" jurisdictions. Zero-tax jurisdictions are those with no CIT system or a zero statutory CIT rate. MNEs with an ultimate parent in the United States are included in this table, for the purpose of comparability with the economic literature.
Source: OECD Secretariat.

239. The amount of shifted profit is also assumed to be a function of the tax rate differential between jurisdictions *i* and *j*: $f(\tau_i - \tau_j)$. The tax rates considered are the statutory CIT rates in "profit origin" jurisdictions, in line with most of the profit shifting literature that focuses on statutory rates, and the ETRs in "profit destination" jurisdictions (with the same data sources as in the rest of this chapter), as ETRs sometimes differ considerably from statutory rates in these jurisdictions. Several shapes of the relationship between profit shifting intensity and tax rate differentials (i.e. of the function $f$) are explored in this chapter, as further discussed below.

240. Finally, the amount of profit shifted depends on an array of $\lambda_{j,k}$ scaling factors, which are specific to each "profit destination"-"ultimate parent" pair of jurisdictions. These scaling factors capture that certain "profit destination" jurisdictions are more attractive to MNEs of a given "ultimate parent" jurisdiction – owing to, for example, geographic proximity or the legal environment – and that tax rate differentials alone do not predict where shifted profits are located. Instead of being taken from the literature, or set at arbitrary levels, these factors are set at the unique level that is consistent with the amount of profit that is deemed shifted in each "profit destination"-"ultimate parent" pair of jurisdictions, as computed in the previous section. Formally, these $\lambda_{j,k}$ factors are computed based on the following formula:

$$\lambda_{j,k} = \frac{\sum_i ProfitShifted_{i,j,k}}{\sum_i Y_{i,k} \cdot f(\tau_i - \tau_j)}$$

241. This way of defining the $\lambda_{j,k}$ factors ensures the consistency of the approach, in the sense that the total profit attributed across "profit origin" jurisdictions – for a given "profit destination"-"ultimate parent" pair of jurisdictions – corresponds exactly to the total profit deemed shifted in that pair of jurisdictions. Ultimately, the average of these $\lambda_{j,k}$ factors can be compared to estimates of the profit sensitivity to tax rate differentials from the literature, as further discussed below.

242. A central question is the shape of the $f$ function, i.e. the relationship between profit shifting and tax rate differentials. This is important for the modelling of profit shifting in this section, but also because this assumption defines the way in which reduced tax rate differentials under Pillar Two will affect profit shifting intensity. The academic literature offers limited insights in this area. Most studies assume a linear

relationship between profit shifting and statutory tax rate differentials and find evidence that this relationship is significant, but do not test empirically for other potential shapes (see for example Bradbury et al. (2018[11]) and Beer et al. (2019[12]) for recent reviews). Such a linear relationship is consistent with the theoretical framework of Huizinga and Laeven (2008[17]), which is based on the underlying assumption that the cost of profit shifting is quadratic. With this assumption, an "interior" solution to the MNE's profit maximisation problem implies that profits are shifted in proportion to tax rate differentials.

243. However, some recent studies suggest that the position is more complex in reality. In particular, Bilicka (2019[18]) and Johannesen et al. (2019[19]) show that many MNE entities report zero profit in higher-tax jurisdictions. This would suggest that these MNEs are able to shift all their profit from these jurisdictions, in which case the solution to the MNE's profit maximisation problem is not always "interior" and the relationship between profit shifting and tax rate differentials is no longer linear. Also, Dowd et al. (2017[20]) find a non-linear relationship according to which US MNEs shift more profits to jurisdictions with very low tax rates than a linear elasticity would imply.[34] However, the question considered in that paper is somewhat different from the one considered in this chapter. Indeed, Dowd et al. (2017[20]) focus on the choice of potential "profit destination" jurisdictions for a given "ultimate parent" jurisdiction (in which case, the fact that MNEs shift as much profit as possible to jurisdictions with the lowest ETRs seems intuitive), while this chapter aims to identify "profit origin" jurisdictions for given "ultimate parent" and "profit destination" jurisdictions.

244. Another insight from the literature is that, all else equal, profit shifting tends to be more intense in lower income jurisdictions than in higher income ones. For example, Fuest et al. (2011[21]), based on German micro-data, find that profit shifting via intra-company loans is approximately twice as intense among the developing countries in their sample compared to other jurisdictions, which they suggest may be due to the limited capacity of these jurisdictions to enforce anti-tax avoidance policies. Johannesen et al. (2019[19]) find that a 10 percentage point decrease in foreign affiliates' tax rates increases the likelihood that an MNE reports zero profits by 3 percentage points in low/middle income countries, but only by 1.7 percentage points in high income countries, based on firm-level data from ORBIS. Finally, Cobham and Janský (2018[22]) relying on macro data, find that "the intensity of losses is substantially greater in low-income and lower middle-income jurisdictions; and in sub-Saharan Africa, Latin America and the Caribbean and in South Asia compared with other regions."

245. Against this background, the baseline assumption in this chapter is that profit shifting is generally proportional to tax rate differentials, but more intense in lower income jurisdictions than in higher income ones. Formally, the function $f$ is assumed to be defined as follows: $f(\tau_i - \tau_j) = \alpha_i.(\tau_i - \tau_j)$ if $(\tau_i - \tau_j)$ is positive, and zero otherwise. The coefficient $\alpha_i$ is equal to 1 in high income jurisdictions, 1.5 in middle income ones and 2 in low income jurisdictions (based on the World Bank classification of jurisdictions by income groups). This shape of the relationship between profit shifting and tax rate differentials is presented in Figure 3.8. As discussed above, the absolute amounts of shifted profit attributed to each "profit origin" jurisdiction will depend on the assumptions presented in this figure, but also on the $\lambda_{j,k}$ factors that capture the amount of deemed shifted profit in each "profit destination" jurisdiction (and for each "ultimate parent" jurisdiction).

Figure 3.8. Stylised shape of relationship between profit shifting intensity and tax rate differentials: Baseline shape

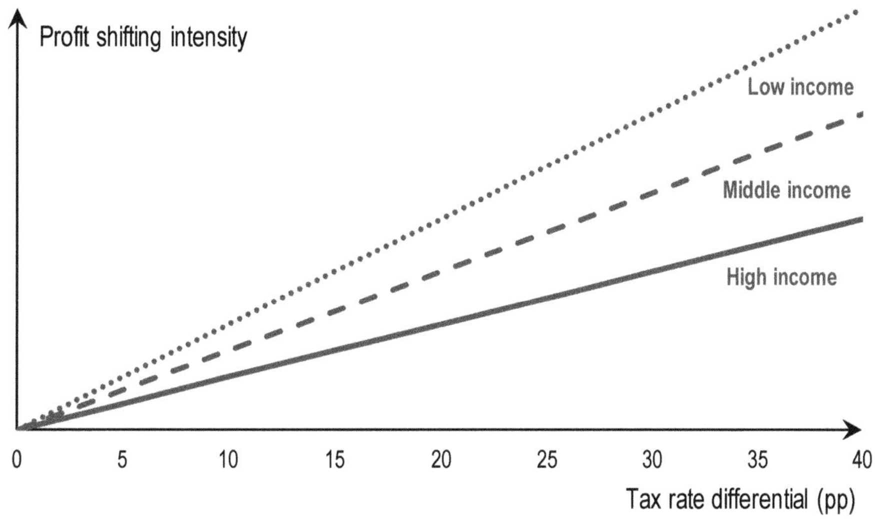


Note: Under the assumptions presented in this figure, the intensity of profit shifting to a jurisdiction is assumed to be proportional to the tax rate differential vis-à-vis this jurisdiction. Profit shifting intensity is assumed to be 1.5 times (resp. 2 times) higher for profit shifted from middle income (resp. low income) jurisdictions compared to high income jurisdictions. The amount of shifted profit (i.e. scale of the Y-axis) will depend on the $\lambda_{j,k}$ factors defined above, which capture the amount of deemed shifted profit in each "profit destination" jurisdiction $j$ (and for each "ultimate parent" jurisdiction $k$).
Source: OECD Secretariat.

### *Profit shifting: Alternative shapes of the relationship between profit shifting and tax rate differentials*

246. To account for potential non-linearities in the shape of the relationship between profit shifting and tax rate differentials, alternative shapes are considered as robustness checks. These shapes are used for the purpose of creating uncertainty ranges around the estimates.

247. Two alternative shapes are considered. The first one is based on the idea that lower income jurisdictions may suffer from profit shifting for tax but also non-tax-related reasons. For example, investors may shift profits away from these jurisdictions due to fears of political instability and/or to circumvent capital controls (this may also be the case in high income jurisdictions, but it seems likely to be less frequent than in lower income jurisdictions). As a result, profit shifting may exist in these jurisdictions even for relatively low tax rate differentials and the subsequent slope of the relationship between profit shifting and tax rate differentials may be less steep than envisaged in the baseline (Figure 3.9, Panel A). This shape also takes into account the assumption that under relatively small tax rate differentials (i.e. less than 5 percentage points), MNEs may generally consider that the costs of profit shifting would exceed the gains (in terms of tax savings). This is why in Figure 3.9 (Panel A) profit shifting intensity does not increase with the tax rate differential as long as this differential remains below 5 percentage points.

248. The second alternative shape takes the same starting point, but also assumes that the slope of the relationship becomes less steep – across all income groups – above a certain level. The idea is that above a certain tax rate differential, MNEs' profit shifting incentives are high anyway and, as a result, these incentives would not be greatly affected by marginal changes in tax rate differentials (Figure 3.9, Panel B).

### Figure 3.9. Alternative shapes of the relationship between profit shifting intensity and tax rate differentials

**Panel A:** Alternative shape No. 1, where lower income jurisdictions suffer from profit shifting due to non-tax factors

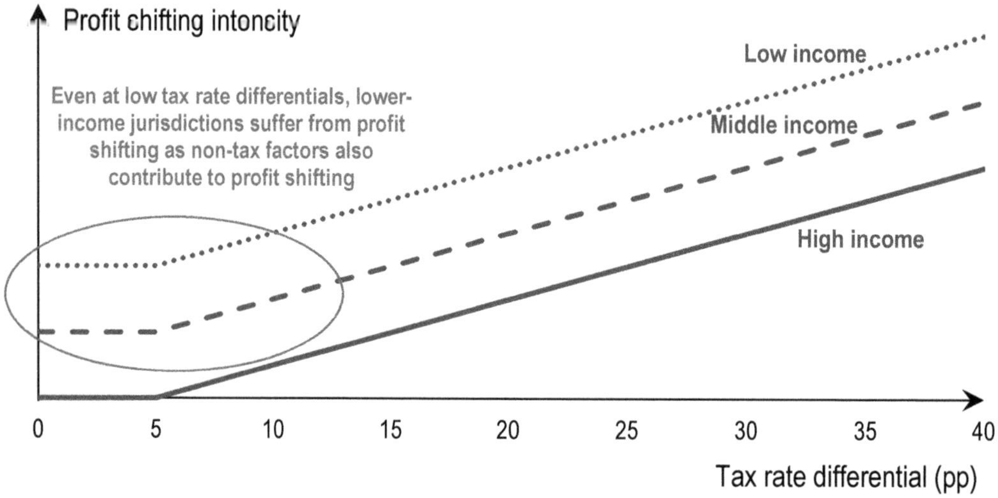


**Panel B:** Alternative shape No. 2, where profit shifting intensity is assumed to become less sensitive to tax rate differentials above a certain tax rate differential

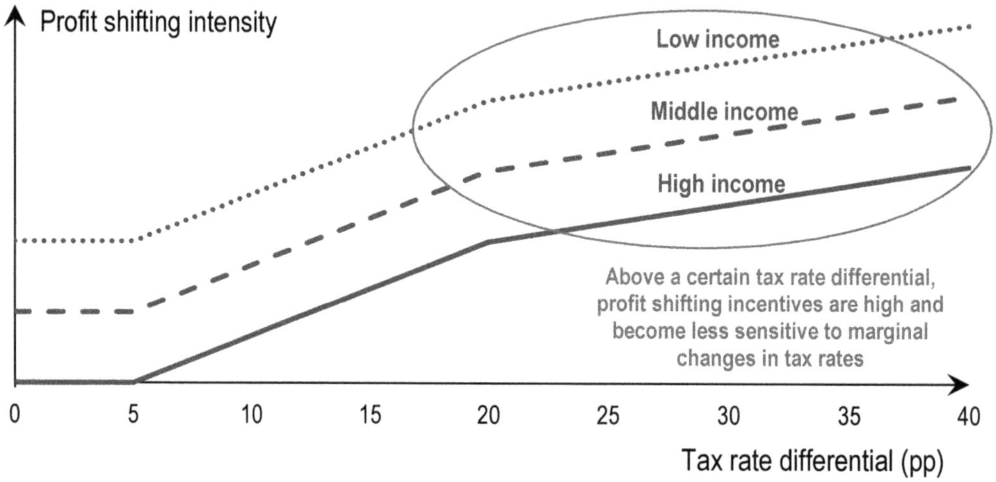


Note: In Panel A, profit shifting intensity is assumed to be higher among lower income jurisdictions than higher income jurisdictions, as in the baseline (Figure 3.8). However, profit shifting in lower income jurisdictions is assumed to be partly driven by non-tax factors, which implies that lower income jurisdictions face profit shifting even under low (or even zero) tax rate differentials. In turn, reducing tax rate differentials in lower income jurisdictions tends to reduce profit shifting less than in the baseline scenario. In Panel B, this assumption is kept, and, in addition, profit shifting intensity is assumed to become less sensitive to tax rate differentials above a certain tax rate differential. This could reflect that for relatively high tax rate differentials, the incentive to shift profit is high anyway, and therefore less influenced by the exact level of the rate differential. In both panels, the amount of shifted profit (i.e. scale of the Y-axis) will depend on the $\lambda_{j,k}$ factors defined above, which capture the amount of deemed shifted profit in each "profit destination" jurisdiction $j$ (and for each "ultimate parent" jurisdiction $k$).
*Source*: OECD Secretariat.

#### *Profit shifting: Comparing the aggregate semi-elasticity with the literature*

249. The estimates obtained with the methodology described in the previous sections can be compared with the existing literature by computing an average aggregate semi-elasticity of profit to tax rate

differentials. In practice, this means computing a weighted average of the $\lambda_{j,k}.\alpha_i$ coefficients. In the baseline case described above, this aggregate profit shifting elasticity is estimated to be about 1.2.[35] This estimate is close to the semi-elasticity of 1 that was found in a recent meta-analysis by Beer et al. (2019[12]). An earlier meta-study found a semi-elasticity of 0.8 (Heckemeyer and Overesch, 2017[23]) The semi-elasticity found in earlier OECD estimates produced in the context of the BEPS Action 11 report was also about 1 (OECD, 2015[24]; Johansson et al., 2017[25]). Overall, this suggests that the methodology to assess profit shifting in this chapter, while based on an approach and on data sources different from most earlier studies, is broadly consistent with these studies in terms of overall results, as suggested as well by the results in Table 3.9.

### 3.6.2. Impact of Pillar Two on tax rate differentials and profit shifting

250. Pillar Two is expected to reduce tax rate differentials between jurisdictions. More precisely, it is expected to reduce the tax rate differential vis-à-vis jurisdictions where the ETR is currently below the minimum rate, by increasing this ETR up to the level of the minimum rate. In a scenario where governments in these jurisdictions do not react, as in Scenario 3, this minimum rate would be paid in another jurisdiction (e.g. the jurisdiction of the ultimate parent in the case of the IIR). If some of the jurisdictions with an ETR below the minimum rate increase their ETR up to the minimum tax rate, as envisaged in Scenario 4, then the tax would be paid in these jurisdictions.

251. In both of these cases, the incentives of MNEs to shift profit to low-tax jurisdictions would be reduced compared to a scenario without Pillar Two. It is also useful to note that these incentives would be the same regardless of whether governments in low-tax jurisdictions increase their ETR or not, since the MNE would face the same amount of tax on its shifted profit (the only difference being where this tax is paid). This is why the order in which the MNE and government reactions are considered in this chapter has relatively little impact on the final outcome, as mentioned earlier.[36]

252. Profit shifting intensity is assumed to be substantially reduced by the decline in tax rate differentials induced by Pillar Two. However, profit shifting is not expected to be completely eliminated by Pillar Two, since some tax rate differentials would persist between the minimum rate and the (higher) rate that applies in the jurisdictions with an ETR above the minimum rate (see stylised example in Figure 3.10). In practice, the decision of an MNE group to continue or not with a certain profit shifting scheme will depend on the tax rate differential after the implementation of Pillar Two and the costs of the profit shifting scheme (e.g. financial and advisory costs associated with setting up the scheme, reputational costs). In some cases, the MNE group may continue with the scheme, while in others it may find that the costs will outweigh the benefits after Pillar Two is introduced. It is difficult to assess how frequent the decision to reduce or even stop profit shifting will be, since the costs of profit shifting are not known with precision and will vary across MNE groups and jurisdictions.

253. In addition, MNE decisions may be more complex than a simple choice between continuing or stopping a profit shifting scheme, as a possible alternative may be to create a different scheme to shift profit to another jurisdiction (e.g. a jurisdiction with a higher ETR but to which the costs of shifting profit are lower) including potentially through changes in corporate structure.[37] These complex reactions will depend on the particular circumstances and choices of each MNE group, and modelling them goes beyond the ambition of this chapter. If MNE reactions depart significantly from the stylised modelling assumptions used in this chapter, which are described below, this could significantly affect the estimated Pillar Two revenue effects, especially at the level of individual jurisdictions. At the global level, or for broad jurisdiction groups, the effect of different profit shifting reactions could partly cancel each other (e.g. if one jurisdiction in the group receives more profit, another jurisdiction in the group may receive less).

## Figure 3.10. Stylised example of the impact of Pillar Two on profit shifting intensity

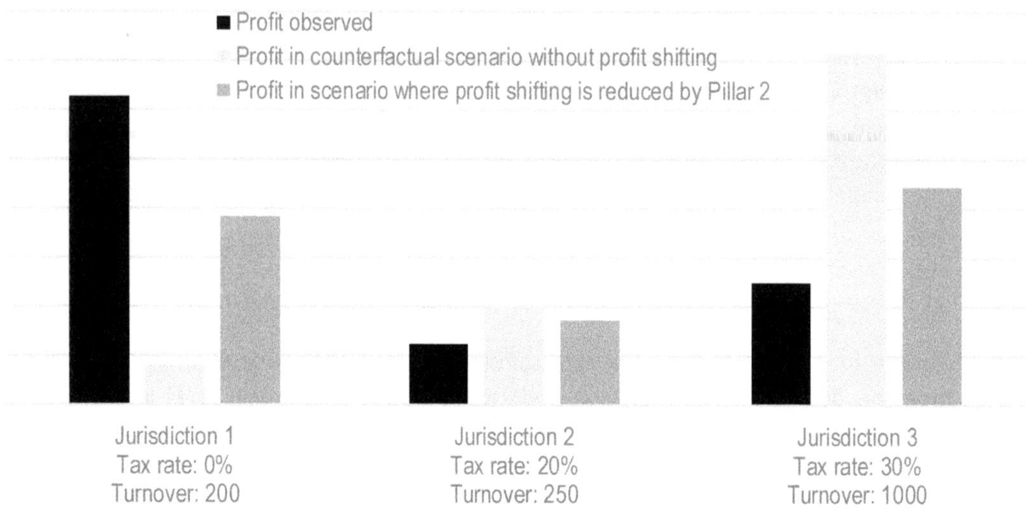


Note: This stylised example, based on fictitious numbers, illustrates how Pillar Two may reduce profit shifting but not eliminate it. In the current situation, most of the profit of the MNE group considered is located in Jurisdiction 1, which has a 0% tax rate. Most of this profit is deemed shifted, which is why little profit remains in Jurisdiction 1 in the counterfactual scenario without profit shifting. This profit is reallocated to Jurisdictions 2 and 3 based on the modelling on profit shifting described above. In the scenario where profit shifting is reduced by Pillar Two (assuming illustratively a 12.5% minimum tax rate), a greater share of profit remains in Jurisdiction 1 as the tax rate differential vis-à-vis Jurisdictions 2 and 3 is reduced but not eliminated.
Source: OECD Secretariat

254. Against this background, the stylised baseline assumption in this chapter is that profit shifting would be reduced proportionally to the reduction in tax rate differential induced by Pillar Two. For example, if Pillar Two reduces the tax rate differential between two jurisdictions by a third, profit shifting between these two jurisdictions is assumed to be reduced by a third. This assumption is consistent with the baseline modelling of profit shifting above.

255. However, this assumption overlooks the fact that (i) some profit shifting in lower income jurisdictions is related to non-tax factors and may persist after the introduction of Pillar Two, and (ii) that for high tax rate differentials, a marginal change in the tax rate differential may not lead to much of a change in the profit shifting intensity, since the profit shifting incentive is high anyway (put differently, the gain from profit shifting outweighs the costs in this case by such a large amount, that a marginal reduction in this gain would not change the choice of the MNE group to engage in profit shifting). These considerations are taken into account in the robustness check scenarios based on the two alternative shapes of the relationship between profit shifting intensity and tax rate differentials (Figure 3.9). In particular, with the second shape, profit shifting incentives become less sensitive to tax rate differentials when these differentials are relatively high. These two robustness check scenarios are used to build the uncertainty ranges around the estimates.

256. Based on the assumptions described above, an adjusted profit matrix taking into account the reduced profit shifting intensity is presented in Table 3.10 for an illustrative minimum tax rate of 12.5%. This is done for the baseline shape of the relationship between profit shifting intensity and tax rate differentials (Panel A) and for the two alternative shapes from Figure 3.9 (Panels B and C). Compared to Table 3.7, the total amount of profit in each column is the same (by construction), but the location of profit has shifted across matrix rows. Broadly speaking, profit has been reallocated away from investment hubs and into the other jurisdiction groups. The amount of profit in investment hubs is reduced by about 9-10% compared to Table 3.7 (depending on the panel considered) and the amount of profit in other jurisdiction groups is increased by 1-8% depending on the group and the panel considered. In particular, middle and

low income jurisdictions tend to regain less profit under the alternative shapes of the relationship between profit shifting intensity and tax rate differentials (Panels B and C) than under the baseline (Panel A), which is consistent with the assumptions underlying these alternative shapes and discussed in the previous section.

### *3.6.3. Implications of a formulaic substance-based carve-out on profit shifting behaviour*

257. The estimates in the previous section are based on a scenario where Pillar Two would not include a formulaic substance-based carve-out. This section discusses how the inclusion of a potential formulaic substance-based carve-out could modify the effect of Pillar Two on MNE profit shifting incentives.

258. A formulaic substance-based carve-out could have two main effects regarding MNE profit shifting behaviour. First, a carve-out might in theory reduce the effect of Pillar Two on profit shifting in specific situations where an MNE group would shift profit to a jurisdiction where it already has a substantial amount of tangible assets and/or payroll. In practice, this is not likely to be the case very often, as profit is frequently (and more likely) shifted to jurisdictions where MNE groups have minimal levels of substantive activity (see Table 3.5 for example). For example, assuming that, after the introduction of Pillar Two, (i) incentives to shift profit are not modified by Pillar Two as long as the shifted profit is ultimately carved out under Pillar Two, and that (ii) Pillar Two has the same effect on the shifting of 'non-carved-out profit' as in the no-carve-out case,[38] then the effect of Pillar Two on the global amount of shifted profit would be reduced by less than 1% compared to a situation where Pillar Two is applied without carve-out.[39]

**Table 3.10. Profit matrix adjusted for reduced profit shifting intensity due to Pillar Two (12.5% minimum tax rate, no carve-out)**

Excluding changes in profit shifting intensity from MNEs with an ultimate parent in the United States

**Panel A**: Assuming baseline shape of relationship between profit shifting intensity and tax rate differentials

| | | Jurisdiction of ultimate parent | | | | |
|---|---|---|---|---|---|---|
| | (USD billion of 2016) | High income | Middle income | Low income | Investment Hubs | Total |
| Jurisdiction of affiliate | High income (64 jurisd.) | 3592.8 | 48.7 | 0.1 | 198.8 | **3840.3** |
| | Middle income (105) | 390.2 | 827.4 | 0.1 | 198.2 | **1415.9** |
| | Low income (29) | 1.7 | 1.3 | 3.1 | 0.5 | **6.7** |
| | Investment Hubs (24) | 602.7 | 59.2 | 0.0 | 256.2 | **918.1** |
| | **Total** | **4587.4** | **936.7** | **3.3** | **653.7** | **6181.1** |

**Panel B**: Assuming alternative shape No. 1 of relationship between profit shifting intensity and tax rate differentials

| | | Jurisdiction of ultimate parent | | | | |
|---|---|---|---|---|---|---|
| | (USD billion of 2016) | High income | Middle income | Low income | Investment Hubs | Total |
| Jurisdiction of affiliate | High income (64 jurisd.) | 3600.8 | 48.8 | 0.1 | 204.5 | **3854.2** |
| | Middle income (105) | 389.5 | 826.3 | 0.1 | 194.4 | **1410.3** |
| | Low income (29) | 1.7 | 1.3 | 3.1 | 0.4 | **6.5** |
| | Investment Hubs (24) | 595.4 | 60.2 | 0.0 | 254.4 | **910.0** |
| | **Total** | **4587.4** | **936.7** | **3.3** | **653.7** | **6181.1** |

**Panel C:** Assuming alternative shape No. 2 of relationship between profit shifting intensity and tax rate differentials

| | | Jurisdiction of ultimate parent | | | | |
|---|---|---|---|---|---|---|
| | (USD billion of 2016) | High income | Middle income | Low income | Investment Hubs | Total |
| **Jurisdiction of affiliate** | High income (64 jurisd.) | 3598.0 | 48.8 | 0.1 | 198.7 | **3845.5** |
| | Middle income (105) | 389.2 | 825.4 | 0.1 | 193.0 | **1407.8** |
| | Low income (29) | 1.7 | 1.3 | 3.1 | 0.4 | **6.5** |
| | Investment Hubs (24) | 598.5 | 61.2 | 0.0 | 261.6 | **921.3** |
| | **Total** | **4587.4** | **936.7** | **3.3** | **653.7** | **6181.1** |

Note: The results in Panel A are based on the baseline relationship between profit shifting intensity and tax rate differentials (presented in Figure 3.8). The results in Panels B and C are based on the alternative relationships presented in Figure 3.9. The results depend on the minimum rate considered. In this Table, a minimum tax rate of 12.5% is assumed and the interaction with Pillar One is taken into account (as in Scenario 2). No carve-out is assumed. The effect of a formulaic substance-based carve-out of profit shifting is further discussed below. Groups of jurisdictions (high, middle and low income) are based on the World Bank classification. Investment hubs are defined as jurisdictions with a total inward FDI position above 150% of GDP. For comparability with the original profit matrix, these tables include MNEs with an ultimate parent in the United States, but potential changes in the profit shifting intensity of these US MNEs are not considered in this table. The effect of Pillar Two on the profit shifting of US MNEs is discussed in Section 3.8.
Source: OECD calculations.

259. Second, the existence of a formulaic substance-based carve-out could encourage MNE groups to relocate tangible assets or employees to low-tax jurisdictions where they already shift profit (or could shift profit in the future) in order to benefit from the carve-out. This effect is difficult to model as it depends on the cost of relocating tangible assets or employees across jurisdictions, which is specific to each MNE group and each jurisdiction. In practice, tangible assets and employees are generally less mobile than intangible assets. Under the carve-out percentages considered in this chapter, it seems unlikely that a substantial amount of relocation would take place.[40] Still, a formulaic substance-based carve-out may trigger attempts by tax planning MNEs to reclassify the location of tangible assets or employees for tax purposes without changing significantly their actual physical location, or to resort to other schemes to try to benefit from the carve-out without actually relocating tangible assets or employees. Reflecting this, it is important that the design of the carve-out is 'abuse-proof', in the sense that it opens carve-out rights only when justified by the actual location of tangible assets and/or employees.

260. Against this background, the estimates in this chapter assume that the effect of Pillar Two on profit shifting intensity are the same in the scenarios with a formulaic substance-based carve-out as in the no-carve-out scenario.

### *3.6.4. Global Pillar Two revenue gains under Scenario 3*

261. Revenue gains from Pillar Two under Scenario 3 are computed based on the assumptions described in the previous sections and presented in Table 3.11. For simplicity, only point estimates are presented, and ranges reflecting uncertainty relative to pockets of low-taxed profits are not included in this table (these ranges are included in the summary tables presented in Section 3.9). The revenue gains consist of two components:

- **Effect of the reduced profit shifting intensity**: Profit that is no longer shifted is assumed to be taxed at the statutory CIT rate in the "profit origin" jurisdictions where it was generated. This assumption is consistent with the literature on profit shifting, which generally assumes that the marginal tax rate that would otherwise be applied to shifted profit is the statutory rate.[41] In contrast, "profit destination" jurisdictions would receive less shifted profit, leading them to lose tax revenues. For these jurisdictions, it is assumed that the shifted profit was taxed at the average ETR on MNE income, reflecting that some of these jurisdictions tax MNE profit at a rate that is well below the statutory rate.[42] Overall, at the global level, the net result is a tax revenue gain, since the tax rate applied in "profit origin" jurisdictions tends is higher than in "profit destination" ones.

- **Revenues collected via the minimum tax**: Even if MNE profit shifting intensity is reduced, some profit would remain located in jurisdictions where the ETR is below the minimum rate. Profit in these jurisdictions would be subject to the IIR and UTPR (except regarding US MNEs, where they would be subject to GILTI), which are modelled with the same assumptions as in Scenarios 1 and 2. The interaction with Pillar One is taken into account in the same way as in Scenario 2, based on the profit matrix adjusted for the new profit shifting patterns.

## Table 3.11. Global Pillar Two revenue gains (Scenario 3), in % of global CIT revenues

Estimates in these tables exclude MNEs with an ultimate parent in the United States

| (in % of global CIT revenues) | Minimum tax rate | 7.5% | 10% | 12.5% | 15% | 17.5% |
|---|---|---|---|---|---|---|
| Baseline | Effect of reduced profit shifting | 0.3% | 0.6% | 0.9% | 1.3% | 1.6% |
| | Revenues from IIR and UTPR | 0.4% | 0.7% | 1.0% | 1.3% | 1.7% |
| | Total | 0.8% | 1.3% | 1.9% | 2.6% | 3.3% |
| Alternative profit shifting shape No. 1 | Effect of reduced profit shifting | 0.4% | 0.7% | 1.0% | 1.4% | 1.7% |
| | Revenues from IIR and UTPR | 0.4% | 0.7% | 1.0% | 1.3% | 1.6% |
| | Total | 0.8% | 1.3% | 2.0% | 2.7% | 3.3% |
| Alternative profit shifting shape No. 2 | Effect of reduced profit shifting | 0.3% | 0.5% | 0.8% | 1.2% | 1.6% |
| | Revenues from IIR and UTPR | 0.4% | 0.7% | 1.0% | 1.4% | 1.7% |
| | Total | 0.7% | 1.2% | 1.9% | 2.6% | 3.2% |

Note: The results in these tables focus on Pillar Two revenue gains under Scenario 3 (i.e. taking into account interaction with Pillar One and MNE reaction). For simplicity, only point estimates are presented, and ranges reflecting uncertainty, including uncertainty relative to pockets of low-taxed profits, are not included in this table (see Section 3.9 for final results including uncertainty ranges). The baseline case corresponds to a situation where profit shifting is assumed to be proportional to tax rate differentials (as in Figure 3.8), while the alternative scenarios correspond to two other versions of the shape of the relationship between tax rate differentials and profit shifting intensity (presented in Figure 3.9). The minimum tax rates considered are illustrative. The results focus illustratively on a scenario assuming a 10% carve-out on payroll and tangible asset depreciation. As discussed above, the effect of Pillar Two on profit shifting intensity is assumed to be the same in both scenarios. Consistent with the assumption that GILTI would coexist with Pillar Two, the estimates in these tables exclude revenues gains related to MNEs with an ultimate parent in the United States (both on the effect of profit shifting and revenues from IIR and UTPR).
Source: OECD Secretariat.

262. To reflect the uncertainties around the estimates, results in the final section of this chapter are presented as ranges. In the case of the effect of reduced profit shifting, the range is defined in the following way: for each jurisdiction, the bottom (top) point of the range is the minimum (maximum) value across the results obtained with the three shapes of the relationship between profit shifting intensity and tax rate differentials considered in this chapter (baseline and alternative shapes No. 1 and No. 2, as described in Figure 3.8 and Figure 3.9).

## 3.7. Scenario 4: Taking into account some government reactions

263. In Scenario 4, it is assumed that certain jurisdictions would change some of their tax rules and/or rates to increase their jurisdiction's ETR on profit that is currently taxed below the minimum rate. The rationale for this reaction is that an ETR increase (up to a rate below or equal to the minimum rate) would not necessarily change the overall amount of tax paid by MNEs, but it would allow the jurisdictions increasing their ETR to capture a greater share of global tax revenues.

264. In practice, whether such an ETR increase would change the overall amount of tax paid by MNEs or not would depend on the design of Pillar Two and of the MNE considered. In particular, assuming that Pillar Two includes a formulaic substance-based carve-out, an ETR increase could increase the overall amount of tax paid by some MNEs, as they would 'lose the benefit' of the carve-out in the jurisdictions increasing their ETR (i.e. they would have to pay the minimum tax rate on all their profit, including the profit that was carved-out under Pillar Two).[43,44] In the case of US MNEs, under the illustrative assumption that GILTI would coexist with Pillar Two, an ETR increase by a low-tax jurisdiction would also lead to a higher overall amount of tax paid.[45]

265. The uncertainty over whether a local ETR increase would increase the global amount of tax paid by MNEs or not makes it difficult to assess with certainty which jurisdictions would decide to increase their ETR in reaction to Pillar Two. Other considerations that are discussed in the next section (e.g. administrative costs of creating a CIT system in a jurisdiction where there is none, possible knock-on effects on taxes paid by non-MNE firms) also add to this uncertainty. Reflecting this, the assumptions presented in the next section should be seen as nothing more than stylised and illustrative assumptions.

### *3.7.1. Assumptions on government reactions*

266. The modelling of Scenario 4 in this chapter is based on the following assumptions on government reactions. These assumptions, which are summarised in Table 3.12, are consistent with those made on Pillar Two implementation in Section 3.4.5 above. They do not depend on the assumption made on a potential formulaic substance-based carve-out, even though, as discussed above, such a carve-out would tend to reduce the incentives for low-tax jurisdictions to increase their ETR.

- **Group 1: Jurisdictions with an average ETR above the minimum rate.** No reaction is modelled. This is because, as discussed above, the potential policy reaction of jurisdictions with an ETR above the minimum rate is a priori ambiguous.[46]
- **Group 2: Jurisdictions with a zero corporate tax rate.** For the purposes of the modelling in this chapter, jurisdictions in this group are not assumed to increase their ETR. The reason is that these jurisdictions generally do not have a CIT system. Introducing a corporate tax system from scratch would generate significant administrative costs, could lead these jurisdictions to be seen as less attractive investment destinations, and could also have spillovers on other sectors of their economies since non-MNE firms would possibly have to be subject to the newly-introduced CIT as well. Assuming that Pillar Two includes a formulaic substance-based carve-out, an additional argument is that an ETR increase would no longer be neutral for the overall amount of tax paid by MNEs, as discussed above. Under the assumption that GILTI would coexist with Pillar Two, the ETR increase would not be neutral for US MNEs either.
- **Group 3: Jurisdictions with an average ETR below the minimum rate, but greater than zero.** Jurisdictions in this group have a CIT system, so it is easier for them to increase their ETR than for jurisdictions in Group 2. Still, it seems plausible that not all of them will increase their ETR, including for the reasons discussed above. In addition, the ETRs faced by MNEs may not be homogeneous, as they reflect the application of different tax provisions (e.g. different kinds of tax deductions and preferential regimes), in which case it may not be straightforward to bring the ETR of all MNE entities up to the level of the minimum rate. Against this background:

- The assumption in this chapter is that half of jurisdictions in Group 3 would increase their ETR on the profit of MNEs up to the level of the minimum rate under Pillar Two, while the other half would not. This is consistent with the assumptions on IIR and UTPR implementation, described in Section 3.4.5, where half of jurisdictions in this group are assumed to implement an IIR and a UTPR. Potential revenue gains related to an increase in the ETR of non-MNE entities are not taken into account in this chapter.
- In practice, and as above, identifying the jurisdictions in Group 3 that would increase their ETR is not straightforward and a similar methodology as used for IIR and UTPR implementation in Scenario 1 is applied. Instead of arbitrarily selecting half of the jurisdictions in the group, a simplifying assumption is made that all jurisdictions in this group increase their ETR to close half of the gap vis-à-vis the minimum rate. Again, this does not aim to be realistic in itself, but rather to be a reasonable proxy for a situation where half of the jurisdictions in this group would increase their ETR to the level of the minimum rate and the other half would not change their ETR. For the purpose of creating uncertainty ranges around the estimates, it is assumed that between one-third and two-thirds of jurisdictions in this group would increase their ETR to the level of the minimum rate (instead of one-half in the baseline).

Table 3.12. Summary of assumptions on government reactions by groups of jurisdictions

| | Definition of group | Implementation of IIR and UTPR under Scenarios 1-4 | ETR increase in Scenario 4 |
|---|---|---|---|
| **Jurisdiction group 1** | Average ETR above minimum rate | Yes | No |
| **Jurisdiction group 2** | Zero tax rate | No | No |
| **Jurisdiction group 3** | Average ETR above zero but below minimum rate | Yes for half of jurisdictions, no for the other half | ETR increase to minimum rate for half of jurisdictions, no reaction for the other |

Note: These assumptions are only used for the purpose of modelling and do not pre-judge governments' actual decisions and reactions. The underlying rationale is discussed in Section 3.4.5 and Section 3.7.1. For jurisdiction group 3, it is assumed that half of the jurisdictions would implement IIR and UTPR and increase their ETR, but identifying which jurisdictions belong to which half is not straightforward. To avoid selecting jurisdictions arbitrarily, a technical assumption (not meant to be realistic in itself) is made that all jurisdictions in this group apply an IIR and a UTPR on half of the relevant profit, and increase their ETR to close half of the gap vis-à-vis the minimum rate.
Source: OECD Secretariat

### *3.7.2. Scenario 4 methodology and results*

267. The methodology to compute revenue gains from Scenario 4 is relatively straightforward, since the location of profit is the same as in Scenario 3 (Table 3.10). The main difference with Scenario 3 is the distribution of revenue gains across jurisdictions, as jurisdictions increasing their ETR capture a greater share of global revenue gains. In practice, jurisdiction-specific gains are computed consistently with Scenarios 1-3 above, with the additional assumption that profit in a jurisdiction increasing its ETR is taxed by this jurisdiction, instead of being subject to the IIRs and UTPRs of other jurisdictions (Figure 3.11).

Figure 3.11. Stylised illustration on Scenario 4 assumptions

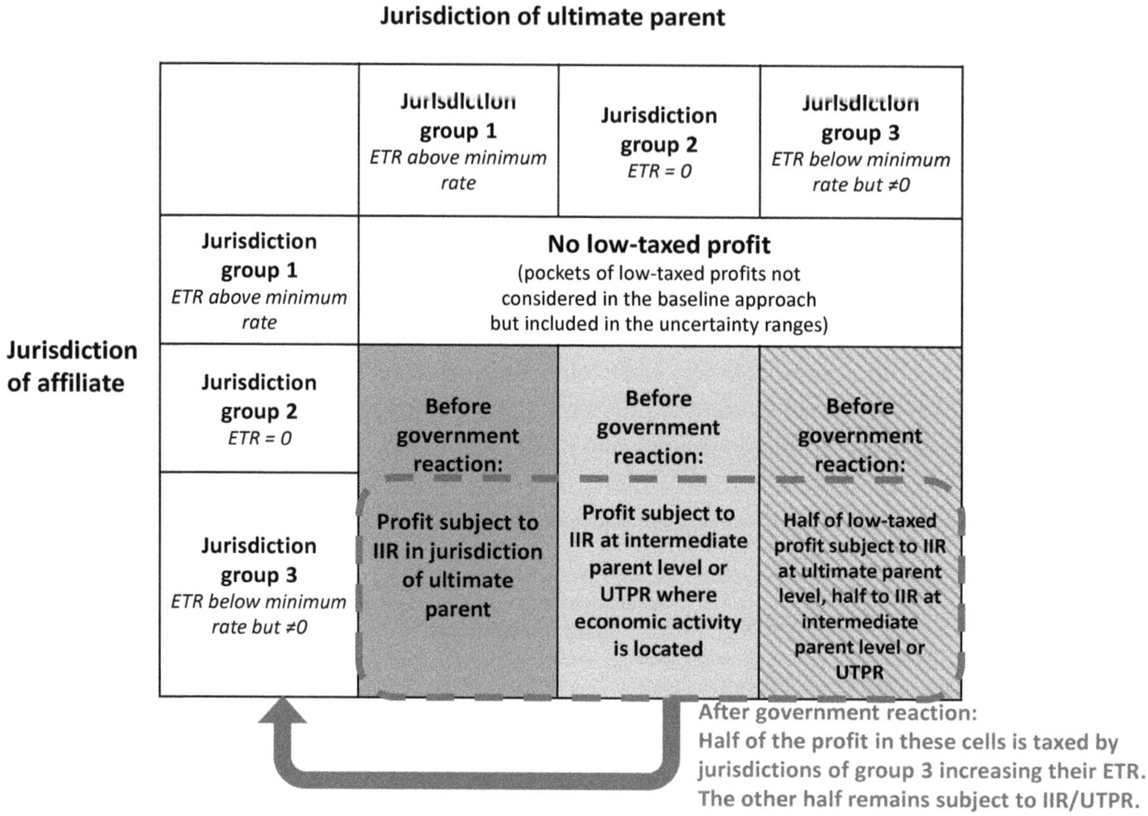


Note: This stylised figure illustrates how the reaction of governments is taken into account in Scenario 4. For the sake of simplicity, this figure focuses on a scenario without formulaic substance-based carve-out. Compared to the similar illustration for Scenarios 1-3 (see Figure 3.5), half of the profit located in countries from group 3 is taxed by these countries as they increase their ETR. The other half of this profit remains subject to IIR and UTPR as in Scenarios 1-3.
Source: OECD Secretariat.

268. Global revenue gains in Scenario 4 are presented in Table 3.13. For simplicity, only point estimates are presented, and ranges reflecting uncertainty relative to pockets of low-taxed profits are not included in this table (these ranges are included in the summary tables presented in Section 3.9). Also for simplicity, results in Table 3.13 only focus on the baseline shape of the relationship between profit shifting intensity and tax rate differentials. Results for the two alternative shapes discussed above are presented in Annex 3.A.

Table 3.13. Global Pillar Two revenue gains (Scenario 4), in % of global CIT revenues

Estimates in these tables exclude MNEs with an ultimate parent in the United States

| Minimum tax rate | 7.5% | 10% | 12.5% | 15% | 17.5% |
|---|---|---|---|---|---|
| Effect of reduced profit shifting | 0.3% | 0.6% | 0.9% | 1.3% | 1.6% |
| Revenues from IIR and UTPR | 0.4% | 0.5% | 0.7% | 0.9% | 1.1% |
| Gains from ETR increases in some jurisdictions | 0.0% | 0.2% | 0.3% | 0.5% | 0.8% |
| Total | 0.8% | 1.3% | 2.0% | 2.7% | 3.5% |

Note: The results in these tables focus on Pillar Two revenue gains under Scenario 4 (i.e. taking into account interaction with Pillar One and MNE reactions) and are based on the baseline relationship between tax rate differentials and profit shifting intensity (presented in Figure 3.8). Results based on the two alternative shapes presented in Figure 3.9 are presented in Annex 3.A. For simplicity, only point estimates are presented, and ranges reflecting uncertainty, including uncertainty relative to pockets of low-taxed profits, are not included in this table (see Section 3.9 for final results including uncertainty ranges). The minimum tax rates considered are illustrative. The results focus illustratively on a scenario assuming a 10% carve-out on payroll and tangible asset depreciation. As discussed above, the effect of Pillar Two on profit shifting intensity is assumed to be the same in both scenarios. Consistent with the assumption that GILTI would coexist with Pillar Two, the estimates in these tables exclude revenue gains related to MNEs with an ultimate parent in the United States (on the effect of profit shifting, revenues from IIR and UTPR and gains from ETR increases).
Source: OECD Secretariat.

## 3.8. Revenue gains relative to MNEs with a US ultimate parent

269. As discussed above, while no decision has been taken by the Inclusive Framework yet, it is illustratively assumed in this chapter that GILTI would coexist with Pillar Two. This is assumed to imply that the United States would collect revenues from GILTI, instead of the IIR, on the low-taxed foreign profit of US MNEs.

270. GILTI shares some common characteristics with GloBE, in the sense that it results in a minimum level of taxation on the foreign profit of US MNEs, but also differs from GloBE in a number of ways. An important difference is the level of blending, as GILTI involves largely, but not completely, global blending of foreign profit, while GloBE (under the illustrative assumptions in this chapter) would entail jurisdictional blending. Other differences (also depending on the final design of GloBE) may notably include the existence of a global revenue threshold, the exact definition of the tax base, the inclusion of loss carry-forward and tax-credit carry-forward provisions, the definition of covered taxes as well as the existence and design of potential carve-outs (see Pillar Two Blueprint report). The GILTI tax rate ranges between 10.5% and 13.125% depending on the amount of foreign taxes paid.[47] These rates are scheduled to increase to 13.125%-16.406% in 2026. GILTI applies to profit in excess of 10% of the carrying cost of tangible assets used in the production of GILTI income reduced by certain interest expense (based on so-called "qualified business asset investment").

271. It goes beyond the ambition of this chapter to model with precision the revenue gains from GILTI, due notably to the many potential rule differences with GloBE. Ex ante estimates of the potential gains from GILTI by the US Joint Committee on Taxation (JCT) are presented in Table 3.14 (US Joint Committee on Taxation, 2017[2]). Over 2018-25, estimated gains represent about USD 9-10 billion per year. Revenue gains are expected to increase to USD 21 billion in 2027, reflecting the scheduled increase in the GILTI tax rate. To date, no ex post assessment of GILTI has been published by the US authorities. Compared to the ex ante assessment by the US JCT, it has been argued that actual revenue gains may be higher (Horst, 2019[26]), as certain provisions of GILTI (notably relating to the allocation of deductible expenses) are stricter than anticipated at the time of the ex ante assessment.

## Table 3.14. Estimated revenue gains from the US GILTI

Ex ante estimates by the US Joint Committee on Taxation

| Fiscal year | 2018 | 2019 | 2020 | 2021 | 2022 | 2023 | 2024 | 2025 | 2026 | 2027 |
|---|---|---|---|---|---|---|---|---|---|---|
| Estimated revenue gains (USD bn) | 7.7 | 12.5 | 9.6 | 9.5 | 9.3 | 9.0 | 9.2 | 9.3 | 15.1 | 21.2 |

Source: https://www.jct.gov/publications.html?func=startdown&id=5053 (section III.B.1)

272. GILTI can be expected to have affected the profit shifting of US MNEs by reducing the potential gains from shifting profit to low-tax jurisdictions, potentially impacting tax revenues in the United States and in other jurisdictions. However, quantifying this effect is complicated by the fact that GILTI was introduced as part of a major and multifaceted US corporate tax reform, involving a reduction in the statutory tax rate as well as a number of other significant provisions (e.g. Foreign-Derived Intangible Income regime, Base Erosion and Anti-abuse Tax) that have also likely affected MNEs' profit shifting incentives. Another complication is that, due to the global blending nature of GILTI, profit shifting incentives are affected differently across firms depending on whether the average ETR on their foreign income is above or below the GILTI rate. For example, GILTI does not reduce the profit shifting incentives of MNEs that have an average ETR on their foreign profit that is above the GILTI rate (even if their ETR in some jurisdictions is below the GILTI rate). In addition, GILTI may also create incentives for more complex reactions, including relocating some tangible assets away from the United States to benefit from a larger carve-out.[48]

273. In the estimates presented in this chapter, MNEs with an ultimate parent in the United States are generally excluded. For the purpose of assessing global revenue gains (including from US MNEs) in section 3.9.2, it is assumed that US gains from GILTI would be in a range between USD 9 billion and USD 21 billion. The use of an uncertainty range reflects both the uncertainty around the ex ante estimates by the JCT and the scheduled rate increase from 2026 onwards.

## 3.9. Overview of the results across the four scenarios

### *3.9.1. Global revenue gains, excluding US MNEs*

274. The estimates of net global revenue effects of Pillar Two across the four scenarios considered – excluding gains related to US MNEs – are summarised in Table 3.15. A range of illustrative minimum rates are included. Results are presented in absence of a formulaic substance-based carve-out (Panel A) or with a 10% carve-out on payroll and tangible asset depreciation (Panel B).

275. Results are presented as ranges to reflect the uncertainty. These ranges take into account the uncertainty around three factors:

- In all four scenarios, the amount of low-taxed profit subject to the IIR or UTPR is assumed to be subject to an uncertainty factor of ±10% around the point estimate. In addition, the upper bound of the range in Scenario 1 is increased by 50% in the case without carve-out, or 40% in the case with a 10% carve-out, to account for the uncertainty around pockets of low-taxed profit in high-tax jurisdictions, as discussed in Section 3.4.3. The lower bound of the range is unchanged. In Scenarios 2-4, the upper bound of the range is increased by the same absolute amount as in Scenario 1, reflecting that the absolute level of uncertainty around these pockets is the same across the four scenarios.

- In Scenarios 3 and 4, the effect of reduced profit shifting is assumed to be in a range between the minimum and the maximum estimates obtained across the three shapes of the relationship between profit shifting intensity and tax rate differentials considered in the analysis (i.e. the baseline shape of Figure 3.8 and the two alternative shapes presented in Figure 3.9). When considering global estimates (as opposed to jurisdiction-group-level estimates), the effects from using these different shapes partly offset each other. For example, when a group of jurisdictions tends to gain more revenues with a shape, the others groups tend to gain less, and the global estimate does not vary strongly (as can be seen in Table 3.11). To avoid that global ranges on the effect of reduced profit shifting would be too narrow because of this effect, an additional ±10% is added on account of the uncertainty (i.e. when building global ranges, -10% is applied to the minimum result across the three profit shifting shapes and +10% to the maximum result).
- In Scenario 4, the share of low-tax jurisdictions (from Group 3) increasing their ETR is assumed to be in a range between one-third and two-thirds. As discussed in Section 3.7.1, the baseline estimate is that half of jurisdictions in this group increase their ETR.

## Table 3.15. Global revenue gains from Pillar Two (excluding US MNEs), in % of global CIT revenues

Estimates in these tables exclude gains related to MNEs with an ultimate parent in the United States

**Panel A**: Assuming no formulaic substance-based carve-out

| Minimum tax rate | 7.5% | 10.0% | 12.5% | 15.0% | 17.5% |
|---|---|---|---|---|---|
| Scenario 1 | 0.5%-0.8% | 0.8%-1.5% | 1.3%-2.3% | 1.8%-3.2% | 2.4%-4.2% |
| Scenario 2 | 0.5%-0.8% | 0.8%-1.5% | 1.3%-2.3% | 1.8%-3.2% | 2.3%-4.2% |
| Scenario 3 | 0.6%-1.1% | 1.1%-2.0% | 1.7%-3.0% | 2.4%-4.1% | 3.0%-5.2% |
| Scenario 4 | 0.6%-1.1% | 1.1%-2.0% | 1.7%-3.0% | 2.4%-4.2% | 3.1%-5.4% |

**Panel B**: Assuming a 10% carve-out on payroll and tangible asset depreciation

| Minimum tax rate | 7.5% | 10.0% | 12.5% | 15.0% | 17.5% |
|---|---|---|---|---|---|
| Scenario 1 | 0.4%-0.7% | 0.8%-1.3% | 1.2%-2.1% | 1.8%-2.9% | 2.3%-3.8% |
| Scenario 2 | 0.4%-0.7% | 0.8%-1.3% | 1.2%-2.0% | 1.7%-2.9% | 2.2%-3.7% |
| Scenario 3 | 0.6%-1.1% | 1.1%-1.9% | 1.7%-2.8% | 2.3%-3.8% | 2.9%-4.7% |
| Scenario 4 | 0.6%-1.1% | 1.1%-1.9% | 1.7%-2.8% | 2.4%-3.9% | 3.0%-5.0% |

Note: All figures are expressed in % of global CIT revenues. Scenario 1 is a static scenario without behavioural reactions. Scenario 2 takes into account the interaction of Pillar Two with Pillar One (without including revenue gains from Pillar One). Scenario 3 adds the reaction of MNEs in the form of lower profit shifting intensity. Scenario 4 adds the reaction of governments, in the form of some jurisdictions with an ETR below the minimum rate increasing their ETR. Consistent with the assumption that GILTI would coexist with Pillar Two, the estimates in these tables exclude revenues gains related to MNEs with an ultimate parent in the United States. The ranges reflect data uncertainty, and the upper bound of the ranges also takes into account uncertainty related to pockets of low-taxed profit in higher-tax jurisdictions.
Source: OECD Secretariat.

276. A more detailed breakdown of the contribution of the different components to this outcome is presented illustratively in Figure 3.12, using the case with a 12.5% minimum rate as an example, either

with no carve-out (Panel A) or with a 10% carve-out on payroll and tangible asset depreciation (Panel B). Overall, these results suggest that the interaction with Pillar One has only a slight impact on the Pillar Two revenue gains (Scenario 2). The reduction in MNE profit shifting intensity leads to a substantial increase in the global revenue gains (Scenario 3). Finally, ETR increases in certain jurisdictions modify global revenue gains only slightly,[49] but change significantly the distribution of these gains across jurisdictions (Scenario 4). Across all four scenarios, the effect of a formulaic substance-based carve-out on the estimated gains is relatively small.

### 3.9.2. Global revenue gains, including US MNEs

277. For the sake of completeness, it is interesting to consider global gains including revenue gains related to US MNEs. The gains related to US MNEs correspond to the effect of GILTI, under the illustrative assumption that GILTI would coexist with Pillar Two, using the estimates from the US JCT described in Section 3.8. An overview of the global results including US MNEs is presented in Table 3.16 for several illustrative minimum tax rates (10%, 12.5% and 15%) in two illustrative scenarios assuming either no carve-out or a 10% carve-out on payroll and tangible asset depreciation. Results focus on Scenario 3 (i.e. including interaction with Pillar One and MNE reaction). For example, assuming a 12.5% minimum tax rate, total gains combining direct and indirect effects of Pillar Two and revenue gains from GILTI could reach about 2.0-3.8% of CIT revenues.

Figure 3.12. Global revenue gains from Pillar Two, in % of global CIT revenues (excluding US MNEs)

Estimates in these figures exclude gains related to MNEs with an ultimate parent in the United States

**Panel A:** Assuming no formulaic substance-based carve-out

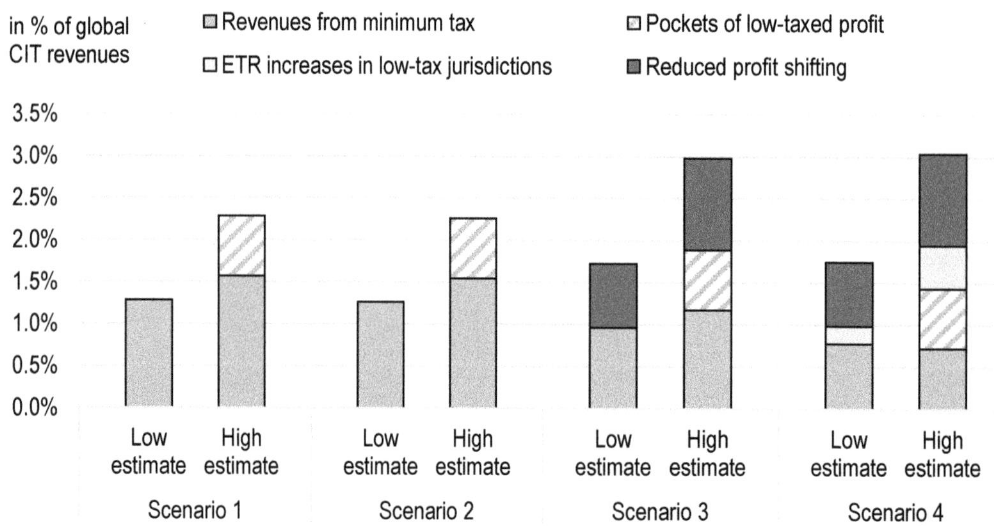

**Panel B:** Assuming a 10% carve-out on payroll and tangible asset depreciation

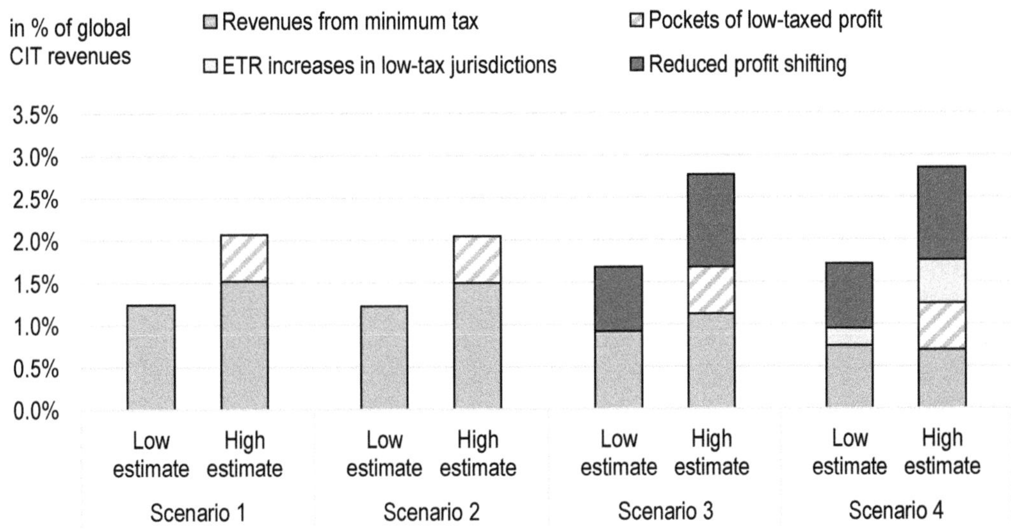


Note: Scenario 1 is a static scenario without behavioural reactions. Scenario 2 takes into account the interaction of Pillar Two with Pillar One. Scenario 3 adds the reaction of MNEs in the form of lower profit shifting intensity. Scenario 4 adds the reaction of governments, in the form of some jurisdictions with an ETR below the minimum rate increasing their ETR to the minimum rate. The results focus illustratively on a scenario assuming a 12.5% minimum rate, with no formulaic substance-based carve-out (Panel A) or a 10% carve-out on payroll and tangible asset depreciation (Panel B). Consistent with the assumption that GILTI would coexist with Pillar Two, the estimates in these figures exclude revenues gains related to MNEs with an ultimate parent in the United States. The ranges between low and high estimates reflect data uncertainty, and the upper bound of the ranges also takes into account uncertainty related to pockets of low-taxed profit in higher-tax jurisdictions.
Source: OECD Secretariat.

## Table 3.16. Global revenue gains from Pillar Two (including US MNEs), in % of global CIT revenues

Illustrative scenario including interaction with Pillar One and MNE reaction (Scenario 3)

| **Minimum tax rate** | 10% | | 12.5% | | 15% | |
|---|---|---|---|---|---|---|
| **Carve-out** | No carve-out | 10% carve-out on payroll and depreciation | No carve-out | 10% carve-out on payroll and depreciation | No carve-out | 10% carve-out on payroll and depreciation |
| **Effect of reduced profit shifting** | 0.5%-0.7% | 0.5%-0.7% | 0.8%-1.1% | 0.8%-1.1% | 1.1%-1.5% | 1.1%-1.5% |
| **Revenues from IIR and UTPR** | 0.7%-1.3% | 0.6%-1.1% | 1.0%-1.9% | 0.9%-1.7% | 1.3%-2.6% | 1.2%-2.3% |
| **Revenues from GILTI** | 0.4%-0.8% | | | | | |
| **Total** | **1.5%-2.8%** | **1.5%-2.7%** | **2.1%-3.8%** | **2.0%-3.6%** | **2.7%-4.9%** | **2.7%-4.6%** |

Note: Contrary to other result tables in this chapter, the estimates in this table include gains related to US MNEs (i.e. revenues from GILTI), based on estimates from the US Joint Committee on Taxation discussed in Section 3.8. Results in this table focus on Scenario 3 (i.e. a scenario taking into account the interaction with Pillar One and MNE reactions). The ranges reflect data uncertainty, and the upper bound of the ranges also takes into account uncertainty related to pockets of low-taxed profit in higher-tax jurisdictions.
Source: OECD Secretariat.

### 3.9.3. Revenue gains for broad jurisdiction groups

278. Results by broad jurisdiction groups across the four scenarios and for several illustrative minimum tax rates (10%, 12.5% and 15%) are presented in Figure 3.13. The results exclude revenue gains related to US MNEs, and the group of high income jurisdictions excludes the United States. Panel A includes all four groups considered in the analysis (high, middle and low income, and investment hubs), while Panel B presents the same results excluding investment hubs (Panel A). Excluding investment hubs makes it possible to use a different scale and increases the readability of the results for the other groups.

279. High, middle and low income jurisdictions would gain revenues from Pillar Two under all four scenarios considered. Revenue gains tend to be larger among high income jurisdictions than lower income ones, reflecting that most MNE group ultimate parents are located in high income jurisdictions, implying that gains from the IIR primarily accrue to these jurisdictions. Still, gains in middle and low income jurisdictions are also significant, especially once the reduced profit shifting intensity of MNEs is taken into account (Scenarios 3 and 4).

280. Investment hubs would gain revenues in Scenarios 1 and 2, while they would gain less revenues on average in Scenario 3. They could even lose revenues in this scenario, depending on the level of the minimum tax rate (Figure 3.13, Panel A). This is because reduced MNE profit shifting would reduce the size of the tax base in a number of investment hubs where profit is currently shifted. However, the magnitude of this average revenue loss is difficult to measure with precision, as it depends on the effective tax rate on this shifted profit. The loss may be compounded by potential knock-on effects of reduced investment in investment hubs on other tax bases, which are not taken into account in the estimates. Also, it is important to note that results vary across investment hubs, which are a relatively heterogeneous group. Finally, in Scenario 4, investment hubs would on average benefit from relatively large revenue gains, reflecting the assumption that a number of them would increase their ETR on low-taxed profit. As investment hubs capture a higher share of global revenue gains, gains in other jurisdiction groups tend to be lower in Scenario 4 than in Scenario 3.

281. Results for hybrid scenarios taking into account MNE and government reactions (as in Scenarios 3 and 4) but not the interaction with Pillar One are presented in Annex 3.B and are qualitatively similar to the results in Figure 3.13. The results in Figure 3.13 assume illustratively a 10% carve-out on payroll and tangible asset depreciation. Results in a scenario without a formulaic substance-based carve-out are presented in Annex 3.E. They are also qualitatively similar to Figure 3.13, but revenue gains across all groups are slightly higher than in the scenario with a carve-out.

### Figure 3.13. Pillar Two revenue gains by broad jurisdiction groups

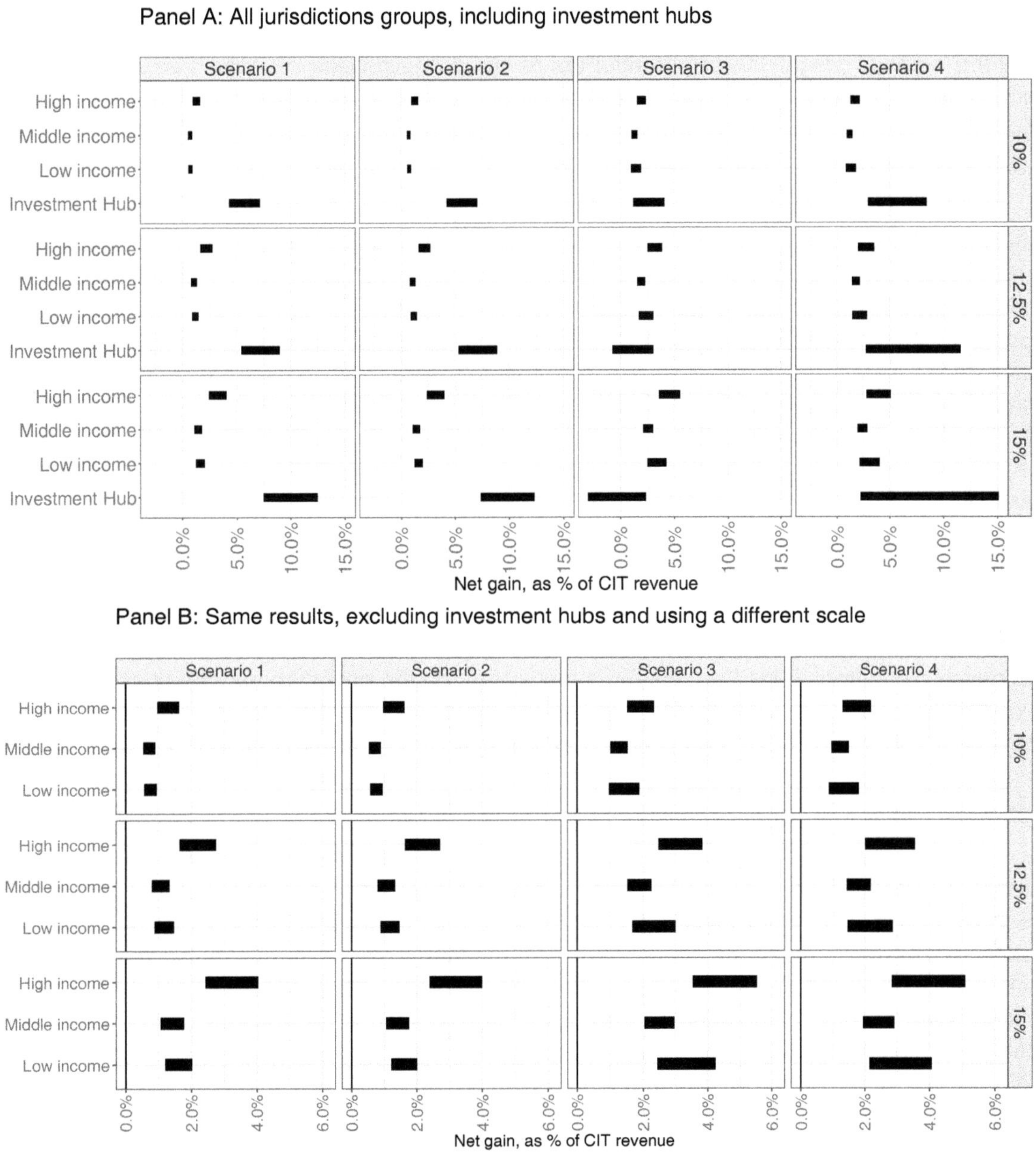


Note: Each facet in the figure correspond to one of four scenarios (in columns) and one of three illustrative minimum tax rates (in rows). Results in Panel B are identical to results in Panel A, except that the investment hubs group is excluded, which makes it possible to use a different scale and increases the readability of results for the other groups. Scenario 1 is a static scenario without behavioural reactions. Scenario 2 takes into account the interaction of Pillar Two with Pillar One. Scenario 3 adds the reaction of MNEs in the form of lower profit shifting intensity. Scenario 4 adds the reaction of governments, in the form of some jurisdictions with an ETR below the minimum rate increasing their ETR to the minimum rate. The results focus illustratively on a scenario with a 10% carve-out on payroll and tangible asset depreciation (results without carve-out are presented in Annex 3.E). Groups of jurisdictions (high, middle and low income) are based on the World Bank classification. Investment hubs are defined as jurisdictions with a total inward FDI position above 150% of GDP. The high income group excludes the United States, in light of the illustrative assumption that GILTI would coexist with Pillar Two. The ranges reflect data uncertainty, and the upper bound of the ranges also takes into account uncertainty related to pockets of low-taxed profit in higher-tax jurisdictions.
Source: OECD Secretariat.

## 3.10. Conclusion

282. This chapter describes the methodology and data sources used by the OECD Secretariat to estimate the order of magnitude of potential tax revenue implications of Pillar Two, across a range of illustrative Pillar Two design and parameter options and under stylised assumptions regarding potential behavioural reactions by MNEs and governments. The chapter also presents the estimated revenue gains at the global level and for broad jurisdiction groups.

283. As discussed in Chapter 1, jurisdiction-level results have been shared on a confidential and bilateral basis with most Inclusive Framework members. The OECD Secretariat has provided estimates to more than 115 jurisdictions at their request. Jurisdiction-specific results were shared in the form of revenue estimation 'tools'. These tools provide jurisdictions with the ability to consider the estimated impact on tax revenues in their jurisdiction of a range of potential Pillar Two parameters (e.g. minimum tax rate, carve-out percentage). Estimates in the tools are presented as ranges to reflect the data uncertainty. After extensive consultation with members of the Inclusive Framework, there was no consensus over whether or not jurisdiction-specific estimates should be publicly released as part of the economic impact assessment. In view of this lack of consensus, no jurisdiction-specific estimates are included in this chapter.

284. The results in this chapter suggest that revenue gains from Pillar Two could be significant across all groups of jurisdictions. Pillar Two would likely reduce MNE profit shifting intensity, which would yield additional tax revenue gains supplementing the direct gains from the minimum tax in many jurisdictions. The interaction of Pillar One with Pillar Two would reduce estimated Pillar Two gains only at the margin. The estimated gains from Pillar Two depend substantially on the minimum tax rate considered, while the effect of the formulaic substance-based carve-out modelled in this chapter on the estimated gains is relatively small. Finally, the distribution of revenue gains across jurisdictions depends on potential government reactions, and in particular on whether governments in some low-tax jurisdictions would increase their ETR in reaction to the introduction of Pillar Two.

285. As discussed in the introduction and throughout the chapter, the estimates rely on a number of simplifying assumptions about Pillar Two design and in the modelling of behavioural reactions to Pillar Two. Behavioural reactions are always difficult to anticipate, especially in an area as complex as MNE profit shifting behaviour. Finally, the data underlying the analysis have a number of limitations. In particular, it inevitably predates the COVID-19 crisis, as well as other important developments such as the implementation of various measures under the OECD/G20 BEPS project and the introduction of the US Tax Cuts and Jobs Act (TCJA). Many key results in this chapter can be expected to remain valid in the post-COVID-19 environment (e.g. on the sensitivity of the outcomes to the various Pillar Two parameter choices, or the implications of the behavioural reactions considered). However, as the profitability of many MNEs is likely to be substantially reduced by the crisis in the short to medium term, the crisis could reduce potential gains from Pillar Two at this horizon. The longer term implications of the crisis for Pillar Two revenue gains will depend on the structural economic changes that the crisis may bring or accelerate, which remain largely uncertain at this stage.

## References


Beer, S., R. de Mooij and L. Liu (2019), “International Corporate Tax Avoidance: A Review of the Channels, Magnitudes, and Blind Spots”, *Journal of Economic Surveys*, pp. 1-29, http://dx.doi.org/10.1111/joes.12305. [12]

Bilicka, K. (2019), “Comparing UK Tax Returns of Foreign Multinationals to Matched Domestic Firms”, *American Economic Review*, Vol. 109/8, pp. 2921-2953, http://dx.doi.org/10.1257/aer.20180496. [18]

Blouin, J. and L. Robinson (2019), “Double Counting Accounting: How Much Profit of Multinational Enterprises Is Really in Tax Havens?”, *SSRN Electronic Journal*, http://dx.doi.org/10.2139/ssrn.3491451. [7]

Bradbury, D., T. Hanappi and A. Moore (2018), “Estimating the fiscal effects of base erosion and profit shifting: data availability and analytical issues”, *Transnational Corporations*, Vol. 25/2, https://dx.doi.org/10.18356/e1d7a8b4-en. [11]

Clausing, K. (2020), “Profit Shifting Before and After the Tax Cuts and Jobs Act”, *SSRN Electronic Journal*, http://dx.doi.org/10.2139/ssrn.3274827. [8]

Clifford, S. (2019), “Taxing multinationals beyond borders: Financial and locational responses to CFC rules”, *Journal of Public Economics*, Vol. 173, pp. 44-71, http://dx.doi.org/10.1016/j.jpubeco.2019.01.010. [27]

Cobham, A., T. Faccio and V. FitzGerald (2019), “Global inequalities in taxing rights: An early evaluation of the OECD tax reform proposals”, *SocArXiv Papers*, http://dx.doi.org/10.31235/osf.io/j3p48. [13]

Cobham, A. and P. Janský (2018), “Global distribution of revenue loss from corporate tax avoidance: re-estimation and country results”, *Journal of International Development*, Vol. 30/2, pp. 206-232, http://dx.doi.org/10.1002/jid.3348. [22]

Damgaard, J., T. Elkjaer and N. Johannesen (2019), “What Is Real and What Is Not in the Global FDI Network?”, *IMF Working Papers*, Vol. 19/274, http://dx.doi.org/10.5089/9781513521527.001. [28]

Devereux, M. et al. (2020), *The OECD Global Anti-Base Erosion (“GloBE”) proposal*, https://www.sbs.ox.ac.uk/sites/default/files/2020-02/OECD_GloBE_proposal_report.pdf. [10]

Dowd, T., P. Landefeld and A. Moore (2017), “Profit shifting of U.S. multinationals”, *Journal of Public Economics*, Vol. 148, pp. 1-13, http://dx.doi.org/10.1016/j.jpubeco.2017.02.005. [20]

Fuest, C., S. Hebous and N. Riedel (2011), “International debt shifting and multinational firms in developing economies”, *Economics Letters*, Vol. 113/2, pp. 135-138, http://dx.doi.org/10.1016/j.econlet.2011.06.012. [21]

Heckemeyer, J. and M. Overesch (2017), “Multinationals’ profit response to tax differentials: Effect size and shifting channels”, *Canadian Journal of Economics/Revue canadienne d’économique*, Vol. 50/4, pp. 965-994, http://dx.doi.org/10.1111/caje.12283. [23]

Hines, J. and E. Rice (1994), “Fiscal Paradise: Foreign Tax Havens and American Business”, *The Quarterly Journal of Economics*, Vol. 109/1, pp. 149-182, http://dx.doi.org/10.2307/2118431. [14]

Horst, T. (2019), "Preliminary Esmates of the Likely Actual Revenue Effects of the TCJA's Provisions", *Tax Notes International*, http://www.horstfrisch.com/pdf/003.pdf. [26]

Huizinga, H. and L. Laeven (2008), "International profit shifting within multinationals: A multi-country perspective", *Journal of Public Economics*, Vol. 92/5-6, pp. 1164-1182, http://dx.doi.org/10.1016/j.jpubeco.2007.11.002. [17]

Johannesen, N., T. Tørsløv and L. Wier (2019), "Are Less Developed Countries More Exposed to Multinational Tax Avoidance? Method and Evidence from Micro-Data", *The World Bank Economic Review*, Vol. 2019, pp. 1-20, http://dx.doi.org/10.1093/wber/lhz002. [19]

Johansson, Å. et al. (2017), "Tax planning by multinational firms: Firm-level evidence from a cross-country database", *OECD Economics Department Working Papers*, No. 1355, OECD Publishing, Paris, http://dx.doi.org/10.1787/9ea89b4d-en. [25]

Keen, M. and K. Konrad (2013), "The theory of international tax competition and coordination", *Handbook of Public Economics*, Vol. 5, pp. 257-328, http://dx.doi.org/10.1016/B978-0-444-53759-1.00005-4. [3]

OECD (2020), "Anonymised and aggregated Country-by-Country Report statistics", *Corporate Tax Statistics - Second Edition*, OECD Publishing, https://www.oecd.org/tax/beps/corporate-tax-statistics-database.htm. [6]

OECD (2020), "Corporate Tax Statistics - Second Edition", OECD Publishing, https://www.oecd.org/tax/tax-policy/corporate-tax-statistics-second-edition.pdf. [9]

OECD (2020), *Tax Challenges Arising from Digitalisation – Report on Pillar Two Blueprint: Inclusive Framework on BEPS*, OECD/G20 Base Erosion and Profit Shifting Project, OECD Publishing, Paris, https://dx.doi.org/10.1787/abb4c3d1-en. [1]

OECD (2015), *Measuring and Monitoring BEPS, Action 11 - 2015 Final Report*, OECD/G20 Base Erosion and Profit Shifting Project, OECD Publishing, Paris, https://dx.doi.org/10.1787/9789264241343-en. [24]

Tørsløv, T., L. Wier and G. Zucman (2019), "The Missing Profits of Nations: 2017 Figures", https://missingprofits.world/wp-content/uploads/2020/04/TWZUpdate.pdf. [15]

Tørsløv, T., L. Wier and G. Zucman (2019), *The Missing Profits of Nations: Updated Figures*, https://missingprofits.world/wp-content/uploads/2019/09/TWZUpdate.pdf. [16]

Tørsløv, T., L. Wier and G. Zucman (2018), "The Missing Profits of Nations", *NBER Working Paper*, No. 24701, http://www.nber.org/papers/w24701.pdf. [5]

US Joint Committee on Taxation (2017), *Estimated budget effects of the conference agreement for H.R. 1, the "Tax Cuts and Jobs Act"*, JCX-67-17, https://www.jct.gov/publications.html?func=startdown&id=5053. [2]

von Schwerin, A. and T. Buettner (2016), *Constrained Tax Competition – Empirical Effects of the Minimum Tax Rate on the Tax Rate Distribution*, Annual Conference 2016: Demographic Change, German Economic Association, http://hdl.handle.net/10419/145642. [4]

# Annex 3.A. Results for alternative assumptions on the shape of profit shifting

## Annex Table 3.A.1. Global Pillar Two revenue gains (Scenario 4) under alternative shapes of profit shifting

Estimates in these tables exclude MNEs with an ultimate parent in the United States

| (% of global CIT revenues) | Alternative profit shifting shape No. 1 | | | | | Alternative profit shifting shape No. 2 | | | | |
|---|---|---|---|---|---|---|---|---|---|---|
| **Minimum tax rate** | **7.5%** | **10%** | **12.5%** | **15%** | **17.5%** | **7.5%** | **10%** | **12.5%** | **15%** | **17.5%** |
| Effect of reduced profit shifting | 0.4% | 0.7% | 1.0% | 1.4% | 1.7% | 0.3% | 0.5% | 0.8% | 1.2% | 1.6% |
| Revenues from IIR and UTPR | 0.4% | 0.5% | 0.7% | 0.9% | 1.0% | 0.4% | 0.6% | 0.7% | 0.9% | 1.1% |
| Gains from ETR increases in some jurisdictions | 0.0% | 0.2% | 0.3% | 0.5% | 0.8% | 0.0% | 0.2% | 0.3% | 0.5% | 0.8% |
| **Total** | **0.8%** | **1.4%** | **2.0%** | **2.8%** | **3.5%** | **0.7%** | **1.3%** | **1.9%** | **2.7%** | **3.5%** |

Note: The results in these tables focus on Pillar Two revenue gains under Scenario 4 (i.e. taking into account interaction with Pillar One and MNE reactions). They are alternative versions of the results in Table 3.13, based on the two alternative relationships between tax rate differentials and profit shifting intensity presented in Figure 3.9. The minimum tax rates considered are illustrative. The results focus illustratively on a scenario assuming a 10% carve-out on payroll and tangible asset depreciation (Panel B). Consistent with the assumption that GILTI would coexist with Pillar Two, the estimates in these tables exclude revenues gains related to MNEs with an ultimate parent in the United States (on the effect of profit shifting, revenues from IIR and UTPR and gains from ETR increases).
Source: OECD Secretariat.

# Annex 3.B. Results excluding the interaction with Pillar One

286. The results in Scenarios 2-4 of this chapter take into account how the interaction with Pillar One would affect Pillar Two results. This annex presents alternative results ignoring the effect of this interaction. Overall, these results are very close to the results taking the interaction into account, reflecting that the effect of this interaction is small under the assumptions on Pillar One and Pillar Two design and parameters considered this chapter.

### Annex Table 3.B.1. Global revenue gains from Pillar Two, with or without Pillar One interaction (including US MNEs)

Illustrative scenario including MNE reaction, 10% carve-out on payroll and tangible asset depreciation

| **Minimum tax rate** | **10%** | | **12.5%** | | **15%** | |
|---|---|---|---|---|---|---|
| **Revenue gains, in % of CIT revenues** | With Pillar One interaction | Without Pillar One interaction | With Pillar One interaction | Without Pillar One interaction | With Pillar One interaction | Without Pillar One interaction |
| Effect of reduced profit shifting | 0.5%-0.7% | | 0.8%-1.1% | | 1.1%-1.5% | |
| Revenues from IIR and UTPR | 0.6%-1.1% | 0.6%-1.1% | 0.9%-1.7% | 0.9%-1.7% | 1.2%-2.3% | 1.2%-2.3% |
| Revenues from GILTI | 0.4%-0.8% | | | | | |
| **Total** | **1.5%-2.7%** | **1.5%-2.7%** | **2.0%-3.6%** | **2.0%-3.6%** | **2.7%-4.6%** | **2.7%-4.6%** |

Note: This table compares the aggregate Pillar Two results presented in Table 3.16 with results excluding the effect of the interaction between Pillar One and Pillar Two. The absence of interaction tends to increase Pillar Two revenues because Pillar One tends to reallocates profit from low-tax to higher-tax jurisdictions where it is not subject to Pillar Two. However, the difference is too small to change the results visibly in this table. The reduced profit shifting is assumed to take place before Pillar One is applied and is therefore not affected by the interaction with Pillar One. The ranges reflect data uncertainty, and the upper bound of the ranges also takes into account uncertainty related to pockets of low-taxed profit in higher-tax jurisdictions.
Source: OECD Secretariat.

## Annex Figure 3.B.1. Estimated revenue gains from Pillar Two by broad jurisdiction groups, with or without Pillar One interaction

Assuming no formulaic substance-based carve out

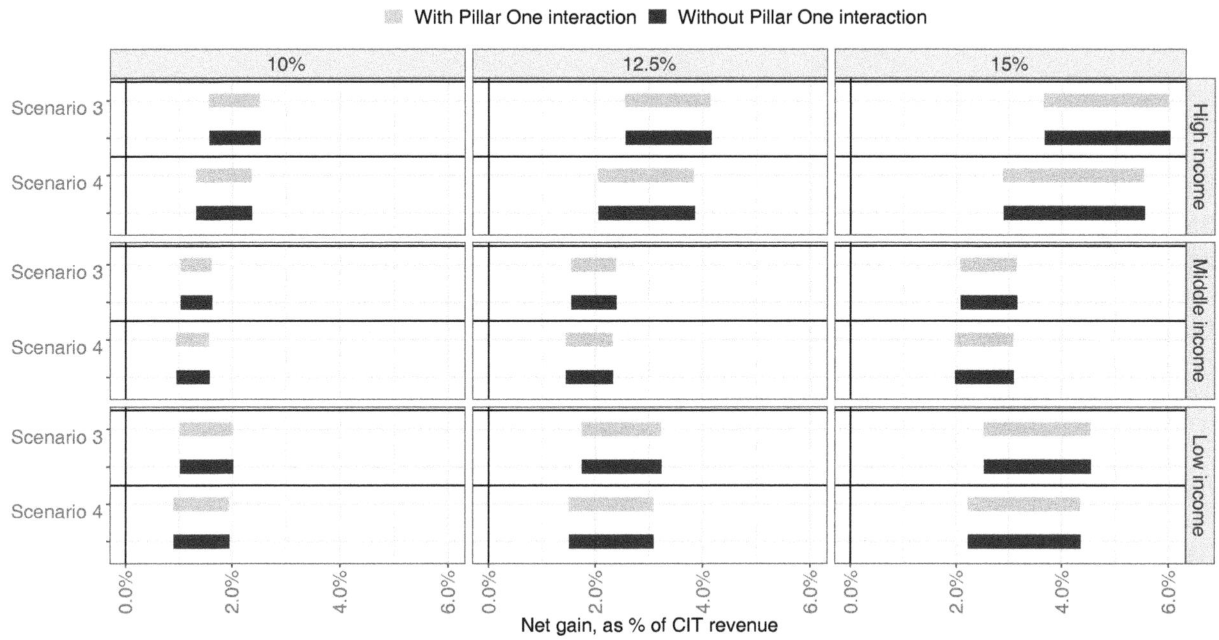


Note: The light blue intervals correspond to the Pillar Two results presented in the main text, which take into account the interaction with Pillar One (see for example Figure 3.13). The dark blue intervals do not take this interaction into account, and can therefore be interpreted as the effect of Pillar Two if it were implemented in isolation. For simplicity, the results focus illustratively on a scenario with no formulaic substance-based carve-out. Only Scenario 3 and Scenario 4 are presented (without Pillar One interaction, Scenario 2 is identical to Scenario 1, which is presented in the main text of this chapter). The high income group excludes the United States, in light of the illustrative assumption that GILTI would coexist with Pillar Two. The ranges reflect data uncertainty, and the upper bound of the ranges also takes into account uncertainty related to pockets of low-taxed profit in higher-tax jurisdictions.
Source: OECD Secretariat.

# Annex 3.C. Robustness of results to using tangible assets or payroll instead of turnover as proxies of economic activity

287. Measures of economic activity are required in two parts of the analysis: (i) as proxy measures to allocate potential revenue gains from the undertaxed payments rule (UTPR), and (ii) as proxy measures to assess where shifted profit originates in the modelling of MNE profit shifting. In both cases, the baseline results in this chapter are relying on turnover as a measure of economic activity. Turnover data are sourced from the turnover matrix described in Chapter 5. Alternative results based on tangible assets or payroll are presented in this annex. The data for tangible assets and payroll are sourced from similar matrices, also described in Chapter 5.

288. The results in this annex focus first on the sensitivity of results to the proxy used for the allocation of gains from the UTPR (Annex Table 3.C.1 and Annex Figure 3.C.1) and second on the sensitivity of results to the proxy used for the profit shifting modelling (Annex Table 3.C.2 and Annex Figure 3.C.2). Overall, results are not very sensitive to these different modelling assumptions.

### Annex Table 3.C.1. Robustness of global results to alternative proxy measures to allocate UTPR gains

Global revenue gains from IIR and UTPR, in % of global CIT revenues, excluding MNEs with an ultimate parent in the United States

| | Minimum tax rate | 7.5% | 10.0% | 12.5% | 15.0% | 17.5% |
|---|---|---|---|---|---|---|
| | **Scenario 1** | | | | | |
| Proxy to allocate UTPR gains | Tangible assets | 0.5% | 0.9% | 1.4% | 1.9% | 2.5% |
| | Payroll | 0.5% | 0.9% | 1.4% | 2.0% | 2.6% |
| | Turnover (baseline) | 0.5% | 0.9% | 1.4% | 2.0% | 2.6% |
| | **Scenario 2** | | | | | |
| Proxy to allocate UTPR gains | Tangible assets | 0.5% | 0.9% | 1.3% | 1.9% | 2.4% |
| | Payroll | 0.5% | 0.9% | 1.4% | 2.0% | 2.5% |
| | Turnover (baseline) | 0.5% | 0.9% | 1.4% | 2.0% | 2.6% |
| | **Scenario 3** | | | | | |
| Proxy to allocate UTPR gains | Tangible assets | 0.4% | 0.7% | 1.0% | 1.4% | 1.7% |
| | Payroll | 0.4% | 0.7% | 1.1% | 1.4% | 1.7% |
| | Turnover (baseline) | 0.4% | 0.7% | 1.1% | 1.4% | 1.8% |
| | **Scenario 4** | | | | | |
| Proxy to allocate UTPR gains | Tangible assets | 0.4% | 0.5% | 0.7% | 0.9% | 1.1% |
| | Payroll | 0.4% | 0.6% | 0.7% | 0.9% | 1.1% |
| | Turnover (baseline) | 0.4% | 0.6% | 0.8% | 1.0% | 1.1% |

Note: The results in these tables focus on Pillar Two revenue gains from IIR and UTPR depending on the variable used to proxy economic activity in order to allocate UTPR revenues. The minimum tax rates considered are illustrative. For simplicity, only point estimates are presented, and ranges reflecting uncertainty relative to pockets of low-taxed profits are not included in this table. The results focus illustratively on a scenario without carve-out. Scenario 1 is a static scenario without behavioural reactions. Scenario 2 takes into account the interaction of Pillar Two with Pillar One. Scenario 3 adds the reaction of MNEs in the form of lower profit shifting intensity. Scenario 4 adds the reaction of governments, in the form of some jurisdictions with an ETR below the minimum rate increasing their ETR. Consistent with the assumption that GILTI would coexist with Pillar Two, the estimates exclude low-taxed profit from MNEs with an ultimate parent in the United States and the associated revenue gains.
Source: OECD Secretariat.

## Annex Figure 3.C.1. Robustness of results by jurisdiction groups to alternative proxy measures to allocate UTPR gains

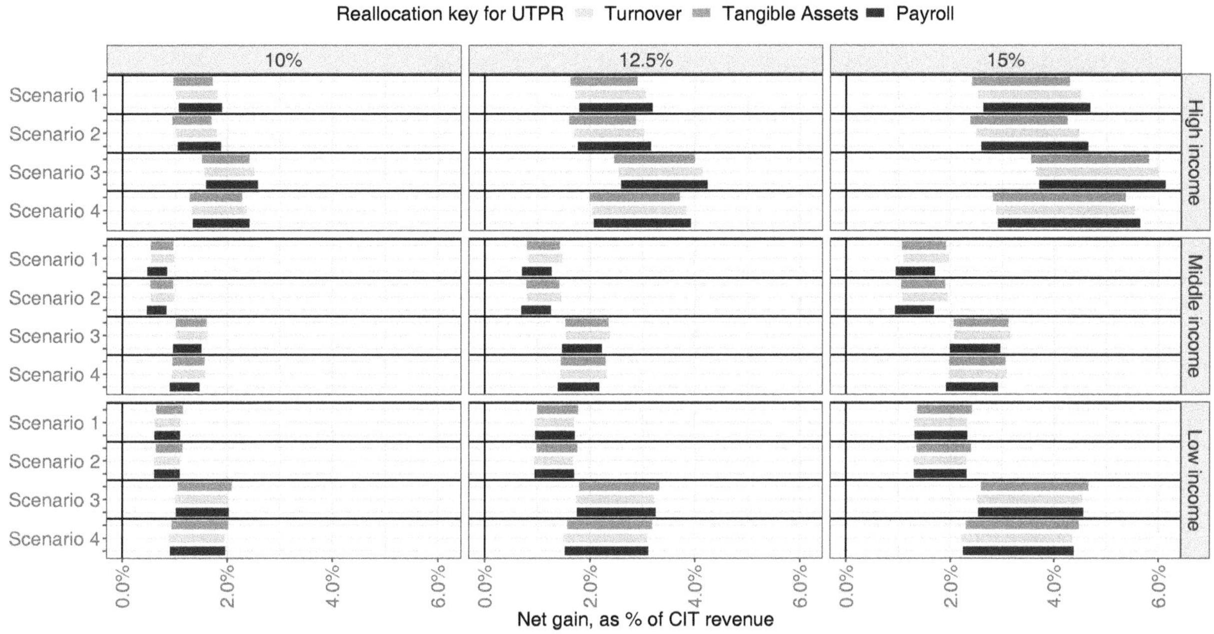


Note: This figure presents Pillar Two estimates by jurisdiction groups, illustrating the implications of using different measures of economic activity to proxy for the allocation of UTPR revenues: turnover (as in the baseline results), tangible assets and payroll. Scenario 1 is a static scenario without behavioural reactions. Scenario 2 takes into account the interaction of Pillar Two with Pillar One. Scenario 3 adds the reaction of MNEs in the form of lower profit shifting intensity. Scenario 4 adds the reaction of governments, in the form of some jurisdictions with an ETR below the minimum rate increasing their ETR. The results focus illustratively on a scenario with no carve out. Investment hubs are excluded to enhance readability of results for the other groups. The high income group excludes the United States, in light of the illustrative assumption that GILTI would coexist with Pillar Two. The ranges reflect data uncertainty, and the upper bound of the ranges also takes into account uncertainty related to pockets of low-taxed profit in higher-tax jurisdictions.
Source: OECD Secretariat.

## Annex Table 3.C.2. Robustness of global results (Scenario 3) to the variable used to allocate the origin of shifted profits

Estimates in these tables exclude MNEs with an ultimate parent in the United States, assume no formulaic substance-based carve out, and are expressed in % of global CIT revenues

| (in % of global CIT revenues) | **Minimum tax rate** | **7.5%** | **10%** | **12.5%** | **15%** | **17.5%** |
|---|---|---|---|---|---|---|
| Shifting origin based on turnover (baseline) | Effect of reduced profit shifting | 0.3% | 0.6% | 0.9% | 1.3% | 1.6% |
| | Revenues from IIR and UTPR | 0.4% | 0.7% | 1.1% | 1.4% | 1.8% |
| | Total | 0.8% | 1.3% | 2.0% | 2.7% | 3.4% |
| Shifting origin based on tangible assets | Effect of reduced profit shifting | 0.4% | 0.6% | 0.9% | 1.3% | 1.7% |
| | Revenues from IIR and UTPR | 0.4% | 0.7% | 1.1% | 1.4% | 1.8% |
| | Total | 0.8% | 1.3% | 2.0% | 2.7% | 3.4% |
| Shifting origin based on payroll | Effect of reduced profit shifting | 0.3% | 0.6% | 0.9% | 1.3% | 1.6% |
| | Revenues from IIR and UTPR | 0.4% | 0.7% | 1.1% | 1.4% | 1.8% |
| | Total | 0.8% | 1.3% | 2.0% | 2.7% | 3.4% |

Note: The results in this table present the sensitivity of estimated Pillar Two gains in Scenario 3, to using alternative proxies for economic activity to assess the origin of MNE shifted profits. Baseline results in this chapter are based on turnover (i.e. assume that MNE profit originates in jurisdictions where MNEs shifting profit have turnover), and alternative results in this table focus on tangible assets and payroll. The profit shifting modelling methodology is the same as described in this chapter, except for the proxy used to assess profit origin. The minimum tax rates considered are illustrative. The results focus illustratively on a scenario with no carve-out. Consistent with the assumption that GILTI would coexist with Pillar Two, the estimates exclude low-taxed profit from MNEs with an ultimate parent in the United States and the associated revenue gains.
Source: OECD Secretariat.

## Annex Figure 3.C.2. Robustness of jurisdiction group results to the variable used to allocate the origin of shifted profits

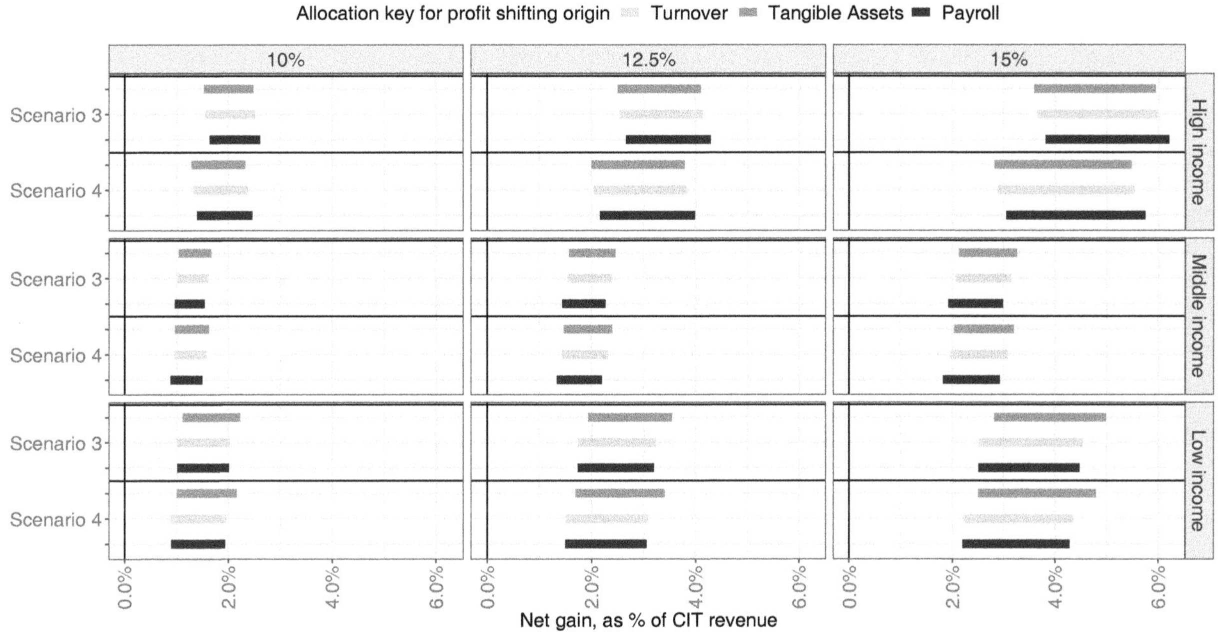


Note: The results in this figure present the sensitivity of estimated Pillar Two gains in Scenario 3 and Scenario 4, to using alternative proxies for economic activity to assess the origin of MNE shifted profits. Baseline results in this chapter are based on turnover (i.e. assume that MNE profit originates in jurisdictions where MNEs shifting profit have turnover), and alternative results in this figure focus on tangible assets and payroll. The profit shifting modelling methodology is the same as described in this chapter, except for the proxy used to assess profit origin. Only Scenario 3 and Scenario 4 are included as Scenarios 1 and 2 do not depend on the profit shifting modelling. The results focus illustratively on a scenario with no carve out. The high income group excludes the United States, in light of the illustrative assumption that GILTI would coexist with Pillar Two. The ranges reflect data uncertainty, and the upper bound of the ranges also takes into account uncertainty related to pockets of low-taxed profit in higher-tax jurisdictions.
Source: OECD Secretariat.

# Annex 3.D. Robustness of results to excluding CbCR as a source of ETR data

289. Jurisdiction-level effective tax rates (ETR) play an important role in the assessment of Pillar Two revenue gains since they are the rates that are compared to the minimum tax, and which can be increased in Scenario 4. They are also included in the tax rate differentials used to assess the origin of shifted profits and the reduction implied by the minimum tax. In the baseline analysis, the average ETR on MNE profit in a jurisdiction is measured as the median estimate obtained across three data sources (see Section 3.4.2) including data from anonymised and aggregated CbCRs.

290. The results in this annex focus on the sensitivity of results to the exclusion of CbCR as a data source on ETRs. Overall, the results suggest that this exclusion would lead to lower estimates of Pillar Two gains, but without changing the broad order of magnitude of the results.

### Annex Table 3.D.1. Robustness of global revenue gains to excluding CbCR as a source of ETR data

Estimates in these tables exclude MNEs with an ultimate parent in the United States, assume no formulaic substance-based carve out, and are expressed in % of CIT revenues

| Panel A: Scenario 3 | | | | | | |
|---|---|---|---|---|---|---|
| (in % of global CIT revenues) | **Minimum tax rate** | **7.5%** | **10.0%** | **12.5%** | **15.0%** | **17.5%** |
| Using median ETR across 3 sources (baseline) | Effect of reduced profit shifting | 0.3% | 0.6% | 0.9% | 1.3% | 1.6% |
| | Revenues from IIR and UTPR | 0.4% | 0.7% | 1.1% | 1.4% | 1.8% |
| | Total | 0.8% | 1.3% | 2.0% | 2.7% | 3.4% |
| Excluding CbCR as a source of ETR data | Effect of reduced profit shifting | 0.3% | 0.5% | 0.7% | 1.0% | 1.4% |
| | Revenues from IIR and UTPR | 0.4% | 0.7% | 0.9% | 1.2% | 1.6% |
| | Total | 0.8% | 1.2% | 1.6% | 2.2% | 3.0% |

**Panel B**: Scenario 4

| (in % of global CIT revenues) | **Minimum tax rate** | **7.5%** | **10.0%** | **12.5%** | **15.0%** | **17.5%** |
|---|---|---|---|---|---|---|
| Using median ETR across 3 sources (baseline) | Effect of reduced profit shifting | 0.3% | 0.6% | 0.9% | 1.3% | 1.6% |
| | Revenues from IIR and UTPR | 0.4% | 0.6% | 0.8% | 1.0% | 1.1% |
| | Gains from ETR increases in some jurisdictions | 0.0% | 0.2% | 0.3% | 0.5% | 0.8% |
| | Total | 0.8% | 1.4% | 2.0% | 2.8% | 3.6% |
| Excluding CbCR as a source of ETR data | Effect of reduced profit shifting | 0.3% | 0.5% | 0.7% | 1.0% | 1.4% |
| | Revenues from IIR and UTPR | 0.4% | 0.5% | 0.7% | 0.9% | 1.1% |
| | Gains from ETR increases in some jurisdictions | 0.1% | 0.1% | 0.3% | 0.4% | 0.7% |
| | Total | 0.8% | 1.2% | 1.7% | 2.3% | 3.2% |

Note: The results in this table present the sensitivity of estimated Pillar Two gains in Scenario 3 and 4 to excluding CbCR as a source when computing the jurisdiction-level ETRs used in the analysis. Baseline results in this chapter compute ETRs by taking the median of three sources (Tørsløv et al. (2018[5]), US BEA data and CbCR data). The robustness check excludes the data from CbCRs from this calculation. The minimum tax rates considered are illustrative. The results focus illustratively on a scenario without carve-out. Consistent with the assumption that GILTI would coexist with Pillar Two, the estimates exclude low-taxed profit from MNEs with an ultimate parent in the United States and the associated revenue gains.
Source: OECD Secretariat.

## Annex Figure 3.D.1. Robustness of jurisdiction group results to excluding CbCR as a source of ETR data

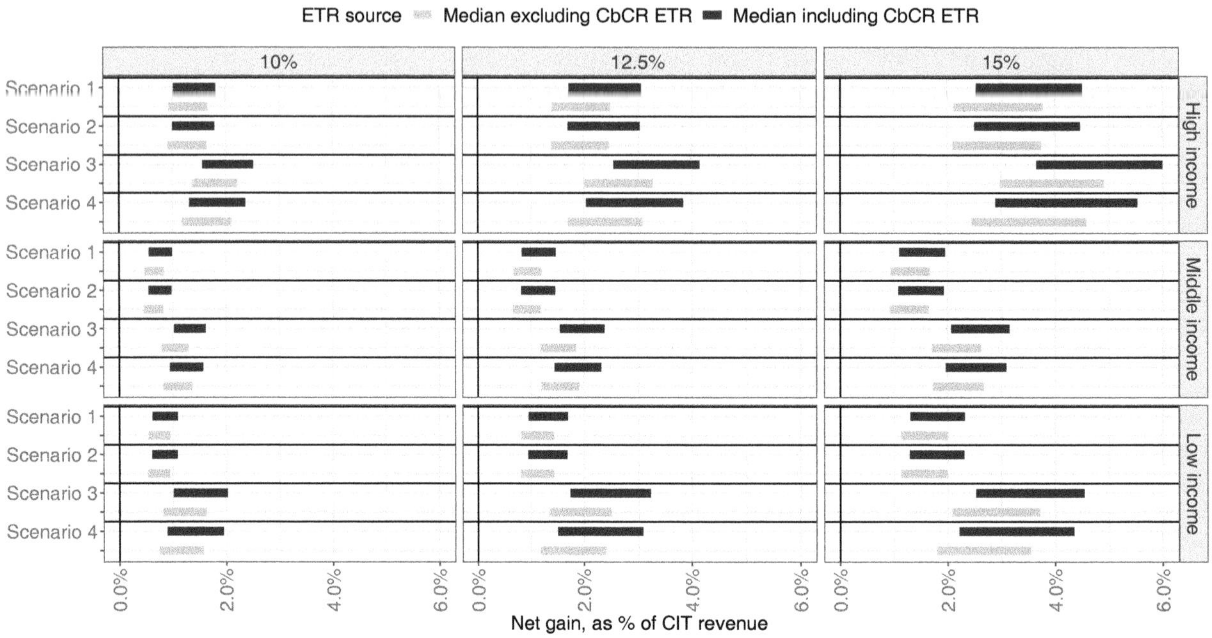


Note: The results in this figure present the sensitivity of estimated Pillar Two gains to excluding CbCR as a source when computing the jurisdiction-level ETRs used in the analysis. Baseline results in this chapter compute ETRs by taking the median of three sources (Tørsløv et al. (2018[5]), US BEA data and CbCR data). The robustness check excludes the data from CbCRs from this calculation. The results focus illustratively on a scenario with no carve out. The high income group excludes the United States, in light of the illustrative assumption that GILTI would coexist with Pillar Two. The ranges reflect data uncertainty, and the upper bound of the ranges also takes into account uncertainty related to pockets of low-taxed profit in higher-tax jurisdictions.
Source: OECD Secretariat.

# Annex 3.E. Pillar Two results by broad jurisdiction groups in the no-carve-out case

Annex Figure 3.E.1. Pillar Two revenue gains by broad jurisdiction groups, assuming no formulaic substance-based carve-out

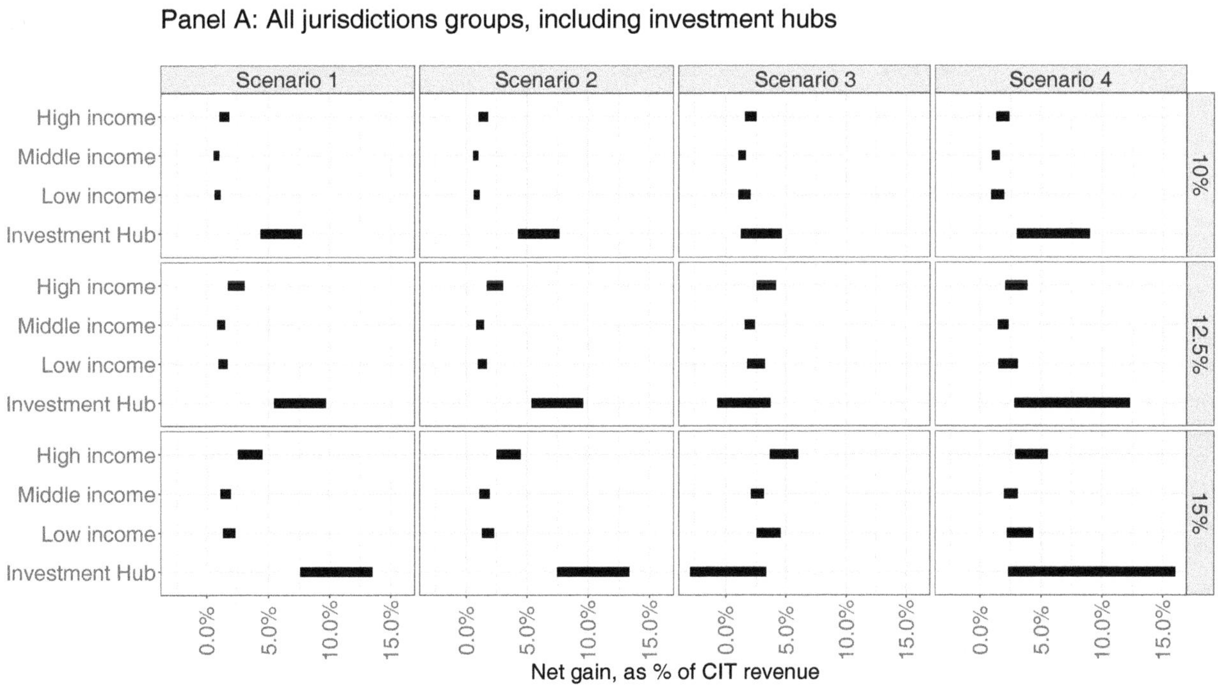

Panel B: Same results, excluding investment hubs and using a different scale

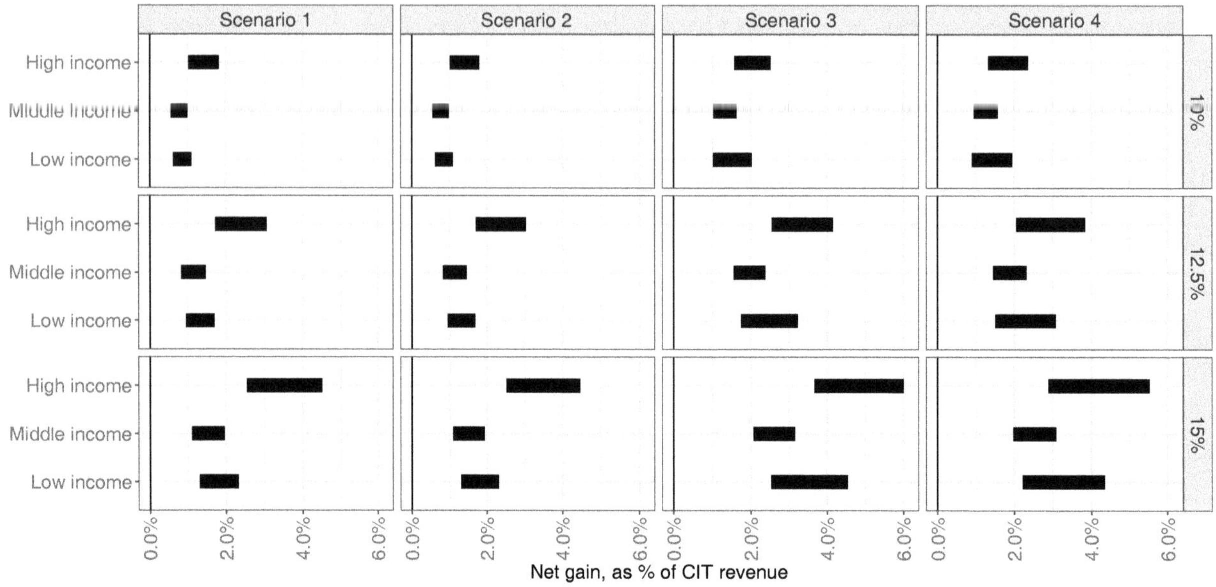


Note: This figure is identical to Figure 3.13, with the difference that it assumes no formulaic substance-based carve out (while Figure 3.13 assumes a 10% carve-out on payroll and tangible asset depreciation). Scenario 1 is a static scenario without behavioural reactions. Scenario 2 takes into account the interaction of Pillar Two with Pillar One. Scenario 3 adds the reaction of MNEs in the form of lower profit shifting intensity. Scenario 4 adds the reaction of governments, in the form of some jurisdictions with an ETR below the minimum rate increasing their ETR. The high income group excludes the United States, in light of the illustrative assumption that GILTI would coexist with Pillar Two. The ranges reflect data uncertainty, and the upper bound of the ranges also takes into account uncertainty related to pockets of low-taxed profit in higher-tax jurisdictions.
Source: OECD Secretariat.

## Notes

[1] In all this chapter, low-tax jurisdictions refers to jurisdictions with an average ETR below the minimum rate (and a variety of potential minimum rates are illustratively considered in this chapter), and higher-tax jurisdictions refers to jurisdictions with an average ETR above the minimum rate.

[2] The OECD/G20 BEPS Package was released in October 2015 and various measures outlined in the package have been implemented in the years that have followed. A range of measures agreed to be implemented by members of the Inclusive Framework continue to be implemented by jurisdictions and, therefore, the full effect of these measures is not captured in the data available at the time of this analysis.

[3] For example, CbCR data, which is an important data source for the analysis, focuses only on one year (2016) and contains no information on whether profit-making MNE sub-groups in a jurisdiction in 2016 have been in a loss position in that jurisdiction in the previous years.

[4] In presence of a formulaic substance-based carve-out, an ETR increase in a low-tax jurisdiction could slightly increase the overall tax payments of an MNE group as it would lose the benefit of the carve-out on the profit in this low-tax jurisdiction. However, as further discussed below, this effect is quantitatively small under the parameters considered in this chapter.

[5] If one assumes a non-cooperative simultaneous rate setting (Nash equilibrium), the introduction of a minimum tax rate tends to lead the higher-tax jurisdiction to increase its rate, while under a sequential rate setting system where the higher-tax jurisdiction is a Stackelberg leader, the higher-tax jurisdiction tends to reduce its rate when the minimum tax is introduced (Keen and Konrad, 2013[3]). In a simultaneous game, the best "response" (in terms of tax rate) of a jurisdiction is usually to increase its tax rate when other jurisdictions' increase their rates, since if the other jurisdictions have higher tax rates, a jurisdiction can increase its own rate to increase revenue without losing its attractiveness. The introduction of a minimum tax tends to increase the "best response" rate of jurisdictions above the minimum tax in this setting. In a sequential game, the first mover takes into account that setting a low tax rate might not be beneficial since the followers can decrease their own. With a minimum tax rate, this "threat" from followers is weaker.

[6] There are two important limitations with CbCR data: (i) there are inconsistencies in the way dividends from affiliates are reported (i.e. sometimes included and sometimes not), and (ii) certain jurisdictions report profit for "stateless" entities, which may correspond to different situations, including "pass-through" entities (see Box 3 in OECD (2020[6]) and https://www.oecd.org/tax/tax-policy/anonymised-and-aggregated-cbcr-statistics-disclaimer.pdf). Reflecting this, the profit of "stateless" entities is not included in the profit matrix. Extensive benchmarking of CbCR data against other sources (e.g. ORBIS) suggests that these issues do not alter substantially the overall picture, as further discussed in Chapter 5.

[7] The amount of losses of loss-making MNE sub-groups in a given year does not clearly indicate how large the effect of a potential loss carry-forward mechanism under Pillar Two would be. For example, it is possible that some MNE sub-groups are persistently in a profit position in a jurisdiction (and therefore never benefit from any loss carry-forward) while others are persistently in a loss position (and never have a Pillar Two liability against which to use their carried-forward losses).

[8] For example, if profit-making sub-groups make a profit of 100 and pay taxes of 20, while loss-making sub-groups make a loss of 15 and pay no taxes, the average ETR of profit-making sub-groups is 20/100=20%, while the average ETR computed across profit-making and loss-making sub-groups is 20/(100-15)=24%. An ETR focusing only on profit-making sub-groups would be more consistent with the Pillar Two analysis in this chapter.

[9] This methodology focusing on foreign taxes and profits of US MNEs is used to compute ETRs in jurisdictions other than the United States. To complement this, an average ETR of (foreign-owned) MNEs in the United States is computed using the same methodology applied to the BEA data on foreign direct investment in the United States.

[10] These other sources are The International Bureau of Fiscal Documentation, and publicly available tax rates from KPMG, EY, and the Tax Foundation.

[11] The estimated gains also take into account the jurisdiction-specific assumptions on Pillar Two implementation described in section 3.4.5, which result in a small share of low-taxed profit not being subject to the top-up tax.

[12] For example, if about 20% of profit in higher-tax jurisdictions is estimated to be carved out, the upper bound of the Pillar Two uncertainty range is increased by 40% (i.e. 50%*(1-20%)) instead of 50%.

[13] These figures are based on the estimates of global CIT revenues in Devereux et al. (2020[10]), which are lower than those in this report due to less extensive geographic coverage and the focus on an earlier year of reference.

[14] The assumption is that ETRs in each jurisdiction follow a bilinear distribution between zero and the statutory rate, centred around the average ETR. This amounts to assuming that a fraction of profit is uniformly distributed between zero and the average ETR, and the rest is uniformly distributed between the average ETR and the statutory rate. The share of profit in each group is determined in a way that ensures that the average of ETRs across the distribution corresponds to the average ETR in the jurisdiction.

[15] This assumes implicitly that the current average ETR in these pockets of low-taxed profit (which is not observed), is the same as the average ETR in low-tax jurisdictions. A different assumption would give different estimates.

[16] In ORBIS, coverage of tangible assets (which is the variable used as a basis to approximate depreciation expenses) is generally better than coverage of payroll.

[17] Indeed, while it is relatively straightforward to compute directly the effect of a combined carve-out with firm-level data in jurisdictions where these data are available, it is more difficult to do it in the jurisdictions where only aggregate data are available.

[18] For example, if the profit of an MNE sub-group is EUR 15, its payroll EUR 100 and its depreciation expenses EUR 100, then a 10% payroll carve-out would carve out an amount of EUR 10 and a 10% depreciation carve-out would also carve out an amount of EUR 10. Summing the two would suggest a total carve-out effect of EUR 20, while the combined carve-out would only carve out an amount of EUR 15 (i.e. the total profit of the sub-group).

[19] The US BEA provides detailed data on depreciation by asset classes in the private sector without distinguishing MNE entities from non-MNE entities (the BEA database on the activity of US MNEs also provides data on depreciation, but does not distinguish between tangible and intangible assets). When considering private non-residential fixed assets (i.e. 'equipment' and 'structures'), the ratio of depreciation expenses to the stock of tangible assets, estimated at current cost, is stable around 6.3-6.5% between 2011 and 2018. Disaggregation by industry at the 2-digit NAICS code suggests heterogeneity across sectors, with the average depreciation rate ranging between 2.6% (real estate and rental and leasing), and 12.7% (construction). One caveat on those numbers is that depreciation in national accounts can differ from depreciation in tax and financial accounts. Table 7.13 of the National Income and Product Accounts relates depreciation and amortisation as reported by the US Internal Revenue Service and as included in the national accounts, and suggests that most of the differences come from a different treatment of intangible assets. Another source of information on depreciation is the balance sheet and income statement data available in ORBIS. ORBIS data contains firm-level information on depreciation of assets, but without distinction between the depreciation of tangible fixed assets and the amortisation of intangible fixed assets. On average, for domestic and multinational firms included in ORBIS, the ratio of depreciation and amortisation on total (tangible and intangible) fixed assets was around 5.8% over the past two decades. Given that tangible fixed assets represent around half of total fixed assets and that the amortisation rate of intangible assets is likely higher than the depreciation rate of tangible assets, this suggests that 10% is indeed an upper bound for the average depreciation rate of tangible fixed assets.

[20] Assuming a linear relationship implies that, above a certain level of the aggregate profitability ratio, no profit at all would be carved-out which is not completely realistic. However, a robustness check assuming that at least a minimum percentage of profit (e.g. 1%) would be carved-out in all jurisdictions suggests that this has little effect on the overall results (i.e. reduction of total Pillar Two revenue gains by less than 2%).

[21] The assumptions on the upper bound of the range to take into account uncertainty related to pockets of low-taxed profit are the following: +50% in a no carve-out scenario (as discussed in Section 3.4.3), +45% when the carve-out percentage is 5%, +40% when the carve-out percentage is 10%, +35% when the carve-

out percentage is 15% and +30% when the carve-out percentage is 20%. These assumptions aim to be relatively simple and at the same time consistent with estimates of the share of carved-out profit in higher-tax jurisdictions. For example, with a 10% carve-out percentage, 16-19% of profit in higher-tax jurisdictions is estimated to be carved-out (see Table 3.5). In turn, assuming that 20% of profit in higher-tax jurisdictions is carved out would lead to an increase in the upper bound of the uncertainty range by 40% (i.e. 50%*(1-20%)) instead of 50% in the no-carve-out scenario.

22 As discussed above, the United States is an exception, as it is assumed in this chapter that GILTI would coexist with Pillar Two and that the United States would apply GILTI (instead of an income inclusion rule) to MNEs with an ultimate parent in the United States (see Section 3.8).

23 As discussed above, the switch-over rule and the subject to tax rule would also contribute to bringing the ETR on low-taxed profit up to the level of the minimum rate, but they are not modelled in this chapter due to data limitations.

24 An alternative approach would be to use bilateral FDI data (e.g. on royalty and interest flows) to identify transactions that may be subject to the UTPR. This may be closer to the actual spirit of the UTPR, but poses other methodological challenges, related to the potential double counting of flows that are channelled through several jurisdictions, as well as data gaps in bilateral FDI flow statistics (see Annex 5.C of Chapter 5).

25 MNE turnover in certain jurisdictions can be inflated as a result of tax planning strategies. To avoid that this has a disproportionate effect on the results, MNE turnover is capped at 100% of GDP in all jurisdictions.

26 In practice, the amount of residual profit relieved under Pillar One is computed for each pair of jurisdictions in the profit matrix in Chapter 2, while the amount of residual profit received is only computed at the level of each receiving jurisdiction (rather than bilaterally). To disaggregate the amount of received residual profit received on a bilateral basis, it is assumed that the residual profit in each column (i.e. each jurisdiction of ultimate parent) is redistributed according to the same distribution key used for the reallocation of the global residual profit in Chapter 2, that is based on the geographical distribution of destination-based sales. This approach ensures that the aggregate numbers obtained in the estimation are consistent with the Pillar One estimates obtained in Chapter 2.

27 For practical reasons, jurisdictions are either considered as profit origin or as profit destination in this chapter, but not both.

28 On the link between high FDI positions and profit shifting, see for example Damgaard et al. (2019[28]).

29 This is because profits shifted to jurisdictions where the average ETR is above the minimum rate would generally not be subject to Pillar Two. However, situations where the ETR on this shifted profit would be below the minimum rate could arise (and these profits would be subject to Pillar Two) due to the existence of pockets of low-taxed profits in higher-tax jurisdictions.

30 It is possible that reduced incentives to shift profit to jurisdictions with an average ETR below the minimum rate could increase MNEs' willingness to shift profit to jurisdictions with an average ETR above the minimum rate. This possibility is not modelled in this chapter, as there is no clear way to identify the magnitude of this effect and the jurisdictions where more profit would be shifted without more granular data on the cost of shifting profit to different jurisdictions.

[31] Other profitability ratios could be considered to define "normal" profit (e.g. profit to total assets). The ratio of profit to turnover was chosen because it could be easily computed across all pairs of jurisdictions based on the data available in the profit and the turnover matrices.

[32] This estimate includes MNEs with an ultimate parent in the United States, for the purpose of comparability with estimates from the economic literature.

[33] On the data sources underlying the turnover matrix and its construction, see Chapter 5.

[34] In contrast, Johansson et al. (2017[25]) tend to find a lower average tax rate semi-elasticity vis-à-vis zero-tax jurisdictions than among jurisdictions with strictly positive tax rates.

[35] This aggregate semi-elasticity is obtained by dividing the share of shifted profits in total profits (observed and shifted) in "profit origin" jurisdictions (12.5%), by the average statutory tax rate differential between "profit origin" jurisdictions and "profit destination" jurisdictions (10.3 percentage points). These tax rates are weighted by turnover. While this chapter uses a combination of statutory and effective tax rates to model profit shifting, this calculation is based exclusively on statutory tax rates for comparability with the literature (which generally relies on statutory rates). The semi-elasticity is estimated with a degree of uncertainty, as it depends among other things on the assumptions on the "normal" profitability level considered, the shape of the relationship between profit shifting and tax rate differentials, or the weights used to aggregate the coefficients.

[36] In presence of a formulaic substance-based carve-out, an ETR increase in a low-tax jurisdiction could result in a slightly higher amount of tax due by an MNE because it would lose the benefit of the substance carve-out included in Pillar Two. However, as further discussed below, this effect is quantitatively small.

[37] For example, Clifford (2019[27]) finds that in response to CFC rules, MNEs redirect profits from subsidiaries below the CFC 'low-tax' threshold into subsidiaries just above the threshold and change incorporation patterns to place fewer subsidiaries below and more above the threshold. Roughly half of the resulting increase in global tax revenue is found to accrue to the rule-enforcing jurisdiction.

[38] This assumption would not be valid if the ETR calculation rules in the presence of a carve-out would not require MNEs to make an adjustment to the covered taxes associated with the carved-out profit.

[39] This calculation assumes illustratively a 12.5% minimum tax rate and a 10% carve-out percentage. The reduction in profit shifting is also very small with other assumptions on the minimum tax and carve-out rates considered in this chapter.

[40] For example, relocating employees representing USD 10 million of payroll into a zero-tax jurisdiction would offer a carve-out of USD 1 million (assuming a 10% carve-out rate), which if used in full would reduce the amount of tax paid under Pillar Two by USD 0.125 million (assuming a 12.5% minimum tax rate). This tax saving seems unlikely to justify the cost of relocation.

[41] This is because the factors that contribute to differences between statutory and effective rates (e.g. depreciation rules, tax deductions, tax credits) are generally linked to real economic activity.

[42] The difference with the reasoning in the previous endnote is that shifted profit may benefit from preferential treatment in "profit destination" jurisdictions, and that the resulting ETR may essentially reflect this preferential treatment, without necessarily being related to the level of the statutory rate in these jurisdictions.

[43] For example, one can consider an MNE group that has a profit of EUR 100, payroll of EUR 40, depreciation expenses of EUR 10, and paid zero tax in a certain jurisdiction. Under Pillar Two, assuming a 12.5% minimum tax rate and a 10% carve-out rate, the MNE would have to pay 12.5%*(100-10%*(40+10))= EUR 11.9. If the jurisdiction increases the ETR of this MNE to 12.5%, the MNE would have to pay this rate on all of its profit (EUR 100), which would result in a tax of 12.5%*100= EUR 12.5, which is higher than the EUR 11.9 paid before the ETR increase.

[44] If jurisdictions increasing their ETRs want to preserve neutrality for the overall amount of tax paid of MNEs, they might try to mimic the functioning of Pillar Two in their tax system, by applying an ETR increase including a carve-out provision that would have the same design and mark-up percentage as the formulaic substance-based carve-out in Pillar Two. In practice however, such a mechanism may not necessarily be straightforward to design or to make consistent with other features of a jurisdiction's corporate tax system.

[45] For MNEs having an average ETR on their foreign profit that is above the GILTI rate (and therefore not paying taxes under GILTI), an ETR increase in a zero-tax jurisdiction would fully translate into an overall tax increase. For MNEs with an average ETR below the GILTI rate, an ETR increase in a zero-tax jurisdiction would also result in an overall tax increase since only 80% of foreign taxes are credited under GILTI in that situation. In that case, the overall tax increase would represent 20% of the liability arising from the ETR increase.

[46] Jurisdictions in this group may consider increasing the ETR on the pockets of low-taxed profit in their jurisdiction if there are some. For simplicity and due to lack of data on these pockets, this potential reaction is not considered in this chapter.

[47] Companies face a US tax liability at a 10.5% rate on the relevant income and a non-refundable tax credit on 80% of foreign taxes paid. If the foreign ETR is 13.125% or above, the tax credit covers the whole US tax liability. By the same logic, the US tax liability at 13.125% starting in 2026 with the same tax credit yields an upper bound of 16.40625%. These are the tax rates determined applying the statutory GILTI rules and do not take into account other features of the US international tax system, such as expense allocation, that may effectively increase a specific taxpayer's overall US tax liability by limiting the creditability of foreign taxes.

[48] A first assessment of the impact of GILTI on profit shifting has been produced by Clausing (2020[8]). She estimates that GILTI could "reduce the corporate profits of US multinational affiliates in 'haven' countries by about 12 to 16 percent", which could bring "an 8 to 9 percent increase in the US entity corporate tax base in foreign jurisdictions above the minimum tax threshold, and a USD 15-30 billion increase in the US corporate tax base each year." However, these results are highly sensitive to the assumptions on the share of US MNEs that have an average ETR on their foreign profit above or below the GILTI rate (see Appendix C in Clausing (2020[8])).

[49] Global revenue gains in Scenarios 3 and 4 are similar, reflecting that the reaction modelled in Scenario 4 primarily changes the distribution of these gains across jurisdictions. Still, there is a slight increase in global revenue gains between Scenarios 3 and 4. This comes from two reasons. First, the ETR increases in Scenario 4 reduce the (relatively small) amount of global low-taxed profit that is not fully taxed under Pillar Two under the assumptions considered in this chapter (see Section 3.7.1 above). For example, this would be the case for the profit in an MNE entity located in a jurisdiction from Group 3 (which would increase its ETR under Scenario 4), if this MNE has an ultimate parent in a jurisdiction from Group 2 (which does not apply an IIR) and its economic activity also in a jurisdiction from Group 2 (which does not apply a UTPR). Second, the ETR increases imply that some low-taxed profit that benefitted from a formulaic substance-based carve-out under Pillar Two would be taxed, leading to larger revenue gains overall.

# 4 Investment Impacts of Pillar One and Pillar Two

## 4.1. Summary

### *4.1.1. New tax rules impact incentive structures of MNEs and governments*

291. **The Pillar One and Pillar Two proposals would introduce significant changes to the international tax rules, affecting global investment through their impacts on the incentives faced by MNEs and governments.** Amount A of Pillar One involves the creation of a new taxing right and the reallocation to market jurisdictions of a share of residual profit determined at the MNE group level, based on a formulaic approach. Pillar Two addresses remaining BEPS challenges and is designed to ensure that large internationally operating businesses pay a minimum level of tax regardless of where they are headquartered or the jurisdictions they operate in. Without prejudging the final design and parameter choices, which are still the subject of discussions among members of the Inclusive Framework on BEPS, the structural changes embedded in these new rules could have substantial direct and indirect effects on investment and economic output.

292. **The new rules will not affect all MNEs, but are targeted to large, highly profitable MNE groups (Pillar One) and large MNE groups with low effective tax rates (Pillar Two).** The inclusion of several scope restrictions would imply that the effects of Pillar One and Pillar Two on investment costs would not affect all firms, but would be targeted to a subset of MNEs. For example, although it remains subject to political decision, the scoping criteria currently being discussed for Amount A of Pillar One only includes businesses or business segments that perform activities within the definitions of the Automated Digital Services (ADS) and Consumer Facing Businesses (CFB) under discussion. Importantly, it includes a profitability threshold that is determined at the MNE group level, which targets the impact of the rules to highly profitable MNEs. Pillar One will also incorporate a global revenue threshold, ensuring that only larger MNE groups are targeted. Pillar Two, on the other hand, is focussed on large MNEs with low effective tax rates, which will mainly affect firms reporting large profits in low-tax jurisdictions. This will especially be the case if a formulaic substance-based carve-out is provided.

### *4.1.2. Investment responses at the MNE entity level*

293. **At the MNE entity level, increases in investment costs could lead to some relocation of investment away from low-tax jurisdictions.** Increases in investment costs are mostly driven by Pillar Two, notably affecting MNE entities that would otherwise have realised effective tax rates (ETRs) below the minimum tax rate. Confirming the established literature, new empirical research on the tax sensitivity of investment suggests that affected MNE entities would be expected to respond to potential cost increases by decreasing or relocating investment, in the absence of other commercial considerations.

294. **Investment relocation across jurisdictions does not necessarily lead to a decrease in global investment if it is linked to an investment increase in another location.** Relocation of MNE activities

can increase the efficiency of capital allocation across jurisdictions, in situations where investment decisions were previously driven mostly by tax considerations. MNEs make investment decisions based on a range of commercial considerations, including taxation. To the extent that taxation has an influence, investment decisions are driven by post-tax rather than pre-tax returns. Given that ETR differentials can be substantial, MNEs could potentially be induced to choose locations where investments yield lower pre-tax, but higher post-tax returns. The Pillar One and Pillar Two proposals reduce ETR differentials across jurisdictions, thus reducing the scope for tax-induced distortions of investment decisions and potentially leading to a more efficient capital allocation and higher global output.

### *4.1.3. Government responses can have indirect effects on investment*

295. **Additional tax revenues can have positive indirect effects on the economy, for example, supporting domestic resource mobilisation in developing countries.** While the optimal level of tax revenues, the optimal tax mix, and the optimal use of public funds depend on the country-specific context, additional tax revenues could have positive effects on the economy, as they can be used, e.g., to support public or private investment, to reduce public debt levels or to finance reductions in other taxes. Lower ETR differentials reduce the potential gains from profit shifting, implying that corporate tax bases may become less elastic and public funds may be able to be raised more efficiently. These positive indirect impacts on fiscal capacity are particularly important for developing countries, which often face more stringent capacity constraints.

296. **Governments' responses to changes in the international tax system could have important indirect effects on the attractiveness of their jurisdiction for foreign investment.** Pillar Two may reduce the effectiveness of certain tax incentives provided through the corporate income tax (CIT) system. Notwithstanding this, governments will continue to be able to draw upon a wide range of tax and non-tax instruments to support policy objectives such as increased innovation or economic development. However, in response to structural changes, some jurisdictions could adapt their policies to improve attractiveness for foreign investment over and above simple tax-cost considerations. For example, a more limited and cost-efficient use of investment tax incentives could strengthen domestic resource mobilisation in developing countries. Both responses would reinforce positive effects on international capital allocation.

### *4.1.4. Investment responses at the MNE group level*

297. **At the MNE group level, the GDP-weighted average increase in effective marginal tax rates could be around 1.4 percentage points, suggesting only limited impacts on global investment levels.** The global GDP-weighted average increase in effective average tax rates (EATRs) is estimated to be around 0.3 percentage points, representing a small impact compared to the weighted average EATR in the sample (24%) or the six percentage point reduction in the unweighted average EATR that was observed between 1999 and 2017. The corresponding increase for effective marginal tax rates (EMTRs) is estimated to be around 1.4 percentage points, again representing a small change compared to the weighted average EMTR of around 25%. These effects represent global averages across all MNEs; the corresponding increase in EATRs and EMTRs would generally be higher for MNEs that are within the scope of Pillar One or Pillar Two. These effects are mostly driven by Pillar Two and are larger for projects located in investment hubs, most of which currently face comparatively low effective tax rates.[1]

298. **The response of investment is expected to be weak for entities in MNE groups affected by the reforms,** as new evidence suggests that MNE entities in more profitable MNE groups are less sensitive to tax increases than entities in MNE groups that are out of scope. Specifically, entities in MNE groups with a profitability rate between 0% and 10% would, on average, reduce their domestic investment rate by around 0.15 percentage points following a one percentage point increase in the jurisdiction's EMTR. The size of this effect is almost half as large for entities in MNE groups with profitability ratios above 10% and more than three times smaller for entities in MNE groups with profitability rates above 15%.

299. **The proposals are expected to produce a more level playing field among MNEs, and vis-à-vis their smaller and domestic competitors.** Pillar One would be targeted towards large and profitable MNEs, while Pillar Two would ensure that all MNEs pay a minimum level of tax in each jurisdiction in which they operate irrespective of where they are based.

### *4.1.5. Impacts on the global economy in case no consensus is reached*

300. **These results must be compared to the implications for the global economy in a counterfactual scenario where a multilateral consensus-based solution cannot be secured**. It would be incorrect to assume that the counterfactual scenario looks like the status quo. Equally important, the evaluation has to acknowledge that the baseline scenario has changed due to the COVID-19 pandemic.

301. **Failure to secure a consensus-based solution would increase the domestic pressures on governments** to address the tax challenges arising from digitalisation unilaterally, and would likely lead to the introduction of digital service taxes or similar measures in a growing number of jurisdictions. An increasing number of jurisdictions have implemented, or are considering the introduction of digital services taxes; other unilateral measures include alternative applications of the permanent establishment threshold, withholding taxes or diverted profit taxes. The introduction of such measures, as well as potentially more aggressive actions by tax administrations, could affect investment indirectly by leading to a rise in disputes between countries and MNEs which generates significant administration and compliance costs.

302. **A proliferation of digital services taxes (DSTs) would lead to economic inefficiencies, reducing global investment and output**. DSTs are not designed as taxes on corporate profits, but as taxes on total revenues associated with specific types of digital transactions. They could lead to positive tax liabilities imposed on loss-making firms as well as to economic double taxation, and are thus more distortive than profit-based taxes, potentially leading to higher prices, lower sales, and less investment in the affected sectors. Since they are typically levied on intermediate services, e.g., online advertisement, these effects are expected to flow through to a much larger number of firms and sectors, an effect that could be larger if intermediate services are provided by online platforms with some degree of market power.

303. **More widespread adoption of DSTs would likely give rise to an increase in trade disputes,** in addition to the immediate negative impacts on economic efficiency.

304. **The negative economic implications of protracted tax- and trade-related conflicts are likely to be significant, ranging between around -0.1% to -1.2% of global GDP**. Based on different DST rates and retaliatory tariffs, global GDP is simulated to be reduced by -0.1% to -0.2% if a smaller group of jurisdictions is involved in the conflict, and between to -0.4% to -1.2% if a larger number is involved, compared to a scenario without tax- and trade-disputes. These results represent a substantial reduction in global GDP, stemming from efficiency losses due to the tariffs compounded with reductions in wages and capital returns as well as a slow-down in investment driven by declining exports. Household income would be impacted to the same extent as GDP, indicating that households would bear most of the costs of the shrinking economy. World trade, measured as real global import volumes, falls by about twice the rate of real GDP.

305. **In contrast, an approximation of the impacts of investment cost increases under the consensus scenario suggests a reduction of less than 0.1% of global GDP,** compared to a hypothetical scenario where failure to secure consensus does not lead to any future tax- and trade-disputes.

### *4.1.6. Overall Assessment against the background of COVID-19*

306. **Under both scenarios, global investment and output are being severely affected by the COVID-19 pandemic**. The COVID-19 crisis is affecting firms, economies and governments in ways that could modify the expected impact of the reform. For example, the economic crisis will have strong negative

effects on the profitability of most MNEs in the short- and possibly medium-term. Under the consensus scenario, loss carry-forward provisions could imply that any impacts of Pillar One and Pillar Two on investment costs, and therefore global investment, are likely to be less than estimated and will take effect over a much longer timeframe. Given the structure of certain highly-digitalised markets, increased demand for digital services could translate into higher profitability for certain large MNE groups, implying that a larger share of profits will likely be subject to Pillar One over time, in line with profitability increases.

307. **Against the background of the COVID-19 crisis, the negative consequences of a failure to secure consensus are likely to be more severe.** As the global economy is very fragile, aggravated tax- and trade disputes could compound the effect of the COVID crisis or hinder the post-crisis recovery. DSTs could lead to double taxation and asymmetric corporate taxation, inducing firms to forego investment opportunities that would be economically viable in the absence of DSTs. Political pressure on governments will increase, as the tax challenges from digitalisation remain unresolved at a time when many highly-digitalised MNEs are experiencing higher sales and rising valuations.

308. **Securing a consensus-based solution to the tax challenges arising from digitalisation will support global investment** compared to alternative counterfactual scenarios, which are likely to exacerbate an already negative economic outlook. While increases in investment costs could slightly weigh on global investment under the consensus scenario, this negative effect would be quantitatively small compared to alternative scenarios capturing the potential costs of the tax- and trade-related conflicts that may arise if a consensus-based solution cannot be secured. In addition, the reform would enhance tax coherence and tax certainty, and the efficiency of capital allocation compared to the no-consensus scenario, which would also support investment and growth.

## 4.2. Introduction

309. The OECD/G20 Inclusive Framework on BEPS adopted a Programme of Work to Develop a Consensus Solution to the Tax Challenges arising from the Digitalisation of the Economy in May 2019 (the Programme of Work) (OECD, 2019[1]), which was approved by the G20 Finance Ministers and Leaders at their meetings in June 2019 meeting. The purpose of the Programme of Work is to develop international corporate tax reform proposals, building on two pillars: Pillar One involves revised profit allocation and nexus rules to reallocate taxing rights to market jurisdictions; and Pillar Two involves rules to ensure a minimum level of effective taxation to address remaining BEPS concerns.

310. As part of the Programme of Work, the Inclusive Framework requested that the OECD Secretariat carry out an economic analysis and impact assessment of the Pillar One and Pillar Two proposals, with an emphasis on both the revenue and investment effects of the proposals. Analysis of the revenue and investment impacts of the proposals will provide valuable information to governments, businesses, civil society organisations and the broader public. In the context of this work, this chapter focusses on the OECD Secretariat's analysis of the effects of the Pillar One and Pillar Two proposals on global investment and economic output.

## 4.3. Conceptual approach

311. The proposals would introduce several novel elements into the international architecture for the taxation of corporate profits that would lead to a number of significant changes in the way multinational enterprises (MNEs) are taxed. While a number of design choices remain open at this point, the most significant changes to the incentives faced by MNEs and governments are expected to come from the following stylised elements.

- Under Pillar One, Amount A involves the creation of a new nexus, not dependent on physical presence, and the reallocation to market jurisdictions[2] of a share of residual profit determined at the MNE group level, based on a formulaic approach.
- Under Pillar Two, a number of interlocking rules seek to address remaining BEPS challenges and ensure that large internationally operating businesses pay a minimum level of tax regardless of where they are headquartered or the jurisdictions they operate in.

312. Notwithstanding other relevant and novel elements of the proposals as well as a number of design choices that remain open at this point, the proposed reforms represent a significant structural reform of the international tax system, which can be expected to have an impact on MNE investment decisions. For example, the implementation of Pillars One and Two could lead to changes in organisational structure and global investment levels, as well as the potential relocation of real economic activities. While these potential behavioural responses[3] of MNEs may not be immediately observable after implementation, the reforms are likely to have effects on global economic growth, as well as public revenues, over the longer term.

313. Analysing the investment impacts of the proposals is a challenging task for a number of reasons. First, some key aspects of policy design are still under development. Second, the proposals that are currently contemplated are ambitious in terms of their underlying policy goals as well as their technical complexity and jurisdiction coverage. Third, the available data is limited and, fourth, the economic impact of the COVID-19 pandemic represents a significant change in the baseline scenario underlying the analysis (see Box 4.1 for a discussion).

## Figure 4.1. Conceptual Approach

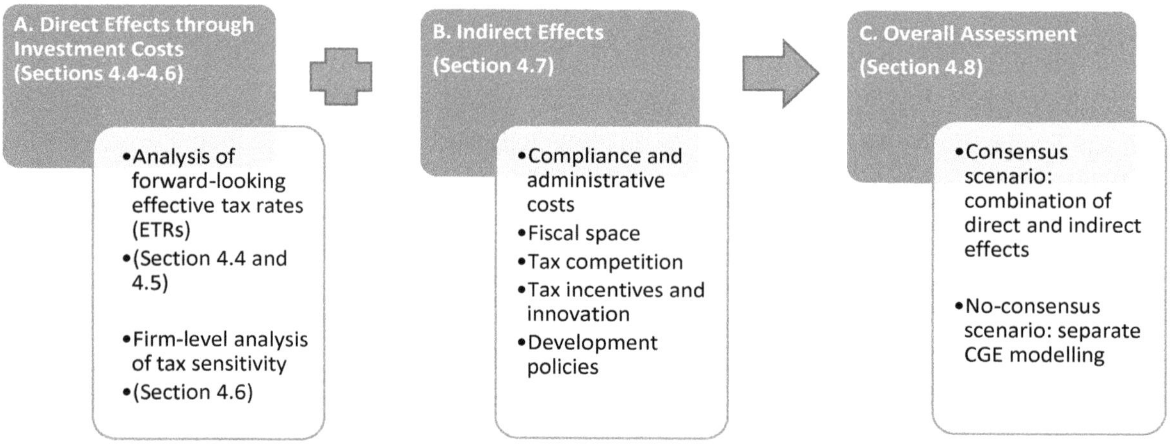


Source: OECD Secretariat.

314. Notwithstanding these challenges, this chapter presents a comprehensive discussion, covering the most pertinent aspects of the ongoing policy debates surrounding the investment impacts of the proposals, based on original research contributions and insights from the relevant economic literature. Conceptually, the analysis builds on three different components, as outlined in Figure 4.1:

- **Investment impacts operating through investment costs:** This component brings together two new empirical studies. The first study estimates the impact of the proposals on forward-looking effective tax rates (ETRs) calculated at the MNE group level. The second study builds on firm-level data to estimate the tax sensitivities of MNE investment at the entity level, taking into account differences in profitability across MNE groups. Taken together, these two studies produce important empirical insights on the effect of the proposals on MNE investment.

- **Indirect effects on MNE investment and economic output**: Drawing upon the existing economic literature, this component analyses the effects of the proposals on MNE investment and economic output operating through a range of indirect channels. For example, substantial impacts could occur through additional fiscal space, compliance and administrative costs or through changes in taxpayer and government behaviour in response to international tax competition, tax incentives and competition between firms.
- **Overall assessment of the investment and growth impacts**: This component brings together the quantitative results on investment costs and additional insights on indirect effects to form an overall assessment of the likely effects of the proposals on MNE investment and growth. This assessment is compared to a range of counterfactual scenarios, which will be modelled using a computable general equilibrium (CGE) model (OECD METRO Trade Model), to assess the trade related implications of a proliferation of unilateral measures that may flow from not reaching international consensus.

315. The Section 4.4 introduces the distinction between MNE investment at the MNE group and entity level. The Section 4.5 discusses the analysis of forward-looking ETRs, while Section 4.6 discusses the firm-level analysis of the tax sensitivity of MNE investment. The Section 4.7 presents the discussion of the indirect effects on MNE investment and economic output. The Section 4.8 presents an overall assessment of the impacts on investment and output with and without a multilateral consensus.

### Box 4.1. Effects of the COVID-19 pandemic on the evaluation

The COVID-19 crisis is affecting firms, economies and governments in ways that could modify the expected impact of the reform, primarily in the short term, but also in the longer term. First, concerns about security of supply in a post COVID-19 environment may induce MNEs to revisit their global value chains (GVCs) to reduce vulnerability to supply disruptions, potentially leading to onshoring or re-shoring of the production of certain goods closer to the markets where they are consumed. Under the consensus scenario, discussed in detail in the Section 4.8, ETR differentials will be lower and the relative weight of non-tax factors in location decisions will be correspondingly higher; as a result, considerations about the vulnerability of supply chains could become a more important factor for location decisions. However, under a scenario where no multilateral consensus is reached this would be less likely be the case; as corporate taxation becomes more incoherent across jurisdictions, MNEs might be more inclined to prioritise tax savings over other considerations.

Second, the economic crisis will have strong negative effects on the profitability of many MNEs in the short and, possibly, medium term. As a result, the amount of residual profit for reallocation under Pillar One is expected to decrease as well as the global amount of MNE profit, thereby reducing the pools of low-taxed profit subject to top-up tax under Pillar Two. While these effects will fade out when economies and MNE profits recover from the crisis, carry-forward provisions allow businesses to offset losses against future profits, which means that any impacts of Pillar One and Pillar Two on investment costs, and therefore global investment, are likely to take effect over a longer timeframe. As a result, even if consensus is reached in 2020 and the reform is implemented swiftly afterwards, any potential effects on investment costs, which are only expected to be small based on this analysis, are only likely to materialise over a period of time, i.e., after MNE profitability has returned to pre-crisis levels.

In contrast, as noted in Section 4.8, failure to secure a consensus-based solution through the multilateral process of the Inclusive Framework could lead to a rapid proliferation of unilateral measures such as DSTs, among others. As the DST is essentially a turnover-based tax, it would impose significant cross-jurisdictional tax liabilities, not only on profitable firms but also on loss-making firms, making recovery much more difficult. In addition, DSTs could lead to double taxation and asymmetric corporate taxation, thus distorting investment decisions away from risky projects, i.e., inducing firms to forego investment opportunities that would be economically viable in the absence of DSTs, at a point in time when additional investment would be most needed. These issues will be particularly acute in the context of the economic crisis resulting from the COVID-19 pandemic.

Third, consumers' and firms' reliance on digital services was already on a rising trend before the crisis. However, the lockdowns and travel restrictions implemented during the crisis have accelerated this structural trend, thus likely leading to a permanent shift towards greater digitalisation and a corresponding increase in the size of the ADS activities. Given the structure of certain highly-digitalised markets, sometimes characterised by winner-takes-most dynamics, increased demand for digital services could translate into higher profitability for certain large MNE groups (Calligaris, Criscuolo and Marcolin, 2018[2]) (Bessen, 2017[3]). Under the consensus scenario, this implies that more MNEs, particularly those engaging in ADS activities, will move into the scope of Pillar One over time, in line with profitability increases. Under the no-consensus scenario, however, political pressure on governments would strongly increase, as the tax challenges from digitalisation remain unresolved at a time when highly-digitalised MNEs are doing increasingly well. As a response, an increasing number of governments might resort to unilateral measures, thus further contributing to the fragmentation of the international tax system and increasing the threat of damaging trade disputes, hampering economic efficiency and undermining the global recovery.

Against the background of the COVID-19 crisis, the negative consequences of a failure to secure a consensus-based solution through the multilateral process of the Inclusive Framework discussed in the Section 4.8 are, therefore, likely to be even more severe. Fragmentation of the international tax system would make the restructuring of GVCs more costly; political pressure would further increase and induce governments to rely increasingly on inefficient unilateral tax measures; and loss-making firms would have to absorb even stronger adverse effects. In addition, the risk of protracted trade disputes would be further heightened, potentially increasing the duration and depth of an already extremely severe worldwide economic crisis.

## 4.4. Investment responses at MNE group and entity level

316. Empirical evidence suggests that taxation is one among many factors, including e.g. political risk, openness, wage levels, infrastructure or the functioning of product markets, affecting MNE investment decisions ( (Hajkova et al., 2006[4]) (Arnold et al., 2011[5]) (Feld and Heckemeyer, 2011[6]) (Sorbe and Johansson, 2017[7])). All else equal, corporate income taxation increases the user cost of capital, i.e., the minimum pre-tax rate of return that a firm needs to earn in order to break even after tax (Creedy and Gemmell, 2017[8]). While other channels through which the reform could affect investment and global output are discussed in the Section 4.7, Section 4.5 focusses on investment impacts operating through investment costs.

317. The introduction of Pillars One and Two could have significant impacts on the taxation of those MNEs that are within the scope of the proposed measures, depending on specific design choices regarding thresholds and carve-outs. Insofar as the proposals lead to changes in their investment costs, MNEs may be expected to respond by adjusting their investment decisions, possibly both in terms of location and scale.

318. In empirical work, impacts of corporate tax reforms on investment costs are often evaluated based on forward-looking effective tax rates (ETRs), i.e., synthetic, model-based tax policy indicators that combine information about corporate tax systems in an internationally comparable framework (Devereux and Griffith (2003[9]); Hanappi (2018[10])). Compared to statutory CIT rates, forward-looking ETRs have the advantage that they also capture standard components of the corporate tax base, e.g. depreciation. In empirical investment studies, forward-looking ETRs are the preferred measure because they avoid endogeneity inherent in backward-looking ETRs, computed as empirically observed taxes paid over a profit measure (Feld and Heckemeyer, 2011[6]).

319. When evaluating the investment impacts of changes in corporate taxation, an important distinction needs to be made between relocation of investment at the MNE entity level and changes in overall investment at the MNE group level.

- **Entity level investment** represents investments undertaken by subsidiaries that are part of an MNE group but not necessarily located in the jurisdiction of the ultimate parent entity; the investment decisions of these subsidiaries tend to consider the prevailing ETRs based on the domestic tax rules of the particular jurisdiction.
- **Group level investment** represents the combined investments of a given MNE group. While the ultimate parent entity of the MNE group will be located in a specific jurisdiction, MNE group level investment aggregates investments undertaken in any other subsidiary entity within the particular MNE group; MNE group level ETRs reflect the organisational structure of the MNE group as well as the relevant tax rules in the respective jurisdictions.

320. Although the empirical literature confirms that entity level investment responds negatively to an increase in the effective marginal tax rate (EMTR) in a given location (Feld and Heckemeyer, 2011[6]), this finding does not necessarily imply that investment at the MNE group level will decline as well. For example, a decrease in investment, which could be observed in response to an increase in the EMTR in a given location, could go together with a relocation of activities to other locations where the MNE group has subsidiaries (or even potentially to a location where the group would establish a new subsidiary). In this case, MNE group level investment would remain at a similar level and global output[4] would remain the same. In fact, this outcome would suggest that taxation has distorted previous location decisions; relocation thus creates the potential for an increase in the efficiency of capital allocation and, in turn, global output due to the relocation.

321. While it is difficult to disentangle entity- and group-level effects with the available data, recent evidence on the effect of the introduction of transfer pricing rules suggests that changes in jurisdiction level tax rules result mainly in a relocation of an MNE's investment rather than a reduction in the MNE group's overall level of investment (de Mooij and Liu, 2020[11]). Although relocation effects are certainly important from the perspective of individual countries, effects on MNE group level investment are likely to be more relevant drivers of global economic growth. The Section 4.5 discusses impacts on investment costs at the MNE group level, while the Section 4.6 focusses on investment responses at the entity level. The indirect effects discussed in the Section 4.7, however, could operate at the MNE entity as well as the group level.

## 4.5. Impacts on MNE group level investment costs

322. To derive an estimate of the impacts of the proposals on MNE group level investment costs, the analysis builds on the theoretical framework for forward-looking effective tax rates developed by Devereux and Griffith (2003[9]) and extends it in two important respects. First, the analysis incorporates the possibility that MNEs use their organisational structure to obtain tax advantages through profit shifting. Second, it evaluates the impact of stylised tax provisions[5] proposed under Pillar One, focusing on Amount A, and Pillar Two. Both extensions are described in detail in Hanappi and González Cabral (2020[12]). The results presented in this chapter are intended to be aligned with the latest discussions of the Inclusive Framework,

as described in the Pillar One and Pillar Two Blueprint reports (OECD, 2020[13]; OECD, 2020[14]), covering the majority of recent design choices. In particular, although political decisions remain to be made, Amount A of Pillar One is assumed to be restricted to Automated Digital Services (ADS) and Consumer-Facing Businesses (CFB); the effects of Pillar Two consider only the impact of the Income Inclusion Rule (IIR, cf. Section 4.7.3) and account for a formulaic substance-based carve-out on depreciation expenses while the impact of a carve-out on payroll cannot be covered in this chapter due to data limitations (see Hanappi and González Cabral (2020[12]) for a detailed description of the modelling approach).[6]

### 4.5.1. Methodological approach

323. Consistent with the MNE group level perspective, the empirical approach considers a stylised organisational structure that is held constant throughout the analysis and calibrated based on jurisdiction-specific data on profit and asset location. For the purposes of the empirical calibration, it is assumed that the ultimate parent entity of the MNE group carries out an investment in the jurisdiction where it is located, conducts operations through its subsidiaries located in other jurisdictions included in the dataset and produces a final consumer good that is sold to a global consumer base. Further assumptions are that the firm is a large MNE in a profit position and that investment is financed by retained earnings; the treatment of loss-making firms is, therefore, not considered. The investment is constructed as an unweighted average across three broad asset categories, non-residential structures, tangibles assets and acquired intangibles; statutory tax rates, depreciation rules and macroeconomic parameters are taken from OECD Corporate Tax Statistics (OECD, 2020[15]).[7] Personal income taxation and other taxes at the international level, e.g., withholding taxes, are not considered.

324. Effective marginal tax rates (EMTRs) and effective average tax rates8 (EATRs) are calculated at the MNE group level with respect to an additional investment in the jurisdiction of the ultimate parent entity[9], assuming that a share of its profits are shifted to other group subsidiaries located in jurisdictions with lower tax rates. The extent to which profits are shifted is approximated based on the consensus estimate from the profit shifting literature (Johansson et al., 2017[16]), (Heckemeyer and Overesch, 2017[17]), (Beer, de Mooij and Liu, 2020[18]). The location of shifted profits as well as the revenue structure are empirically calibrated, consistent with the data matrices constructed for the development of the tax revenue estimates (see Chapter 5), and shifted profits are taxed at the respective statutory CIT rates (see Hanappi and González Cabral (2020[12]) for a sensitivity analysis). This approach ensures that cross-country heterogeneity in the activities of MNEs, and thus in the potential impact of the proposals, is reflected in the analysis.

325. To capture the impact of the proposals, ETRs are first calculated[10] for a baseline case with profit shifting, building on data from 2019 on corporate tax rates and bases as published in OECD Corporate Tax Statistics (OECD, 2020[19]). Holding organisational structure and profit location constant, the baseline case is then compared to the post-implementation case to determine ETR changes at the MNE group level. Pillars One and Two include several design features that determine the extent to which the MNE group level ETRs will be affected. While the specific parameters are yet to be determined, the analysis relies on a set of assumptions, on a without prejudice basis, to model the expected effects of both pillars.[11] The specification underlying the analysis discussed below assumes[12] that Amount A[13] under Pillar One entails a 10% profitability threshold based on profit before tax over turnover, a 20% reallocation percentage to market jurisdictions and a restriction to ADS and CFB. In considering Pillar Two, a 12.5% rate with jurisdiction blending is assumed; the carve-out on depreciation expenses is assumed to be 10% and approximated using the value and location of tangible assets while the carve-out on payroll cannot be covered in this chapter due to data limitations. A revenue threshold of EUR 750 million is modelled for both Pillars. Using these parameters, the share of firms and profits that are in scope of Pillar One and Pillar Two are calibrated using jurisdiction-specific, firm-level data.[14] Additional results for a range of design options and parameter values are presented in Hanappi and González Cabral (2020[12]).

### 4.5.2. Empirical results

326. Consistent with the assumptions about stylised organisational structures, the results in Figure 4.2 identify MNE group level changes in ETRs associated with real investments in the jurisdiction of the ultimate parent entity.[15] Changes in profit shifting due to the implementation of the proposals are not captured in the calculation of the MNE group level ETRs. As discussed in Chapter 3, the new provisions are expected to reduce the amount of profits shifted to low-tax jurisdictions; this means that overall effective taxation would increase, on average, while tax liabilities under Pillar Two would fall if changes in profit shifting are accounted for. Insofar as that is the case, the direct impact of minimum effective taxation on the group level ETR would be lower. Following the approach taken with respect to the revenue results, the jurisdiction-specific results are aggregated into three groups based on GDP per capita: high income jurisdictions, low and middle income jurisdictions, and investment hubs.[16] GDP-weighted aggregated results are shown, for each of the three groups as well as the global average, in Figure 4.2.

327. Several initial insights emerge from the analysis of MNE group level ETRs. First, the share of MNEs that will be unaffected by the new rules is significant due to the revenue threshold and various scope restrictions.[17] Second, the results suggest small effects of Pillars One and Two on MNE group level effective average tax rates (EATRs) and effective marginal tax rates (EMTRs), based on an average across all MNEs. The global GDP-weighted average change in the EATRs from Pillar One and Two is estimated to be just over 0.3 percentage points (Panel A), representing a small impact compared to 24%, i.e., the weighted average EATR in the sample, or the 6 percentage point reduction in the EATR observed over 1999-2017 (Section 4.7.3). The corresponding change for the EMTR is around 1.4 percentage points, again representing a small change compared to the weighted average EMTR of around 25%. Third, much of this increase is driven by Pillar Two. While the global weighted-average change in the EATR due to Pillar One is close to zero (0.01 percentage points), the change due to Pillar Two is estimated to be around 0.3 percentage points. The same pattern is observed for the EMTR (Panel B in Figure 4.2). Fourth, the effect of the new rules on ETRs realised on investments in investment hubs is larger compared to investments in other jurisdictions.

#### Figure 4.2. Changes in Effective Tax Rates due to Pillars One and Two

ETRs are calculated at the MNE group level assuming an investment in the jurisdiction of the ultimate parent entity; the vertical axis shows GDP-weighted average changes in ETRs in percentage points by income groups.

*Panel A: Effective Average Tax Rates*

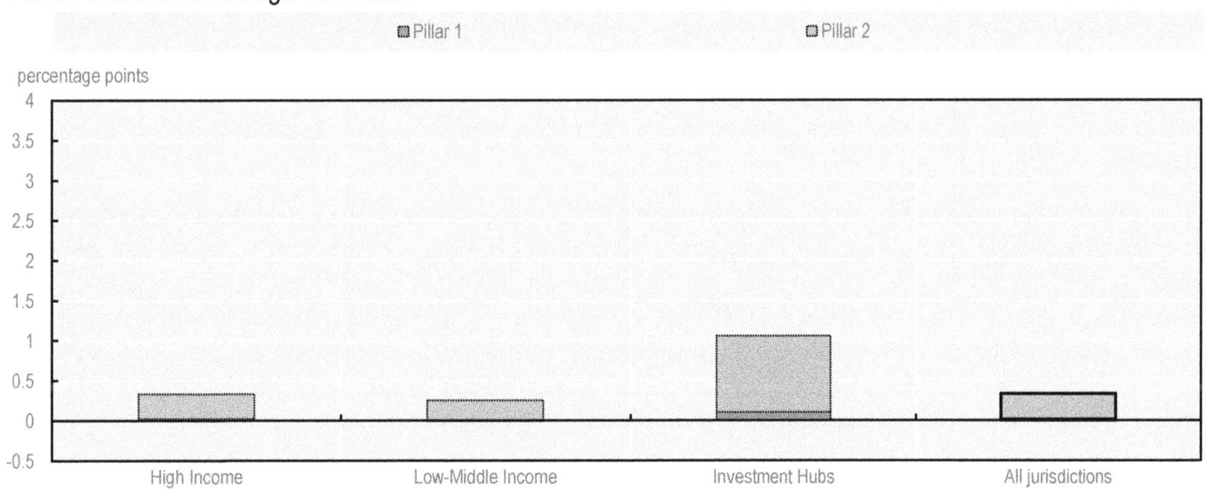

*Panel B: Effective Marginal Tax Rates*

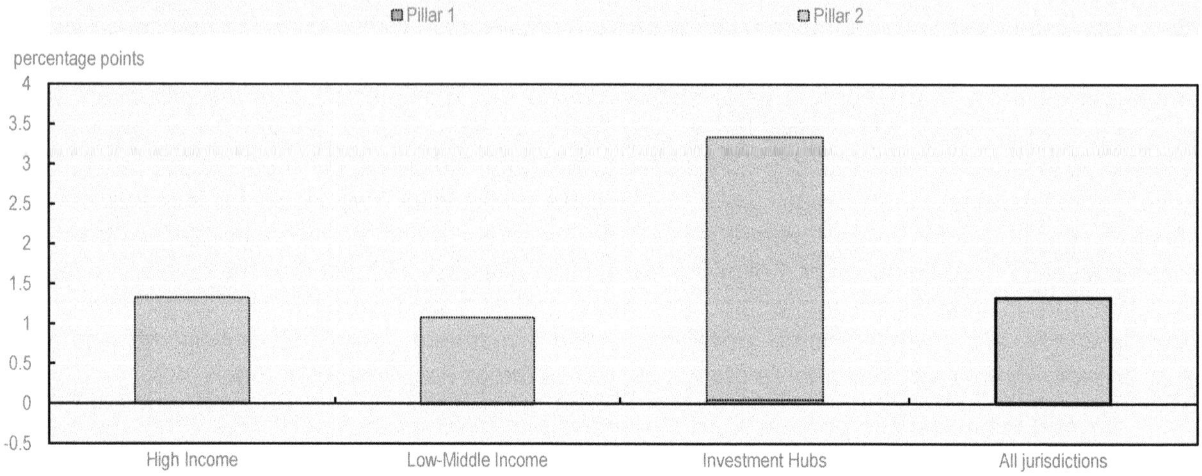


Note: Pillar One (Amount A only) considers a 10% profitability threshold on Profit/Turnover, 20% reallocation percentage to market and a scope that is restricted to ADS and CFB. Pillar Two considers a 12.5% rate with jurisdiction blending and a 10% carve-out on depreciation expenses (approximated using the value of tangible assets). In addition, it is assumed that an MNE group that claims the benefit of the carve-out should be required to make a corresponding and proportional adjustment to the covered taxes for the calculation of the ETR. The alternative option (i.e. not making a corresponding and proportional adjustment to the covered taxes) would be difficult to model with the available data. See Chapter 3 for more details. As described in endnote 12, real investments in jurisdictions without a full-fledged CIT system are not considered; those jurisdictions are thus excluded from the Figure, but profits can still be shifted to these jurisdictions. A revenue threshold of EUR 750 million is assumed, on a without prejudice basis, for the modelling of both Pillars. The combined effect does not include interaction effects of both Pillars. The results in the Figure reflect the average effects across all MNEs. The number of jurisdictions is restricted to those available in the OECD's Corporate Tax Statistics (OECD, 2020[19]), with the exception of Estonia and Latvia where profits are only taxed upon distribution. Jurisdiction groups are based on the World Bank classification of countries by income group. Investment hubs are defined as jurisdictions with a total inward FDI position above 150% of GDP, based on raw FDI data.
Source: Hanappi and González Cabral (2020[12]).

328. A range of further issues should be considered when interpreting these results in terms of their impacts on investment and global output. Although the quantitative analysis discussed above focuses on group level ETRs, some additional insights on entity level ETRs emerge as a corollary; in particular, both Pillars narrow the dispersion of entity and group level EATRs and EMTRs across jurisdictions. The reduced dispersion in tax rates reduces the tax gains from profit shifting, thus likely resulting in a corresponding reduction in the amount of shifted profits. As the marginal gain from profit shifting falls, corporate tax bases may become less elastic and, as a consequence, a given tax rate increase may be associated with lower costs in terms of tax base lost due to relocation – governments may thus be able to raise funds more efficiently.

329. In addition, a reduction in ETR differentials across jurisdictions is likely to improve the efficiency of the international allocation of capital (Englisch and Becker, 2019[20]). Firms make investment decisions based on post-tax rather than pre-tax returns. If profits are taxed at source and foreign income is tax-exempt, as is increasingly the case,[18] ETR differentials can be substantial, potentially inducing firms to choose locations where investments yield lower pre-tax, but higher post-tax returns. As entity level ETR differentials decrease due to the new tax rules, there is less scope for tax-induced distortions and global output[19] could thus increase as capital allocation across jurisdictions becomes more efficient.[20]

### *4.5.3. Tax Incidence*

330. The tax incidence of the reform can impact economic agents and their investment behaviour and should thus be considered in the evaluation. As opposed to statutory incidence (i.e., the legal obligation to remit a tax), the economic incidence associated with a new corporate tax liability may be borne by shareholders or may be shifted onto other economic agents, e.g., workers or consumers, through price adjustments. The extent to which these different economic agents bear the incidence of the reform could affect the impact of cost increases on firms' investment, therefore having important implications for the assessment of the new rules in terms of efficiency.[21] For example, if an increase in investment costs would fall mostly on workers or consumers, it could lead to a smaller reduction in firms' investment compared to the case where a larger share is borne by shareholders.

331. In general, the extent to which the economic incidence can be shifted onto others depends on a range of factors including supply and demand elasticities as well as market structure (Fullerton and Metcalf, 2002[21]) (Auerbach, 2006[22]). In the context of corporate taxation, it is typically assumed that in open economies (with competitive product markets), where capital is relatively mobile across jurisdictions while labour tends to be less mobile, firms will be able to shift a comparatively large share of the burden onto workers through wage decreases. However, only a few empirical papers directly investigate these theoretical insights and subsequent research has questioned the underlying assumptions, suggesting that, based on empirical estimates, shareholders bear a larger share of the economic incidence than previously assumed (see Gravelle (2013[23]), Clausing (2012[24]) (2013[25]) and references therein).

332. While empirical research on tax incidence is not conclusive due to the scarcity of disaggregated firm-level data, recent studies suggest that price adjustments to tax changes often follow more complex patterns, specifically when standard theoretical assumptions are not fully satisfied. For example, if firms earn more than the normal return to capital, e.g., due to their dominant position in a given market, corporate tax would fall, at least in part, on economic rents; as a consequence, capital allocation would be less distorted and downward pressure on wages would be lower (Auerbach, 2006[22]). Furthermore, Clausing (2013[25]) argues that profit-shifting allows multinational firms to decouple the location where profits are reported from the location of economic activities, thus partially insulating workers in high-tax jurisdictions from adverse wage effects associated with a given corporate tax increase. In addition, recent studies based on disaggregated data suggest that firm-level heterogeneity and rent-sharing between workers and shareholders could have implications for tax incidence (Arulampalam et al. (2012[26]); Serrato and Zirdar (2016[27]); Fuest, Peichl and Siegloch (2018[28])). Furthermore, the evidence discussed in Section 4.6 suggests that investment of entities in more profitable MNE groups is less sensitive to taxation, a result that could also be driven by the existence of economic rents at the MNE group level.

333. The literature on corporate tax incidence often assumes that product markets are competitive in which case it is impossible for firms to shift incidence onto consumers. Although this assumption may be warranted in more general settings, it is less likely to be the case in the context of highly-digitalised firms operating in markets characterised by winner-takes-all (or winner-takes-most) dynamics. In particular, the presence of multi-sided markets could have implications for tax incidence analysis, thereby potentially affecting investment decisions. Theoretical research suggests that in multisided markets optimal prices do not necessarily correspond to marginal costs (Rochet and Tirole (2003[29]), (2006[30])). If this is indeed the case, it is possible that tax changes induce an adjustment in the optimal price structure, for example, if the digital platform has some degree of market power and is sharing economic rents with different groups of end users. However, the academic literature on this particular topic is still limited and recent contributions suggest that there is a considerable degree of uncertainty with respect to tax incidence in multisided markets (Kind, Koethenbuerger and Schjelderup (2008[31]), (2010[32]), Belleflamme and Toulemonde (2016[33]), Kind and Koethenbuerger (2017[34]), Tremblay and Tremblay (2017[35]), Bourreau, Caillaud and De Nijs (2018[36]), Cui (2019[37]), Bibler, Teltser and Tremblay (2019[38])).

334. Compounding these considerations, the new rules are likely to elicit additional behavioural changes by MNEs and governments that could lead to further indirect effects on efficiency and global output relating, as discussed in the Section 4.7.

## 4.6. Tax sensitivity of MNE investment

335. While these results suggest that group level ETRs are expected, at the global average, to increase slightly, the impact of this increase on economic growth will depend on whether MNEs respond by adapting their investment behaviour. In particular, increases in group level ETRs could in turn affect the investment decisions of MNEs, with potential impacts on global investment and the location of investment across jurisdictions. Over the longer term, these changes in investment patterns could have impacts on global growth.

336. As discussed in the Section 4.4 by reducing after-tax returns on investment, higher corporate income tax can lead firms to forgo, downscale or relocate some investment projects. A corporate tax increase in one country, all else being equal, tends to result in lower MNE investment in that country (Sorbe and Johansson, 2017[7]; Feld and Heckemeyer, 2011[6]). However, the sensitivity of firm investment to corporate tax rates depends on the type of firm considered. Evidence from previous literature suggests that this sensitivity depends, for example, on characteristics such as investment financing structure and liquidity constraints (Zwick and Mahon, 2017[39]), market structure, in particular firm market power (Kopp et al., 2019[40]), and – more specifically for MNEs – tax planning possibilities (Sorbe and Johansson, 2017[7]).

337. Recent literature has documented the rise of 'superstar firms', i.e., highly productive and innovative firms, which often rely intensively on intangible assets. These firms typically operate globally and increasingly dominate certain product markets, especially in digitalised industries and industries characterised by winner-takes-all or winner-takes-most dynamics (Calligaris, Criscuolo and Marcolin, 2018[2]; Bajgar et al., 2019[41]; Gutiérrez and Philippon, 2019[42]; Autor et al., 2017[43]). In the context of the international tax proposals currently under discussion, these patterns could be of particular importance, given the scope of the reform proposals.

338. In particular, entities in more profitable MNE groups could react differently to taxation from entities in less profitable groups for several reasons. First, more profitable groups are likely to have higher financial resources (e.g. available liquidities) than less profitable groups, which makes them less credit constrained and thus less sensitive to a potential increase in taxation. Second, their high profitability rates may be related to monopolistic or oligopolistic positions, in which case incidence tends to fall on monopoly rents rather than on normal returns to capital (see Section 4.5.3), which may induce smaller behavioural responses in investment decisions (Kopp et al., 2019[40]). Moreover, these monopolistic positions may have been acquired thanks to significant past investments (e.g. through the grant of patents, or under winner-takes-all or winner-takes-most dynamics), in which case MNE groups might be reluctant to reduce future investment as this would threaten their dominant position in the market. Finally, more profitable groups may have greater opportunities and incentives to engage in tax planning.[22] For example, as these firms will often rely more on intangible assets, they have a greater opportunity to engage in tax planning activities through the strategic location of intangible assets. In addition, the fixed costs of tax planning may reduce the incentives for less profitable groups to engage in some profit shifting strategies.

339. For instance, recent evidence on US firms' reactions to the Tax Cuts and Jobs Act suggests that superstar firms, which are generally characterised by very high mark-ups and profitability rates, are indeed likely to react differently from other firms to changes in corporate taxation (Kopp et al., 2019[40]). Since these firms are also more likely than the average firm to be impacted by the international tax reforms currently under discussion, the variation in tax sensitivity between these firms and others could have substantial implications on the overall investment effects of the reform.

Figure 4.3. Tax Sensitivity of Investment by Profitability at the MNE Group Level

Change in the investment rate (ratio of investment to lagged capital stock), in percentage point, after a 1-percentage point increase in the EMTR; Profitability at the MNE group level measured by profit before tax over turnover

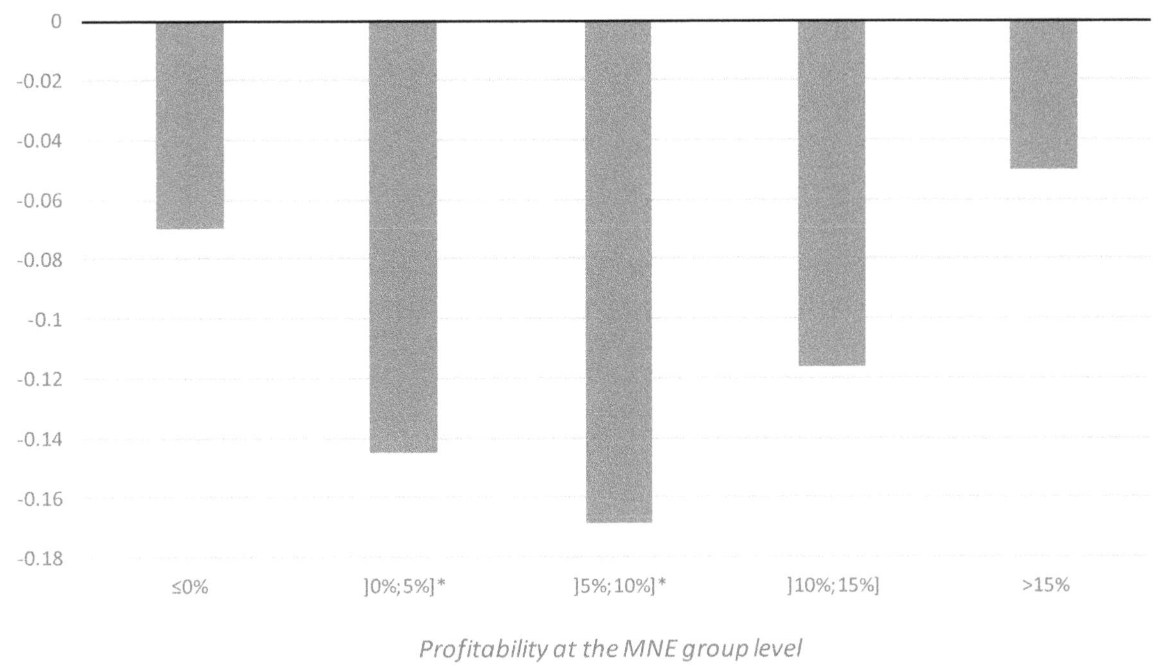


Note: Estimates based primarily on firm-level data from the ORBIS database, as well as ZEW ETR data. The estimated effects for profitability groups marked with a star (*) are statistically significantly different from zero at the 10% level, whereas the effects for other profitability groups are not.
Source: See Millot et al. (2020[44]).

340. Under Pillar One, new tax liabilities would arise only above a certain defined profitability threshold, e.g., in relation to profit before tax over turnover. More profitable MNEs are also more likely to have shifted profits to low-tax jurisdictions; this implies, all else equal, that they will also likely be more affected by minimum effective taxation under Pillar Two. To study the potential impacts of the reform, additional empirical analysis has been conducted. In Millot et al. (2020[44]), further insights on the effect of corporate taxes on MNE investment at the entity level have been produced, focussing on the variation in the tax sensitivity of investment across MNE groups, in particular, depending on the profitability rate of the group.

341. Relying on a firm-level econometric framework estimated on a panel of about 26,000 MNE entities located in 17 predominantly European countries over the period 2007-2016, the analysis confirms the earlier findings in the literature that MNE investment in a given jurisdiction responds negatively to increases in the jurisdiction level EMTR.[23]

342. Going one step further, the results of the analysis suggest that the short-term[24] tax sensitivity of MNE investment is lower among entities belonging to groups that have a relatively high profitability. As shown in Figure 4.3, the tax sensitivity of entities in an MNE group with profitability above 15%, computed as profit-before-tax to turnover, would be considerably lower than that of an entity in a group with profitability between 0% and 10%. Specifically, it is estimated that entities in MNE groups with a profitability rate between 0% and 10% would on average reduce their domestic investment rate by around 0.15 percentage points following a one percentage point increase in the jurisdiction's EMTR. However, this effect is almost half as large for entities in MNE groups with profitability ratios above 10% and more than

three times smaller for entities in MNE groups with profitability rates above 15%. The difference between the estimated sensitivities for the different profitability groups is moreover statistically significant when controlling for all potential sources of unobserved heterogeneity through fixed effects at the firm and country-year level. Additional regression results suggest that this lower tax sensitivity among entities from high-profitability MNE groups can be related to the lower liquidity constraints likely faced by these groups.

343. Overall, these results suggest that entities in MNE groups that are more likely to be impacted by the new tax rules proposed under Pillars One and Two may be less sensitive to taxes in their investment behaviour than entities in an average MNE.

## 4.7. Indirect effects on MNE investment and economic output

344. As discussed in the Sections 4.4 and 4.5, the new tax rules affect real investment directly through their impact on investment costs. However, the proposals include several novel elements that are likely to elicit behavioural responses by MNEs and governments. Amount A of Pillar One involves the creation of a new nexus and the reallocation to market jurisdictions[25] of a share of residual profit determined at the MNE group or segment level, based on a formulaic approach. Pillar Two seeks to address remaining BEPS challenges and ensure that large internationally operating businesses pay a minimum level of tax regardless of where they are headquartered or the jurisdictions they operate in. Without prejudging the final design and parameter choices, it is clear that the structural changes embedded in these new rules could have additional indirect effects on investment and economic output through various channels. To bring these indirect effects into the analysis this section builds on the economic literature, discussing relevant empirical and theoretical insights with a view towards the overall assessment presented in the Section 4.8.

345. Figure 4.4 illustrates the most relevant indirect effects. To start with, additional fiscal space generated by the tax revenues from Pillar One and Pillar Two could have positive indirect effects on investment. Since the analysis of investment costs in Section 4.5 focusses only on tax-induced cost increases, any other additional cost changes faced by taxpayers and governments also need to be accounted for in the overall assessment, notably compliance and administrative costs. On the business side, compliance costs are discussed in a separate subsection; on the government side, administrative costs are included in the broader discussion on fiscal space.

346. Adding to these effects, the introduction of novel elements is also expected to change the incentive structure underlying the international tax system, potentially affecting capital allocation across projects or locations and thus overall economic output. For example, strategic interactions in tax policy design can give rise to fiscal externalities when the government's tax policy choices in one jurisdiction affect the optimal response of other governments in terms of their tax policies. Introducing novel elements into the international tax system could alter the structure of these fiscal externalities, thus changing governments' optimal tax policy choices as well as firms' responses to a changing tax policy landscape. Indirect effects operating through such fiscal externalities are discussed in the subsection on international tax competition.

Figure 4.4. Overview: Indirect Effects on Investment and Economic Output

This figure illustrates the quantitatively most relevant indirect channels through which global investment could be affected by the new tax rules.

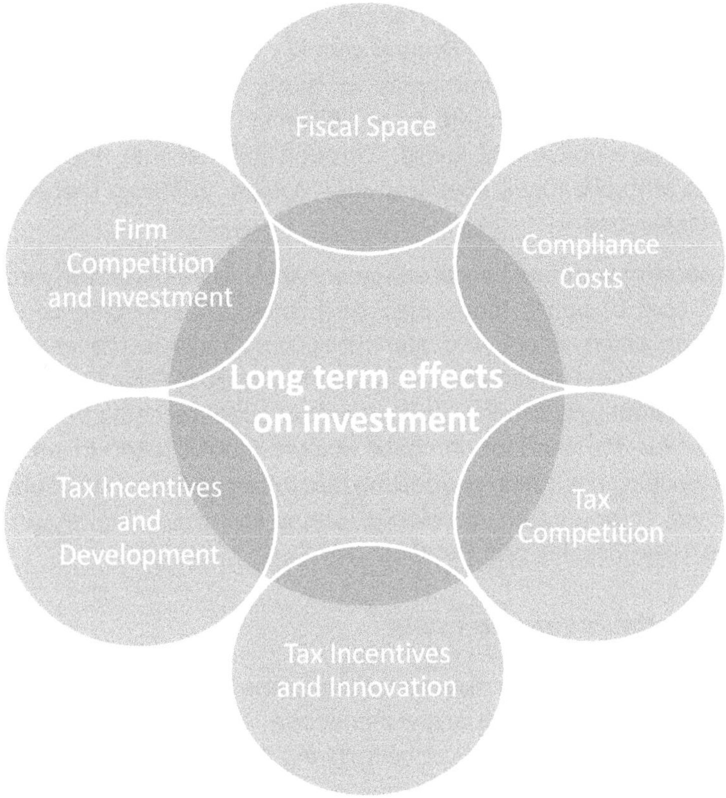


Source: OECD Secretariat.

347. In some policy areas the existence of market failures or positive externalities provides a policy rationale to support specific investment projects. Since public support is often delivered through the corporate tax system, the new rules, in particular minimum effective taxation under Pillar Two, could reduce the policy options available to governments possibly leading to under-investments in projects that would otherwise have received more public support. The two main policy areas where tax incentives are often rationalised based on this argument are innovation and economic development; both of these policy areas are discussed in separate subsections.

348. Finally, an increase in market power, e.g. measured as firm concentration within a given market or industry, can under some circumstances decrease the firms' incentives to innovate and invest. If the new rules contribute to a more level playing field between firms, a potential reduction in market power could have positive indirect effects on innovation and investment – an argument that is examined in a separate subsection.

### *4.7.1. Fiscal space*

349. Having already accounted for the corresponding direct effects on investment in the Section 4.5, the overall assessment of the new rules also has to account for the expected increases in fiscal space. As discussed in the revenue analyses, the new tax rules are expected to directly increase tax revenues for most governments (see Chapter 2 and Chapter 3). While the optimal use of additional fiscal space depends on the country-specific context, an increase in tax revenues, having already accounted for the change in

investment costs, is likely to have positive effects on the economy, as it can be used, e.g., to support public or private investment or to reduce public debt levels.

350. Furthermore, the reduction in ETR differentials noted in the Section 4.5 affects not only real investment, but it also reduces the potential gains from profit shifting. As a result, MNEs would be expected to engage in less tax evasion and corporate tax bases may become less elastic on average, e.g., if the sensitivity of profits to tax is increasing non-linearly with tax rate differentials. A given tax rate increase would, therefore, be associated with lower costs in terms of tax base lost due to relocation and governments may thus be able to raise funds more efficiently; e.g., tax administrations could raise the same revenue with lower tax enforcement levels. Through this channel, the new tax rules would thus reduce the marginal cost of public funds (Slemrod and Wilson, 2009[45]), thereby further strengthening fiscal space across all jurisdictions.

351. The positive impacts of increased fiscal space are likely to be particularly important for developing countries. The marginal cost of public funds may be higher in developing countries due to capacity constraints in terms of tax enforcement and administration (Dabla-Norris et al., 2019[46]; Keen et al., 2015[47]). Insofar as compliance and administration functions related to Pillar One and Pillar Two are carried out by entities in ultimate parent jurisdictions, additional tax revenues could be raised at a lower cost per unit of public funds. Moreover, the need for domestic resource mobilisation to support public investments tends to be greater in developing countries, suggesting that public investments could yield stronger positive effects in those countries compared to developed countries where the return on additional public investment is likely to be lower (Besley and Persson, 2014[48]).

### *4.7.2. Compliance and administration costs*

352. Introducing new tax provisions to implement Pillars One and Two will increase filing requirements, and compliance costs, for those MNEs that are within scope. As discussed in Chapter 2 and Chapter 3, the policy design includes several scope restrictions implying that only large and relatively profitable MNEs will be in scope. This means that increases in compliance costs will be borne mostly by those firms that currently have the lowest compliance costs measured as a proportion of turnover (see Box 4.2). In addition to this, some tax administrations may experience increases in administration costs as a result of implementing the new rules. Simplified administrative processes currently under discussion for various components of both Pillars would help to limit these costs.

### Figure 4.5. Trends in Multilateral Agreement Procedure (MAP) cases for OECD Countries

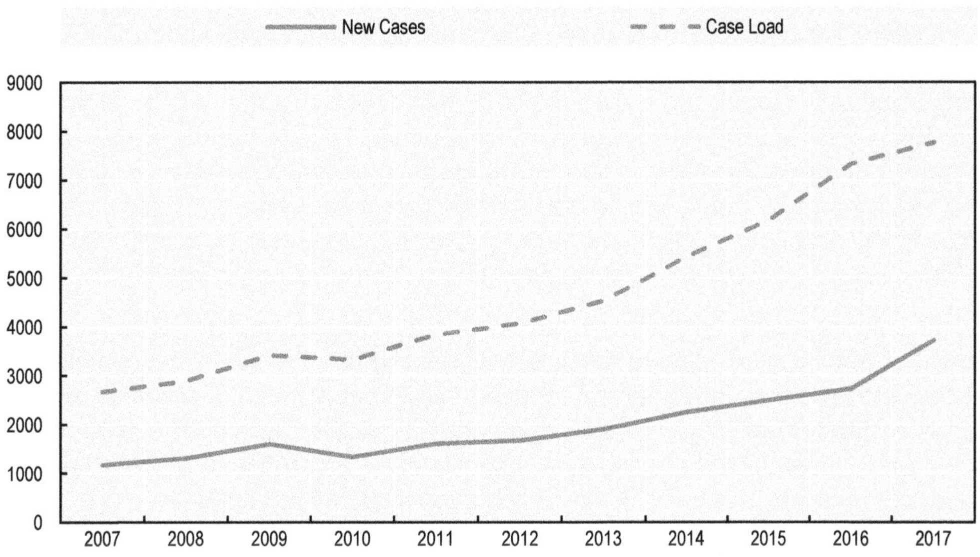


Source: OECD calculations based on MAP Statistics at: https://www.oecd.org/ctp/dispute/

To ensure a balanced panel, data are provided only for the following countries: Australia, Austria, Belgium, Canada, Chile, Czech Republic, Denmark, Estonia, Finland, France, Germany, Greece, Hungary, Iceland, Ireland, Israel, Italy, Japan, Korea, Luxembourg, Mexico, the Netherlands, New Zealand, Norway, Poland, Portugal, Slovak Republic, Slovenia, Spain, Sweden, Switzerland, Turkey, the United Kingdom, and the United States.

### Figure 4.6. Time to closure of cases under Multilateral Agreement Procedure

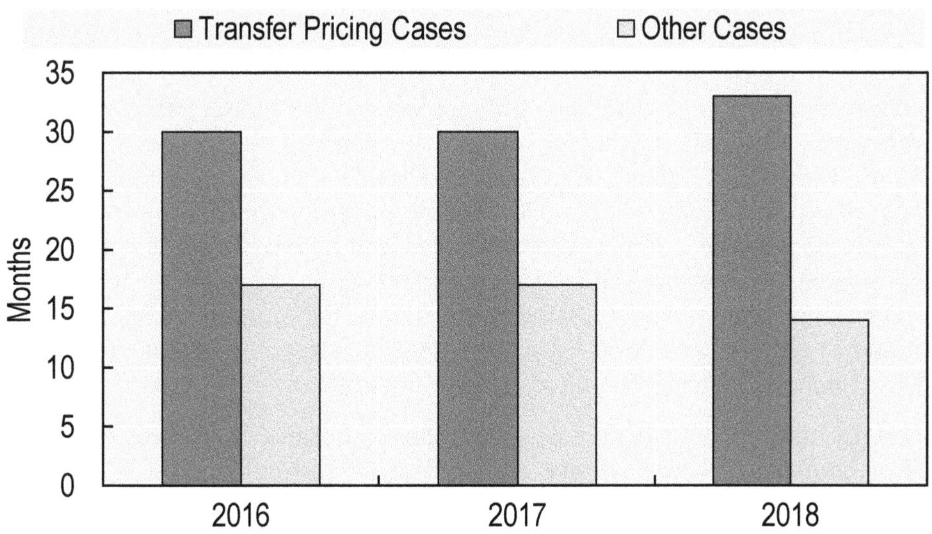


Source: OECD calculations based on MAP Statistics at: https://www.oecd.org/ctp/dispute/

353. Several indirect effects on firm behaviour could, at least partially, attenuate the expected increase in compliance costs. First, tax planning represents a larger proportion of the administrative costs of large MNEs relative to smaller firms (see Box 4.2). It is expected that the new rules will reduce the incentives for MNEs to engage in profit shifting. To the extent that firms reduce or abandon the use of complex tax

planning structures, in the medium term this could reduce compliance costs for firms and administration costs for tax authorities.

354. Second, there has been an expansion of Mutual Agreement Procedure (MAP) cases and an increasing volume of outstanding MAP cases in the international tax system (Figure 4.5). These cases are already creating significant compliance costs for MNEs. It is noteworthy that a large share of these MAP cases (51% in 2018) are transfer-pricing cases, which typically take much longer to close (Figure 4.6). While time-to-closure remains high for transfer pricing cases, it has recently been reduced for other, non transfer-pricing-related cases. Some of the transfer pricing cases refer to related party distributors, especially limited-risk distributors. By standardising the remuneration of related party distributors, Amount B of Pillar One would reduce the likelihood of these cases ending up in MAP. [26]

355. Third, the reforms considered under Pillars One and Two are expected to include an expansion and improvement of dispute prevention procedures, suggesting that the additional compliance burden of implementing the proposals may be somewhat reduced. MNEs would need to allocate fewer resources to appeals, litigation and audits than would be the case in the absence of these additional procedures. These aspects, coupled with a potential reduction in MAP disputes due to simplifications under Amount B of Pillar One, may attenuate any increases in compliance costs for MNEs that result from the implementation of the new rules.

356. As the implementation of the proposals creates additional compliance costs for MNEs that are within scope, they may also lead to additional administration costs for tax authorities. As is the case for MNEs, a reduction in disputes due to expanded dispute prevention and resolution procedures may reduce administration costs. Simplification measures (such as Amount B) may also obviate transfer pricing disputes in certain areas. However, the overall level of administration costs may nonetheless rise as a result of the implementation of the proposals. Additional administration costs may be larger for those administrations that act as the lead tax administration as part of the proposed centralised and simplified administration system, and so may not be equal across jurisdictions.

### Box 4.2. Compliance costs

Measuring compliance costs is challenging and subject to significant uncertainty. Most studies examining compliance costs rely on survey data with relatively small samples (Eichfelder and Vaillancourt, 2014[49]). It is also difficult to generalise findings that relate to the subcomponents of compliance costs, which impact different firms in different ways and to different degrees. Much of the existing literature on compliance costs focuses on small and medium sized enterprises, with fewer studies (e.g. Slemrod and Venkatesh (2002[50]) and Erard (1997[51])) focusing on larger firms. There is evidence that compliance costs can vary significantly across firms, including by age, firm size, the number of members in a group, and firms' legal form (see Stamatopoulos, Hadjidema and Eleftheriou (2017[52]) and Eichfelder and Vaillancourt (2014[49]) for reviews).

In spite of these uncertainties, the literature suggests that compliance with taxes forms a substantial part of the overall compliance burden. Large companies are generally found to have greater total compliance costs than small firms in absolute terms. However, as a proportion of turnover, the literature suggests that compliance costs are greater for smaller firms than for larger firms (Eichfelder and Vaillancourt, 2014[49]; Slemrod and Venkatesh, 2002[50]; Ariff, Cheung and Chan, 1999[53]). Higher proportionate burdens for small businesses are in part due to the fixed costs of compliance. Compliance costs are thus regressive due to these diseconomies of scale.

The overall tax compliance burden is also disaggregated in the literature. Studies suggest that major components of compliance costs are the costs of filing tax returns and the costs of record keeping (Lignier and Evans, 2012[54]; Colmar Brunton, 2005[55]). For many firms, a key burden in their overall financial compliance is the preparation of financial accounting information (Asatryan and Peichl, 2018[56]; Eichfelder and Vaillancourt, 2014[49]).

Tax planning itself is a key component of the compliance costs of large firms. The literature suggests that tax planning is a larger cost component of the compliance cost of large businesses relative to small businesses (Slemrod and Venkatesh, 2002[50]), which may be a result of the fact that tax planning is more cost effective for large businesses.

Tax audits and tax appeals are also key drivers of compliance costs and tax complexity (Hoppe et al., 2019[57]), which in turn can reduce investment (Hoppe et al., 2020[58]). Concerns over the inconsistent approaches of different tax authorities towards the application of international tax standards have been expressed by businesses as key drivers of tax uncertainty (IMF-OECD, 2017[59]).

The economic literature suggests that the costs of engaging in audit, appeal and litigation increase as a share of the total compliance burden with business size (Eichfelder and Vaillancourt, 2014[49]). Slemrod and Blumenthal (1996[60]) suggest that about one quarter of total compliance costs for large businesses can be allocated to appeals, litigation and audits – excluding any potential reputational costs. This could be driven by economies of scale in the compliance process, a higher probability of audit for large firms, and a higher willingness of large firms to take on legal disputes. Audits may be linked to increased tax planning by large multinational firms and the ability of governments to gain large amounts of tax revenue from these audits.

In addition to costs associated with business compliance, it is also important to consider cost increases from the perspective of tax administrations. While compliance can be a significant burden on businesses, complex taxes can also be more difficult and costly to administer for tax administrations. There is evidence that corporate taxes are among the most complex taxes for tax administrations to administer, and that audits and investigations are a significant burden on tax administrations (Díaz de Sarralde Miguez, 2018[61]). Developing countries may suffer more from the burden of administering complex taxes (Dabla-Norris et al., 2019[46]; Keen et al., 2015[47]), and are less able to bear the costs of complex tax enforcement. Nonetheless, investments in tax administrations often yield benefits well in excess of their costs (Chatib Basri et al., 2019[62]), especially in low-capacity contexts. Implementation of simplified tax regimes may reduce costs for tax administrations.

### *4.7.3. International tax competition*

357. Empirical evidence generally supports the view that jurisdictions use their CIT system, including statutory rates as well as the definition of corporate tax bases, to compete for MNE investment and the tax revenue it generates over time (see Box 4.3). First, statutory CIT rates have been declining since the mid-1980s, not only in OECD countries but also in many developing and emerging economies (Devereux et al., 2002[63]) (Klemm and Van Parys, 2012[64]). In particular, the unweighted average statutory CIT rate in OECD countries has declined from above 32% in 2000 to around 23% in 2020, and from around 28% to just below 21% in a sample covering more than 90 developing and developed countries over the same time horizon (see Figure 4.7 based on OECD Corporate Tax Statistics (2020[19])). Second, available data on forward-looking effective average tax rates[27] (EATRs), capturing not only the statutory rates but also standard components of the corporate tax base, show a decline in the unweighted effective average tax rate from 29% to around 23% in a balanced panel of OECD and G20 countries over the period 1999 to 2017. An alternative data source covering mostly European countries shows a similar decline in the unweighted EATR from 24% to 20% over the years 2005 to 2018 (Figure 4.8).

358. In addition, empirical research has also identified strategic interactions in tax policy design across jurisdictions, implying that the policy choices of governments regarding tax rates and bases are affected by other governments' tax policy choices (see Annex 4.A). Interactions can arise in many different areas, going beyond statutory CIT rates and bases; for example, policy decisions on preferential regimes, CFC rules or double tax agreements can have implications for policy design in other jurisdictions. Ultimately, these strategic responses to tax competition produce negative fiscal externalities (or spillovers) that could drive corporate effective tax rates below their optimal level and lead to inefficiently high taxation of less mobile tax bases such as labour or consumption. In this case, unilateral (or uncoordinated) policy design is likely to produce a globally inefficient outcome, i.e., a reduction in global economic output compared to the case with multilateral (or coordinated) policy design (Gupta et al., 2014[65]).

359. However, the theoretical literature reviewed in Annex 4.A also provides some arguments for the potentially efficiency-enhancing effects of tax competition. For example, competitive pressure could have positive efficiency effects if capital becomes partially immobile once the location decision has been taken and governments cannot credibly commit to keeping effective tax rates stable in the absence of tax competition. Alternatively, positive efficiency effects could also materialise if competitive pressure limits public sector growth that is driven by rent-seeking or self-interested behaviour by political leaders and government officials.

## Figure 4.7. Combined statutory CIT rates 2000 to 2020, by Region (unweighted)

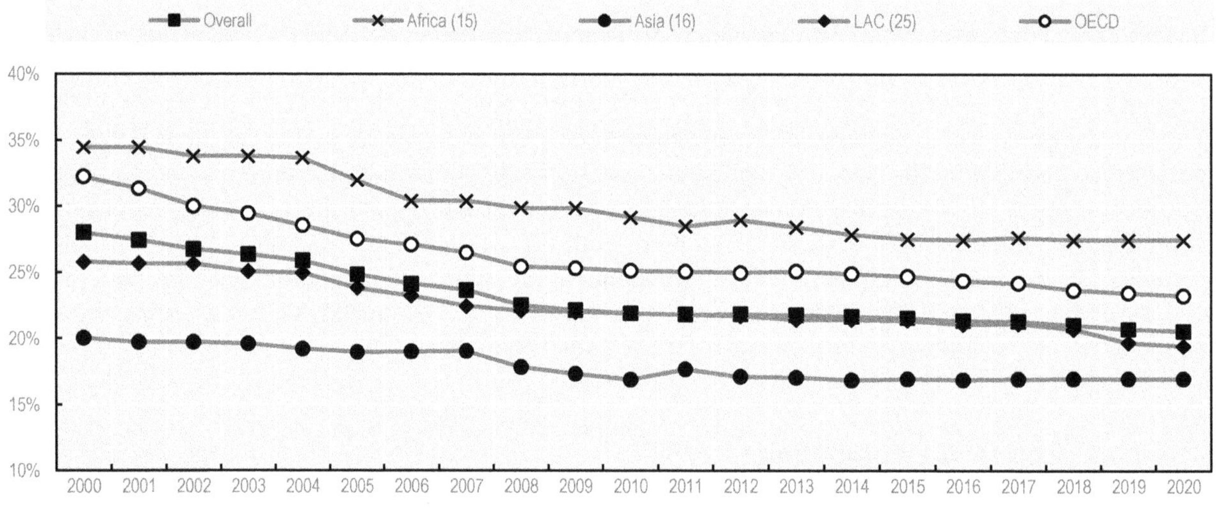


Note: The data series represent unweighted average combined CIT rates across all countries covered in the second edition of OECD Corporate Tax Statistics; zero-tax jurisdictions are included; in the case of progressive tax systems the highest applicable rate is used.
Source: OECD Corporate Tax Statistics (2020[19])).

360. The new tax rules introduced under Pillar One and Pillar Two will affect the strategic interactions in tax policy design across jurisdictions, potentially reducing the extent to which governments engage in tax competition. Under Pillar One, the share of the corporate tax base within the scope of Amount A is determined by reference to profitability at the MNE group level; a fraction of this share is then allocated to market jurisdictions[28] and taxed there at prevailing rates. This approach is likely to reduce competitive pressure on governments through two different channels. First, consumers and users can generally be considered as relatively immobile; the allocation of a share of the corporate tax base to market jurisdictions thus directly reduces the tax base that can be attracted through lower effective taxation. Second, assessing corporate tax bases at the MNE group level, rather than on a separate basis for each of the entities of the

MNE group, is likely to reduce the sensitivity of MNE investment with respect to tax rates in specific locations. As the amount of investment that can be attracted through a given reduction in the effective tax rate will be lower, governments will have some scope to retain higher levels (or resist pressure to implement lower levels) of effective taxation compared to the case without an MNE group-level assessment.

361. Under Pillar Two, minimum taxation is implemented by introducing four new rules (see Chapter 1), leading to significant implications for governments' optimal tax policy choices. The objective of the new provisions is to ensure that the effective tax rate on MNE profit that would otherwise be taxed below an agreed minimum rate is brought up to this minimum rate, which has to be decided by the Inclusive Framework. The income inclusion rule (IIR) will allow jurisdictions where ultimate parent entities are located to top-up taxes on low-taxed profits earned by subsidiaries in other jurisdictions such that effective tax rates are brought up to a given minimum rate. In the absence of complementary rules, MNEs could have incentives to invert, i.e., to change their residence for tax purposes, in order to avoid minimum taxation if some jurisdictions do not adopt the IIR (see Annex 4.C). To avoid creating such an incentive, the undertaxed payments rule (UTPR) would allocate top-up tax proportionately among entities applying UTPR in a co-ordinated way first to those entities making direct payments to the low-tax MNE entity and then amongst all entities in the group that have net intra-group expenditure (Englisch and Becker, 2019[20]). Furthermore, two additional components, the switch-over rule and the subject to tax rule, complement these rules, contributing to the objective of ensuring minimum effective taxation.

362. Pillar Two introduces a lower bound on the effective tax rates that governments can offer in order to attract foreign investment, thereby limiting the extent to which competition can take place through the corporate tax system. However, it is possible that competitive pressure persists and some governments respond by providing other forms of public support. In some cases (e.g., grants or subsidies), this support will be more transparent than if it was delivered through the tax system. In addition, the existence of a lower bound does not necessarily imply that effective tax rates will remain stable (or even increase) across all participating jurisdictions. As reviewed in Annex 4.A, some theoretical models[29] suggest that a reduction in the effective tax rate in jurisdictions with relatively high rates could, under certain assumptions, become more attractive with minimum effective taxation because it is common knowledge that low-tax jurisdictions cannot lower their rates below a certain minimum. However, it is unclear whether this theoretical result is empirically relevant, given that recent evidence at the German subnational level points in the opposite direction (Schwerin and Buettner, 2016[66]).

## Figure 4.8. Effective Average Tax Rates (EATRs), by Data Source (unweighted)

Time series data on EATRs is currently available from two different sources, the Oxford Centre for Business Taxation (CBT) and the Leibniz Centre for European Economic Research (ZEW); the unweighted averages shown in this graph are computed for balanced panels covering 38 and 35 countries respectively.

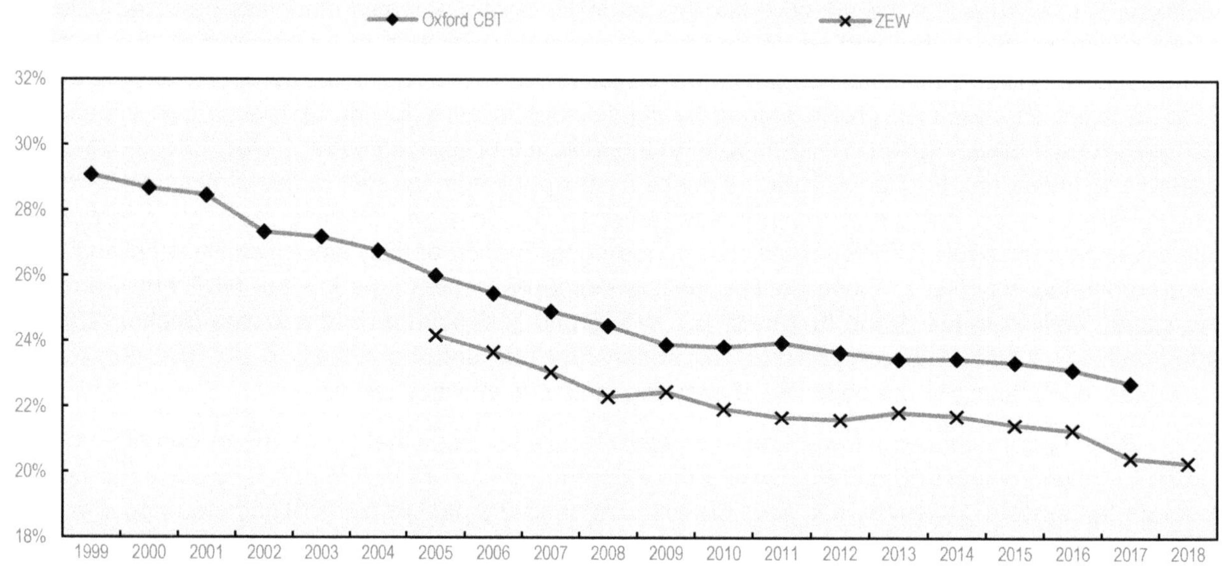


Note: The ZEW time series covers 35 mostly European countries over 2005 to 2018: Austria, Belgium, Bulgaria, Canada, Switzerland, Cyprus[30], Czech Republic, Germany, Denmark, Estonia, Spain, Finland, France, UK, Greece, Croatia, Hungary, Ireland, Italy, Japan, Lithuania, Luxembourg, Latvia, Macedonia, Malta, Netherlands, Norway, Poland, Portugal, Romania, Sweden, Slovenia, Slovak Republic, Turkey and the USA. The time series from the Oxford University Centre for Business Taxation covers 38 countries over 1999 to 2017: Argentina, Austria, Brazil, Belgium, Bulgaria, Canada, Switzerland, Chile, Germany, Denmark, Estonia, Spain, Finland, France, UK, Greece, Hungary, Indonesia, Ireland, Israel, India, Iceland, Italy, Japan, Republic of Korea, Luxembourg, Mexico, Netherlands, Norway, New Zealand, Poland, Portugal, Russia, Sweden, Slovenia, Turkey, USA and South Africa.

Source: ZEW rates are based on the European Union (EU) Commission project TAXUD/2018/DE/307; Oxford CBT rates have been sourced from the website.

363. A different strand of the theoretical literature investigates the role of zero-tax jurisdictions specialised in attracting accounting profits that are shifted outwards from other jurisdictions. On the one hand, the existence of such jurisdictions increases the marginal cost of public funds faced by other jurisdictions, thus implying a net loss in global economic output (Slemrod and Wilson, 2009[45]). On the other hand, it has also been argued that allowing for a certain amount of profits to be shifted outwards could be an efficient strategy in a context where governments compete for mobile and immobile tax bases but tax policy cannot discriminate between the two (Dharmapala, 2020[67]).

364. Taken together, these theoretical and empirical insights suggest that the new rules will not put an end to tax competition, but they are likely to dampen the downward pressure on effective tax rates across many jurisdictions, mostly due to the reduction in ETR differentials. While the provisions envisaged under Pillar One clearly reduce negative fiscal externalities, scope restrictions will limit the overall impacts of these changes in the incentive structure at the global level. Minimum effective taxation under Pillar Two introduces a lower bound to tax competition; however, the resulting changes in the incentive structure are complex and optimal policy responses will depend on a range of other factors such as the size and structure of the economy, regional interactions or the general tax structure.

**Box 4.3. Empirical evidence on tax competition**

The secular downward trend in statutory CIT rates provides initial empirical evidence of international tax competition, understood as the interdependent setting of corporate income tax rates and tax bases by national governments (Devereux and Loretz, 2013[68]). Early theoretical contributions, notably Zodrow and Mieskowski (1986[69]) and Wilson (1986[70]), suggest that statutory CIT rates are, under certain conditions, strategic complements in the sense that a decrease in one country induces decreases in other countries (and vice versa), potentially leading to inefficiently low CIT rates and an under-provision of public goods due to a lack of fiscal space.

Empirical research has often started from the assumption that economic integration increases over time, raising competitive pressures on CIT rates (see Devereux and Loretz (2013[68]) for a review of various empirical strategies). Recent empirical contributions typically aim at identifying the slope of the government reaction function directly, following Devereux, Lockwood and Redoano (2008[71]). Although Chirinko and Wilson (2017[72]) suggest that reaction functions of US state governments may be downward sloping, the vast majority of empirical studies confirm that government reaction functions are positively sloped, i.e., that there is strategic complementarity between CIT rates across countries (Leibrecht and Hochgatterer (2012[73]); Davies and Voget (2011[74]); Costa-Font, De-Albuquerque and Doucouliagos (2014[75]); Redoano (2014[76])). The most recent study, Lee (2020[77]), investigates tax competition on CIT rates in 67 countries between 1981 and 2015, again confirming upward sloping reaction functions.

While most of the empirical literature on tax competition assumes that governments respond simultaneously to other governments' rate setting choices, it has been recognised that tax competition could also be sequential (Gordon (1992[78]); Keen and Konrad (2013[79])). In particular, larger countries, such as the United States, could lead by first setting their own rate, while other countries follow by choosing their rate depending on the leader's choice. In such a model (i.e., applying the Stackelberg equilibrium concept), countries would choose higher tax rates than in the standard model with simultaneous choices (i.e., applying the Nash equilibrium concept). Altshuler and Goodspeed (2015[80]) are the first to provide an empirical test for the sequential model, providing evidence for positive reaction functions and finding that the United States has acted as a leader in CIT rate setting using data from 1968 to 2008; the results reject leadership roles for Germany or the United Kingdom over the same time horizon.

While the sequential model allows for the possibility that a minimum tax could induce leader and follower countries to choose lower CIT rates (Konrad (2009[81]); Kiss (2012[82])), empirical evidence at the German subnational level seems to contradict this finding (Schwerin and Buettner, 2016[66]). Specifically, Schwerin and Buettner (2016[66]) exploit a recent business tax reform in the German Federation that introduced a minimum tax with the aim of reducing tax competition among subnational governments; quasi-experimental evidence suggests that subnational municipalities competing with lower-tax subnational regions responded to the reform by increasing their business tax rates.

### *4.7.4. Tax incentives to support innovation*

365. Innovation is a key driver of productivity, investment and growth at the firm level as well as for entire economies. However, due to the intrinsic nature of innovation, there are reasons to believe that individual entrepreneurs and businesses are likely to generate less innovation than would be socially optimal, in the absence of government intervention (see Box 4.4).

366. To support innovation and innovation activities[31] such as research and development (R&D), governments have a wide array of policies at their disposal. Targeted policies can take the form of direct support via grants or public procurement of R&D services, or indirect support via the tax system, i.e., R&D tax incentives. While governments often opt for a mix of direct and indirect measures, the use of indirect

support instruments has generally increased across the OECD in recent years. In some cases, governments combine tax incentives that provide preferential treatment to the inputs to innovation, e.g., R&D expenditure such as the wage of researchers; with tax incentives providing preferential treatment to the output of innovation, e.g., the income from a patent (Appelt, Galindo-Rueda and González Cabral, 2019[83]) (see Box 4.4). However, despite the increased use of tax incentives in policy, evidence on their effectiveness is mixed, appearing more positive for input-based incentives than for output-based incentives (see Annex 4.Bs). [32] Moreover, providing preferential treatment to the income from a highly mobile asset has been found to lead to the strategic location of IP assets, a key profit shifting channel identified in the literature (Beer, de Mooij and Liu, 2020[18]).

### Box 4.4. Government support for business R&D and innovation

Several reasons are often referred to in the literature to support the proposition that, in the absence of government intervention, markets will generate less innovation than would be optimal. First, knowledge is in principle non-rival. Innovation activities generate unpriced spillovers to other agents in the economy, preventing the full appropriability of the returns to innovation (Romer, 1990[84]; Aghion and Howirrt, 1992[85]). Second, the risky and uncertain nature of innovation that cannot be fully insured against or diversified away may also lead to an under-allocation of resources to innovative activities (Arrow, 1962[86]). Third, as a result of the latter, the cost of financing of these investments will be higher compared to alternative investment opportunities that do not pose the same level of risk and uncertainty, which particularly affects financially constrained firms. This issue is of particular concern for young firms and SMEs that lack both the collateral and the track record to obtain external funding (Hall and Lerner, 2010[87]). Fourth, underinvestment might be frequent in research areas of public interest that are non-rival and non-excludable, e.g., public goods such as climate change or health (Hall, 2019[88]).

Governments can offer direct support for business R&D and innovation via grants or public procurement of R&D services; or indirect support via the tax system in the form of tax incentives. These two instruments are, however, different in nature. Direct funding is discretionary, and allows governments to fund specific areas of research with high spillovers. It is often targeted towards basic research, encouraging radical rather than incremental innovation (Akcigit, Hanley and Serrano-Velarde, 2013[89]).

Tax incentives are typically a non-discretionary, market-based, policy instrument; they do not discriminate across firms or activities, all firms that qualify for the incentive will be able to benefit from the tax break, making such support easier to administer than direct support measures. Therefore, tax incentives are well suited to promote R&D and innovation across industries and firm types. However, they may not be as well-suited as a targeted measure to stimulate areas of potential underinvestment where higher social returns could be expected. In addition, concerns are sometimes raised over the ability of tax administrations to distinguish claims that pertain to R&D vs. non-R&D related activities, i.e., relabelling of non-R&D activities as R&D.

R&D tax incentives may provide enhanced relief to the inputs to innovation, i.e., to R&D expenditure such as the wage of R&D researchers, and/or to the output, i.e., to the income from R&D and other innovation activities such as income from a patent. Input-based R&D tax incentives have a more direct impact on the decision of the firm to engage and perform innovation activities, as relief is granted to the expenditure that is within the firm's control. Output-based tax incentives, as a relief on the outcome, are only granted in cases where the innovation has been successful, which depends on factors that may be beyond the firm's control. The latter might induce firms to seek patent protection for innovations that would not have been patented in the absence of the policy, i.e., so-called zombie patents; or to other unintended behaviours such as patent trolling (Appelt et al., 2016[90]; Klemens, 2016[91]; Gaessler, Hall and Harhoff, 2018[92]).

367. Notwithstanding the impact that the broader tax environment has on innovation, a key change that the new rules under Pillars One and Two introduce is the potential limitation of the use of targeted measures such as expenditure- or income-based tax incentives to foster innovation. In particular, minimum effective taxation, as proposed under Pillar Two, will limit the potential tax benefits that governments can provide through these instruments. The extent of the tax benefits offered will depend both on the design of the incentive and the general characteristics of the tax system (see Annex 4.B). Therefore, this potential reduction in generosity will only come to bear in situations where tax incentives drive effective taxation at the jurisdiction[33] level, i.e., taking into account taxation on other non-qualifying income, below the minimum threshold. In cases where the minimum threshold limits the benefits of tax incentives under Pillar Two, only a subset of large MNEs would be affected while domestic and potentially also smaller multinational firms would still be able to benefit from tax incentives as before. As the final design parameters under Pillar Two are still under discussion, the introduction of carve-outs would also reduce the number of firms affected and limit the reduction in tax benefits from Pillar Two to an even smaller number of cases.

368. The provisions envisaged under Pillar One will have much less direct effect on the use of tax incentives to support innovation. Both types of tax incentives, expenditure- and income-based, decrease the effective taxation of innovative projects, thus increasing their profitability. To the extent that the reallocation of a percentage of residual profits under Pillar One leads to an increase in the tax rates applicable to the income derived from innovative projects, the new rules could lessen the reduction in effective taxation intended by tax incentives. This effect would be more likely in the case of income-based incentives.[34] However, given the size of the reallocation percentage currently under discussion, the generosity and effectiveness of expenditure- and income-based tax incentives are unlikely to be significantly altered by this potential interaction with a reallocation of tax bases under Pillar One. Overall, only a relatively narrow subset of large and highly profitable MNE groups will be subject to these effects as determined by the scope of Pillar One.

## Figure 4.9. Business R&D expenditures, by type of expenditure

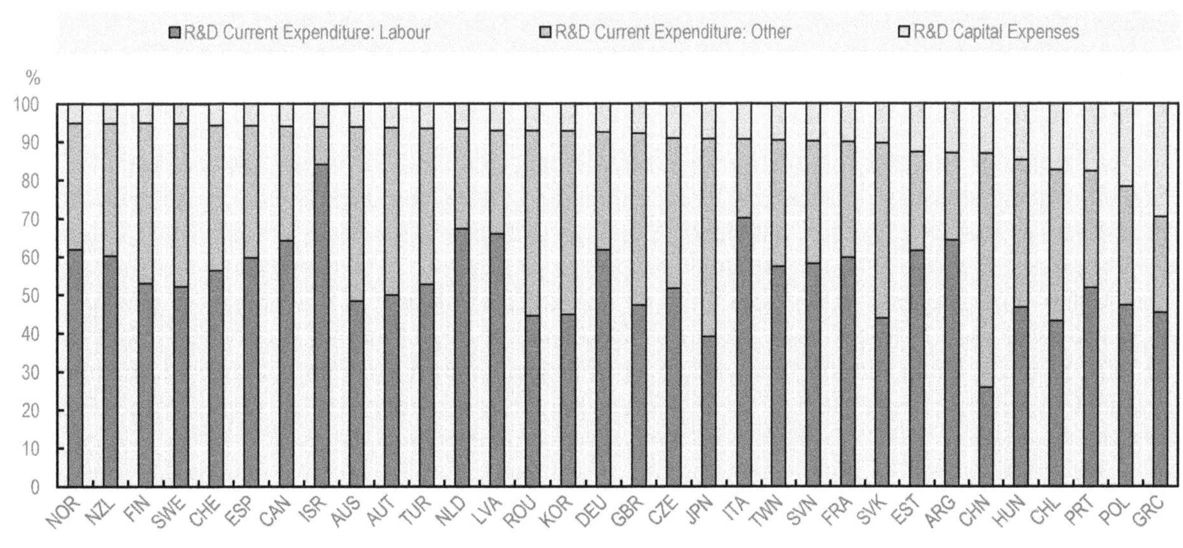


Note: The definitions used in the graph are based on the Frascati Manual. Current expenditures are composed of labour costs of R&D personnel and other current costs used in R&D. Other current expenditures are defined in the Frascati Manual 4.23 as those non-capital purchases of materials, supplies, equipment and services to support R&D, including external R&D personnel. Country coverage for this indicator is limited to those available in the OECD R&D Statistics. The underlying data refers to the latest year available, mostly to the year 2017. The data in the graph refers to 2018 for Chinese Taipei, Japan and Korea, 2016 for Argentina, Chile, Estonia, Latvia, Poland and United Kingdom; to 2013 France and New Zealand; to 2011 for China; and to 2009 for the Netherlands.
Source: OECD, R&D Statistics, September 2020.

369. The set of available innovation policies is broad enough to enable governments to respond flexibly and adapt their policy mix to these structural changes in the international tax environment if there is a concern about the level of innovation in their economies.[35] After all, incentives through the tax system are only one instrument in the policy toolbox of governments. For example, direct support measures could still be employed.[36] However, even within the tax system, tax incentives delivered through the CIT are not the only instruments available to governments to support innovation. First, expenditure-based tax incentives that provide relief to payroll taxes or social security contributions will, in principle, be unaffected, as they do not depend on corporate income taxes. These types of incentives provide an immediate subsidy to labour costs, a key component for R&D making up around 60% in R&D statistics, as shown in Figure 4.9.

Figure 4.10. R&D active innovative firms as a percentage of innovation-active firms, 2016

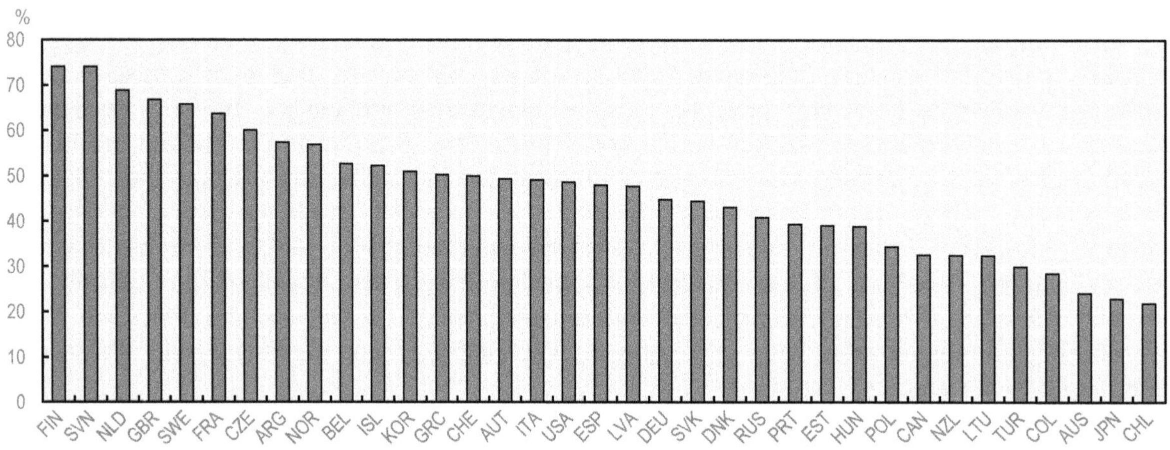


Note: The indicator refers to product or process innovative firms. Data covers OECD and partner economies. Data on Israel, Mexico, Ireland and Luxembourg are not available. The statistics for Colombia and Argentina refer to the manufacturing sector.
Source: OECD, based on the 2019 OECD survey of national innovation statistics and the Eurostat's Community Innovation Survey (CIS-2016), http://oe.cd/inno-stats, January 2020. Data and notes available here: https://www.oecd.org/sti/inno/innovation-indicators-2019.zip

370. Second, there are other tax instruments beyond targeted R&D tax incentives that can be used to promote innovation activities. In fact, the type of innovation activities firms conduct varies by country, across industries and firm types (Castellacci, 2008[93]; Galindo-Rueda and Verger, 2016[94]; Galindo-Rueda, Verger and Ouellet, 2020[95]), and thus the optimal policy mix. Among innovation–active firms, the share engaging in R&D averages 47% for OECD countries for which data is available, with great variability across jurisdictions, see Figure 4.10.[37] This only highlights the role of innovation activities beyond R&D. The acquisition of capital assets and knowledge typically represent a significant share of total innovation expenditures, reaching around 50% of innovation expenditures among EU jurisdictions for which this breakdown is available, with significant variation across jurisdictions (Eurostat, 2020[96]). Accelerated depreciation schemes that seek to reduce the cost of acquiring new equipment, such as hardware or software, and that appear to be effective tools in promoting investment (Ohrn, 2019[97]; Zwick and Mahon, 2017[39]) could be considered as part of the policy-mix.[38]

371. Taxation is ultimately one among many factors affecting innovation decisions. Well-functioning product, labour and capital markets, with regulations that do not overly penalise failure may all act to increase the returns to innovation (Andrews, Criscuolo and Menon, 2014[98]). A skilled workforce, an intensive innovative environment, stable macroeconomic and regulatory conditions, competition and openness to trade and policies that help surmount innovation barriers (e.g., regulatory barriers to competition or insufficient human capital) are all key elements in the development of a sound innovation

environment (Bloom, Van Reenen and Williams, 2019[99]; OECD, 2015[100]; OECD, 2010[101]). Notwithstanding the limitations that the Pillar One and Pillar Two reforms will impose upon the use of CIT-related tax incentives, governments will continue to be able to draw upon a wider range of instruments to rebalance the innovation policy-mix to mitigate any impact on the support that firms affected by the new rules are receiving, if deemed necessary.

372. Although the new rules, especially minimum effective taxation under Pillar Two, could limit the generosity of some tax incentives for R&D and innovation under specific conditions, they will also curtail the potential tax gains from profit shifting through the strategic location of IP assets. This will dampen the incentives for governments to engage in tax competition over mobile tax bases. To the extent to which the location of R&D and innovation-related activities was previously driven by tax considerations, rather than other commercial considerations, the new rules would, therefore, be expected to support an efficiency-increasing relocation of these activities. This effect further strengthens and reinforces the impacts of the reduction in ETR differentials on the efficiency of the international allocation of capital, as discussed in Section 4.4. Taken together, these changes in the incentive structure faced by MNEs and governments are thus likely to lead to a more efficient location of innovation activities, and investments more generally, which would be more strongly affected by non-tax considerations related to wider business and economic conditions.

### *4.7.5. Tax incentives to support economic development*

373. Foreign Direct Investment (FDI) can play an important role in promoting economic development due to its potential to generate positive external effects in the local economy, e.g., through a spillover in knowledge and expertise to local workers and businesses. Governments use investment tax incentives to influence the size as well as the sectoral or regional location of FDI, with the aim[39] of, e.g., creating jobs and boosting exports in their jurisdiction (see Box 4.5).[40]

374. Jurisdictions differ with respect to their general tax structures and the type of incentives used. Low income jurisdictions (or developing countries), in particular, collect much less tax revenue as a share of GDP compared to higher income jurisdictions, an empirical finding that is often related to a lack of administrative capacity (Besley and Persson, 2014[48]). Given prevailing differences in public infrastructure, human capital and the general business environment, their comparative advantage are typically cost-related, e.g., larger labour cost differentials or lower corporate taxation (Vukšić, 2013[102]). Against this background, high income jurisdictions tend to rely more on R&D-related tax incentives, which are typically narrower in scope and more reliant on administrative capacity, while low income jurisdictions often resort to more generous tax incentives such as, e.g., tax holidays or exemptions, which are broader in scope but require less capacity to administer (IMF-OECD-UN-World Bank, 2015[103]). In some cases, tax incentives are combined with other measures, e.g., policies aimed at creating a favourable business and legal environment, in a Special Economic Zone (SEZ), an approach that is also more prevalent in low- and middle-income jurisdictions (Figure 4.11).

Figure 4.11. Special economic zones (SEZs) by income group

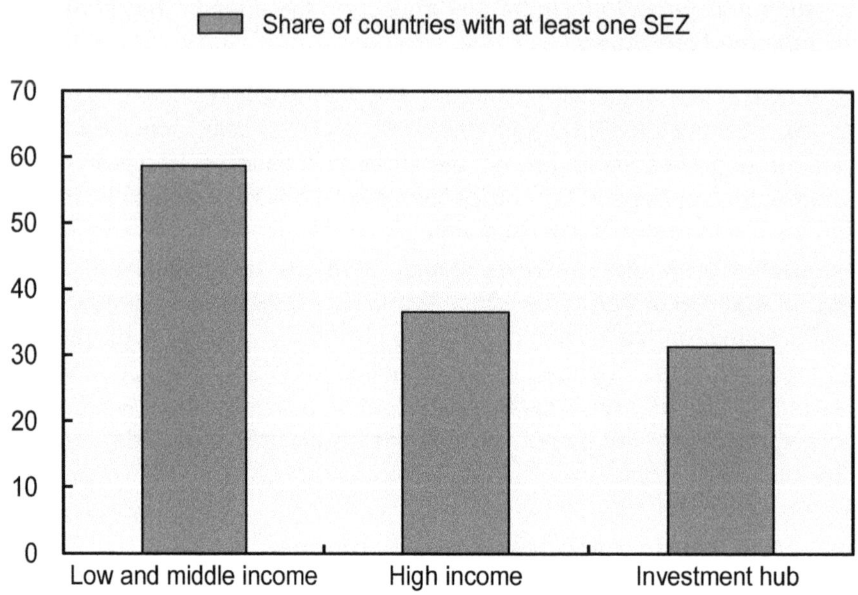


Source: UNCTAD (2019).
Note: Special economic zones does not include logistic hubs.

375. Under certain conditions the new tax rules proposed could serve to limit the ability of government to provide generous tax incentives, including investment tax incentives. In particular, tax provisions under Pillar Two are aimed at ensuring a minimum level of effective taxation. This implies that the maximum level of tax benefits that governments can provide to foreign investors will be limited because other jurisdictions (e.g., in the case of the application of the IIR, the ultimate parent jurisdiction) will be able to apply a top-up tax to the low-taxed profits in order to bring effective tax rates at the jurisdictional level up to the minimum rate. While the minimum tax rate could also become binding in the case of very generous credits and allowances, this effect will be most significant for the most generous tax incentives, such as corporate tax holidays and exemptions, which often reduce CIT liabilities to zero, either indefinitely or for a defined period. Tax provisions introduced under Pillar One are less likely to limit the tax benefits obtained through investment tax incentives since a potential reallocation of tax bases will be determined at the MNE group or segment level and entail the reallocation of only a share of residual profit. However, even after the implementation of Pillar One and Pillar Two, governments will still be able to use tax incentives as before to attract FDI as long as effective tax rates do not fall below the minimum rate at the jurisdictional level.

376. Although the potential limitation in the generosity of tax incentives could reduce the scope of policy instruments available to governments to attract foreign investment, it is unlikely to produce efficiency losses at the jurisdiction or global level. First, the effect of tax incentives on cost differentials across jurisdictions could be smaller than anticipated if tax competition induces an increasing number of jurisdictions to offer incentives, leading to a level effect without creating a comparative advantage for any particular jurisdiction. Second, tax incentives may induce distortions across different investments and may result in windfall gains for projects that would already have taken place in absence of the incentives. Third, competitive pressure is likely to be stronger in developing countries due to the resource requirements associated with the administration, auditing and evaluation of targeted regimes based on a narrower scope, thus further limiting potential resource mobilisation. Fourth, reductions in domestic resources available to governments in developing countries are unlikely to be compensated by increases at the global level if investment is merely

relocated to other jurisdictions with similar economic characteristics. There is therefore a risk that tax incentives fail to achieve the stated policy objectives at the jurisdictional level while at the same time leading to a globally inefficient allocation of capital.

377. In line with these arguments, the literature finds only limited evidence of the effectiveness of tax incentives in terms of attracting additional FDI. On the one hand, the existing literature typically does not investigate whether investment tax incentives obtained in a specific jurisdiction lead to an increase in global investment of a given MNE group, e.g., driven by a reduction in the effective tax rate at the group level. On the other hand, even at the jurisdiction level, there is only mixed evidence of their effectiveness in attracting foreign investment (Box 4.5 and Hajkova et al. (2006[4])).

378. However, even if they succeed in attracting investment, tax incentives are not necessarily the most cost-efficient use of public funds dedicated to investment promotion. The net benefits of investment tax incentives, taking into account forgone tax revenue, are often not well understood, due to capacity constraints and/or lack of thorough evaluation. These constraints are of particular relevance for developing countries, where reliable information on revenue forgone is often not available. As tax revenues are a key source of finance to deliver often lacking public goods and services in developing countries, such as education and skills development, health and infrastructure, it is possible that alternative policies[41] would deliver superior results in terms of investment, growth and sustainable development.

Figure 4.12. Distribution of statutory CIT rates by income group

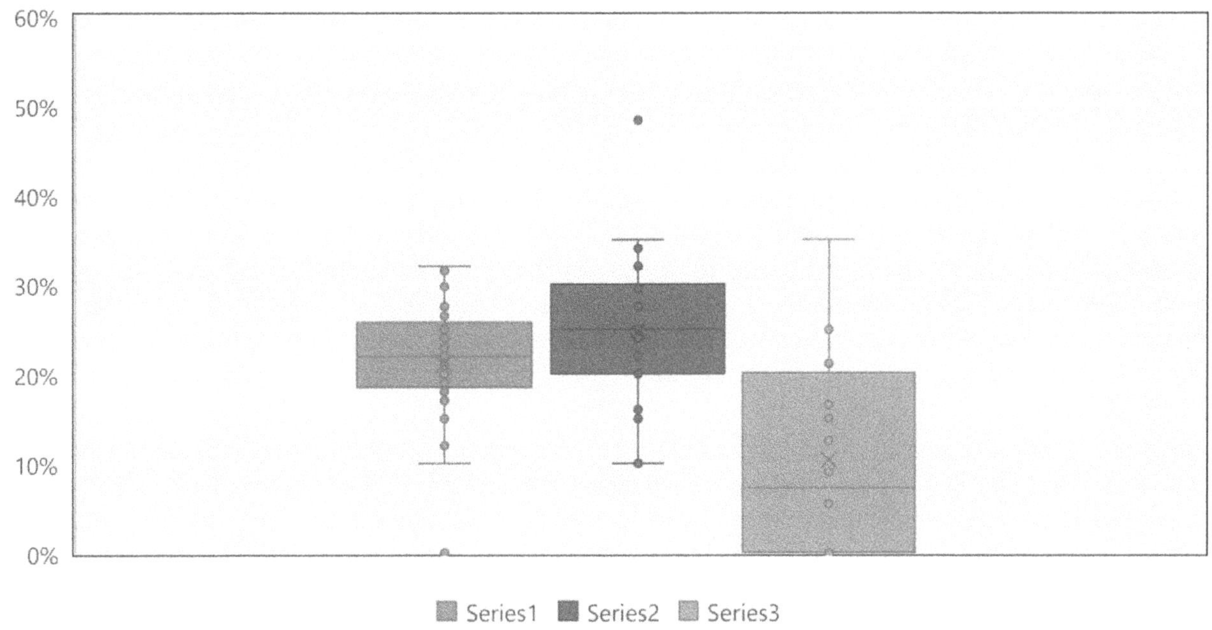


Note: For each of the income groups, the boxplot shows the 25th percentile (lower edge of the box), the median (straight line in the box) and the 75th percentile (upper edge of the box); the mean is indicated by a cross and each circle corresponds to an observation.
Source: OECD Corporate Tax Statistics.

379. Irrespective of the cost-efficiency and effectiveness of tax incentives in general, developing countries will have substantial policy space to support foreign investment through their corporate tax systems, even after the introduction of the proposed rules. Figure 4.12 shows that, based on the most recent available data, statutory CIT rates are highest, on average, in lower and lower middle income countries; forward-looking effective average tax rates, taking into account standard components of corporate tax bases, also tend to be higher in developing countries (OECD, 2020[15]). On average, in developing countries both types of rates are generally well above the minimum effective tax thresholds that are currently being debated (Figure 4.12). Developing countries therefore retain considerable policy

space for the use of tax incentives, even after the implementation of Pillar One and Two, especially compared to emerging or advanced economies. As with R&D tax incentives discussed above, governments will continue to be able to rely upon investment tax incentives to incentivise the location of FDI in their jurisdiction as long as the resulting effective tax rates do not fall below the minimum threshold. Given that in a number of developing countries current incentive regimes are very generous, e.g. relying mainly on tax holidays and exemptions, an adaptation of investment promotion strategies towards a cost-efficient use of tax incentives could thus be a key priority for developing countries aiming to promote economic development in the context of the evolving international tax system.

380. Taken together, the available evidence suggests that, in the absence of otherwise attractive economic conditions, the cost-efficiency and effectiveness of tax incentives is limited. Moreover, tax incentives could increase tax competition and undermine domestic revenue mobilisation efforts, especially in developing countries. Against this background, the introduction of the new tax rules under Pillar One and Pillar Two could strengthen the bargaining position of developing countries wanting to move away from certain, particularly costly, policy choices that deliver unclear net benefits. A reduced reliance on tax incentives would imply, in turn, that MNE location decisions are more affected by commercial considerations, instead of tax considerations, thereby potentially reinforcing positive effects on the efficiency of international capital allocation, as discussed in the context of R&D tax incentives and, more generally, in the Section 4.4.

### Box 4.5. Investment tax incentives and sustainable development

Foreign direct investment (FDI) can play an important role in promoting development. FDI can serve as a conduit for the diffusion of technology and skills that can raise productivity, create jobs, boost exports, trigger innovation and, more generally, advance progress towards sustainable development (Javorcik, 2004[104]; Farole and Winkler, 2014[105]; OECD, 2019[106]).

Tax incentives are widely used policy tools – in developed and developing countries – to attract investment and influence its size, location or industry. Low and middle-income countries – with on average, higher statutory CIT rates (Figure 4.12) – tend to offer higher tax reductions to attract investment (IMF-OECD-UN-World Bank, 2015[103]). Competition among developing countries to attract investment has resulted in increasingly generous special tax regimes, as jurisdictions move to match or surpass tax incentives offered by other jurisdictions and bring ETRs faced by some firms to very low levels (Abbas and Klemm, 2013[107]; World Bank, 2017[108]; Wiedemann and Finke, 2015[109]; World Bank, 2017[108]).

However, developing and developed economies' tax incentives regimes typically differ in design, with the former relying more on tax holidays, exemptions and reduced rates, and the latter offering less generous allowances and credits often linked to specific R&D-related activities (James, 2013[110]). These design differences have been found to play a significant role in determining the effectiveness of tax incentives in terms of achieving their intended policy objectives (IMF-OECD-UN-World Bank, 2015[103]; OECD, 2015[111]; Wells et al., 2001[112]).

Empirical findings on the effectiveness of tax incentives in attracting FDI in developing countries is mixed, which, in part, may be due to the difficulty in disentangling the relevance of taxation within the broader policy mix and accurately capturing their net cost-benefit (Feld and Heckemeyer, 2011[6]) (Redonda and Neubig, 2018[113]). According to one study, lower statutory CIT rates and longer tax holidays are associated with additional FDI in Latin America and the Caribbean (LAC) countries, but not among African ones, indicating that additional factors may interact with how effective incentives are (Klemm and Van Parys, 2012[64]). Although a positive correlation has also been found in studies, the boost to investment provided by tax incentives appears to occur at a low rate (Abbas and Klemm, 2013[107]). FDI motivation may play a role in explaining the variation in findings across studies. For example, export-platform FDI of US MNEs was found to be more sensitive to host country taxation, particularly in developing countries (Mutti and Grubert, 2004[114]; Azémar and Desbordes, 2010[115]).

Competition may lead to only a limited relative change in the tax rate differential across jurisdictions, i.e., their competitive advantage in terms of investment costs. In Asia-Pacific, for example, special tax regime ETRs were found to result in a reduction of a similar magnitude across jurisdictions compared to their statutory rates - a parallel downward shift (Wiedemann and Finke, 2015[109]). Li (2016[116]) confirms this idea, finding evidence of a parallel downward shift of sub-central tax rates within countries due to regional competition.

International investors typically do not cite tax incentives among the most important factors to determine investment location decisions, relative to the infrastructure they offer, as well as the simplified regulatory framework that facilitates creating and running businesses (UNIDO, 2013[117]; IMF-OECD, 2017[118]; Canh et al., 2013[119]). Soft and hard infrastructure were found to be highly correlated with the presence of a foreign investor, in particular export-oriented ones based on firm-level data from 77 developing countries (Kinda, 2010[120]). Countries are likely to benefit most from tax incentives when combined with a strong investment climate, macroeconomic stability, market access and clear intellectual property rights (Thomsen, 2004[121]).

Special economic zones (SEZs) – more common in low and middle-income countries (Figure 4.11) – often provide the most generous special tax regime within a country. SEZs offer a package of benefits to investors including tax incentives (98% of SEZs), special customs regimes (94%) and others (UNCTAD, 2019[122]). SEZs can act as hubs to attract FDI and when linkages develop with the rest of economy, generate economic growth and positive spillovers on the broader economy (Wang, 2013[123]; Chaurey, 2017[124]). Despite their prevalence, econometric studies find limited evidence of tax incentives as the main determinant for investing in the zone (Hsu et al., 2019[125]; Lin and Wang, 2014[126]) or of their positive spillovers on the rest of the economy.

### *4.7.6. Firm competition and investment*

381. Recent research suggests that structural economic changes related to digitalisation and globalisation have important effects on firm concentration and price-cost mark-ups at market and industry level. While the debate on these effects is not settled, evidence from the last several decades suggests that, in certain countries and industries, fewer firms account for a higher share of revenues, output and/or employment (see Box 4.6). In particular, several empirical studies suggest that these developments are mostly driven by the highly digitalised sectors of the economy, as network effects give rise to winner-takes-all (or winner-takes-most) dynamics allowing some firms to gain competitive advantages (Bauer and Latzer, 2016[127]) (OECD, 2018[128]) (OECD, 2019[129]). To the extent that these findings are associated with a decrease in the intensity of competition among firms,[42] they could imply a reduction in consumer welfare, as well as business investment, innovation and productivity growth (Gutiérrez and Philippon, 2017[130]).

382. The Pillar One and Pillar Two proposals are not targeted to influence competition dynamics among firms, as this is primarily the focus of competition and regulatory policies rather than tax policy. Nevertheless, from a tax perspective, Pillar One and Pillar Two would contribute to a more even playing field among MNEs, and between MNEs and non-MNE firms. In turn, this could contribute to reducing, or at least slowing down the trend towards greater concentration and other potentially adverse effects associated with such concentration.

383. The impact of the proposals differs across firms due to the thresholds and scope restrictions embedded in the new provisions. The design of Pillar One is targeted towards MNEs based on their size, through the global revenue threshold, and their profitability, through the profitability threshold (see Pillar One Blueprint report (OECD, 2020[13])) in addition, its application is potentially limited to businesses providing automated digitalised services (ADS) and consumer facing businesses (CFB). The new provisions under Pillar One, therefore, target the largest and most profitable MNEs - these are the firms that have been most strongly associated with the secular trends towards firm concentration and price-cost

mark-ups (Calligaris, Criscuolo and Marcolin (2018[2]); Bailin Rivares et al. (2019[131])). Under Pillar Two, no sector-specific scope restrictions are considered. However, the new provisions introduced to ensure minimum effective taxation will imply that those MNEs engaging in profit shifting to low-tax jurisdictions will experience larger increases in their tax liabilities under Pillar Two, in line with the policy intention to address remaining concerns about base erosion and profit shifting (BEPS). Since larger MNEs tend to engage more in tax planning and related tax savings could be used to crowd out other firms (Sorbe and Johansson, 2017[132]), the expected reduction in profit shifting due to the new tax rules, and Pillar Two in particular, could further counteract the observed trends in concentration.

384. The impacts of Pillars One and Two reinforce each other, possibly contributing to a dampening of the trend towards greater concentration at market and industry level. As large and profitable MNEs, especially those who are engaging in profit shifting, will be affected the most, the new rules are expected to produce a more level playing field among MNEs, and vis-à-vis their smaller and domestic competitors, as well as those firms not engaging in profit shifting. If less concentrated markets and industries are indeed associated with more business investment and innovation, the reform could have additional positive effects on growth through this channel. However, tax policy is only one among many factors affecting concentration dynamics; its quantitative impact also depends on the wider competition and regulatory policy context.

### Box 4.6. Firm competition and investment

An avenue through which the proposals could affect investment and growth is through their impacts on competition intensity and market power and, as a consequence, on investment. The proposals are likely to impact firms that are able to impose mark-ups by virtue of their strong market positions, and firms that have more opportunities to engage in tax planning. To the extent that the proposals reduce incentives and opportunities to engage in profit shifting, and raise effective tax rates on those firms earning higher mark-ups, they may level the playing field between different kinds of firms. As firms may have lower incentives to invest and innovate where they have a dominant market position, this more level playing field may in turn raise investment levels (Gutiérrez and Philippon, 2019[42]).

There is an expanding literature pointing to increasing market concentration and declining competition intensity, although this topic is still the subject of extensive academic debate (see Syverson (2019[133]) for a review). Furman and Orszag (2015[134]) and Autor et al. (2017[43]) (2020[135]) point to evidence of increased concentration and declining competition intensity in the United States in particular. Bajgar et al. (2019[41]), find that increased concentration is also present outside the United States. De Loecker, Eeckhout and Unger (2020[136]) point to increased market power by examining both mark-ups and profitability, and find a reallocation of market share from firms with low mark-ups to those with high mark-ups.

Several recent empirical papers suggest that increases in market power are more pronounced in highly digitalised sectors of the economy. Network effects in the digital sector may mean that some firms are able to gain competitive advantages over other firms and discourage entry by smaller firms (Bauer and Latzer, 2016[127]) (OECD, 2018[128]) (OECD, 2019[129]). For example, Bailin Rivares et. al. (2019[131]) find high levels of concentration among online platforms. Calligaris, Criscuolo and Marcolin (2018[2]) point to evidence of higher mark-ups in digital-intensive sectors as evidence of reduced competition. Some papers in the literature have also related higher mark-ups to tax planning. Sorbe and Johansson (2017[132]) find that tax-planning multinationals have higher mark-up rates than other firms, even after controlling for other factors influencing mark-ups. They note that the direction of causality is difficult to establish, since a high mark-up can be a factor encouraging a firm to engage in tax planning.

This expanding evidence of increased industry concentration, market power and higher mark-ups has been related by some authors to investment. Gutiérrez and Philippon (2019[137]; 2017[130]) attribute low investment levels to a variety of factors, significant among which is expansion of market concentration and a weakening of the competitive environment. They find that firm concentration and governance issues account for 75% of the investment gap in their analysis, and that those industries with higher degrees of concentration are characterised by lower levels of investment, even after controlling for current market conditions and the intangible intensity of the industry. They also find that firms driving the investment gap return a disproportionate amount of free cash flow to shareholders. Increased concentration patterns have also been found in Europe. However, other papers suggest that market power may be a result of increased investment in intangibles by some firms, which may be efficiency enhancing (Crouzet and Eberly, 2019[138]).

Pillar Two focuses on firms with lower ETRs, which are likely to be firms engaging in aggressive tax planning and profit shifting. This suggests that the implementation of the proposals could help level the playing field between firms with better access to tax planning opportunities, and more specifically, those engaging in profit shifting compared to other firms. For the reasons set out above regarding the potential linkages between market concentration and investment levels, this may in turn have a positive impact on investment.

## 4.8. Impacts on investment and output with and without a multilateral consensus

385. Sections 4.3 to 4.7 have been devoted to a detailed discussion of the investment effects of the proposals, based on new empirical research as well as insights drawn from the economic literature. This section brings together the main results from these analyses to form an overall assessment of these proposals if they were to become a consensus-based solution. This consensus scenario also assumes the withdrawal of existing DSTs as well as a commitment to refrain from introducing such measures in the future. To conduct a meaningful evaluation of the consensus scenario, however, this assessment needs to compare this outcome with a plausible counterfactual. It would be incorrect to assume that this counterfactual looks like the status quo; instead, the consensus scenario should be evaluated against a scenario reflecting the projected state of the global economy in the event that a consensus-based solution to address the tax challenges arising from digitalisation cannot be secured through the multilateral process of the Inclusive Framework. Equally important, both sets of scenarios should acknowledge the fact that the baseline scenario, reflecting the situation before potential implementation of the reforms, has changed due to the COVID-19 pandemic. While Box 4.1 discusses how the pandemic and its economic implications affect the evaluation, the following two subsections provide a qualitative discussion of the consensus and no-consensus scenarios before developing quantitative estimates for both sets of scenarios by drawing on a range of additional modelling tools as well as results from the related literature.

### *4.8.1. Global economic implications if consensus is reached*

386. Taking stock of the findings presented in Sections 4.3 to 4.7, several main insights emerge in relation to the expected investment effects at the group and entity level, as summarised in Figure 4.13. To begin with, it is worth highlighting that the proposals operate at the MNE group level, determining tax bases based on the global performance of the MNE group as a whole rather than on a separate entity basis. Depending on the final policy design, the inclusion of a number of scope restrictions would imply that the effects of Pillar One and Pillar Two on investment costs would be limited to a subset of MNEs. It is currently proposed that the scope of Pillar One is limited to MNE groups that perform ADS and CFB activities, and by a profitability threshold that targets the impact of the rules to more profitable MNEs, and by a revenue threshold that targets larger MNE groups. Pillar Two, on the other hand, is focussed on large MNEs

achieving low effective tax rates at the jurisdictional level. Particularly, where a formulaic substance-based carve-out is provided, it is likely that these rules will mainly affect firms engaging in profit shifting.

### *MNE responses at entity level*

387. Additional tax liabilities at the MNE group level lead to higher tax payments by some affiliated entities, thereby increasing investment costs at the entity level within the affected MNE groups.[43] In the case of Pillar Two, MNE entities that would otherwise have realised ETRs below the minimum threshold could face an increase in investment costs. In line with the literature on the tax sensitivity of foreign and domestic investment, the empirical estimates suggest that affected MNEs will respond to potential cost increases by reducing or relocating some of their investments. As a consequence, the proposals could lead to investment relocation away from low-tax jurisdictions, however, relocation across jurisdictions does not necessitate a reduction in global investment if it is linked to an investment increase in another location.[44] As discussed in Section 4.4, relocation can increase the efficiency of capital allocation across jurisdictions, in situations where investment decisions were previously driven by tax considerations. A more cost-efficient use of tax incentives could reinforce positive effects on capital allocation. In addition, entities in more profitable MNE groups may be less sensitive to tax increases, suggesting that relocation of investments may be lower for entities in MNE groups affected by the reforms compared to entities in an average MNE group – as discussed in Section 4.6.

### *Government responses and other indirect effects on investment*

388. As the discussion in Section 4.7 shows, potential indirect effects on investment are typically context-specific. Furthermore, indirect effects could interact, positively or negatively, with each other, thus either reinforcing or offsetting overall effects on investment at the jurisdiction level; the overall direction of these effects at the jurisdiction level therefore depends mostly on government responses to the evolving international tax system. For example, increased fiscal space could be used to increase support for business innovation or to expand tax administrations with the aim of lowering compliance costs; a more level playing field for domestic and multinational firms could be combined with additional support for young, innovative firms; lower competitive pressure on effective tax rates could facilitate the development of a different investment promotion strategy. A successful adaptation of domestic policies to the changing incentive structure could, therefore, lead to additional positive effects on global investment and economic output.

389. In particular, the analysis highlights several policy areas where the response of individual governments to the changes in the international tax system could have important effects on investment at the jurisdiction and, ultimately, the global level. To start with, investment costs would increase in jurisdictions where firms were subject to ETRs below the minimum threshold prior to the reform, either due to minimum effective taxation under Pillar Two or because low-tax jurisdictions increase their domestic ETRs. As a result, ETR differentials across jurisdictions would decrease, implying lower tax gains from relocation and thus higher relevance of non-tax factors for location decisions. In addition, lower profit shifting incentives would reduce the cost of public funds to the extent that tax administrations need to spend less on enforcement activities. Responding to this structural change, low-tax jurisdictions could decide to adapt their broader policy strategies to improve their attractiveness for foreign investment, over and above pure cost considerations. As discussed in Section 4.7, a similar response could be adopted by countries, including developing countries, where they have previously chosen to grant generous, and often inefficient, tax incentives to attract FDI, but can strengthen domestic resource mobilisation and open up more fiscal space for public investments.

390. Moreover, specific consideration should be given to policy areas where investments yield positive externalities, as tax policies are often used to address concerns about underinvestment in such contexts. While spillover effects from FDI could also yield positive effects on local economies, the main policy area

where external effects are expected to be quantitatively relevant is innovation and, in particular, business R&D. Section 4.7 has presented in-depth discussions of various tax and non-tax policies aimed at supporting innovation and their effectiveness based on empirical evidence. This analysis suggests that, while policy strategies may need to be adapted in certain jurisdictions, e.g., to bring preferential regimes in line with recommendations of the OECD/G20 Base Erosion and Profit Shifting project or to shift public support from indirect to direct support measures, a wide array of policy instruments remain available to governments after the implementation of Pillar One and Pillar Two in order to achieve their intended policy objectives.

391. Although the changing incentive structure could thus induce behavioural reactions by MNEs and governments, leading to a more efficient allocation of capital across jurisdictions, and therefore, an increase in global economic output, as summarised in Table 4.2, it is beyond the scope of this overall assessment to quantify these effects. However, in the event that some positive efficiency effects are realised at the global level due to the implementation of Pillar One and Pillar Two, these effects could be expected to, at least partially, offset any negative effects associated with higher investment costs at the MNE group level.

### Figure 4.13. Investment effects at MNE group and entity level

MNE responses at the group level and their impacts on global GDP

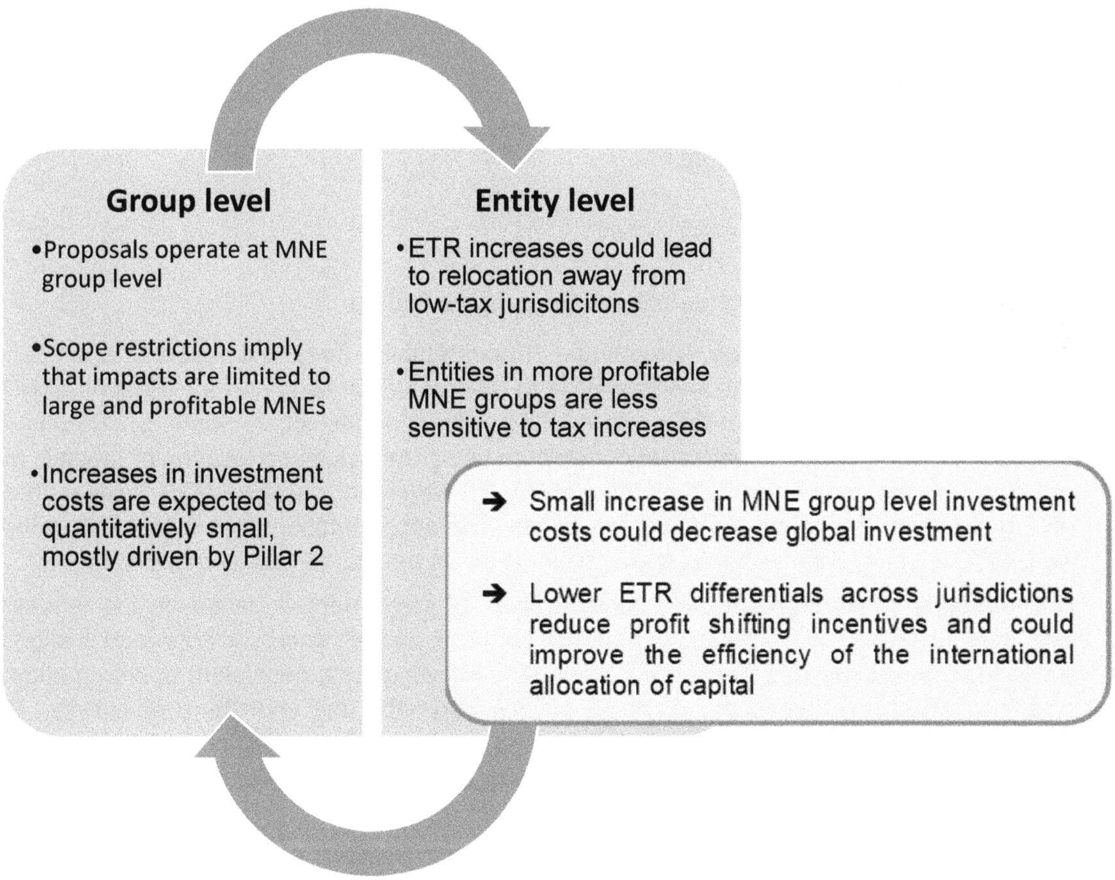


392. Turning to the analysis of investment costs at the MNE group level, the empirical results show that, on average, there are only small effects of Pillars One and Two on EATRs and EMTRs.[45] The global GDP-weighted average change in the EATRs is estimated to be just around 0.35 percentage points; the

corresponding change for the EMTR is around 1.40 percentage points, with Pillar Two driving most of this increase. Moreover, the effect on investment costs is larger for projects located in investment hubs, most of which have comparatively low effective tax rates. These results rely on the following illustrative assumptions on the design of Pillar One and Pillar Two. In Pillar One, only Amount A is modelled, assuming a 10% profitability threshold based on profit before tax over turnover, a 20% reallocation percentage to market jurisdictions and a scope restriction to ADS and CFB sectors. In modelling Pillar Two, a 12.5% rate with jurisdictional blending is assumed, including a 10% carve-out on depreciation expense (approximated using the value and location of tangible assets).

393. These results provide a starting point to explore the extent to which an eventual implementation of the Pillar One and Pillar Two proposal could lead to a reduction in the global level of MNE investment. In particular, a quantitative approximation of the overall impact on global output in the medium to long run (i.e. 10 years following implementation) can be derived by combining the empirical results from Sections 4.5 and 4.6 with additional assumptions and modelling techniques. To provide a quantitative approximation of the investment effects that is consistent with the OECD model for long-run projections,[46] an estimate of the change in the total business investment rate can be derived - this calculation is illustrated in Figure 4.14.

Figure 4.14. Estimating the change in the total business investment rate

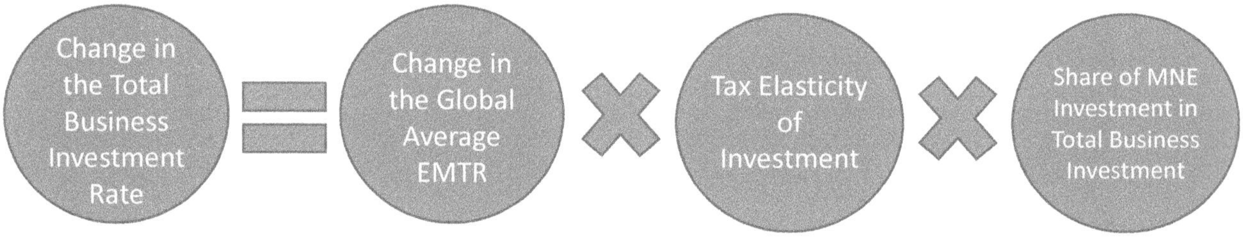


Source: OECD illustration.

394. The calculations are based on the following aggregate figures.

- **Global average EMTR change**. Assuming a 10% profitability threshold based on profit before tax over turnover, a 20% reallocation percentage to market jurisdictions and a restriction to ADS and CFB for Amount A under Pillar One and a 12.5% rate with jurisdiction blending, including a 10% carve-out on depreciation expense (approximated using the value and location of tangible assets), for Pillar Two, the combined effect on the global GDP-weighted average EMTR,[47] measured at the MNE group level, is about 1.4 percentage points. The approximation uses the EMTR, rather than the EATR, to better align with the empirical literature on the tax sensitivity of investment.
- **Tax elasticity of investment**. The tax sensitivity of investment is based on the industry-level estimates developed by Sorbe and Johansson (2017[7]), as their empirical approach is aligned with the estimates discussed in Section 4.6 while also allowing for a consistent approximation of the long-term effects on investment. Building on this approach, the short-term sensitivity, -0.05, is translated into a long-term sensitivity of -0.12, and adjusted downwards to -0.08 to account for the empirical finding that tax sensitivities are on average around 35% lower among MNE groups with profitability above 10%.[48]
- **Share of MNE investment**. The empirical results from Sections 4.5 and 4.6 refer to investment costs and elasticities of MNEs; however, not all business investment comes from MNEs. Since the MNE share in global business investment is not directly observed in the data, it is approximated[49] based on the global average MNE share in gross value added (32%), including domestic and foreign MNEs, using data from the Analytical AMNE[50] database.

395. Bringing the aggregate figures together, as shown in Figure 4.14, suggests that increasing investment costs would lead to a decline in the total business investment rate of around 0.04 percentage points (1.4*-0.08*0.32=-0.04). Although this approximation accounts for lower tax sensitivities among the MNE groups targeted by the new rules, it corresponds to an upper bound, given that the tax sensitivity does not take into account that group level responses are likely to be smaller due to relocation of investment within the group. Further, this tentative approximation is subject to a number of caveats that have been highlighted in relation to the underlying empirical work discussed throughout this chapter (Millot et al. (2020[44]), Hanappi and González Cabral (2020[12]).

396. Once the change in the total business investment rate has been estimated, it can be used to approximate the GDP change, using a stylised framework consistent with the OECD model for long-run economic projections (see Box 4.7 for a brief description of the modelling approach). Based on this approach the change in the investment rate, -0.04, thus translates into a reduction in GDP of around 0.07% over a medium- to long-term horizon.

397. While the above calculation represents only a simple approximation of the likely effects on GDP, a sensitivity analysis can be conducted to understand how the quantitative result would change with respect to some of the underlying assumptions. Specifically, the same calculation can be done using the average tax sensitivity of investment, -0.12, without adjusting downwards to account for the lower tax sensitivity of highly profitable MNEs. In this case, the change in the investment rate is estimated to be -0.05 (1.4*-0.12*0.32=-0.05), leading to a slightly higher reduction in GDP, i.e., 0.11% over the same horizon. Alternatively, the change in the EATR can be used, instead of the EMTR, to approximate the impacts of the proposals on backward-looking ETRs. Using the change in the global GDP-weighted average EATR, 0.35 percentage points, as a basis for the approximation would result in a significantly less negative effect on GDP, i.e., -0.02% over the same horizon.

### Box 4.7. Assumptions to model long-run economic impacts

The impacts of a reduction in the investment rate on GDP can be assessed based on the following framework that can be seen as a stylised and simplified version of the OECD model for long-run economic projections. Production in the economy is assumed to be a Cobb-Douglas function of capital $K$ and labour $L$, with labour share, $1-\alpha$.

$$Y_t = AK_t^{\alpha}L^{1-\alpha}$$

In this equation, $A$ represents total factor productivity (TFP). Capital depreciates at a constant rate, $\delta$, so that its evolution is determined by the accumulation equation.

$$K_{t+1} = (1-\delta)K_t + I_{t+1}$$

$I_{t+1}$ represents investment, which is assumed to be a constant share, $\gamma$, of GDP, $I_{t+1} = \gamma Y_t$. Given that in the steady state the investment rate is fixed to the level of the depreciation rate, $\frac{I}{K} = \delta$, the fall in investment is implemented as a permanent reduction in the investment-to-GDP ratio, $\gamma$. To align the parameters with the OECD long-term model, it is assumed that the capital-to-output ratio equals 1.5, $\frac{K}{Y} = 1.5$, implying that a shock of $\epsilon$ on the investment rate, $\frac{I}{K}$, as derived in the econometric estimations, can be translated as a permanent reduction in $\gamma$ of $1.5 \cdot \epsilon$ . The shock is implemented starting from a situation where the economy is in its steady state, with the initial parameters set at $\alpha = 0.24$, $\delta = 5\%$ (per year) and $\gamma = 7.5\%$ before the shock.

398. Taken together, the two main channels through which the proposals affect global investment and output are, first, an increase in investment costs at the MNE group level, reducing global investment levels and, second, a reduction in ETR differentials, reducing profit shifting and improving the global capital

allocation across jurisdictions. The first effect is negative and a tentative quantification suggests that it could lead to a reduction of global GDP by less than 0.1%. However, there could be a second, countervailing effect on global GDP if capital allocation across jurisdictions becomes more efficient; however, the extent to which this would be the case depends on individual governments' policy responses to the evolving international tax system as well as on MNE responses along other decision margins, e.g., with respect to their organisational structure. Since these effects are difficult to quantify, only the effect of the first channel has been modelled in this quantitative assessment.

### Table 4.1. Consensus scenario: Summary

| Direct Effects on Investment | Indirect Effects | Summary |
|---|---|---|
| Scope restrictions imply that many MNEs will be unaffected and increases in investment costs are targeted to highly-profitable MNE groups and those engaged in profit shifting | Fiscal space increases for most jurisdictions and lower profit shifting incentives could make it easier to raise additional public funds | Increases in investment costs could induce a small reduction in global investment |
| Increases in investment costs are expected to be quantitatively small, mostly driven by Pillar Two | Compliance and administration costs could increase, but this potential increase would likely be lower than in a situation without agreement | This could lead to a reduction in global GDP by less than 0.1%, which may be partly or fully offset by positive indirect effects |
| ETR increases at the entity level may lead to some relocation away from low-tax jurisdictions | Indirect effects are often context-specific and adaptation of policy mixes may be required in certain jurisdictions | Policy adaptations may be needed in certain jurisdictions in response to changes in the international tax system |
| Entities in more profitable MNE groups are less sensitive to tax increases | Many policy instruments remain available after implementation of Pillar One and Pillar Two to achieve intended policy objectives | |
| Reduction in ETR differentials across jurisdictions is likely to reduce the incentives for profit shifting and could improve the efficiency of the international allocation of capital | Economic efficiency could increase, e.g., if firm competition is strengthened | A consensus-based multilateral solution would lead to a more favourable environment for investment and growth than would likely be the case in the absence of an agreement |

Source: OECD illustration.

### *4.8.2. Global economic implications if no consensus is reached*

399. The tax challenges arising from digitalisation were described in detail in the BEPS Action 1 Report (OECD, 2015[139]). Although the report considered several options to address these challenges, no agreement was reached at the time. Subsequently, the *Tax Challenges Arising from Digitalisation – Interim Report 2018* noted that changes to the international tax rules were required and that a coherent and concurrent review of two key aspects of the existing framework, the nexus and profit allocation rules, should be undertaken with the view towards a global consensus in 2020 (OECD, 2018[128]).

400. As stated in the Interim Report, some jurisdictions adopted the position that, in the absence of a consensus-based global solution, interim measures to address concerns about the tax challenges arising from digitalisation would likely be implemented on a unilateral basis. Notwithstanding the fact that diverging positions existed on both the merits of and the need for interim measures such as transaction-specific digital services taxes (DSTs), an increasing number of jurisdictions have implemented or are considering the implementation of DSTs. In addition, a number of jurisdictions have introduced other unilateral measures including alternative applications of the permanent establishment (PE) threshold, withholding taxes or specific regimes targeting large MNEs, e.g., diverted profit taxes. While these additional unilateral measures are not included, Table 4.2 presents an overview of jurisdictions that have either legislated or are considering the implementation of a DST or similar measure.

## Table 4.2. Digital services taxes and similar measures

| Jurisdiction | Measure | Rate | Status |
|---|---|---|---|
| Austria | Digital Advertisement Tax | 5.0% | Effective |
| France | Digital Services Tax | 3.0% | Effective (collection postponed) |
| Hungary | Digital Advertisement Tax | 7.5% | Effective (0% until Dec 2022) |
| India | Equalisation levy | 2 and 6% | Effective |
| Indonesia | Electronic transaction tax | TBD | Legislated |
| Italy | Digital Services Tax | 3.0% | Effective |
| Tunisia | Digital Services Tax | 3.0% | Legislated |
| Turkey | Digital Services Tax | 7.5% | Effective |
| United Kingdom | Digital Services Tax | 2.0% | Legislated |
| Australia | Tax on digital services or similar measure in the event of no international solution | - | Under Consideration |
| Belgium | Tax on digital services or similar measure at EU level in the event of no international solution | - | Under Consideration |
| Bulgaria | Tax on digital services or similar measure at EU level in the event of no international solution | - | Under Consideration (EU) |
| Brazil | Digital Services Tax | 1 to 5% | Under Consideration |
| Croatia | Tax on digital services or similar measure at EU level in the event of no international solution | - | Under Consideration (EU) |
| Cyprus[51] | Tax on digital services or similar measure at EU level in the event of no international solution | - | Under Consideration (EU) |
| Czech Republic | DST or similar measure at EU or national level in the event of no international solution | 7.0% | Under Consideration |
| Denmark | Tax on digital services or similar measure at EU level in the event of no international solution | - | Under Consideration (EU) |
| Estonia | Tax on digital services or similar measure at EU level in the event of no international solution | - | Under Consideration (EU) |
| Finland | Tax on digital services or similar measure at EU level in the event of no international solution | - | Under Consideration (EU) |
| Germany | Tax on digital services or similar measure at EU level in the event of no international solution | - | Under Consideration (EU) |
| Greece | Tax on digital services or similar measure at EU level in the event of no international solution | - | Under Consideration (EU) |
| Ireland | Tax on digital services or similar measure at EU level in the event of no international solution | - | Under Consideration (EU) |
| Israel | Tax on digital services or similar measure in the event of no international solution | 3 or 5% | Under Consideration |
| Kenya | Digital Services Tax | 1.5% | Under Consideration |
| Latvia | DST or similar measure at EU or national level in the event of no international solution | 3.0% | Under Consideration |
| Lithuania | Tax on digital services or similar measure at EU level in the event of no international solution | - | Under Consideration (EU) |
| Luxembourg | Tax on digital services or similar measure at EU level in the event of no international solution | - | Under Consideration (EU) |
| Malta | Tax on digital services or similar measure at EU level in the event of no international solution | - | Under Consideration (EU) |
| Netherlands | Tax on digital services or similar measure at EU level in the event of no international solution | - | Under Consideration (EU) |
| New Zealand | Tax on digital services or similar measure in the event of no international solution | 3.0% | Under Consideration |
| Norway | Tax on digital services or similar measure in the event of no international solution | - | Under Consideration |
| Philippines | Digital Services Tax | - | Under Consideration |
| Poland | Tax on digital services or similar measure at EU level in the event of no international solution | - | Under Consideration |

| | | | |
|---|---|---|---|
| Portugal | Tax on digital services or similar measure at EU level in the event of no international solution | - | Under Consideration (EU) |
| Romania | Tax on digital services or similar measure at EU level in the event of no international solution | - | Under Consideration (EU) |
| Russia | Tax on digital services or similar measure in the event of no international solution | | Under Consideration |
| Slovakia | Tax on digital services or similar measure at EU level in the event of no international solution | - | Under Consideration (EU) |
| Slovenia | DST or similar measure at EU or national level in the event of no international solution | 3.0% | Under Consideration |
| Spain | DST or similar measure at EU or national level in the event of no international solution | 3.0% | Under Consideration |
| Sweden | Tax on digital services or similar measure at EU level in the event of no international solution | - | Under Consideration (EU) |
| Zimbabwe | Tax on digital services or similar measure | - | Under Consideration |

Note: The table lists jurisdictions where a digital services tax (DST) has been implemented and is effective, as well as those jurisdictions where a DST or similar measure is under consideration (or has been) by the government or legislature.
Source: OECD Secretariat.

### *Digital services taxes*

401. Against the background of these developments, a failure to secure a consensus-based solution through the Inclusive Framework's multilateral process would significantly increase the domestic pressures on governments to address the tax challenges arising from digitalisation unilaterally, and would likely lead to the introduction of DSTs or similar measures in a growing number of jurisdictions. Given the uncoordinated nature of these unilateral policy responses, it is not possible to model the impacts of the various measures, including their interactions, on investment and economic output with the same amount of detail as has been done for the Pillar One and Pillar Two proposals. However, the evaluation of the consensus scenario requires a comparison with a counterfactual capturing the main implications for the global economy of the absence of a consensus-based solution to the tax challenges arising from digitalisation.

402. Most importantly, the number of jurisdictions considering the introduction of a DST or similar measure can be expected to increase significantly in the absence of a global solution, thus increasing tax-related distortions of MNE behaviour and reducing global economic output. Although design elements differ across jurisdictions, DSTs are, broadly speaking, taxes on revenue earned by certain highly-digitalised MNEs from transactions linked to online activities of users resident in the taxing jurisdiction. As taxable transactions are typically determined based on the user's location, e.g., the jurisdiction of the viewer of an advertisement or the recipient of an online service, DSTs tend to apply to resident and non-resident MNEs irrespective of the extent of their physical presence in the taxing jurisdiction (OECD, 2018[128]).

403. From an economic perspective, DSTs are subject to a number of deficiencies. In contrast to the corporate income tax (CIT), DSTs are a tax on revenues rather than a tax on corporate profits (i.e., total revenues minus total costs). Total revenues associated with specific types of digital transactions are within the scope of the tax, regardless of the costs incurred in providing the respective digital services, leading, for example, to positive tax liabilities imposed on loss-making firms. Economic double taxation could arise if DSTs are levied on residents and non-residents with no ability to credit the tax against CIT levied on the same income. Consequently, DSTs are more distortive than profit-based taxes, leading to higher prices, lower quantities and less investment in the affected sectors (Lowry, 2019[140]). Since they are typically levied on intermediate services, e.g., online advertisement, the negative effects of economic double taxation could flow through to a much larger number of firms and sectors. As discussed in 4.5.3, the extent to which this effect is potentially passed through depends on a range of other factors such as the degree

of market power and the prevalence of economic rents, and is difficult to assess especially in the context of multisided markets.

404. Another major implication of a failure to secure a consensus-based solution through the multilateral process of the Inclusive Framework would be an increasing fragmentation of international taxation, driven by the proliferation of various unilateral measures, compounded by substantial increases in compliance costs for taxpayers and administrative costs for governments. Due to their selective targeting of specific digital services, a more widespread adoption of DSTs, in particular, would introduce additional distortions across projects and business models,[52] contributing to further fragmentation. In addition, tax uncertainty would increase relative to the consensus scenario, as governments fail to coordinate their policy responses. Such negative fiscal spillovers could give rise to globally inefficient outcomes (see Section 4.7). Relatedly, ETR differentials across firms are likely to increase as a consequence of a growing number of transaction-specific DSTs, leading to potential inefficiencies in capital allocation across jurisdictions.

### *The risk of entering into trade-related disputes*

405. Apart from immediate impacts on economic efficiency, a failure to secure a consensus-based solution through the multilateral process of the Inclusive Framework could have broader geopolitical implications feeding back into the economic evaluation of the counterfactual. In particular, a more widespread adoption of DSTs would likely give rise to an increase in trade disputes. The potential for such an escalation has been highlighted in the context of France's introduction of a DST. In that case, the United States responded to the introduction of the French DST, with the US Trade Representative (USTR) launching an investigation under Section 301 of the US Trade Act 1974.

406. Following its investigation launched in July 2019, the USTR published a report on the French DST in December 2019 (USTR, 2019[141]). The document highlighted what the USTR considered to be the "discriminatory, unreasonable and burdensome aspects of France's DST".53 In its Notice of Determination and Request for Comments Concerning Action Pursuant to Section 301: France's Digital Services Tax (USTR, 2019[142]), the USTR noted that section 301(c)(1)(B) of the Trade Act authorises the USTR to impose duties on the goods of the foreign country subject to the investigation and stated that, pursuant to sections 301(b) and (c), the USTR proposed to determine that action was appropriate in respect of the French DST. At the time, he provided that appropriate action could include the imposition of additional ad valorem duties of up to 100 percent on certain products of France and outlined a preliminary list of 63 tariff subheadings, with an estimated import trade value for calendar year 2018 of approximately USD 2.4 billion, corresponding to an amount approximately five times the total expected revenues from the first year of the French DST's operation.54 On 10 July 2020, the USTR referred to the investigation of the French DST and announced that his office would take action in the form of additional duties of 25 percent on French products, targeting 21 tariff subheadings, with an estimated trade value for calendar year 2019 of approximately USD 1.3 billion, corresponding to an amount approximately proportional to the revenues expected to be raised by the French DST in its first year from US MNEs (USTR, 2020[143]).

407. On several occasions, the European Commission responded to these developments by emphasising its commitment to a common EU-level response. In January 2020, the EU Trade Commissioner issued a statement stating that he views "the investigation as a European matter and, as in all trade-related matters, the EU will act and react as one" (EU Commission, 2020[144]). More recently, the EU Commissioner for the Economy announced that "the commission stands as one with EU countries facing the threat of US sanctions because they have moved forward with their own digital services taxes. If needed, we will react as one" (EU Commission, 2020[145]).

408. Following these developments, the United States has agreed to suspend the application of additional tariffs while France has postponed the collection of revenues from the DST, however, in the absence of an international agreement through the multilateral process of the Inclusive Framework, the number of countries involved in similar disputes could increase significantly. In parallel to these

developments, on 2 June 2020, the USTR announced that his office had initiated investigations under Section 301 of the 1974 Trade Act into DSTs or similar measures that have been adopted or are being considered by a number of US trading partners, namely with respect to Austria, Brazil, the Czech Republic, the European Union, India, Indonesia, Italy, Spain, Turkey, and the United Kingdom (USTR, 2020[146]). While these additional investigations have only just commenced, these recent developments suggest that a failure to secure a consensus-based solution on the tax challenges arising from digitalisation through the multilateral process of the Inclusive Framework would significantly heighten the risk of protracted trade disputes involving several major economies, including members of the G20.

### *Modelling the economic implications of tax and trade disputes*

409. The counterfactual scenarios aim to consider the potential state of the global economy assuming the failure to secure an agreement on international taxation. As mentioned above, such an agreement is assumed to entail a consensus on the design of the proposals as well as a commitment to withdraw any existing DSTs and to refrain from implementing such measures in the future. In contrast, the counterfactual scenarios not only capture the economic impacts of unilateral measures on global investment and output, but also the potential trade-related ramifications of an increasing fragmentation of the international tax system and, in particular, their feedback effects on economic outcomes. To this end, the following analysis builds on a cooperation with the OECD's Trade and Agriculture Directorate using the OECD METRO Trade Model,55 a computable general equilibrium (CGE) model, capable of simulating economic impacts of taxes as well as tariff retaliation in a consistent framework.

410. The OECD METRO Trade Model is routinely used to study changes in trade policy and other factors (see Annex 4.D and the model documentation (OECD, 2020[147])). It covers 65 countries and regional aggregates and 65 commodities across the global economy, based on external and internal data sources such as the Trade in Value Added[56] (TiVA) database, to analyse how production and trade are linked in global value chains and how resources such as labour, capital and natural resources are allocated across economic activities. It allows for the simulation of the economic impacts of a wide range of trade policies, including border tariff rates, non-tariff measures, export restrictions, domestic taxes and support programs.

**Box 4.8. Digital services taxes and retaliatory tariffs in the OECD METRO Trade Model**

The DST is implemented as an ad valorem tax on intermediate sales from the business services sector to all buyers, assuming that the revenues from digitally delivered services, such as revenues from advertising on a digital platform, are located exclusively in that sector.[57]

While the DST is not the focus of the analysis, its implementation by the respective country grouping in each scenario anchors the size of the tariff retaliation and the counter-retaliation. To calibrate the DST rate, the French case serves as a benchmark based on the observation that the 3% DST in France is expected to generate revenues of around EUR 450 million in its first year. With that information, and taking the value of intermediate sales of business services in France as the benchmark, a corresponding DST rate on the business services sector can be approximated for either a 3% or a 5%[58] rate for each country, however, it is not possible to model revenue or income thresholds, as the model does not distinguish individual firms.

Given this approach, the French DST rate of 3% translates into a 0.12% tax on the entire business services sector – i.e., the DST-equivalent sector-level tax rate. Hence, the implicit assumption is that roughly 1/30 of the intermediate sales of business services correspond to digitally delivered services under the scope of the DST. This DST-equivalent tax rate is applied to intermediate sales of business services in all countries that are simulated to implement a DST, yielding the targeted tax revenues as shown in Annex Table 4.D.1 and Annex 4.D.

The retaliating region, i.e., the United States, implements retaliatory tariffs on targeted sectors to match the DST revenues in countries that implement a DST, times a retaliation factor of either one or five. The size of the (ad valorem) retaliatory tariff rate is thus a function of the DST revenues in the implementing country, the imports into the United States of the targeted sectors in the baseline data and the size of the retaliation factor. Tariffs are simulated on trade in non-service sectors that are known to be typically targeted for tariff action and are symmetrically applied to the same products, which makes the results comparable between countries.

Based on these assumptions, the retaliatory tariffs increase with the DST rate and the retaliation factor, leading to a set of calibrated tariff rates. Counter-retaliatory tariffs are assumed to match US retaliatory tariffs exactly in terms of revenues, without an additional counter-retaliatory mark up (see OECD (2018[148]) and Annex 4.D). All counterfactual tax and tariff rates are assumed to be permanent and calculated on baseline data, i.e., without taking reactions and adjustments into account that will occur once a tax or tariff is put in place.

411. Although the DST is not included in the set of standard trade policy measures, it can be incorporated in a stylised way as an ad valorem tax on the share of digitally delivered intermediate sales from the business services sector to other sectors. As described in Box 4.8, its design is calibrated using French DST provisions and revenue estimates to produce an approximation of the DST base. In line with the variation in DSTs across jurisdictions, the DST rate is assumed to be either 3% or 5% (Table 4.2). Retaliatory tariffs are a standard feature of trade modelling that is captured within the existing framework. In the calibration used for this analysis, a range of plausible retaliation factors is considered. At the higher end, a worst-case scenario with a retaliation factor of five is considered, reflecting the broad magnitude of the tariff retaliation that was initially announced in the dispute between France and the United States. At the lower end, a proportional retaliation scenario is considered, broadly in line with the tariff response announced by the USTR on 10 July 2020 (see Annex 4.D for sensitivity analyses).

## Figure 4.15. Trade retaliation: sequence of events

Simulation of the different cases follow a three-step sequence of events.

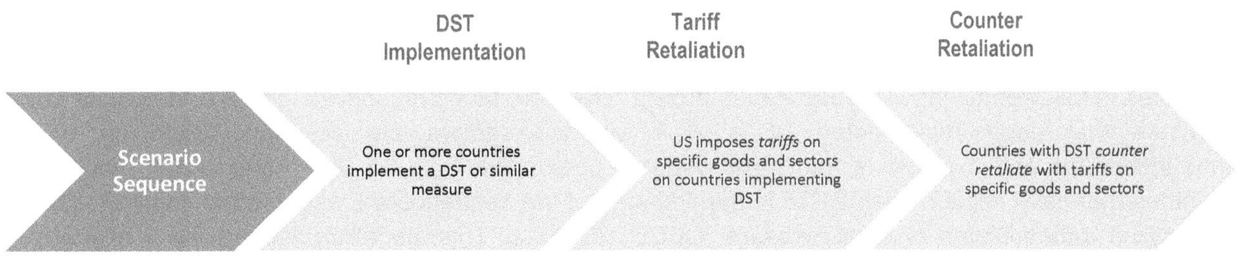


Source: In each of the cases, the number of countries implementing a DST or similar measure varies; the group of countries counter retaliating varies accordingly. The country groups are described in Table 4.3 and Table 4.4.

412. Figure 4.15 outlines the sequence of DST implementation, tariff retaliation and counter-retaliation underlying the counterfactual simulations presented in this section (see Annex 4.D for a description of additional simulation results). To capture a broad range of possible trade developments, as discussed above, two cases are distinguished, each corresponding to a different group of countries implementing a DST. In the case with narrow DST implementation, only those jurisdictions that have already legislated a DST or are subject to USTR Section 301 investigations are assumed to adopt such a policy in the event

that the multilateral process does not reach a consensus, i.e., groups 1, 2 and 3 in Table 4.3. In the case[59] with broad DST implementation, all jurisdictions in the model except for the United States, the People's Republic of China and Hong Kong (China) implement a DST or similar measure, i.e., groups 1, 2, 3 and 6 in Table 4.3.[60]

### Table 4.3. Country groupings

The following country groups are used to construct the policy simulations in Table 4.4.

| Group | Label | Countries | Share in global GDP |
|---|---|---|---|
| 1 | DST legislated and/or effective | France | 4% |
| 2 | Section 301 investigation underway - EU | Austria, Czech Republic, Hungary, Italy, Spain, Belgium, Bulgaria, Croatia , Cyprus[61], Denmark, Estonia, Finland, Germany, Greece, Ireland, Latvia, Lithuania, Luxembourg, Malta, Netherlands, Poland, Portugal, Romania, Slovakia, Slovenia, Sweden | 16% |
| 3 | Section 301 investigation underway – non-EU | Brazil, India, Indonesia, Turkey, United Kingdom | 12% |
| 4 | Retaliating | United States | 22% |
| 5 | No DST, no retaliation | China, Hong Kong (China) | 14% |
| 6 | Other (no DST except in the case with broad implementation) | Rest of the World | 33% |

Note: In the case with narrow DST implementation, only those jurisdictions that have already legislated a DST or are subject to USTR Section 301 investigations are assumed to adopt such a policy in the event that the multilateral process does not reach a consensus, i.e., groups 1, 2 and 3. In the case with broad DST implementation, all jurisdictions in the model except for the United States, the People's Republic of China and Hong Kong (China) implement a DST or similar measure, i.e., groups 1, 2, 3 and 6. Group 6 includes the following countries: Australia, Canada, Israel, New Zealand, Norway, Philippines, Tunisia, Russia, Kenya, Japan, Korea, Brunei Darussalam, Cambodia, Philippines, Singapore, Viet Nam, Argentina, Chile, Colombia, Peru, Costa Rica, Switzerland, Kazakhstan, Saudi Arabia, Morocco, South Africa, Malaysia, Mexico, Thailand as well as an aggregate category covering the remainder of the global economy.
Source: OECD.

413. In each of the two cases, it is assumed that the unilateral implementation of DSTs or similar measures is followed by the United States imposing retaliatory tariffs on specific goods and sectors in the countries that have implemented DSTs. The targeted sectors are selected based on official announcements and experience from past trade disputes (see Box 4.8 and Annex 4.D). Finally, the countries that have implemented DSTs in the first step of the sequence are assumed to counter-retaliate against the United States in equal measure (OECD, 2018[148]). This modelling assumption is also based on public statements made by French and European Union officials. Again, the targeted sectors are selected based on official announcements and past experience.

## Table 4.4. Overview of the simulated cases

Different DST rates and retaliation factors are simulated for both cases. Group numbers refer to country groups in Table 4.3.

| Case | DST rate | Tariff Retaliation Factor | Simulations |
|---|---|---|---|
| Narrow DST implementation | 3%, 5% | 1, 5 | DST implemented: group 1,2,3<br>Tariff retaliation: group 4<br>Tariff counter-retaliation: group 1,2,3 |
| Broad DST implementation | 3%, 5% | 1, 5 | DST implemented: group 1,2,3,6<br>Tariff retaliation: group 4<br>Tariff counter-retaliation: group 1,2,3,6 |

Note: As sensitivity analysis, additional scenarios have been simulated and are described in Annex 4.D.
Source: OECD

### *Tax and trade disputes: impacts on global GDP*

414. The results show that the simulated trade disputes could have substantial impacts on global GDP, measured in real terms. Depending on the combination of DST rates and retaliation factors, global GDP is simulated to be reduced by -0.09% to -0.24% in the case with narrow DST implementation (relative to a no-tax-and-trade-dispute scenario), and by to -0.44% to -1.21% in the case with broad DST implementation (Table 4.5).[62] These results represent a potentially substantial negative effect on the level of global GDP, stemming from efficiency losses due to the tariffs compounded by reductions in wages and capital returns as well as a slow-down in investment driven by declining exports. Household income decreases at similar rates, indicating that households would bear most of the costs of the shrinking economy, as tariff increases affect households through two channels. First, their purchases become more expensive, as tariff-ridden import prices increase, and, second, factor income falls as the economy contracts. World trade, measured as real global import volumes, falls by about twice the rate of real GDP.

## Table 4.5. Trade retaliation: simulation results (weighted percent changes)

Effects on macroeconomic indicators in percent for selected scenarios compared to a situation without DSTs and trade retaliation.

| | Narrow DST Implementation | | | | Broad DST Implementation | | | |
|---|---|---|---|---|---|---|---|---|
| **US tariff retaliation factor** | 1 | | 5 | | 1 | | 5 | |
| **DST rate** | **3%** | **5%** | **3%** | **5%** | **3%** | **5%** | **3%** | **5%** |
| Global GDP (real) | -0.09 | -0.15 | -0.15 | -0.24 | -0.44 | -0.72 | -0.73 | -1.21 |
| Global Household income | -0.08 | -0.14 | -0.14 | -0.23 | -0.38 | -0.64 | -0.64 | -1.07 |
| Global Imports (real) | -0.17 | -0.28 | -0.34 | -0.53 | -0.68 | -1.14 | -1.25 | -2.04 |

Note: As sensitivity analyses, additional results corresponding to retaliation factors of 0.5 and 4 are shown in Annex 4.D.
Source: METRO v3 database, OECD calculations.

415. Comparison of the two cases suggests that economic costs increase as DST implementation and subsequent tariff retaliation become more widespread. However, additional results presented in Annex 4.D reveal considerable heterogeneity across country groups. In particular, the countries engaging in unilateral actions are most negatively affected, while those that are not engaged in the dispute initially benefit from shifts of economic activity towards them. However, as the tax and trade dispute involves an increasing number of countries, the options for reallocation of trade and production between countries become fewer.

The shrinking size of the economies engaged in tariff retaliation generates progressively larger negative impacts. As their trade declines, income declines and demand for imports falls further. In line with these results, bilateral trade between the countries engaged in the dispute could shrink by double-digit numbers. While countries that are not engaged in the dispute would expand exports slightly, including trade amongst themselves, their trade into the countries that are affected by the tariff increases is only expanding marginally. As a consequence, trade diversion is limited, as import demand is falling in step with the overall economic contraction. Table 4.6 summarises direct and indirect effects on investment under the no-consensus scenario.

## Table 4.6. No-consensus scenario: Summary

| Direct Effects on Investment | Indirect Effects | Summary |
|---|---|---|
| Unilateral measures, such as digital services taxes and similar measures, increase investment costs for specific businesses | Additional fiscal space could have positive indirect effects on investment and economic output | Higher investment costs have a negative effect on global investment and output |
| Trade disputes could lead to a sequence of retaliatory tariffs, adding to investment cost increases | Profit shifting incentives remain high and could potentially increase due to increasing fragmentation and incoherence of international taxation | Trade disputes are likely to emerge, with the potential to significantly reduce global investment and output |
| Jurisdictions engaging in unilateral actions are most negatively affected, with bilateral trade potentially falling by double-digit numbers | Compliance and administrative costs are likely to increase more strongly due to an increasingly incoherent tax system | Economic impacts of trade disputes could entail a reduction in global GDP by around -0.1% to -0.2% if a smaller number of jurisdictions is involved, rising to -0.4% to -1.2% if more jurisdictions are involved |
| ETR differentials across firms are likely to increase due to fragmentation and incoherence of international taxation (e.g., transaction-specific DSTs) | Competition over mobile tax bases could intensify, potentially impacting economic efficiency | |
| DSTs could lead to double taxation, adding to increases in investment costs and distorting investment decisions | Turnover taxation, e.g., taxation of loss-making firms, reduces economic efficiency and global output, especially during periods of economic recession | Increasing uncertainty, fragmentation, incoherence of international taxation due to increasing reliance on turnover taxation |

Source: OECD secretariat.

## References


Abbas, S. and A. Klemm (2013), "A partial race to the bottom: corporate tax developments in emerging and developing economies", *Int Tax Public Finance*, Vol. 20, pp. 596–617, http://dx.doi.org/10.1007/s10797-013-9286-8. [107]

Acemoglu, D. et al. (2018), "Innovation, Reallocation, and Growth †", *American Economic Review*, Vol. 108/11, pp. 3450-3491, http://dx.doi.org/10.1257/aer.20130470. [186]

Aghion, P. and P. Howirrt (1992), "A Model of Growth Through Creative Destruction", *Econometrica*, Vol. 60/2, pp. 323-351, http://dx.doi.org/10.3386/w3223. [85]

Aguiar, A. et al. (2019), "The GTAP Data Base: Version 10", *Journal of Global Economic Analysis*, Vol. 4/1, pp. 1-27, http://dx.doi.org/10.21642/JGEA.040101AF. [195]

Akcigit, U. et al. (2018), "Taxation and Innovation in the 20th Century", *NBER Working Paper*, No. 24982, National Bureau of Economic Research, Cambridge, MA, http://dx.doi.org/10.3386/w24982. [209]

Akcigit, U., D. Hanley and N. Serrano-Velarde (2013), "Back to Basics: Basic Research Spillovers, Innovation Policy and Growth", *NBER Working Paper*, No. 19473, National Bureau of Economic Research, Cambridge, MA, http://dx.doi.org/10.3386/w19473. [89]

Almus, M. and D. Czarnitzki (2003), "The effects of public R and D subsidies on firms' innovation activities: The case of Eastern Germany", *Journal of Business and Economic Statistics*, Vol. 21/2, pp. 226-236, http://dx.doi.org/10.1198/073500103288618918. [177]

Alstadsaeter, A. et al. (2015), "Patent Boxes Design, Patents Location and Local R&D", *IPTS Working Papers on Corporate R&D and Innovation*, No. 6/2015, https://ec.europa.eu/jrc/sites/jrcsh/files/JRC96080_Patent_boxes.pdf. [174]

Altshuler, R. and T. Goodspeed (2015), "Follow the Leader? Evidence on European and US Tax Competition", *Public Finance Review*, Vol. 43/4, pp. 485-504. [80]

Andrews, D., C. Criscuolo and C. Menon (2014), "Do resources Flow to Patenting Firms?", *OECD Economics Department Working Papers*, No. 1127, OECD, http://dx.doi.org/10.1787/5JZ2LPMK0GS6-EN. [98]

Appelt, S. et al. (2016), "R&D Tax Incentives: Evidence on design, incidence and impacts", in *OECD Science, Technology and Industry Policy Papers*, OECD Publishing, Paris, https://doi.org/10.1787/5jlr8fldqk7j-en. [90]

Appelt, S., F. Galindo-Rueda and A. González Cabral (2019), "Measuring R&D tax support: Findings from the new OECD R&D Tax Incentives Database", *OECD Science, Technology and Industry Working Papers*, No. 2019/06, OECD Publishing, Paris, https://dx.doi.org/10.1787/d16e6072-en. [83]

Ariff, M., D. Cheung and S. Chan (1999), "Compliance costs of corporate taxation in Hong Kong", *International Tax Journal*, Vol. 25, https://research.monash.edu/en/publications/compliance-costs-of-corporate-taxation-in-hong-kong. [53]

Arnold, B. et al. (2011), "Tax Policy for Economic Recovery and Growth", *Economic Journal*, Vol. 120/550, pp. F59-F80. [5]

Arrow, K. (1962), "Economic Welfare and the Allocation of Resources for Invention", in *The Rate and Direction of Inventive Activities: Economic and Social Factors*, Princeton University Press, Princeton, NJ, http://www.nber.org/chapters/c2144. [86]

Arulampalam, W., M. Devereux and G. Maffini (2012), "The direct incidence of corporate income tax on wages", *European Economic Review*, Vol. 56/6, pp. 1038-1054. [26]

Asatryan, Z. and A. Peichl (2018), "Responses of Firms to Tax, Administrative and Accounting Rules: Evidence from Armenia", *CESifo Working Paper Series*, No. 6754, https://papers.ssrn.com/sol3/papers.cfm?abstract_id=3106710. [56]

Auerbach, A. (2006), "Who Bears the Corporate Tax? A Review of What We Know", in *Tax Policy and the Economy*, National Bureau of Economic Research, https://www.nber.org/chapters/c0065. [22]

Autor, D. et al. (2020), "The Fall of the Labor Share and the Rise of Superstar Firms", *The Quarterly Journal of Economics*, Vol. 135/2, pp. 645-709, http://dx.doi.org/10.1093/QJE/QJAA004. [135]

Autor, D. et al. (2017), "The Fall of the Labor Share and the Rise of Superstar Firms", *NBER Working Papers*, No. 23396, http://www.nber.org/papers/w23396.pdf. [43]

Azémar, C. and R. Desbordes (2010), "Short-run Strategies for Attracting Foreign Direct Investment", *The World Economy*, Vol. 33/7, https://doi.org/10.1111/j.1467-9701.2010.01226.x|. [115]

Bailin Rivares, A. et al. (2019), "Like it or not? The impact of online platforms on the productivity of incumbent service providers", *OECD Economics Department Working Papers*, No. 1548, OECD Publishing, Paris, https://dx.doi.org/10.1787/080a17ce-en. [131]

Bajgar, M. et al. (2019), "Industry Concentration in Europe and North America", *OECD Productivity Working Papers*, No. 18, OECD Publishing, Paris, https://dx.doi.org/10.1787/2ff98246-en. [41]

Baldwin, R. and P. Krugman (2004), "Agglomeration, integration and tax harmonisation", *European Economic Review*, Vol. 48/1, pp. 1-23. [151]

Bauer, J. and M. Latzer (2016), "The economics of the Internet: an overview", in *Handbook on the Economics of the Internet*, Edward Elgar Publishing, http://dx.doi.org/10.4337/9780857939852.00007. [127]

Becker, J. and N. Riedel (2012), "Cross-border tax effects on affiliate investment - Evidence from European multinationals", *European Economic Review*, Vol. 56. [206]

Beer, S., R. de Mooij and L. Liu (2020), "International Corporate Tax Avoidance: A review of the channels, magnitudes and blind spots", *Journal of Economic Surveys*, Vol. 34/3, pp. 660-688, http://dx.doi.org/10.1111/joes.12305. [18]

Belleflamme, P. and E. Toulemonde (2016), "Tax Incidence on Competing Two-Sided Platforms: Lucky Break or Double Jeopardy", *CESifo Working Paper 5882*. [33]

Benz, S. and F. Gonzales (2019), "Intra-EEA STRI Database: Methodology and Results", *OECD Trade Policy Papers*, No. 223, OECD Publishing, Paris, http://dx.doi.org/10.1787/2aac6d21-en. [197]

Benz, S. and A. Jaax (2020), "The costs of regulatory barriers to trade in services: New estimates of ad valorem tariff equivalents", *OECD Trade Policy Papers*, No. 238, OECD Publishing, Paris, http://dx.doi.org/10.1787/bae97f98-en. [198]

Bermejo Carbonell, J. and R. Werner (2018), "Does Foreign Direct Investment Generate Economic Growth? A New Empirical Approach Applied to Spain", *Economic Geography*, Vol. 94/4, pp. 425-456. [203]

Besley, T. and T. Persson (2014), "Why do developing countries tax so little?", *Journal of Economic Perspectives*, Vol. 28/4, pp. 99-120. [48]

Bessen, J. (2017), "Information Technology and Industry Concentration", *Law and Economics Research Papers*, Vol. 17-41. [3]

Bibler, A., K. Teltser and M. Tremblay (2019), "Inferring Tax Compliance from Pass-through: Evidence from Airbnb Tax Enforcement Agreements", *CESifo Working Papers 7747*. [38]

Bloom, N., M. Schankerman and J. Reenen (2013), "Identifying Technology Spillovers and Product Market Rivalry", *Econometrica*, Vol. 81/4, pp. 1347-1393, http://dx.doi.org/10.3982/ecta9466. [182]

Bloom, N., J. Van Reenen and H. Williams (2019), *A toolkit of policies to promote innovation*, American Economic Association, http://dx.doi.org/10.1257/jep.33.3.163. [99]

Blundell, R., R. Griffiths and J. Van Reenen (1999), "Market Share, Market Value and Innovation in a Panel of British Manufacturing Firms", *Review of Economic Studies*, Vol. 66/3, pp. 529-554, http://dx.doi.org/10.1111/1467-937X.00097. [184]

Bourreau, M., B. Caillaud and R. De Nijs (2018), "Taxation of a digital monopoly platform", *Journal of Public Economic Theory*, Vol. 20/1, pp. 40-51. [36]

Brennan, G. and J. Buchanan (1980), *The Power to Tax: Analytic Foundations of a Fiscal Constitution*, Cambridge University Press. [160]

Busom, I. (2000), "An Empirical Evaluation of The Effects of R&D Subsidies", *Economics of Innovation and New Technology*, Vol. 9/2, pp. 111-148, http://dx.doi.org/10.1080/10438590000000006. [176]

Cadot, O. et al. (2018), "Estimating Ad Valorem Equivalents of Non-Tariff Measures: Combining Price-Based and Quantity-Based Approaches", *OECD Trade Policy Papers*, No. 215, OECD Publishing, Paris, http://dx.doi.org/10.1787/f3cd5bdc-en. [196]

Calligaris, S., C. Criscuolo and L. Marcolin (2018), "Mark-ups in the digital era", *OECD Science, Technology and Industry Working Papers*, No. 2018/10, OECD Publishing, Paris, https://dx.doi.org/10.1787/4efe2d25-en. [2]

Canh, N. et al. (2013), "Measuring the Effectiveness of Corporate Income Tax Investment Incentives for Domestic Companies in Vietnam", *Journal of Emerging Issues in Economics, Finance and Banking*, Vol. 1/1. [119]

Cappelen, Å., A. Raknerud and M. Rybalka (2012), "The effects of R&D tax credits on patenting and innovations", *Research Policy*, http://dx.doi.org/10.1016/j.respol.2011.10.001. [171]

Castellacci, F. (2008), "Technological paradigms, regimes and trajectories: Manufacturing and service industries in a new taxonomy of sectoral patterns of innovation", *Research Policy*, Vol. 37/6-7, pp. 978-994, http://dx.doi.org/10.1016/j.respol.2008.03.011. [93]

Castellacci, F. and C. Lie (2015), *Do the effects of R&D tax credits vary across industries? A meta-regression analysis*, Elsevier B.V., http://dx.doi.org/10.1016/j.respol.2015.01.010. [167]

Chalk, N., M. Keen and V. Perry (2018), "The Tax Cuts and Jobs Act: An Appraisal", *IMF Working Papers*, No. 18/185. [211]

Chatib Basri, M. et al. (2019), "Tax administration vs. Tax Rates: Evidence from Corporate Taxation in Indonesia", No. 26150, NBER Working Papers, http://www.nber.org/papers/w26150.ack. [62]

Chaurey, R. (2017), "Location-based tax incentives: Evidence from India", *Journal of Public Economics*, Vol. 156, pp. 101-120, https://doi.org/10.1016/j.jpubeco.2016.08.013. [124]

Chirinko, R. and D. Wilson (2017), "Tax competition among U.S. states: Racing to the bottom or riding on a seesaw?", *Journal of Public Economics*, Vol. 155, pp. 147-163. [72]

Ciaramella, L. (2017), "Patent Boxes and the Relocation of Intellectual Property", *SSRN Electronic Journal*, http://dx.doi.org/10.2139/ssrn.2943435. [175]

Clausing, K. (2013), "Who Pays the Corporate Tax in a Global Economy?", *National Tax Journal*, Vol. 66/1, pp. 151-184. [25]

Clausing, K. (2012), "In Search of Corporate Tax Incidence", *Tax Law Review*, Vol. 65. [24]

Clausing, K., T. Miller and W. Mintz (2014), *Corporate Inversions*, Tax Policy Center, https://www.taxpolicycenter.org/sites/default/files/alfresco/publication-pdfs/413207-Corporate-Inversions.PDF. [188]

Clifford, S. (2019), "Taxing multinationals beyond borders: Financial and locational responses to CFC rules", *Journal of Public Economics*, Vol. 173, pp. 44-71, http://dx.doi.org/10.1016/j.jpubeco.2019.01.010. [193]

Colmar Brunton (2005), *Measuring the tax compliance costs of small and medium-sized businesses-a benchmark survey*, Inland Revenue, Wellington. [55]

Congressional Budget Office (2017), *An analysis of corporate inversions*, http://www.cbo.gov/publication/53093. [187]

Congressional Research Service (2019), *Corporate Expatriation, Inversions, and Mergers: Tax Issues*, https://crsreports.congress.gov. [190]

Costa-Font, J., F. De-Albuquerque and H. Doucouliagos (2014), "Do jurisdictions compete on taxes? A meta-regression analysis", *Public Choice*, Vol. 161/3-4, pp. 451-470. [75]

Covarrubias, M., G. Gutiérrez and T. Philippon (2019), "From Good to Bad Concentration? U.S. Industries over the Past 30 Years", *National Bureau of Economic Research*, http://dx.doi.org/10.3386/w25983. [137]

Creedy, J. and N. Gemmell (2017), "Taxation and the User Cost of Capital", *Journal of Economic Surveys*, Vol. 31/1, pp. 201-225, http://dx.doi.org/10.1111/joes.12137. [8]

Crouzet, N. and J. Eberly (2019), *Understanding Weak Capital Investment: the Role of Market Concentration and Intangibles*, National Bureau of Economic Research, Cambridge, MA, http://dx.doi.org/10.3386/w25869. [138]

Cui, W. (2019), "The Digital Services Tax on the Verge of Implementation", *Canadian Tax Journal/Revue fiscale canadienne*, Vol. 67/4, pp. 1135-1152. [37]

Czarnitzki, D., P. Hanel and J. Rosa (2011), "Evaluating the impact of R&D tax credits on innovation: A microeconometric study on Canadian firms", *Research Policy*, Vol. 40/2, pp. 217-229, http://dx.doi.org/10.1016/j.respol.2010.09.017. [169]

Dabla-Norris, E. et al. (2019), "The quality of tax administration and firm performance: evidence from developing countries", *International Tax and Public Finance*, pp. 1-38, http://dx.doi.org/10.1007/s10797-019-09551-y. [46]

Davies, R. and J. Voget (2011), "Tax Competition in an Expanding European Union", *GEE Papers*, No. 33, https://www.gee.gov.pt/RePEc/WorkingPapers/GEE_PAPERS_33.pdf. [74]

de Boer, P. et al. (2019), *Evaluation Dutch R&D tax credit scheme (WBSO) 2011-2017*, https://www.dialogic.nl/wp-content/uploads/2019/04/Evaluation-WBSO-2011-2017-Summary-8-03-2019-def.pdf. [165]

De Loecker, J. and J. Eeckhout (2017), *The Rise of Market Power and the Macroeconomic Implications*, National Bureau of Economic Research, Cambridge, MA, http://dx.doi.org/10.3386/w23687. [185]

De Loecker, J., J. Eeckhout and G. Unger (2020), "The Rise of Market Power and the Macroeconomic Implications", *The Quarterly Journal of Economics*, Vol. 135/2, pp. 561–644, https://doi.org/10.1093/qje/qjz041. [136]

de Mooij, R. and L. Liu (2020), "At a Cost: The Real Effects of Transfer Pricing Regulations", *IMF Economic Review*, Vol. 68, pp. 268-306, http://dx.doi.org/10.1057/s41308-019-00105-0. [11]

Dechezleprêtre, A. et al. (2016), "Do tax incentives for research increase firm innovation? An RD design for R&D", in *National Bureau of Economic Research*, http://dx.doi.org/10.3386/w22405. [168]

Dernis, H. et al. (2019), "World Corporate Top R&D investors: Shaping the Future of Technologies and of AI. A joint JRC and OECD report.", *Publications Office of the European Union*, http://dx.doi.org/10.2760/16575. [180]

Desai, M., C. Foley and J. Hines (2006), "The demand for tax haven operations", *Journal of Public Economics*, Vol. 90/3, pp. 513-531. [155]

Desai, M. and J. Hines (2002), "Chains of Ownership, Regional Tax Competition, and Foreign Direct Investment", *National Bureau of Economic Research*, http://dx.doi.org/10.3386/w9224. [200]

Desai, M. and J. Hines (2002), *Expectations and Expatriations: Tracing the Causes and Consequences of Corporate Inversions*, National Bureau of Economic Research, Cambridge, MA, http://dx.doi.org/10.3386/w9057. [191]

Devereux, -. et al. (2002), "Corporate Income Tax: Reforms and International Tax Competition", *Economic Policy*, Vol. 17/35, pp. 449-495. [63]

Devereux, M. and R. Griffith (2003), "Evaluating Tax Policy for Location Decisions", *International Tax and Public Finance*, Vol. 10/2, pp. 107-126, http://dx.doi.org/10.1023/A:1023364421914. [9]

Devereux, M., B. Lockwood and M. Redoano (2008), "Do countries compete over corporate tax rates?", *Journal of Public Economics*, Vol. 92/5-6, pp. 1210-1235. [71]

Devereux, M. and S. Loretz (2013), "What Do We Know About Corporate Tax Competition?", *National Tax Journal*, Vol. 66/3, pp. 745-774. [68]

Dharmapala, D. (2020), "Do Multinational Firms Use Tax Havens to the Detriment of Other Countries?", *CESifo Working Paper Series*, No. 8275, https://www.cesifo.org/DocDL/cesifo1_wp8275.pdf. [67]

Dharmapala, D. (2008), "What problems and opportunities are created by tax havens", *Oxford Review of Economic Policy*, Vol. 24/4, pp. 661-679, http://dx.doi.org/10.1093/oxrep/grn031. [152]

Dharmapala, D. and J. Hines (2006), "Which Countries Become Tax Havens?", *NBER Working Paper*, No. 12802, http://dx.doi.org/10.3386/w12802. [154]

Díaz de Sarralde Miguez, S. (2018), *Tax Administrations: Collection, Costs and Personnel Evidence for the CIAT Countries with data of ISORA*, Interamerican Center of Tax Administration - CIAT. [61]

Edwards, J. and M. Keen (1996), "Tax competition and Leviathan", *European Economic Review*, Vol. 40, pp. 113-134. [161]

Egger, P., K. Erhardt and C. Keuschnigg (2018), "Heterogeneous Tax Sensitivity of Firm-level Investments", *CEPR Discussion Papers*. [201]

Eggert, W. and P. Sørensen (2008), "The effects of tax competition when politicians create rents to buy political support", *Journal of Public Economics*, Vol. 92/5-6, pp. 1142-1163. [162]

Eichfelder, S. and F. Vaillancourt (2014), "Tax Compliance Costs: A Review of Cost Burdens and Cost Structures", *SSRN Electronic Journal*, http://dx.doi.org/10.2139/ssrn.2535664. [49]

Englisch, J. and J. Becker (2019), "International effective minimum taxation-the GLOBE proposal", *World Tax Journal*, Vol. 11/4. [20]

Erard, B. (1997), *The income tax compliance burden on Canadian big business*, prepared for the Technical Committee on Business Taxation, Department of Finance, Ottawa., https://www.researchgate.net/publication/228582929_The_income_tax_compliance_burden_on_Canadian_big_business. [51]

Ernst, C. and C. Spengel (2011), "Taxation, R&D Tax Incentives and Patent Application in Europe", *ZEW Discussion Papers*, No. 11-024, ftp://ftp.zew.de/pub/zew-docs/dp/dp11024.pdf. [170]

EU Commission (2020), *Extract of remarks by Commissioner Phil Hogan at exchange with press in Paris*, https://ec.europa.eu/commission/commissioners/2019-2024/hogan/announcements/extract-remarks-commissioner-phil-hogan-exchange-press-paris_en. [144]

EU Commission (2020), *Paolo Gentiloni - Press Conference*. [145]

Eurostat (2020), *Community Innovation Survey 2016*. [96]

Farole, T. and D. Winkler (2014), *Making Foreign Direct Investment Work for Sub-Saharan Africa*, World Bank,, http://dx.doi.org/10.1596/978-1-4648-0126-6. [105]

Feld, L. and J. Heckemeyer (2011), "FDI and taxation: A meta-study", *Journal of Economic Surveys*, Vol. 25/2, pp. 233-272, https://doi.org/10.1111/j.1467-6419.2010.00674.x. [6]

Forslid, R. (2005), "Tax competition and agglomeration: Main effects and empirical implications", *Swedish Economic Policy Review*, Vol. 12.2005, pp. 113-137. [149]

Fuest, C., A. Peichl and S. Siegloch (2018), "Do Higher Corporate Taxes Reduce Wages? Micro Evidence from Germany", *American Economic Review*, Vol. 108/2, pp. 393-418. [28]

Fullerton, D. and G. Metcalf (2002), "Tax Incidence", *NBER Working Paper*, No. 8829, https://www.nber.org/papers/w8829.pdf. [21]

Furman, J. and P. Orszag (2015), "A Firm-Level Perspective on the Role of Rents in the Rise in Inequality for US", in *Toward a Just Society: Joseph Stiglitz and Twenty-First Century Economics*, https://www.hks.harvard.edu/publications/firm-level-perspective-role-rents-rise-inequality (accessed on 24 April 2020). [134]

Gaessler, F., B. Hall and D. Harhoff (2018), *Should There Be Lower Taxes on Patent Income?*, National Bureau of Economic Research, Cambridge, MA, http://dx.doi.org/10.3386/w24843. [92]

Galindo-Rueda, F. and F. Verger (2016), "OECD Taxonomy of Economic Activities Based on R&D Intensity", *OECD Science, Technology and Industry Working Papers*, No. 2016/4, OECD Publishing, Paris, https://dx.doi.org/10.1787/5jlv73sqqp8r-en. [94]

Galindo-Rueda, F., F. Verger and S. Ouellet (2020), "Patterns of innovation, advanced technology use and business practices in Canadian firms", *OECD Science, Technology and Industry Working Papers*, No. 2020/02, OECD Publishing, Paris, https://dx.doi.org/10.1787/6856ab8c-en. [95]

Gordon, R. (1992), "Can Capital Income Taxes Survive in Open Economies?", *The Journal of Finance*, Vol. 47/3, pp. 1159-1180. [78]

Gravelle, J. (2013), "Corporate Tax Incidence: Review of General Equilibrium Estimates and Analysis", *National Tax Journal*, Vol. 66/1, pp. 185-214. [23]

Griffith, R., H. Miller and M. O'Connell (2014), "Ownership of intellectual property and corporate taxation", *Journal of Public Economics*, Vol. 112, pp. 12-23, http://dx.doi.org/10.1016/j.jpubeco.2014.01.009. [173]

Gupta, S. et al. (2014), "Spillovers in International Corporate Taxation", *IMF Policy Papers*, No. 2014/071, http://dx.doi.org/10.5089/9781498343367.007. [65]

Gutiérrez, G. and T. Philippon (2019), "Fading Stars", *NBER Working Papers*, No. 25529, National Bureau of Economic Research, https://www.nber.org/papers/w25529?utm_campaign=ntwh&utm_medium=email&utm_source=ntwg22. [42]

Gutiérrez, G. and T. Philippon (2017), "Investmentless Growth: An Empirical Investigation", *BPEA Conference Drafts*, https://www.brookings.edu/wp-content/uploads/2017/09/2_gutierrezphilippon.pdf. [130]

Hajkova, D. et al. (2006), "Taxation, Business Environment and FDI Location in OECD Countries", *OECD Economics Department Working Papers*, No. 502, http://dx.doi.org/10.1787/874058477248. [4]

Hall, B. (2019), *Tax Policy for Innovation*, National Bureau of Economic Research, Cambridge, MA, http://dx.doi.org/10.3386/w25773. [88]

Hall, B. and J. Lerner (2010), "The financing of R&D and innovation", in *Handbook of the Economics of Innovation*, Elsevier B.V., http://dx.doi.org/10.1016/S0169-7218(10)01014-2. [87]

Hall, B. and A. Maffioli (2008), *Evaluating the Impact of Technology Development Funds in Emerging Economies: Evidence from Latin America*, National Bureau of Economic Research, Cambridge, MA, http://dx.doi.org/10.3386/w13835. [178]

Hall, B. and J. Van Reenen (2000), "How effective are fiscal incentives for R&D? A review of the evidence", *Research Policy*, Vol. 29/4-5, pp. 449-469. [163]

Hanappi, T. (2018), "Corporate Effective Tax Rates: Model Description and Results from 36 OECD and Non-OECD Countries", *OECD Taxation Working Papers*, No. 38, http://dx.doi.org/10.1787/a07f9958-en. [10]

Hanappi, T. and A. González Cabral (2020), "The impact of the pillar one and pillar two proposals on MNE's investment costs : An analysis using forward-looking effective tax rates", *OECD Taxation Working Papers*, No. 50, OECD Publishing, Paris, https://dx.doi.org/10.1787/b0876dcf-en. [12]

Heckemeyer, J. and M. Overesch (2017), "Multinationals' profit response to tax differentials: Effect size and shifting channels", *Canadian Journal of Economics/Revue canadienne d'économique*, Vol. 50/4, pp. 965-994, http://dx.doi.org/10.1111/caje.12283. [17]

Hines, J. and J. Park (2019), "Investment ramifications of distortionary tax subsidies", *Journal of Public Economics*, Vol. 172, pp. 36-51. [202]

Hong, Q. and M. Smart (2010), "In praise of tax havens: International tax planning and foreign direct investment", *European Economic Review*, Vol. 54/1, pp. 82-95, http://dx.doi.org/10.1016/j.euroecorev.2009.06.006. [156]

Hoppe, T. et al. (2020), "The Relation between Tax Complexity and Foreign Direct Investments: Evidence Across Countries", *SSRN Electronic Journal*, http://dx.doi.org/10.2139/ssrn.3526177. [58]

Hoppe, T. et al. (2019), "Measuring Tax Complexity Across Countries: A Survey Study on MNCs", *SSRN Electronic Journal*, http://dx.doi.org/10.2139/ssrn.3469663. [57]

Hsu, M. et al. (2019), "Tax incentives and foreign direct investment in China", *Applied Economics Letters*, Vol. 26/9, pp. 777-780, http://dx.doi.org/10.1080/13504851.2018.1495817. [125]

Huizinga, H. and S. Nielsen (2008), "Must losing taxes on saving be harmful?", *Journal of Public Economics*, Vol. 92/5-6, pp. 1183-1192. [150]

IMF-OECD (2017), *Report for the G20 Finance Ministers on Tax Certainty*, https://www.oecd.org/tax/tax-policy/tax-certainty-report-oecd-imf-report-g20-finance-ministers-march-2017.pdf. [59]

IMF-OECD (2017), *Tax certainty*, IMF/OECD Report for the G20 Finance Ministers. [118]

IMF-OECD-UN-World Bank (2015), *Options for Low Income Countries' Effective and Efficient Use of Tax Incentives for Investment*, A report prepared for the G-20 Development Working Group by the IMF, OECD, UN and World Bank., http://www.imf.org/external/pp/ppindex.aspx. [103]

James, S. (2013), *Tax and Non-Tax Incentives and Investments: Evidence and Policy Implications*, http://ssrn.com/abstract=2401905http://ssrn.com/abstract=2401905. [110]

Javorcik, B. (2004), "Does Foreign Direct Investment Increase the Productivity of Domestic Firms? In Search of Spillovers Through Backward Linkages", *American Economic Review*, pp. 605-627. [104]

Johannesen, N. (2010), "Imperfect tax competition for profits, asymmetric equilibrium and beneficial tax havens", *Journal of International Economics*, Vol. 81/2, pp. 253-264. [157]

Johansson, Å. et al. (2017), *Tax planning by multinational firms: firm-level evidence from a cross-country database*, OECD, http://www.oecd.org/eco/workingpapers. [16]

Joint Committee of Taxation (2011), *Background and Selected Issues Related to the U.S. Internaitonal Tax System and Systems that Exempt Foreign Business Income*, https://www.jct.gov/publications.html?func=startdown&id=3793. [210]

Keen, M. (2001), "Preferential Regimes Can Make Tax Competition Less Harmful", *National Tax Journal*, Vol. 14/4. [158]

Keen, M. and K. Konrad (2013), *The theory of international tax competition and coordination*, Elsevier B.V. [79]

Keen, M. et al. (2015), "Current Challenges in Revenue Mobilisation: Improving Tax Compliance", *IMF Staff Report*, https://www.imf.org/external/np/pp/eng/2015/020215a.pdf. [47]

Kinda, T. (2010), "Investment Climate and FDI in Developing Countries: Firm-Level Evidence", *World Development*, Vol. 38/4, pp. 498-513, https://doi.org/10.1016/j.worlddev.2009.12.001. [120]

Kind, H. and M. Koethenbuerger (2017), "Taxation in digital media markets", *Journal of Public Economic Theory*, Vol. 1. [34]

Kind, H., M. Koethenbuerger and G. Schjelderup (2010), "Tax responses in platform industries", *Oxford Economic Papers*, Vol. 62/4. [32]

Kind, H., M. Koethenbuerger and G. Schjelderup (2008), "Efficiency enhancing taxation in two-sided markets", *Journal of Public Economics*, Vol. 92/5-6. [31]

Kiss, Á. (2012), "Minimum taxes and repeated tax competition", *International Tax and Public Finance*, Vol. 19/5, pp. 641-649. [82]

Klemens, B. (2016), "A Boxing Match: Can Intellectual Property Boxes Achieve Their Stated Goals?", *SSRN Electronic Journal*, http://dx.doi.org/10.2139/ssrn.2822575. [91]

Klemm, A. and S. Van Parys (2012), "Empirical Evidence on the Effects of Tax Incentives", *International Tax and Public Finance*, Vol. 19/3, pp. 393-423. [64]

Konrad, K. (2009), "Non-binding minimum taxes may foster tax competition", *Economics Letters*, Vol. 102/2, pp. 109-111. [81]

Kopp, E. et al. (2019), "U.S. Investment Since the Tax Cuts and Jobs Act of 2017", *IMF Working Papers*, No. 19/120, https://www.imf.org/en/Publications/WP/Issues/2019/05/31/U-S-46942. [40]

Lee, Y. (2020), "Competition in Corporate and Personal Income Tax: Evidence from 67 Developed and Developing Countries", *Korean Economic Review*, Vol. 36, pp. 101-133, http://dx.doi.org/10.1016/j.euroecorev.2009.06.006. [77]

Leibrecht, M. and C. Hochgatterer (2012), "Tax competition as a cause of falling corporate income tax rates: A survey of empirical literature", *Journal of Economic Surveys*, Vol. 26/4, pp. 616-648. [73]

Lignier, P. and C. Evans (2012), "The Rise and Rise of Tax Compliance Costs for the Small Business Sector in Australia", *Australian Tax Forum*, Vol. 27/3, https://papers.ssrn.com/sol3/papers.cfm?abstract_id=2128418. [54]

Lin, W. and J. Wang (2014), "Do Tax Incentives Encourage Direct Investment in China by Taiwanese Enterprises?", *Journal of Accounting and Taxation*, Vol. 6/2, pp. 38–53, http://dx.doi.org/10.5897/JAT2014.0143. [126]

Li, Q. (2016), "Fiscal decentralization and tax incentives in the developing world", *Review of International Political Economy*, Vol. 23/2, pp. 232-260, https://doi.org/10.1080/09692290.2015.1086401. [116]

Lowry, S. (2019), *Digital Services Taxes (DSTs): Policy and Economic Analysis.* [140]

Mairesse, J. and P. Mohnen (2010), *Using Innovations Surveys for Econometric Analysis*, National Bureau of Economic Research, Cambridge, MA, http://dx.doi.org/10.3386/w15857. [164]

Millot, V. et al. (2020), "Corporate Taxation and Investment of Multinational Firms: Evidence from Firm-Level Data", *OECD Taxation Working Papers*, No. 51, OECD Publishing, Paris, https://dx.doi.org/10.1787/9c6f9f2e-en. [44]

Mohnen, P., P. Vankan and B. Verspagen (2017), "Evaluating the innovation box tax policy instruments in the Netherlands, 2007-13", *Oxford Review of Economic Policy*, Vol. 33/1, pp. 141-156, https://doi.org/10.1093/oxrep/grw038. [172]

Mongrain, S. and J. Wilson (2017), *Tax Competition with Heterogeneous Capital Mobility*, https://www.cesifo.org/DocDL/cesifo1_wp5688.pdf. [159]

Mutti, J. and H. Grubert (2004), "Empirical Asymmetries in Foreign Direct Investment and Taxation", *Journal of International Economics*, Vol. 62/2, pp. 337-358, http://dx.doi.org/10.1016/S0022-1996(03)00016-3. [114]

OECD (2020), *Corporate Tax Statistics database*, https://oe.cd/corporate-tax-stats. [19]

OECD (2020), *Corporate Tax Statistics. Corporate Effective Tax Rates: Explanatory Annex.*, https://www.oecd.org/tax/tax-policy/explanatory-annex-corporate-effective-tax-rates.pdf. [15]

OECD (2020), *METRO Version 3: Model Documentation*, OECD Publishing, Paris, https://one.oecd.org/document/TAD/TC/WP/RD(2020)1/FINAL/en/pdf. [147]

OECD (2020), *Tax Challenges Arising from Digitalisation – Report on Pillar One Blueprint: Inclusive Framework on BEPS*, OECD/G20 Base Erosion and Profit Shifting Project, OECD Publishing, Paris, https://dx.doi.org/10.1787/beba0634-en. [13]

OECD (2020), *Tax Challenges Arising from Digitalisation – Report on Pillar Two Blueprint: Inclusive Framework on BEPS*, OECD/G20 Base Erosion and Profit Shifting Project, OECD Publishing, Paris, https://dx.doi.org/10.1787/abb4c3d1-en. [14]

OECD (2020), "The effects of R&D tax incentives and their role in the innovation policy mix: Findings from the OECD microBeRD project, 2016-19", *OECD Science, Technology and Industry Policy Papers No. 92*, https://doi.org/10.1787/65234003-en. [166]

OECD (2019), *FDI Qualities Indicators: Measuring the sustainable development impacts of investment*, OECD Publishing. [106]

OECD (2019), *OECD R&D Tax Incentive Database*, http://oe.cd/rdtax. [179]

OECD (2019), "OECD time series estimates of government tax relief for business R&D", No. TAX4INNO Project 674888, http://www.oecd.org/sti/rd-tax-stats-tax-expenditures.pdf. [181]

OECD (2019), *Programme of Work to Develop a Consensus Solution to the Tax Challenges Arising from the Digitalisation of the Economy, OECD/G20 Inclusive Framework on BEPS*, OECD, Paris, https://www.oecd.org/tax/beps/programme-of-work-to-develop-a-consensus-solution-to-the-tax-challenges-arising-from-the-digitalisation-of-the-economy.pdf. [1]

OECD (2019), "Vectors of Digital Transformation", *OECD Digital Economy Papers*, No. 273, http://dx.doi.org/10.1787/5ade2bba-en. [129]

OECD (2018), *Tax Challenges Arising from Digitalisation – Interim Report 2018*, OECD, https://doi.org/10.1787/9789264293083-en. [128]

OECD (2018), *Trade Facilitation and the Global Economy*, OECD Publishing, Paris, http://dx.doi.org/10.1787/9789264277571-en. [199]

OECD (2018), *Trade Policy and the Global Economy - Scenario 2: Increasing Tariffs*, https://issuu.com/oecd.publishing/docs/oecd-trade-scenario-2-increasing_ta?e=3055080/65009159. [148]

OECD (2015), *Addressing the Tax Challenges of the Digital Economy, Action 1 - 2015 Final Report*, OECD. [139]

OECD (2015), *Designing Effective Controlled Foreign Company Rules, Action 3 - 2015 Final Report*, OECD/G20 Base Erosion and Profit Shifting Project, OECD Publishing, Paris, https://dx.doi.org/10.1787/9789264241152-en. [192]

OECD (2015), *Policy Framework for Investment, 2015 Edition*, OECD Publishing, Paris, https://dx.doi.org/10.1787/9789264208667-en. [111]

OECD (2015), *The Innovation Imperative: Contributing to Productivity, Growth and Well-Being*, OECD Publishing, Paris, https://dx.doi.org/10.1787/9789264239814-en. [100]

OECD (2010), *The OECD Innovation Strategy: Getting a Head Start on Tomorrow*, OECD Publishing, Paris, https://dx.doi.org/10.1787/9789264083479-en. [101]

OECD-WTO-IMF (2020), *Handbook on Measuring Digital Trade.* [204]

Ohrn, E. (2019), "The effect of tax incentives on U.S. manufacturing: Evidence from state accelerated depreciation policies", *Journal of Public Economics*, Vol. 180, p. 104084, http://dx.doi.org/10.1016/j.jpubeco.2019.104084. [97]

Redoano, M. (2014), "Tax competition among European countries. Does the EU matter?", *European Journal of Political Economy*, Vol. 34, pp. 353-371. [76]

Redonda and Neubig (2018), *Assessing Tax Expenditure Reporting in G20 and OECD Economies*, Council on Economic Policies. [113]

Rochet, J. and J. Tirole (2006), "Two-sided markets: a progress report", *RAND Journal of Economics*, Vol. 37/3, pp. 645-667. [30]

Rochet, J. and J. Tirole (2003), "Platform Competition in Two-Sided Markets", *Journal of the European Economic Association*, Vol. 1/4, pp. 990-1029. [29]

Romer, P. (1990), "Endogenous technological change", *Journal of Political Economy*, Vol. 98/5, pp. S71-S102, http://dx.doi.org/10.3386/w3210. [84]

Schwerin, V. and A. Buettner (2016), *A Service of zbw Leibniz-Informationszentrum Wirtschaft Leibniz Information Centre for Economics*. [66]

Serrato, J. and O. Zidar (2016), *Who benefits from state corporate tax cuts? A local labor markets approach with heterogeneous firms*, American Economic Association. [27]

Slemrod, J. (2008), "Why Is Elvis on Burkina Faso Postage Stamps? Cross-Country Evidence on the Commercialization of State Sovereignty", *Journal of Empirical Legal Studies*, Vol. 5/4, pp. 683-712. [153]

Slemrod, J. and M. Blumenthal (1996), "The Income Tax Compliance Cost of Big Business", *Public Finance Review*, Vol. 24/4, pp. 411-438, http://dx.doi.org/10.1177/109114219602400401 (accessed on 23 April 2020). [60]

Slemrod, J. and V. Venkatesh (2002), "The Income Tax Compliance Cost of Large and Mid-Size Businesses", No. 914, Ross School of Business Paper, http://dx.doi.org/10.2139/ssrn.913056. [50]

Slemrod, J. and J. Wilson (2009), "Tax competition with parasitic tax havens", *Journal of Public Economics*, Vol. 93/11-12, pp. 1261-1270. [45]

Sorbe, S. and Å. Johansson (2017), "International tax planning and fixed investment", *OECD Economics Department Working Papers*, No. 1361, OECD Publishing, Paris, https://dx.doi.org/10.1787/83239540-en. [7]

Sorbe, S. and Å. Johansson (2017), "International tax planning, competition and market structure", *OECD Economics Department Working Papers* No. 1358. [132]

Squicciarini, M. and H. Dernis (2013), "A Cross-Country Characterisation of the Patenting Behaviour of Firms based on Matched Firm and Patent Data", *OECD Science, Technology and Industry Working Papers*, No. 05, http://dx.doi.org/10.1787/5k40gxd4vh41-en. [183]

Stamatopoulos, I., S. Hadjidema and K. Eleftheriou (2017), "Corporate income tax compliance costs and their determinants: Evidence from greece", *Advances in Taxation*, Vol. 24, pp. 233-270, http://dx.doi.org/10.1108/S1058-749720170000024006. [52]

Suárez Serrato, J. (2018), "Unintended Consequences of Eliminating Tax Havens", *NBER Working Papers*, Vol. 24850. [205]

Syverson, C. (2019), *Macroeconomics and market power: Context, implications, and open questions*, American Economic Association, http://dx.doi.org/10.1257/jep.33.3.23. [133]

Thierfelder, K. and S. Mcdonald (2012), *Globe v1: A SAM Based Global CGE Model using GTAP Data*, https://www.usna.edu/EconDept/RePEc/usn/wp/usnawp39.pdf. [194]

Thomsen, S. (2004), *Investment Incentives and FDI in Selected ASEAN Countries*, OECD Publishing. [121]

Tremblay, M. and V. Tremblay (2017), "Tax Incidence and Demand Convexity in Cournot, Bertrand, and Cournot–Bertrand Models", *Public Finance Review*, Vol. 45/6. [35]

U.S. Department of the Treasury (2016), *Treasury Announces Additional Action to Curb Inversions, Address Earnings Stripping*, https://www.treasury.gov/press-center/press-releases/Pages/jl0405.aspx. [208]

U.S. Department of the Treasury (2014), *Fact Sheet: Treasury Actions to Rein in Corporate Tax Inversions*, https://www.treasury.gov/press-center/press-releases/Pages/jl2645.aspx. [207]

UNCTAD (2019), *World Investment Report 2019: Special Economic Zones*, United Nations Conference on Trade and Development, http://dx.doi.org/ISBN 978-92-1-112949-6. [122]

UNIDO (2013), *Africa Investor Survey*, United Nations Industrial Development Organization, http://dx.doi.org/978-92-1-106450-6. [117]

USTR (2020), *Initiation of Section 301 Investigations of Digital Services Taxes*. [146]

USTR (2020), *Notice of Action in the Section 301 Investigation of France's Digital Services Tax*. [143]

USTR (2019), *Notice of Determination and Request for Comments Concerning Action Pursuant to Section 301: France's Digital Services Tax*. [142]

USTR (2019), *Report on France's Digital Services Tax Prepared in the Investigation under*. [141]

Voget, J. (2011), "Relocation of headquarters and international taxation", *Journal of Public Economics*, Vol. 95/9-10, pp. 1067-1081, http://dx.doi.org/10.1016/j.jpubeco.2010.11.019. [189]

Vukšić, G. (2013), "Developing countries in competition for foreign investment", *Journal of International Trade and Economic Development*, Vol. 22/3, pp. 351-376. [102]

Wang, J. (2013), "The economic impact of Special Economic Zones: Evidence from Chinese municipalities", *Journal of Development Economics*, Vol. 101, pp. 133-147, https://doi.org/10.1016/j.jdeveco.2012.10.009. [123]

Wells, L. et al. (2001), *Using tax incentives to compete for foreign investment - Are they worth the costs?*, http://documents.worldbank.org/curated/en/164401468770722428/Using-tax-incentives-to-compete-for-foreign-investment-Are-they-worth-the-costs. [112]

Wiedemann, V. and K. Finke (2015), *Taxing investments in the Asia-Pacific region: The importance of cross-border taxation and tax incentives*, ZEW Discussion Paper No. 15-014, http://ftp.zew.de/pub/zew-docs/dp/dp15014.pdf. [109]

Wilson, J. (1986), "A Theory of Interregional Tax Competition", *Journal of Urban Economics*, Vol. 19/3, pp. 296-315, http://dx.doi.org/10.1016/0094-1190(86)90045-8. [70]

World Bank (2017), *Corporate Tax Incentives and FDI in Developing Economies*, World Bank, https://doi.org/10.1596/978-1-4648-1175-3. [108]

Zodrow, G. and P. Mieszkowski (1986), "Pigou, Tiebout, Property Taxation, and the Underprovision of Local Public Goods", *Journal of Urban Economics*, Vol. 19/3, pp. 356-370, http://dx.doi.org/10.1016/0094-1190(86)90048-3. [69]

Zwick, E. and J. Mahon (2017), "Tax policy and heterogeneous investment behavior", *American Economic Review*, Vol. 107/1, pp. 217-248, http://dx.doi.org/10.1257/aer.20140855. [39]

# Annex 4.A. Tax Competition: Theoretical Insights

416. This annex provides an overview of the recent developments in the theoretical tax competition literature. It complements Box 4.3 that focuses mostly on empirical studies.

417. Earlier contributions to the theoretical literature on tax competition, reviewed by Forslid (2005[149]), Keen and Konrad (2013[79]) or Devereux and Loretz (2013[68]) among others, have produced insights and stimulus for empirical research. Huizinga and Nielsen (2008[150]), for example, construct a model in which multinational production creates economic rents and firm ownership is diversified across domestic and foreign owners. Extending the standard framework in this way highlights that governments may have incentives to increase source-based CIT rates to tax some of the economic rent accruing to foreign owners; this effect, in turn, weakens competitive pressure on CIT rates. Baldwin and Krugman (2004[151]) question the idea that economic integration necessarily increases competitive pressure on corporate tax rates. Their model allows for location-specific rents to arise from economic agglomeration, i.e., the emergence of highly-productive nodes within the world economy. Similar to Huizinga and Nielsen (2008[150]), location-specific rents may induce governments to set higher CIT rates, thus dampening tax competition; as intensifying economic integration first increases and then decreases economic agglomeration, they find that the relation between economic integration and tax competition could be non-linear.

418. The theoretical literature has also investigated the role of certain zero-tax jurisdictions specialised in attracting accounting profits that are shifted outwards from other jurisdictions – in the context of these models. The existence of zero-tax jurisdictions and investment hubs can have an impact on tax competition for real investments occurring between other countries (see Dharmapala (2008[152]) for a review). The distinguishing feature of this literature is that it introduces the possibility for MNEs to relocate accounting profits from one jurisdiction to another while keeping real production decisions unchanged; it views zero-tax jurisdictions and investment hubs typically as jurisdictions with a small (or negligible) real economy, specialised in attracting accounting profits from other countries in return for a small payment. Slemrod (2008[153]) argues that this strategy corresponds to a commercialisation of a jurisdiction's sovereignty that comes at the cost of a significant loss in reputation; as a result, mostly countries with small population sizes adopt this strategy (Dharmapala and Hines, 2006[154]).

419. Slemrod and Wilson (2009[45]) formalise this idea in the context of a tax competition model; their results highlight that tax avoidance activities, e.g., tax consultants helping to shift profits to low-tax jurisdictions, represent a net social loss to the economy, and that higher shifting costs reduce the marginal cost of public funds. Other studies have challenged this view, arguing that the existence of low-tax jurisdictions allows other jurisdictions to offer lower effective marginal tax rates (at the MNE group level) when tax policy cannot discriminate between mobile and immobile tax bases. According to this argument, the existence of low-tax jurisdictions therefore has the potential to induce an increase in real investment that could outweigh other costs associated to them (Desai, Foley and Hines (2006[155]); Hong and Smart (2010[156])). Finally, Johannesen (2010[157]) further explores the effects on tax competition, suggesting that the existence of zero-tax jurisdictions and investment hubs could force countries with lower effective taxation to choose whether to pursue a zero-tax strategy. As a result, the remaining jurisdictions would have incentives to coordinate towards a higher-tax strategy, implying lower levels of tax competition.

420. Keen (2001[158]) argues that a differentiation of tax rates on mobile and immobile tax bases, through preferential regimes, can increase competition for mobile bases while decreasing it for immobile bases, possibly leading to an overall positive impact on revenues. Mongrain and Wilson (2017[159]) build on this approach, introducing a model where tax policy makers cannot directly observe tax base mobility. As discrimination between tax bases becomes more costly within this framework, countries could decide

against the introduction of preferential regimes leading to, under certain conditions, higher overall tax revenues.

421. Another strand of the theoretical literature on tax competition has focussed on the political processes underlying national tax policy choices, i.e., dropping the assumption that government acts as a benevolent planner. Instead, this literature introduces the effects of electoral policies or self-interested policy-making by politicians into the modelling framework, studying how these assumptions affect tax competition (e.g., Brennan and Buchanan (1980[160]) or Edwards and Keen (1996[161])). Eggert and Soerensen (2008[162]), more recently, develop a model where vote-maximising politicians have an incentive to increase the size of the public sector to create economic rents for public sector employees; in this setting, tax competition is found to be potentially welfare-enhancing due to the fact that it restricts this type of self-interested behaviour.

# Annex 4.B. Tax Incentives to Support Innovation

## Evidence on the use and effectiveness of R&D tax incentives

422. The effectiveness of government support for R&D can be evaluated from an input perspective, in terms of its capacity to generate additional R&D investment, or from an output perspective, in terms of its capacity to generate innovation.

423. Expenditure-based R&D tax incentives have proven effective in generating both additional R&D investment by firms (i.e., input additionality), as well as an increase in innovation (i.e., output additionality), although evidence on the latter is more scarce. The most recent estimates find that a euro of R&D tax relief offered by governments translates into at least one euro extra of R&D investment by firms (Hall and Van Reenen, 2000[163]; Mairesse and Mohnen, 2010[164]; de Boer et al., 2019[165]; OECD, 2020[166]). In addition, the input additionality of expenditure-based R&D tax incentives is found to be larger for young and small- and medium-sized enterprises (SMEs) than for larger firms (Castellacci and Lie, 2015[167]; Dechezleprêtre et al., 2016[168]). These estimates would overstate the additionality of expenditure-based R&D tax incentives if there is relabelling of non-R&D expenditure as R&D expenditure to benefit from the tax relief or if these incentives incite the relocation of R&D activity rather than an increase in global R&D (Bloom, Van Reenen and Williams, 2019[99]). Output additionality is more difficult to measure due to the possible lag between R&D and innovation, the imperfect nature of innovation indicators and measurement difficulties related to potential spillover effects (Appelt et al., 2016[90]; Mairesse and Mohnen, 2010[164]). Several studies find positive evidence pointing to increased innovative sales, new products and patenting activity (Czarnitzki, Hanel and Rosa, 2011[169]; Ernst and Spengel, 2011[170]; Cappelen, Raknerud and Rybalka, 2012[171]) in response to the tax break.

424. While the evidence is more positive and conclusive on the effectiveness of expenditure-based R&D tax incentives, this is not the case for income-based R&D tax incentives. From the input-side, evidence on the ability of income-based incentives to induce additional business R&D spending is mixed (Mohnen, Vankan and Verspagen, 2017[172]; Gaessler, Hall and Harhoff, 2018[92]). From the output-side, the measurement of their impact on innovation poses methodological challenges due to the secular upward trend in patenting and the lack of sources of variation across countries and time, which may explain differences in results in prior literature (Gaessler, Hall and Harhoff, 2018[92]; Hall, 2019[88]). However, while income-based R&D tax incentives are designed to promote the output from R&D, recent evidence suggests that patented inventions do not show a statistically significant increase in countries offering intellectual property (IP) regimes compared to those that do not; on the contrary, some findings suggest a small negative impact on the numbers of patented inventions (Gaessler, Hall and Harhoff, 2018[92]). This apparent failure to achieve the stated policy goal, combined with limited evidence on their effectiveness, casts doubt over the rationale for this policy instrument (Gaessler, Hall and Harhoff, 2018[92]; Bloom, Van Reenen and Williams, 2019[99]).

425. The mobile nature of intangible assets makes it easier for multinational firms to strategically determine the location, and thus the income derived from them, in response to preferential income treatment in order to minimise their global tax liabilities (Griffith, Miller and O'Connell, 2014[173]). Evidence suggests that the location and transfer of patents is responsive to preferential tax rates, offered through IP regimes, if no domestic development conditions are required (Alstadsaeter et al., 2015[174]; Ciaramella, 2017[175]). As part of the Base Erosion and Profit Shifting (BEPS) project, government efforts have been directed towards a reduction in the use of these incentives for harmful purposes, which resulted in the nexus requirements introduced under BEPS Action 5 and other recommendations regarding controlled-

foreign company (CFC) rules under BEPS Action 3. The introduction of development conditions as a prerequisite to providing benefits from the income-based incentives has been found to mitigate the transfer of patents for purely tax purposes (Gaessler, Hall and Harhoff, 2018[92]).

426. Aside from indirect support through the tax system, direct government support via, for example, grants are found to have positive impacts on both R&D investment and innovation output output (Busom, 2000[176]; Almus and Czarnitzki, 2003[177]; Hall and Maffioli, 2008[178]; OECD, 2020[166]).

## Design considerations: how much, to whom and why?

427. The design of R&D tax incentives plays a major role in determining how generous tax benefits are expected to be and to which firm types, and types of activity, the benefits are directed.

428. First, alongside the general characteristics of tax systems, the design of R&D tax incentives influences the generosity of these provisions. A comparison across countries yields a very heterogeneous landscape, with the implied R&D subsidy rate provided through expenditure-based R&D tax incentives ranging from somewhere close to 0 to 0.41 euros for an extra euro of R&D invested by large profitable firms (OECD, 2019[179]). The generosity of these schemes has also been growing over time, with the average implied subsidy rising from 0.03 in 2000 to 0.14 in 2019 for large profitable firms. The trends are similar for firms of different types and levels of profitability (Appelt, Galindo-Rueda and González Cabral, 2019[83]).

429. Second, although tax incentives are non-discretionary instruments, governments can design R&D tax incentives to target certain activities or firm types to address specific market failures. In some jurisdictions, preferential treatment is granted to young as well as small- and medium-sized enterprises through preferential rates; more generous provisions are sometimes applied in case of insufficient tax liabilities, e.g., refund provisions or more generous carry-over provisions, or to projects conducted in collaboration, e.g., with universities. In some countries, ceilings are used to limit the generosity of the provisions, particularly to large claimants, and to shelter public finances. In contrast to volume-based incentives that provide relief to the full R&D expenditure, incremental tax incentives provide enhanced relief to R&D above a certain base amount to avoid funding R&D that would have been undertaken in the absence of support, in an effort to protect public finances (Appelt et al., 2016[90]).

430. Beyond the design of R&D tax incentives, it is crucial to analyse the use of these provisions to assess whether the intended policy goal is achieved. The distribution of tax support across firms and activities ultimately depends on the types of firm that are using the incentives as well as the interaction of their characteristics with the design of the incentive, e.g., the benefits for loss-making firms will depend on whether carry-over or refundability provisions are available (Appelt, Galindo-Rueda and González Cabral, 2019[83]).

431. Recent literature has shed light on some of these questions, producing several important insights:

- **Innovation, R&D and government support are highly concentrated:** The top 2000 R&D performers account for almost two thirds of patents filed at the largest five IP offices worldwide (Dernis et al., 2019[180]). In addition, large taxpayers also benefit from the majority of government support – both direct grants and tax support – despite constituting a smaller number of claims (OECD, 2019[181]). Taken together, the evidence on the concentration of patents, especially high-revenue patents, among a small number of large MNEs suggests that the benefits from preferential regimes accrue mainly to multinational firms.

  The rationale for channelling government support to large performers is attached to their ability to generate larger spillover effects and externalities, particularly if directed to basic research activities (Bloom, Schankerman and Reenen, 2013[182]; Akcigit, Hanley and Serrano-Velarde, 2013[89]).[63]

- **The extent of government support to MNEs might be higher than intended:** The expansion of global value chains provides MNEs with the opportunity to locate their activity, including their R&D activities and intangible assets, in a tax efficient manner (Ernst and Spengel, 2011[170]). This may boost the return to innovation that MNEs are able to secure relative to domestic performers, who could face comparative disadvantages due to these policies, an effect that might not have been intended when the policy was designed. With rising levels of the generosity of R&D tax incentives and with firms becoming increasingly more global, this concern is likely to become increasingly salient. In addition, the transfer of patents to other jurisdictions might also result in situations where the jurisdictions granting tax relief to R&D cannot secure the intended benefits, as spillovers materialise outside the domestic economy (OECD, 2015[100]).
- **Young firms and SMEs play a key role in spurring innovation**: Looking at patenting activity as an imperfect measure for innovation, first-time patenting occurs typically within ten years of the existence of the firm (Squicciarini and Dernis, 2013[183]) and young firms are more likely to introduce radical innovations (Andrews, Criscuolo and Menon, 2014[98]). These findings highlight the importance of facilitating entry of young firms and SMEs into the market, both of whom tend to face greater difficulties in accessing finance (Hall and Lerner, 2010[87]), as well as greater fixed costs of entry, as regulatory compliance costs are typically regressive in size.
- **Established performers may have an incentive to innovate to preserve their market position:** Although incumbents benefitting from monopoly rents may not have an incentive to innovate per se, the challenge posed by new entrants, who have incentives to capture the rents, may induce them to innovate to protect their dominant market position (Blundell, Griffiths and Van Reenen, 1999[184]). This effect might be particularly relevant in highly digitalised and intangible-intensive sectors in which market concentration has been found to increase more strongly than in other sectors (De Loecker and Eeckhout, 2017[185]; Autor et al., 2020[135]; Calligaris, Criscuolo and Marcolin, 2018[2]). Subsidising large incumbent firms might be counterproductive if it encourages the survival of firms with low innovative capacity preventing resources from being allocated to firms with high innovation capacity (Acemoglu et al., 2018[186]).

# Annex 4.C. Corporate Inversions

432. As discussed in the Section 4.7, the implementation of an income inclusion rule (IIR) acts as a top-up to low-taxed profits earned by subsidiaries. Taken in isolation, MNEs could have incentives to invert, i.e. to change their tax residence, in order to escape the tax liability. The under-taxed payment rule (UPR) acts to prevent such an incentive. This appendix provides a review of the literature on corporate inversions by MNEs in the context of recent policy developments.

433. The international operations of MNEs allow them to utilise a variety of strategies to change how and where their income is taxed. Corporate inversions are one of these strategies, by which an MNE engages in a transaction that changes the location of its ultimate parent entity and consequently, its tax residence, to a foreign jurisdiction. While corporate inversions can be motivated by many factors, some inversions are motivated by tax considerations. Companies inverting out of the United States between 1994 and 2014 are estimated to have reduced their worldwide tax expense to earnings ratio by an average of 9 percentage points, i.e. from an average of 29% prior to the inversion to 18% the year after the inversion (Congressional Budget Office, 2017[187]).64

434. Several corporate inversions have been documented during the last decade; however, anecdotal evidence points towards a slowdown in recent years (Clausing, Miller and Mintz, 2014[188]; Voget, 2011[189]; Congressional Budget Office, 2017[187]; Congressional Research Service, 2019[190]).65 Recent developments in international and domestic taxation and the increased use of anti-inversion regulations are likely to have driven this most recent trend. Overall, incentives for corporate inversions may vary across jurisdictions according to the structure and level of taxation as well as the stringency of regulations against base erosion and profit shifting (BEPS).

435. First, in worldwide tax systems, taxes on foreign active income can typically be deferred until repatriation. Such a system may lead MNEs to accumulate large amounts of unrepatriated profits in foreign jurisdictions, increasing the motivation for corporate inversions (Clausing, Miller and Mintz, 2014[188]; Desai and Hines, 2002[191]).66 This effect becomes more salient, the higher the taxation is at the level of the headquarter jurisdiction. Evidence suggests that a 10 percentage points increase in repatriation taxes is estimated to increase the share of relocating MNEs by 2.2 percentage points (Voget, 2011[189]). However, in recent years there has been a clear shift towards territoriality with only four out of 37 OECD countries67 retaining worldwide taxation. Under territorial tax systems, incentives for inversions are much weaker as active income from their foreign subsidiaries is exempt upon repatriation.

436. Second, the move towards territorial taxation has increased pressure on curbing base erosion and profit shifting. Under territorial taxation, the exemption of foreign active income creates incentives to shift income to low-tax jurisdictions. This has led to coordinated international efforts to introduce anti-BEPS rules that seek to protect corporate tax bases. As an example, controlled foreign company (CFC) rules allow the parent to bring low-taxed passive income into the domestic tax base, thus reducing the incentive to relocate profits (OECD, 2015[192]).68 Indeed, CFC rules appear to induce MNEs to locate not only less profit but also fewer subsidiaries in jurisdictions below the CFC threshold, moving the income to higher-taxed environments (Clifford, 2019[193]). However, the presence of CFC rules appears to also increase the likelihood of headquarter relocations (Voget, 2011[189]).69

437. Third, some jurisdictions have sought to reinforce domestic regulations in order to hinder the ability of corporations to invert with the purpose of obtaining a tax advantage. These include regulations that tighten restrictions over how companies are classified as foreign, e.g., including stricter criteria on control or economic substance; as well as regulations to close strategies that firms use to erode the tax base (Congressional Research Service, 2019[190]).70 However, measures to deter corporate inversions are

dependent on the regulatory framework of the jurisdiction enacting them; e.g., in the European Union freedom of establishment is one of the fundamental freedoms of the European single market.

438. Although changes in organisational structures are pursued to obtain a tax advantage, corporate inversions are associated with considerable costs and uncertainties. Aside from the costs required to establish the organisational structure, the restructuring might trigger additional tax liabilities on other tax bases, e.g., transaction taxes or capital gains[71] taxes, depending on the regulatory framework in the respective jurisdictions. Inversions have consequences beyond taxation stemming from: the change in control of the company whereby shareholders could lose their influence over the future of the company; the new regulatory environment of the country where the company inverts to; and the reputational costs that might be attached to inverted companies (Congressional Budget Office, 2017[187]). In many cases, these hidden costs associated with corporate inversions could outweigh the tax advantages from restructuring.

# Annex 4.D. Trade Simulations

439. This annex provides some further results regarding the empirical calibration of the trade simulations discussed in the Section 4.8, exploring the effects of tariff retaliation on non-service trade against DSTs unilaterally imposed by a subset of countries. The numerical results are obtained using the OECD METRO model, which is a computable general equilibrium model (CGE) that traces complex international interdependencies in a theoretically and empirically consistent framework.[72]

## Model description

440. The METRO model is calibrated for this analysis to 6 regions (Table 4.3), 19 sectors, and 8 production factors (OECD, 2020[147]). The simulations represent short-to-medium term shocks where production factors are mobile across sectors, but the overall endowment of labour remains fixed while allowing for unemployment, and capital stocks respond to investment.

441. METRO, like many CGE models, relies on a comprehensive specification of all economic activity within and sometimes between countries (and therefore the different inter-linkages that tie these together). The model builds on the GLOBE model developed by McDonald and Thierfelder (2012[194]). The novelty and strength of METRO lies in the detailed trade structure and the differentiation of commodities by end use. Specifically, commodities and thus trade flows are distinguished by whether they are destined for intermediate use, for use by households, for government consumption, or as investment commodities.

442. The underlying framework of METRO consists of a series of individually specified economies interlinked through trade relationships. As is common in CGE models, the price system is linearly homogeneous, with a focus on relative, not absolute, price changes. Each region has its own numeraire, typically the consumer price index, and a nominal exchange rate (an exchange rate index of reference regions serves as model numeraire). Prices between regions change relative to the reference region.

443. The database of the model relies on the GTAP v10 database (Aguiar et al., 2019[195]) in combination with the OECD Inter-Country Input-Output Tables, which are the main source of the OECD Trade in Value Added Indicators and allows the model to distinguish trade for use in intermediate production or final demand. Policy information combines tariff and tax information from GTAP with OECD estimates of non-tariff measures on goods (Cadot et al., 2018[196]), services (Benz and Gonzales, 2019[197]) (Benz and Jaax, 2020[198]), trade facilitation (OECD, 2018[199]) and export restricting measures. The METRO database contains 65 countries and regional aggregates and 65 commodities.

444. The model is firmly rooted in microeconomic theory, with firms maximising profits and creating output from primary inputs (i.e., land, natural resources, labour and capital), which are combined using constant elasticity of substitution (CES) technology, and intermediate inputs in fixed shares (Leontief technology). Households are assumed to maximise utility subject to a Stone-Geary utility function, which allows for the inclusion of a subsistence level of consumption. All commodity and activity taxes are expressed as ad valorem tax rates, and taxes are the only income source to the government.

445. In the simulations for this analysis, the trade balance is fixed and the nominal exchange rate is flexible. Wages are assumed downwardly rigid, but remuneration rates of all other factors (i.e., land, capital, natural resources) are assumed to adjust. All tax and tariff rates are exogenous and fixed, government expenditures are fixed at base levels in value terms (i.e., there are no budgetary reallocations). Government surplus or deficit is flexible and adjusts with changes in tax and tariff revenues. The overall savings rate is fixed for each country group.

## Calibration: digital service taxes and tariff retaliation

446. As described in Box 4.8, the DST is implemented as an ad valorem tax on intermediate sales from the business services sector to all buyers, using the French DST as benchmark. The DST-equivalent sector-level tax rates are applied permanently to all countries included in the simulations. Annex Table 4.D.2 shows the respective tax revenues generated in each of the country groups. Tariffs are simulated on trade in non-service sectors that are known to be typically targeted for tariff action and are symmetrically and permanently applied to the same products, which makes the results comparable between countries (Annex Table 4.D.1).[73]

### Annex Table 4.D.1. Sectors targeted for tariff retaliation or counter retaliation

Targeted sectors are subject to tariff retaliation or counter retaliation.

| All Sectors | Targeted Sectors |
|---|---|
| Cereal grains | *Cereal grains* |
| Other agriculture and food | |
| Beverages and tobacco products | *Beverages and tobacco products* |
| Oil seeds | *Oil seeds* |
| Natural resources | |
| Meats | *Meats* |
| Mineral and metal products | |
| Motor vehicles and parts | *Motor vehicles and parts* |
| Transport equipment | *Transport equipment* |
| Electronic equipment | *Electronic equipment* |
| Machinery and equipment | *Machinery and equipment* |
| Other manufacturing | |
| Transportation services | |
| Communication services | |
| Financial services | |
| Insurance | |
| Business services | |
| Education services | |
| Public Administration and defence | |

Source: METRO v3 simulations and database, OECD calculations.

### Annex Table 4.D.2. DST revenues targeted for tariff retaliation

| US retaliation factor | 0.5 | | 1 | | 4 | | 5 | |
|---|---|---|---|---|---|---|---|---|
| DST rate | 3% | 5% | 3% | 5% | 3% | 5% | 3% | 5% |
| Model DST tax parameter | 0.12% | 0.20% | 0.12% | 0.20% | 0.12% | 0.20% | 0.12% | 0.20% |
| 1 DST legislated | 454 | 757 | 454 | 757 | 454 | 757 | 454 | 757 |
| 2 Section 301 EU Countries | 2167 | 3612 | 2167 | 3612 | 2167 | 3612 | 2167 | 3612 |
| 3 Section 301 non-EU Countries | 824 | 1373 | 824 | 1373 | 824 | 1373 | 824 | 1373 |
| 6 Other | 2460 | 4101 | 2460 | 4101 | 2460 | 4101 | 2460 | 4101 |

Source: METRO v3 database, OECD calculations.

447. In the retaliating region, i.e., the United States, the size of the ad valorem tariff rate depends on the DST revenues in the implementing country, the imports into the United States of the targeted sectors in the baseline data and the size of the retaliation factor. The average retaliatory tariffs by country group

are shown in Annex Table 4.D.3. The calibrated tariff rates are generally close between country groups, except for country group 6 that contains a very mixed set of economies at different stages of development. As a result, the average level of servicification in this group is lower than in the other groups, and hence the revenues from a tax on digital services at a given tax rate are also lower compared to their weight in the global economy (see GDP shares in Table 4.3 and DST revenues in Annex Table 4.D.2). This results in a relatively lower level of retaliatory tariffs.

### Annex Table 4.D.3. US Retaliatory tariffs on targeted sectors

The table shows the unweighted average tariff rate across all targeted sectors (Annex Table 4.D.1) corresponding to the respective DST revenue volume (Annex Table 4.D.2) and retaliation factor.

| **US retaliation factor** | **0.5** | | **1** | | **4** | | **5** | |
|---|---|---|---|---|---|---|---|---|
| **DST rate** | **3%** | **5%** | **3%** | **5%** | **3%** | **5%** | **3%** | **5%** |
| Model DST tax parameter | 0.12% | 0.20% | 0.12% | 0.20% | 0.12% | 0.20% | 0.12% | 0.20% |
| 1 DST legislated | 1.1% | 1.8% | 2.1% | 3.6% | 8.6% | 14.3% | 10.7% | 17.9% |
| 2 Section 301 EU Countries | 0.9% | 1.4% | 1.7% | 2.8% | 6.8% | 11.4% | 8.5% | 14.2% |
| 3 Section 301 non-EU Countries | 1.1% | 1.8% | 2.2% | 3.7% | 8.8% | 14.7% | 11.1% | 18.4% |
| 6 Other | 0.3% | 0.4% | 0.5% | 0.9% | 2.1% | 3.5% | 2.6% | 4.4% |

Source: METRO v3 database, OECD calculations.

448. In scenarios with counter-retaliation, countries react to the retaliatory tariff imposed by the United States such that the counter-retaliation matches retaliation in terms of tariff revenues, without an additional mark up. The counter-retaliatory tariffs, shown in Annex Table 4.D.4, are close, but not equal, to the initial retaliatory tariffs imposed by the United States because the size of the import flow into the counter-retaliating countries does not generally match the size of their exports on which the initial US retaliatory tariff is based.

### Annex Table 4.D.4. Counter-retaliatory tariffs on targeted sectors

The table shows the unweighted average tariff rate across all targeted sectors (Annex Table 4.D.1) corresponding to the respective DST revenue volume (Annex Table 4.D.2) and retaliation factor.

| **US retaliation factor** | **0.5** | | **1** | | **4** | | **5** | |
|---|---|---|---|---|---|---|---|---|
| **DST rate** | **3%** | **5%** | **3%** | **5%** | **3%** | **5%** | **3%** | **5%** |
| Model DST tax parameter | 0.12% | 0.20% | 0.12% | 0.20% | 0.12% | 0.20% | 0.12% | 0.20% |
| 1 DST legislated | 1.4% | 2.3% | 2.8% | 4.6% | 11.1% | 18.4% | 13.8% | 23.0% |
| 2 Section 301 EU Countries | 1.7% | 2.8% | 3.3% | 5.5% | 13.3% | 22.1% | 16.6% | 27.6% |
| 3 Section 301 non-EU Countries | 1.0% | 1.7% | 2.1% | 3.4% | 8.2% | 13.7% | 10.3% | 17.2% |
| 6 Other | 0.3% | 0.5% | 0.6% | 1.0% | 2.4% | 4.0% | 3.0% | 4.9% |

Source: METRO v3 database, OECD calculations.

## Additional results

449. The series of simulations for each parameter combination follows the sequence outlined in Annex Table 4.D.5. First, the implementation of the DST is simulated (S0); second, the new equilibrium after the DST implementation is taken as a starting point to simulate tariff retaliation (S1); third, starting again with the new equilibrium after tariff retaliation has taken place, counter-retaliation is simulated according to the case with narrow DST implementation (S2) and so on. Between each of the steps, the economy settles

into a new equilibrium, which reflects the adjustments in trade, production and prices that result from the respective policy development.

### Annex Table 4.D.5. Overview of the simulated cases

Two different DST rates and retaliation factors are simulated for cases S1, S2 and S3. Group numbers refer to country groups in Table 4.3; the sequence of events is outlined in Figure 4.15.

| Case | DST rate | Tariff Retaliation Factor | Simulations |
|---|---|---|---|
| First step in the sequence (S0) | 3%, 5% | - | DST implemented, group 1 |
| First and second step in the sequence (S1) | 3%, 5% | 0.5, 1, 4, 5 | DST implemented, group 1<br>Tariff retaliation , group 4 |
| Narrow DST implementation – full sequence (S2) | 3%, 5% | 0.5, 1, 4, 5 | DST implemented: group 1,2,3<br>Tariff retaliation: group 4<br>Tariff counter-retaliation: group 1,2,3 |
| Broad DST implementation – full sequence (S3) | 3%, 5% | 0.5, 1, 4, 5 | DST implemented: group 1,2,3,6<br>Tariff retaliation: group 4<br>Tariff counter-retaliation: group 1,2,3,6 |

Note: The main text only refers to the cases with narrow and broad DST implementation; the additional cases are discussed only in this annex.
Source: OECD.

450. Aggregate results are discussed in the main text (Table 4.5) and Annex Table 4.D.6. However, there is considerable heterogeneity across country groups that is not visible from the global averages of GDP changes. That heterogeneity stems from various sources: the trade linkages with the United States; the trade linkages between and among country groups; the weight of the tariff-targeted sectors in the economy; and, importantly, the sequence of policy developments. Annex Figure 4.D.1 illustrates the distribution of GDP changes by scenario and across all parameter combinations.

451. The impact of the implementation of the DST in one county (S0) is very small and concentrated on the implementing country. Subsequent tariff retaliation (S1) spreads the negative effects more widely. Both countries engaged in this stage experience negative effects from the tariffs with the GDP of the DST implementing country (France) declining by between -0.1% to -0.3% and that of the retaliating country (US) by up to -0.08%. Other county groups would be either positively or negatively affected as trade is diverted away from the two countries engaged in the retaliation. For example, other EU countries would pick up some of the lost trade from the DST implementing country, while global value chain linkages would harm the trade from some EU and non-EU countries that flows through the DST implementing EU country and subsequently to the United States.

452. When the implementation of the DST, the tariff retaliation and the counter-retaliation becomes more widespread (S2) the economic cost increases and the variation across countries becomes more pronounced. The countries engaged in tariff retaliation are subject to larger negative effects, while those not engaged in the dispute could pick up some of the trade and economic activity. At this stage, two country groups would see a GDP increase, making up 0.38% or less for group 5 (China and Hong-Kong) and +0.32% or less for group 6 (including all other countries). In spite of this substantial reallocation, average global GDP would be lower, as shown in Table 4.5 in the main text and Annex Table 4.D.6.

453. As the implementation of a DST and tariff retaliation generalizes to even more countries (S3), the options for reallocation become fewer and global GDP would decline by up to -1.2% with very wide variations across country groups. The shrinking size of the economies engaged in tariff retaliation generates progressively negative effects. As their trade declines, incomes decline and demand for imports falls further. Country group 5, which is the only one not engaged in the dispute, picks up some of the economic activity (with GDP growth up to 1.3%) but obviously it cannot absorb all of the strain put on the global economy.

454. Standing by and not engaging in the tax and trade dispute generally appears to pay off. While some positive spillovers on countries not engaged in the trade dispute are always to be expected, the positive effects on country group 6 in the case where they are engaged in the dispute is not evident (Annex Figure 4.D.2). One reason for this finding is that they would benefit from reallocation of activities during the previous stages of the simulation (S0 through S2). The tariffs imposed when they enter in the last stage (S3) do not wipe out those previous gains, even if the incremental effects between S2 and S3 are negative for them. Another reason is that their tariff rates are comparatively lower than those imposed by other country groups (Annex Table 4.D.3 and Annex Table 4.D.4).

## Annex Table 4.D.6. Simulation results (weighted percent changes)

| | Narrow DST implementation (S2) | | | | | | | | Broad DST implementation (S3) | | | | | | | |
|---|---|---|---|---|---|---|---|---|---|---|---|---|---|---|---|---|
| Tariff ret. factor | 0.5 | | 1 | | 4 | | 5 | | 0.5 | | 1 | | 4 | | 5 | |
| DST rate | 3% | 5% | 3% | 5% | 3% | 5% | 3% | 5% | 3% | 5% | 3% | 5% | 3% | 5% | 3% | 5% |
| Real GDP | -0.08 | -0.14 | -0.09 | -0.15 | -0.13 | -0.22 | -0.15 | -0.24 | -0.40 | -0.66 | -0.44 | -0.72 | -0.66 | -1.08 | -0.73 | -1.21 |
| Real HH income | -0.08 | -0.13 | -0.08 | -0.14 | -0.13 | -0.21 | -0.14 | -0.23 | -0.35 | -0.59 | -0.38 | -0.64 | -0.57 | -0.95 | -0.64 | -1.07 |
| Real Imports | -0.14 | -0.23 | -0.17 | -0.28 | -0.30 | -0.48 | -0.34 | -0.53 | -0.61 | -1.02 | -0.68 | -1.14 | -1.11 | -1.81 | -1.25 | -2.04 |

Source: METRO v3 simulations and database. OECD calculations.

## Annex Figure 4.D.1. Distribution of GDP changes by scenario, relative to base data (%)

GDP changes by scenario across all parameter combinations.

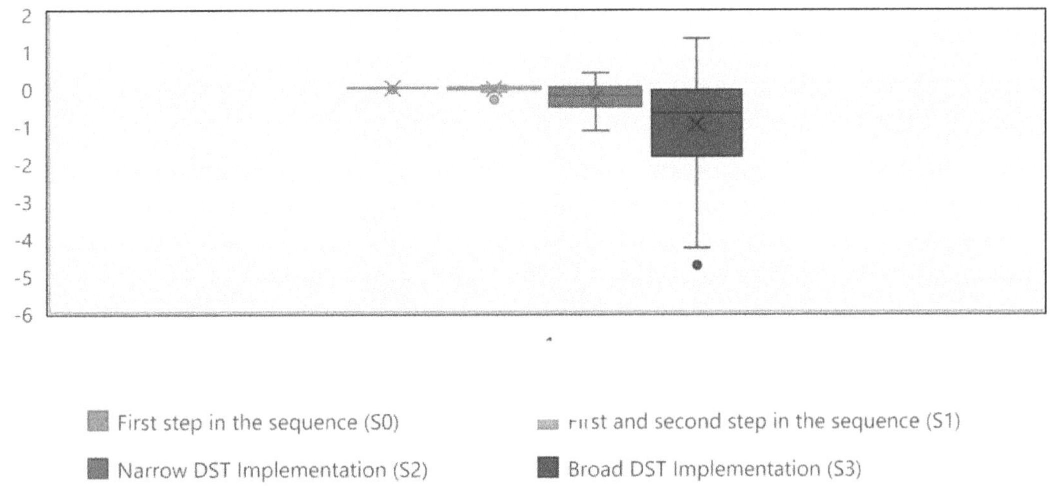


Note: The upper edge of the box corresponds to the 75th percentile; the lower end of the box corresponds to the 25th percentile; the middle line in the box is the median while the unweighted average is shown as a cross.
Source: METRO v3 simulations and database. OECD calculations.

Annex Figure 4.D.2. Distribution of GDP changes by jurisdiction group, relative to base data (%)

GDP changes by scenario across all parameter combinations.

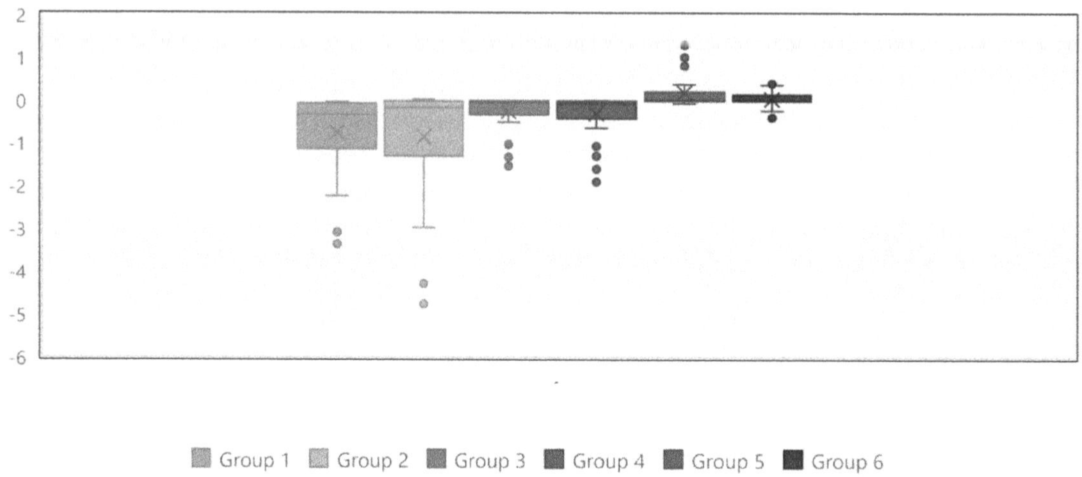


Note: The upper edge of the box corresponds to the 75th percentile; the lower end of the box corresponds to the 25th percentile; the middle line in the box is the median while the unweighted average is shown as a cross.
Source: METRO v3 simulations and database. OECD calculations.

455. The broader the spread of tariffs and counter tariffs, the more widespread the slowdown in trade becomes (Annex Table 4.D.7). Bilateral trade in the case with narrow DST implementation (S2) between the countries imposing tariffs on each other could shrink by double-digit numbers. For example, the exports from EU countries to the United States could shrink by 10.8%, while the corresponding opposite trade flow could shrink by 11.5%. In this scenario, the countries not engaged in the dispute would expand exports slightly, including trade amongst themselves. Their trade into the countries that are affected by tariffs is only expanding marginally, however. Trade diversion is limited, because import demand is falling in step with the overall economic contraction.

456. Falling exports are not only the result of retaliatory tariffs imposed by trade partners, but are also a consequence of the export taxing effect of import tariffs (Lerner effect).

457. In the case with broad DST implementation (S3), when country group 6 also enters into the dispute, they would lose markets globally, except for the intra-group trade and trade with the countries not participating in the trade dispute; country group 5, (China and Hong Kong (China)). Their trade to other regions would collapse further as the global decline of economic activity aggravates.

## Annex Table 4.D.7. Change in bilateral trade matrix (DST rate = 5%, Retaliation factor = 5), relative to base (%)

| **Narrow DST implementation** | | | | | | |
|---|---|---|---|---|---|---|
| to: | 1 DST | 2 Section 301 EU Countries | 3 Section 301 non-EU Countries | 4 Retaliating | 5 No DST, no retaliation | 6 Other |
| from: | | | | | | |
| 1 DST | 0.0 | -0.4 | -0.4 | -25.0 | -2.0 | -1.0 |
| 2 Section 301 EU Countries | -1.0 | -0.7 | -0.2 | -10.8 | -0.1 | -0.1 |
| 3 Section 301 non-EU Countries | -0.7 | -0.4 | -0.1 | -8.1 | 0.5 | 0.3 |
| 4 Retaliating | -14.8 | -11.5 | -9.0 | 0.0 | 1.1 | 0.9 |
| 5 No DST, no retaliation | -0.6 | 0.1 | 0.7 | 1.0 | 0.0 | 0.4 |
| 6 Other | -0.7 | -0.3 | 0.0 | 1.3 | 0.7 | 0.5 |
| **Broad DST implementation** | | | | | | |
| to: | 1 DST | 2 Section 301 EU Countries | 3 Section 301 non-EU Countries | 4 Retaliating | 5 No DST, no retaliation | 6 Other |
| from: | | | | | | |
| 1 DST | 0.0 | -4.4 | -2.7 | -26.7 | -3.3 | -2.6 |
| 2 Section 301 EU Countries | -4.7 | -5.7 | -3.6 | -13.7 | -2.7 | -3.0 |
| 3 Section 301 non-EU Countries | -2.1 | -3.2 | -1.1 | -9.2 | 1.0 | -0.1 |
| 4 Retaliating | -15.5 | -13.3 | -9.4 | 0.0 | 2.0 | -4.2 |
| 5 No DST, no retaliation | -0.4 | -1.0 | 1.4 | 3.1 | 0.0 | 1.7 |
| 6 Other | -1.2 | -2.1 | 0.1 | -2.5 | 2.4 | 1.6 |

Source: METRO v3 simulations and database. OECD calculations.

## Notes

[1] This specification models only Amount A under Pillar One, assuming a 10% profitability threshold based on profit before tax over turnover, a 20% reallocation percentage to market jurisdictions and a restriction to ADS and CFB. In modelling Pillar Two, a 12.5% rate with jurisdiction blending is assumed, including a 10% carve-out on depreciation expenses (approximated using the value and location of tangible assets).

[2] For the purpose of this chapter, user/market jurisdictions (henceforth "market jurisdictions") are jurisdictions where an MNE group sells its products or services or, in the case of highly digitalised businesses, provides services to users or solicits and collects data or content contributions from them.

[3] The analysis of the revenue effects of the Pillar Two proposals in Chapter 3 covered certain scenarios including behavioural responses by governments and MNEs. On the government side, these responses covered only increases in effective tax rates in half of the jurisdictions where the average backward-looking effective tax rate on MNE profits is currently below the minimum rate but not zero and in none of the zero-tax jurisdictions - situations where the respective profits would otherwise be taxed at the minimum rate in another jurisdiction. On the business side, it included only changes in the intensity of profit shifting, e.g., when an MNE decides to shift fewer profits to lower-tax jurisdictions due to the introduction of the minimum tax. The revenue analysis presented so far has not taken into account impacts on real economic activities by MNEs, notably the impacts of the proposals on growth and investment.

[4] If the relocation implies a decrease in production efficiency, global output could still decrease; however, the effects of changes in production efficiency are difficult to evaluate because the extent to which capital allocation is distorted before (and after) the relocation takes place is unknown.

[5] Given that discussions on policy design and key parameters are still taking place through the Inclusive Framework, any modelling assumptions are made on a without prejudice basis.

[6] The required data on depreciation expenses are not readily available across jurisdictions. In the ETR calculations the impact of a carve-out on depreciation expenses is therefore approximated using the value and location of tangible assets. The carve-out on payroll expenses cannot be adequately modelled in this framework. See Hanappi and González Cabral (2020[12]) for more detail.

[7] The required data from OECD Corporate Tax Statistics is available for 72 jurisdictions (excluding Estonia and Latvia).

[8] The literature generally distinguishes effective average tax rates (EATRs) and effective marginal tax rates (EMTRs). EMTRs measure the extent to which taxation increases the pre-tax rate of return required by investors to break even. This indicator is used to analyse how taxes affect the incentive to expand existing investments given a fixed location (along the intensive margin). EATRs reflect the average tax contribution a firm makes on an investment project earning above-zero economic profits. This indicator is used to analyse discrete investment decisions between two or more alternative projects (along the extensive margin).

[9] Throughout this analysis the MNE organisational structure is kept constant and empirical calibrations are based on the assumption that the investment is undertaken in the jurisdiction of the ultimate parent entity. However, the empirical calibration could be adjusted to analyse investments in the location of any given subsidiary, assuming that the ultimate parent entity is located in another jurisdiction; in theory, this approach would then need to consider all parent and subsidiary jurisdictions in the data to take into account the full set of combinations. While this approach may be conceptually appealing, data limitations imply that the results are likely to be less reliable than those based on the narrower but more accurate approach proposed here.

[10] The ETRs in OECD Corporate Tax Statistics are based on information obtained directly from the respective delegate for each of the participating jurisdictions, including several rounds of feedback and quality assurance. However, data comparability at the jurisdiction level could be affected if asset classes are interpreted differently across jurisdictions.

[11] For the purposes of the ETR analysis, possible interaction effects between Pillar One and Pillar Two are not taken into account. Modelling the effects of both Pillars simultaneously would complicate the formal derivations significantly without necessarily providing further insights, over and above the empirical results described in the revenue analysis.

[12] As shown in Corporate Tax Statistics (OECD, 2020[15]), certain jurisdictions lack the tax provisions and administrative infrastructure to operate a full-fledged CIT system; this is typically the case in jurisdictions where the statutory rate is zero and there is thus no need to establish much infrastructure. Given this lack of infrastructure in zero-tax jurisdictions, the impact of the proposals on real investment, as opposed to profit shifting, in those jurisdictions will strongly depend on the tax policy responses by the respective government following the implementation of the Pillar One and Pillar Two proposals. For this reason, and to operate on a without prejudice basis, the empirical modelling does not consider the impact of such, more wide-ranging, tax policy changes in the case of zero-tax jurisdictions. The impact of the proposals on foreign profits shifted into these jurisdictions is, nonetheless, accounted for.

[13] Amount B is not modelled within the ETR framework due to methodological challenges. More specifically, modelling Amount B would require a comprehensive cross-country dataset of entity level data combining

information on (i) the nature of the activities of each entity (to identify which entities would be affected by Amount B) and (ii) their financial information (to quantify the effect of applying Amount B).

[14] As described in Chapter 5, the firm level data for this calibration has been collected from several sources including the ORBIS database, Worldscope and other sources; from ORBIS only consolidated financial account data have been used for this part of the analysis, making concerns about country coverage less pertinent given that coverage of consolidated accounts is much more extensive across countries than coverage of unconsolidated accounts.

[15] As discussed in endnote 9, this approach is mainly driven by the need for empirical calibration and is likely to produce the most accurate results given the data limitations.

[16] Jurisdiction groups are based on the World Bank classification of countries by income group. Investment hubs are defined as jurisdictions with a total inward FDI position above 150% of GDP, based on raw FDI data.

[17] When looking in isolation to the subset of firms affected by Pillar One (with revenues over EUR 750 million, in CFB or ADS and with residual profits defined using a 10% threshold), the change in ETRs is estimated to be of 0.12 percentage points for the EATR and 0.07 percentage points for the EMTR. However, these figures fail to reflect the scope restrictions of Pillar One that will only target a subset of MNEs. The turnover of firms in-scope of Pillar One as defined above, which is used to weight the impact of Pillar One on ETRs, only accounts for 10% of the turnover of all MNEs in the analysis. The same applies to the scope of Pillar Two. The modelling assumes that Pillar Two only applies to MNEs with revenues above EUR 750 million, and thus the impact of Pillar Two on ETRs is weighted by the share of turnover from MNEs above the EUR 750 million threshold. While this subset of MNEs still includes over 90% of the turnover of all firms in the economy, only those with low-taxed profits will be affected by Pillar Two.

[18] Only 4 out of 37 OECD countries retain a worldwide taxation system in 2020. These are Chile, Israel, Mexico and South Korea. These are jurisdictions not offering participation exemptions for foreign capital gains and dividends.

[19] However, policy priorities and tax structures differ across jurisdictions; the costs associated with different distortions may thus be assessed differently across jurisdictions, thereby affecting optimal policy choices at the jurisdiction level.

[20] In fact, a reduction in tax rate differentials can be interpreted as a move towards capital export neutrality (CEN).

[21] More generally, tax incidence also has obvious implications on the progressivity of corporate taxation; however, an analysis of the impacts of the new rules on progressivity of existing tax systems is outside the scope of this chapter.

[22] The empirical findings discussed in this paragraph could be driven by several underlying effects, e.g., liquidity constraints, economic rents or profit shifting among others. Since it is difficult to disentangle the effects empirically, it is not possible to determine at this point whether and to what extent the elimination of a specific effect (among many) would change the findings.

[23] The firm-level analysis relies on firm-level data from ORBIS. While ORBIS covers a large number of countries, the final sample of countries is driven by the availability of financial data at the entity level. Although the sample at the entity level is restricted to 17 – mostly European – countries, the results are likely to be applicable to other countries given that the model estimates firm-level effects of corporate tax

everything else being equal, and that the list of countries covered (including for example Nordics, Eastern and Southern European countries, and big European Union countries) is relatively varied both in terms of taxation and economic structure.

[24] Due to limitations of the available data, the analysis focuses on the short-term reaction of investment to tax changes. The economic literature suggests that investment is lumpy and that reactions to tax rate changes are larger in the long term than in the short term (Sorbe and Johansson, 2017[7]). The fact that profitable MNE groups are less sensitive to taxes than less profitable groups in the short term suggests that this may be the case in the long term as well.

[25] In some business models, the reallocation of residual profit will be to the jurisdiction of the user rather than the consumer.

[26] Depending on the final design of the proposals, there may be a risk of additional disputes stemming from the interaction of Amounts A and B with the existing transfer pricing system.

[27] Available evidence also suggests that EMTRs have fallen over the observed period (Devereux et al., 2002[63]).

[28] For the purpose of this chapter, "market jurisdictions" are jurisdictions where an MNE group sells its products or services or, in the case of highly digitalised businesses, provides services to users or solicits and collects data or content contributions from them.

[29] Assuming simultaneous tax rate setting (i.e., a Nash equilibrium), the introduction of minimum taxation leads the high-tax jurisdiction to increase its rate. Assuming sequential tax rate setting with the high-tax jurisdiction being the leader (i.e., Stackelberg equilibrium), the high-tax jurisdiction tends to reduce its rate when minimum effective taxation is introduced (Keen and Konrad, 2013[79]). In a simultaneous game, the best response of a given jurisdiction, in terms of the effective tax rate, is increasing to the level of other jurisdictions' effective tax rates; i.e., a jurisdiction can increase its own rate without losing its attractiveness as long as other jurisdictions have higher effective tax rates. In this setting, the introduction of minimum effective taxation increases the optimal tax rate chosen by jurisdictions with rates above the minimum. However, in a sequential game, the leader takes into account that setting a lower tax rate might not be beneficial because the followers can decrease theirs. With a minimum effective tax rate, this threat from the followers is weaker.

[30] Note by Turkey: The information in this document with reference to "Cyprus" relates to the southern part of the Island. There is no single authority representing both Turkish and Greek Cypriot people on the Island. Turkey recognises the Turkish Republic of Northern Cyprus (TRNC). Until a lasting and equitable solution is found within the context of the United Nations, Turkey shall preserve its position concerning the "Cyprus issue".

Note by all the European Union Member States of the OECD and the European Union: The Republic of Cyprus is recognised by all members of the United Nations with the exception of Turkey. The information in this document relates to the area under the effective control of the Government of the Republic of Cyprus.

[31] Innovation activities are defined as "all scientific, technological, organisational, financial and commercial steps which actually, or are intended to, lead to the implementation of innovations" and the Oslo Manual recognises eight different categories, of which investment in research and development (R&D) is only one of them. Among the other innovation activities recognised in the Oslo Manual are: engineering, design and other creative work activities; marketing and brand equity activities; intellectual property related activities;

employee training activities; software development and database activities; activities related to the acquisition or lease of tangible assets and innovation management activities. Note that innovation activities may or may not lead to innovations.

[32] The focus on the targeted tax provisions is due to their direct interaction with the new Pillar One and Pillar Two rules.

[33] Under the assumption that Pillar Two operates with jurisdictional blending.

[34] For example, a share of the profits previously attributed to preferential regimes could become subject to reallocation, and therefore higher taxation, under Pillar One, however, this effect is highly dependent on the design of Pillar One, in particular the rules for double tax relief, and relevant only for the qualifying share of income as defined in the preferential regime.

[35] It is important to note that even though innovation appears responsive to taxation, heterogeneity in firms' responses is to be expected. This might be due to the industry and markets where they operate, the type of business model, the organisational, management and ownership structure, the technology they use (Desai and Hines, 2002[200]; Egger, Erhardt and Keuschnigg, 2018[201]; Griffith, Miller and O'Connell, 2014[173]). Agglomeration effects also diminish the sensitivity of firms to taxation (Akcigit et al., 2018[209]).

[36] Depending on the design of the rules, there might be instances where the benefits granted through direct support measures are curtailed. Tax incentives targeted to younger or smaller firms that are out of scope of the new provisions will most likely be unaffected by these developments.

[37] This indicator refers to innovation-active firms in product and process. Innovation is defined following the Oslo Manual 2005 edition. Product innovation is defined as the introduction of a good or service that is new or significantly improved with respect to its characteristics or intended uses. This includes significant improvements in technical specifications, components and materials, incorporated software, user friendliness or other functional characteristics. Process innovation is defined as the implementation of a new or significantly improved production or delivery method. This includes significant changes in techniques, equipment and/or software. Further information on this indicator is available in the data link provided in the note to Figure 4.10.

[38] The degree of acceleration granted to these investments will affect the generosity of these incentives and if deemed too generous could potentially drive ETRs below the minimum threshold. However, this effect will be less pronounced than in the case of enhanced provisions that provide relief over and above the value of the investment.

[39] However, recent empirical research suggests that the effects of FDI on growth could be lower than previously thought (Bermejo Carbonell and Werner, 2018[203]).

[40] Similarly, investment tax incentives are sometimes used to stimulate domestic investment in specific, less-advanced regions within a country.

[41] Alternative policies include investment promotion and facilitation measures to simplify administrative procedures for companies in their operations in sometimes complex legal and institutional environments. They also include infrastructure provision and institutional stability.

[42] Increasing market concentration is not synonymous with weakening competition. For example, a large firm with many small competitors may be subject to less competitive pressure than a large firm with only a few similarly large competitors. In addition, in existing studies concentration is typically measured at an aggregate industry level, which is unlikely to be reflective of the competitive dynamics within markets.

[43] Different policy options to achieve this are still under discussion.

[44] The extent to which investment would be relocated remains an open question. If investment in one foreign affiliate can be substituted by investing in another affiliate, overall effects on group level investment would be small, however, negative effects on group level investment would be relatively larger if foreign and domestic investment were complements (Becker and Riedel, 2012[206]) (Suárez Serrato, 2018[205]).

[45] Group level EATRs and EMTRs are computed for a stylised investment in the ultimate parent jurisdiction taking into account the possibility to shift profits to other locations within the MNE group.

[46] The model is described online at: https://www.oecd.org/economy/growth/scenarios-for-the-world-economy-to-2060.htm#papers.

[47] This result corresponds to the MNE group level effect for a stylised investment project, including a combination of assets, i.e., non-residential structure, tangible assets and acquired intangibles. The empirical calibration assumes that the investment takes place in the ultimate parent jurisdiction, such that the empirically observed location of profits and tangible assets matches an ultimate parent entity headquartered in the respective jurisdiction. As discussed in Hanappi and González Cabral (2020[12]), the aggregate figure is constructed as a GDP-weighted average across the jurisdiction level results.

[48] As discussed in Millot et al. (2020[44]), the tax sensitivity of entities in MNE groups with profitability above 10% is estimated to be -0.085, while the tax sensitivity in average MNE groups is estimated to be -0.131. The short-term tax sensitivity is thus around 35% lower for entities in more profitable MNE groups. The adjustment assumes that this difference also holds in the long term.

[49] The MNE shares in business investment and value added may differ; however, additional cross-checks show that the share of foreign MNEs in business investment and value added are almost identical in the European Union (see Eurostat data on the structure and activity of foreign affiliates).

[50] The Analytical AMNE database is accessible online at https://www.oecd.org/industry/ind/analytical-amne-database.htm.

[51] Note by Turkey: The information in this document with reference to "Cyprus" relates to the southern part of the Island. There is no single authority representing both Turkish and Greek Cypriot people on the Island. Turkey recognises the Turkish Republic of Northern Cyprus (TRNC). Until a lasting and equitable solution is found within the context of the United Nations, Turkey shall preserve its position concerning the "Cyprus issue".

Note by all the European Union Member States of the OECD and the European Union: The Republic of Cyprus is recognised by all members of the United Nations with the exception of Turkey. The information in this document relates to the area under the effective control of the Government of the Republic of Cyprus.

[52] Hines and Park (2019[202]) investigate the effects of tax subsidies for investments in specific assets (but not others), suggesting that such a selective approach leads to substitution effects that could largely offset positive effects on investment. If such substitution effects would materialise also in response to a DST, e.g., from digital advertisements to other forms of advertisement, a similar effect could undermine DST revenue.

[53] The concerns raised focused on the following points: (i) the potentially discriminatory nature of the DST; (ii) the retroactivity; (iii) the DST's application to revenue rather than income; (iv) its application to revenues unconnected to a physical presence in France; and (v) its application to a small group of digital companies.

[54] Given that the French DST is expected to raise around EUR 450-500 million in its first year, the proposed US response, which amounts to USD 2.4 billion corresponds to approximately a fivefold increase in revenues compared to the revenues raised from the DST.

[55] A brief description of the model is available online.

[56] The database is accessible online, including documentation.

[57] It should be noted that the statistical classification of digital services is still subject to considerable discussion, and the choice made in this study follows closely the insights in the Handbook on Measuring Digital Trade, Version 1, OECD, WTO and IMF (2020[204]) and mapping into the GTAP v10 sector aggregation which is used as input in the METRO database. More information is available at https://www.oecd.org/sdd/its/Handbook-on-Measuring-Digital-Trade.htm.

[58] The 5% rate is also modelled on the basis that a number of jurisdictions have proposed DSTs with a higher rate than France (see Table 4.1 above).

[59] Each simulated case takes the new equilibrium reached under the previous simulation as a starting point; see Annex 4.D for a detailed description.

[60] Given the opposition to DSTs and similar measures expressed by the United States and its clearly stated policy position of reacting to such measures through trade retaliation, it is assumed to never introduce a DST, but always retaliate where a DST or similar measure has been introduced. China has also expressed very strong public opposition to DSTs and similar measures, although it has not publicly stated that it would take any trade related actions in response to the introduction of such measures. On this basis, China is not considered to implement a DST, even under the scenario with broad DST implementation, nor is it assumed that China implements a retaliatory trade response under any of the scenarios.

[61] Note by Turkey: The information in this document with reference to "Cyprus" relates to the southern part of the Island. There is no single authority representing both Turkish and Greek Cypriot people on the Island. Turkey recognises the Turkish Republic of Northern Cyprus (TRNC). Until a lasting and equitable solution is found within the context of the United Nations, Turkey shall preserve its position concerning the "Cyprus issue".

Note by all the European Union Member States of the OECD and the European Union: The Republic of Cyprus is recognised by all members of the United Nations with the exception of Turkey. The information in this document relates to the area under the effective control of the Government of the Republic of Cyprus.

[62] Although GDP effects are not linear with respect to modelling parameters in the OECD METRO Model, intermediate scenarios, e.g., when different groups of jurisdictions implement DSTs or different DST rates or retaliation factors are chosen, are likely to produce GDP effects between the ranges mentioned in this paragraph.

[63] Although high costs of financing is one of the reasons behind the policy support for innovation, large performers do not particularly observe high costs of financing established and thus government

intervention towards large performers on these grounds does not appear justified (Hall and Lerner, 2010[87]).

64 This estimate obtained by the CBO considers companies that reported positive income in the financial year pre and post the inversion. There is variability across firms' experiences post inversion.

65 Voget (2011[189]) finds that 6% of multinationals relocated their headquarters from 1997–2007. The CBO (2017[187]) identified sixty inversions from the US from 1983 through 2015. Fourteen inversions have been proposed between 2014 and 2017, with eleven being completed by 2016. Although seemingly small in numbers, a more informative metric for corporate inversions might be the level of total assets held by inverting companies, e.g. in 2001 three US companies inverted with total assets amounting to $22 billion compared to six in 1999 that had total assets of $13 billion. In 2014, 10 corporations considering inversions in the US amounted to USD 300 billion in total assets and had a much larger share of foreign profits than previous inverted companies, which would turn into permanently reinvested earnings and would not be taxed again in the US. Only four companies completed the inversion after tightening of inversion rules in 2014 announced by the Treasury (U.S. Department of the Treasury, 2014[207]).

66 For certain types of passive income that are highly mobile, taxation occurs on a current basis, i.e. not deferred. This is through the application of controlled-foreign-corporation rules. Territorial systems in practice do not provide a full exemption of foreign income and certain types of income, e.g. passive income are taxed as worldwide income (Joint Committee of Taxation, 2011[210]).

67 These are Chile, Israel, Mexico and South Korea. These jurisdictions are not offering participation exemptions for foreign capital gains and dividends.

68 These rules however move the tax system away from a purely territorial system to tax certain types of income at a worldwide level.

69 Independent of the system of taxation, CFC rules makes the tax liability current and therefore there is no possibility of further deferral.

70 Examples of these are the American Jobs Creation Act of 2004 and the regulations issued by the Treasury in 2014 and 2016; as well as the most recent measures introduced as part of the Tax Cut and Jobs Act in the US (U.S. Department of the Treasury, 2014[207]) (U.S. Department of the Treasury, 2016[208]) (Chalk, Keen and Perry, 2018[211]).

71 It has been suggested that inversions might be responsive to changes in these taxes, i.e. inversions might be more prone when there is an expected hike in the capital gains tax rate for the sale of the stock that leads to the inversion or during economic downturns when the amount of realised capital gains would be lower.

72 See https://www.oecd.org/trade/topics/metro-trade-model/ for an overview.

73 The results clearly depend on the choice of those sectors. The alternative would be to design a rule that selects sectors for each country based on some objective criteria such as their weight in a county's export bundle or in value added. Even with such a rule, one would likely miss the details of tariffs that are set at a very disaggregate level (for example, a tariff on cognac is very targeted, but the beverage is contained in the more aggregate 'agriculture and food' category of the model database. The approach in this analysis bypasses those intricacies, but nonetheless addresses the sectors where historically trade disputes have been most frequent. A recently published piece under the auspices of the OECD Trade Committee follows essentially the same approach (with the exception of electronics): https://issuu.com/oecd.publishing/docs/oecd-trade-scenario-2-increasing_ta?e=3055080/65009159.

# 5 Construction of the data "matrices" underlying the impact assessment

## 5.1. Introduction and overview

458. Having good data on the location of profit and economic activity of multinational enterprises (MNEs) is key to assessing the implications of international corporate tax reforms, such as the Pillar One and Pillar Two proposals currently being discussed by the OECD/G20 Inclusive Framework on Base Erosion and Profit Shifting (BEPS). However, while a range of data sources provide valuable insights on the profit and activities of MNEs, no existing data source is sufficiently comprehensive in its geographic coverage and in terms of variables available to be used in isolation for a comprehensive reform impact assessment covering all 137 jurisdictions in the OECD/G20 Inclusive Framework on BEPS (Inclusive Framework).

459. Against this background, the OECD Secretariat has undertaken to combine a range of existing data sources into a consistent framework, which serves as a central instrument supporting the impact assessment analysis in this report. The framework consists of a set of four matrices: a profit matrix, focusing on the location of the profit of MNEs across jurisdictions, and three matrices focusing on indicators of the economic activity of MNEs (turnover, tangible assets and payroll). Each matrix contains data spanning more than 200 jurisdictions (each jurisdiction corresponding to a matrix *row*) and broken down across more than 200 jurisdictions of ultimate parent of the MNE considered (each jurisdiction of ultimate parent being a matrix *column*). Each matrix therefore takes the form of a square table with more than 200 rows and more than 200 columns. For example, the France-United States cell in the profit matrix would represent the profit of US MNEs (i.e. MNEs with an ultimate parent in the United States) in France.

460. The matrices combine data from a range of sources, and build on earlier efforts to map the profit and activity of MNEs for the analysis of profit shifting (Tørsløv, Wier and Zucman, 2018[1]) and the study of global value chains (GVCs) (Cadestin et al., 2018[2]). A primary source of data used in the matrices is the newly available anonymised and aggregated Country-by-Country Report (CbCR) data,[1] which have been collected as a result of the implementation of the 2015 BEPS Action Plan and were published for the first time by the OECD in July 2020 (OECD, 2020[3]). Other sources include the ORBIS database of firm-level financial accounts (in jurisdictions where ORBIS coverage is good), the OECD AMNE database (which includes data from the Eurostat FATS database and from the US Bureau of Economic Analysis) and the OECD Analytical AMNE database (Cadestin et al., 2018[2]), which builds upon and complements the OECD AMNE database. The data considered focus essentially on year 2016, which is the latest available year across all the data sources used.

461. These various data sources complement each other as they have different geographic coverage and include different variables, meaning that the combined dataset is richer than any data source taken individually. These sources also have substantial overlap in their coverage. This overlap is used to benchmark sources against each other, in order to address the limitations of individual data sources and ensure the overall consistency of the approach, as further discussed below. The methodology aims to

make data across the four matrices as comparable as possible, so as to enable the joint use of the matrices (e.g. using simultaneously the profit and turnover matrices to compute average profitability). To this end, efforts have been made to rely as much as possible on comparable data sources for the same cell across the different matrices. For example, if a cell is filled with CbCR data in the profit matrix (e.g. profit of US MNEs in France), the aim has been to use CbCR data to fill the corresponding cell in the other matrices (e.g. turnover of US MNEs in France).

462. In matrix cells where no source of 'hard' data is available, estimates are based on extrapolations relying on macroeconomic data (e.g. FDI data, GDP, GDP per capita). The extrapolation methodology builds on the information contained in the matrix cells filled with hard data, which aims to ensure consistency *within* each matrix. The extrapolation methodology is also designed to make the data *across* the four matrices as comparable with each other as possible. For example, extrapolations in the tangible assets and payroll matrices are based on data from the turnover matrix.

463. Among the four variables considered in the matrices, profit is arguably the most difficult to extrapolate when it is not observed in hard data, because the profit of MNEs may not always be located in the same jurisdiction as their economic activity. To overcome this issue, a sophisticated extrapolation methodology based on foreign direct investment (FDI) data has been developed. This methodology, inspired by Damgaard and Elkjaer (2017[4]) and Casella (2019[5]), involves various steps to identify the ultimate foreign investor into a jurisdiction, based on successive iterations on the existing data on 'immediate' foreign investors, and to eliminate 'pass-through FDI' from the data. One of the intermediate outputs of this procedure is a full matrix of FDI by jurisdiction of ultimate investor, which is interesting in its own right.

464. Overall, the various extrapolations ensure that all of the cells in the matrices can be filled, which makes it much easier to use the matrices for economic analysis. Extrapolated data are more fragile than hard data, but extrapolations represent a moderate share of the total amounts in the matrices (on average 25% across the four matrices), meaning that the information in the matrices is based predominantly on hard data. There are important geographic differences in the share of extrapolated values. This share is relatively low in high-income jurisdictions, higher in middle-income jurisdictions, and very high in low-income jurisdictions.[2] In investment hubs, the share of extrapolated values, while substantial (e.g. close to 40% in the profit matrix), is much lower than it would have been in the absence of the CbCR data, highlighting the importance of CbCR as a key new source of data on the amount of profit in investment hubs.

465. The various data sources mobilised to build the matrices have limitations, as is the case for any source of economic data. More specifically, CbCR data on profit have issues related to ambiguities in the treatment of intra-company dividends as well as 'stateless' entities, these ambiguities being related to the fact that 2016 was the first year in which the data was collected (OECD, 2020[3]). This may give rise to cases of double-counting of profit and revenues.[3] Another limitation of the data sources is that ORBIS unconsolidated account data has uneven coverage across jurisdictions. Reflecting this, ORBIS is used to fill the matrices only in jurisdictions where coverage is deemed sufficiently good, but even in these jurisdictions, coverage is not always exhaustive. A limitation of the OECD Analytical AMNE database is that some values are based on imputations and alternative sources to fill coverage gaps in the underlying data (Cadestin et al., 2018[2]). Finally, a limitation of the OECD AMNE database is that it does not include the financial sector in its data on inward investment in European jurisdictions.

466. To assess the implications of these limitations, improve data quality and ensure consistency across the various data used in the matrices,[4] extensive benchmarking and quality checks have been undertaken in this chapter. The benchmarking primarily takes advantage of the fact that, in many matrix cells, several data sources are simultaneously available, making it possible to assess their consistency. Data in the matrices have also been cross-checked against other relevant sources, including tax or financial account data shared with the OECD Secretariat by jurisdiction representatives. Overall, the

consistency checks reveal some inconsistencies, but suggest good overall data comparability across sources. For example, the correlation between CbCR data and estimates based on ORBIS, computed across the matrix cells where both of these sources are available, exceeds 90% in the profit and turnover matrices, and the correlation of estimates based on extrapolations with those from hard data ranges between 64% and 96% across the four matrices and the various hard data sources considered.

467. The four matrices have been used extensively by the OECD Secretariat in its assessment of the estimated effect of Pillar One and Pillar Two on tax revenues (Chapters 2 and 3 of this report) and MNE investment behaviour (Chapter 4). In the case of Pillar One, the profit and turnover matrices were used primarily to assess the location of the residual profit of MNE groups (in the form of a 'residual profit matrix'), so as to identify jurisdictions that would provide double tax relief, i.e. from which residual profit would be reallocated under Pillar One (see Chapter 2).

468. In the case of Pillar Two, the profit matrix was used, in combination with data on effective tax rates, to assess the amount and the location of the 'low-taxed' profit of MNEs (i.e. profit that is currently taxed at an effective rate below the potential minimum tax rate). The profit and turnover matrices have also been used to assess the extent of MNE profit shifting and how profit shifting could be reduced by the introduction of Pillar Two (the tangible assets and payroll matrices have also been used instead of the turnover matrix for the purpose of robustness checks), and, in turn, how this could affect tax revenues across jurisdictions (see Chapter 3). In addition, the turnover matrix has been used to proxy where some of the revenues from the minimum tax would accrue (here as well, the tangible assets and payroll matrices have been used for the purpose of robustness checks).[5] Finally, the tangible assets and payroll matrices were used to model the implications of potential 'carve-outs' to the minimum tax based on economic substance.[6]

469. In the investment impact analysis, the matrices were used to calibrate the framework used to assess the impact of Pillar One and Pillar Two on forward-looking effective tax rates (see Chapter 4 and Hanappi and González Cabral (2020[6])).

470. This chapter contains a preliminary version of the four matrices, presented at a certain level of aggregation (i.e. by income groups and broad geographic regions). After extensive consultation with members of the Inclusive Framework, there was no consensus over whether or not jurisdiction-specific data in the four matrices should be publicly released as part of the economic impact assessment. In view of this lack of consensus, no jurisdiction-specific data are included in this chapter.

471. Looking ahead, the matrices presented in this chapter could be used in the future for a range of other purposes, in the area of tax policy analysis and beyond, as discussed in the conclusion of this chapter.

## 5.2. Main existing data sources on MNE profit and activities

472. A number of data sources are available to assess the location of the profit and economic activity of MNEs, with different strengths, limitations and coverage, as discussed for example in OECD (2015[7]) and OECD (2018[8]). This section gives a brief overview of the main existing data sources, with the aim to provide useful background to the methodology underlying the construction of the matrices. Indeed, all of the sources presented in this section are mobilised – to different degrees – to build and benchmark the matrices presented in this chapter. More precisely, CbCR data, ORBIS data and data from the OECD AMNE and Analytical AMNE databases are used directly in the matrices, and used to benchmark each other. FDI data are used for the purpose of the extrapolations in the profit matrix. Finally, data from the US Bureau of Economic Analysis (BEA) are used only for the purpose of benchmarking. This section gives general information on these data sources, while the precise way in which they are used in the matrices (e.g. preference order, extrapolation methodology) is presented in the following sections.

### 5.2.1. Anonymised and aggregated Country-by-Country Report (CbCR) data

473. The obligation for MNE groups with global revenues above EUR 750 million to report their profit and economic activities on a country-by-country basis was introduced in 2016 as part of the implementation of the OECD/G20 BEPS Project, in order to support jurisdictions in combating BEPS. While the main purpose of CbCRs is to support tax administrations in the high-level detection and assessment of transfer pricing and other BEPS-related risks, data collected from CbCRs also offer great potential for the economic analysis of BEPS and MNEs in general.

474. MNE groups file their CbCRs with tax administrations, typically in the jurisdiction of their ultimate parent entity. While the individual CbCRs of MNE groups are generally not public, it was decided as part of the work on Action 11 of the OECD/G20 BEPS Project that jurisdictions would compile and provide aggregated and anonymised CbCR statistics to the OECD for publication (OECD, 2015[7]).

475. The first vintage of aggregated and anonymised CbCR statistics was published in July 2020 as part of the 2020 edition of the OECD's Corporate Tax Statistics (OECD, 2020[3]). The dataset focuses on year 2016 and includes nearly 4 000 MNE groups from 26 ultimate parent jurisdictions (see list in Annex 5.A). This dataset contains a vast array of information on the global financial and economic activities of these MNE groups, including information on the number of employees, related and unrelated party revenues, profits and taxes paid (generally based on financial accounting data), as well as the main business functions across jurisdictions or jurisdiction groups.

476. The way the data is collected ensures that all activities and profits of the covered MNE groups are included, even in jurisdictions that are often subject to coverage issues (e.g. zero-tax jurisdictions and investment hubs). This makes CbCR data a key new source of information compared to existing sources, especially for the analysis of BEPS. As any data source, the CbCR data are subject to a number of limitations. One limitation of this first vintage is that several countries, including large ones, have not submitted aggregated CbCR statistics to the OECD for publication. Another issue is that due to lack of clarity in the expected treatment of intra-company dividends and 'stateless entities', the profit and to a lesser extent revenue variables may be subject to some double counting.[7] A full description of the CbCR dataset, including a presentation of the collection and aggregation methodology, a discussion of the main data limitations and high-level summary statistics based on the data can be found in OECD (2020[3]).

### 5.2.2. The ORBIS database

477. The ORBIS database, provided by Bureau van Dijk (BvD), is the largest cross-country database of ownership information and financial accounts of firms worldwide. It relies on information from various underlying sources, including credit rating agencies (e.g. Cerved in Italy) and national banks (e.g. National Bank of Belgium). ORBIS contains firm-level data for both publicly listed and privately owned companies. The available variables typically include balance sheet information (e.g. assets, liabilities), information from the profit and loss statement (e.g. turnover, cost of employees, earnings before interest and taxes (EBIT), profit before tax), data on the number of employees, and ownership information (e.g. direct and ultimate owners of an entity, ownership shares).

478. ORBIS contains financial account data both at the consolidated (i.e. MNE group) and unconsolidated (i.e. entity) level. The coverage of consolidated account data is good in most jurisdictions of ultimate parent, while the coverage of unconsolidated account data is very uneven across jurisdictions. For example, unconsolidated account data coverage is good in many European jurisdictions, while it is poor in the United States and most developing economies, zero-tax jurisdictions and investment hubs. In this chapter, ORBIS unconsolidated level data have only been used in jurisdictions with good coverage (see list in Annex 5.A). Despite the uneven coverage of unconsolidated account data, ownership information is comprehensive in ORBIS, as the global ultimate owner (GUO) of each entity is generally identified, even if it is located in a jurisdiction with poor coverage of unconsolidated financial accounts.[8]

This enables a comprehensive identification of the jurisdiction of ultimate parent of the MNE entities in ORBIS.

479. Given that ORBIS data are not primarily collected for statistical analysis, important processing and cleaning work is required to enhance data reliability (e.g. eliminating duplicates and reporting errors). The ORBIS dataset used to build the matrices in this chapter has benefitted from extensive cleaning of both ownership data and financial data, building on longstanding OECD expertise with ORBIS (see Annex 5.B for details).

### *5.2.3. The OECD AMNE database*

480. The OECD AMNE database contains data on the activities of foreign-owned affiliates in OECD countries ('inward' data), and also on the foreign activities of affiliates of MNEs headquartered in OECD countries ('outward' data). The OECD AMNE database is based on data reported to the OECD and other institutions, including Eurostat (where it is included in the Eurostat FATS database) and the US BEA (where is it included in the US AMNE database), in the framework of annual surveys on the activities of foreign-owned enterprises and foreign affiliates abroad controlled by residents of the compiling country.

481. The AMNE database contains 17 variables broken down by country of origin (inward investment) or destination (outward investment) and by industrial sector (50 industries) for 31 OECD countries. The available variables include, among others, production, value added, employment, labour compensation, research and development expenditures, exports, gross investment in tangible goods and gross operating surplus. Gross operating surplus is the closest measure of profit among these variables, but it nevertheless has important conceptual differences with profit before tax as reported in firms' financial accounts. In particular, gross operating surplus is based on a national account methodology to account for depreciation, and interest paid is not subtracted from profit.

482. The main limitations of the AMNE database for the purpose of the analysis are (i) that it does not contain data on domestic-owned MNE entities, and (ii) that financial sectors are excluded from the scope of the data in certain jurisdictions (e.g. EU countries). In addition, there are a number of data gaps in the bilateral AMNE data, reflecting notably confidentiality issues as certain values at the country-pair level contain information related to a small number of MNEs. Inward and outward data also do not provide the same set of variables, as for instance outward data does not include gross operating surplus.

### *5.2.4. The OECD Analytical AMNE database*

483. The OECD Analytical AMNE database contains a full bilateral matrix of the output of foreign affiliates in 59 countries plus a 'rest of the world' aggregate. Data is broken down by host and parent country and by industry (across 34 industrial sectors of the NACE Rev. 2 classification (Eurostat, 2008[9])). Analytical AMNE also contains data on value-added, exports and imports of intermediate inputs at the host country and industry level, which provides information on the contribution of foreign MNEs to those variables but without a breakdown by country of ultimate parent. In addition, the data contains a second set of tables providing information on output, value-added, exports and imports of intermediate inputs of domestic MNEs and non-MNE domestic firms.

484. The OECD Analytical AMNE database was constructed using the OECD AMNE database (see previous section) as a starting point. In order to estimate the missing information in the OECD AMNE database across countries and industries, additional national sources have been used and various statistical methodologies applied (see Cadestin et al. (2018[2]) for more details).

485. The main limitation of Analytical AMNE data for the purpose of this chapter is that it focuses on a limited number of variables, and does not contain an indicator of profit (unlike the OECD AMNE database, which contains data on gross operating surplus), tangible assets or payroll. Another limitation relates to the fact that the underlying AMNE data focuses on foreign-owned MNEs, which implies that the information

on domestic-owned MNEs in Analytical AMNE tends to be more fragile than the information on foreign-owned MNEs, as it tends to rely more on other (potentially less harmonised) sources as well as imputations.

### *5.2.5. Foreign Direct Investment (FDI) data*

486. Several international organisations (e.g. OECD, IMF, UNCTAD) publish bilateral FDI data across a wide range of jurisdictions. These data are generally collected as part of the balance of payments statistics. FDI data contain information about investment positions (i.e. stocks) and investment flows across borders, focusing on investments involving a long-term relationship and reflecting a lasting interest and a degree of control (based on a 10% ownership threshold). Financial flows consist of equity transactions, reinvestment of earnings, and intercompany debt transactions. FDI data also contain information on investment income (dividends, interest) as well as royalty flows. Bilateral FDI data are typically reported by both the investor and the recipient jurisdiction, but different values may be reported for the same data point due to methodological differences between reporting jurisdictions.[9]

487. For the purpose of this chapter, one advantage of FDI data is their wide geographic coverage, as most pairs of jurisdictions with significant cross-border investment are covered. Data on FDI position and FDI income can be used to build proxy measures of MNE profit in foreign jurisdictions. In contrast, FDI data lack direct information on turnover, tangible assets or payroll. The well-known fact that BEPS behaviour can distort FDI data is an issue for the analysis of 'real' investment activity based on FDI (Damgaard, Elkjaer and Johannesen, 2019[10]), but it is not necessarily an issue to assess profit location across jurisdictions, which is the goal of the profit matrix. Indeed, FDI data are known to provide some information on the location of shifted profits of MNEs (Bolwijn, Casella and Rigo, 2018[11]).

488. One important limitation of FDI data is that they traditionally focus on direct investors into a jurisdiction, as opposed to ultimate investors. This can be an issue especially since certain investments can go through several jurisdictions before they reach their final destination (Borga and Caliandro, 2018[12]), especially in the context of profit shifting schemes. In recent years, the OECD started publishing inward FDI position statistics by ultimate (as opposed to immediate) investor for a subset of 15 recipient jurisdictions (OECD, 2015[13]). When using FDI data, this chapter makes use of these data by ultimate investor where available. In other recipient jurisdictions, it relies on a sophisticated methodology, inspired by Damgaard and Elkjaer (2017[4]) and Casella (2019[5]), to iterate on direct FDI data and eliminate 'pass-through' (or 'conduit') FDI to measure FDI positions by ultimate investor (see Annex 5.C).

### *5.2.6. Data from the US Bureau of Economic Analysis*

489. National sources can contain additional data on the activity and profit of MNEs, even though they lack the cross-country perspective of the sources listed above. The most detailed national source is the US Bureau of Economic Analysis (BEA). As part of the Activities of US Multinational Enterprises database, the BEA provides statistics on the worldwide activities of US MNEs, including balance sheet data, income statement data, data on employment and compensation of employees, data on trade in goods and services, and expenditures for research and development. Data are disaggregated by both affiliate jurisdiction and economic sector, with different levels of disaggregation (geographic and sectoral) depending on the table considered. Part of the BEA data on US MNEs is the basis for the OECD AMNE data for the United States, but the BEA data is in many respects more detailed than the OECD AMNE data relative to US MNEs.

490. Two indicators of profit are included in the BEA data: (i) net income, from the income statement (Table II.D 1 of the BEA database), which has been identified as involving some double counting of equity income (Blouin and Robinson, 2019[14]) and (ii) 'profit-type' return, from the decomposition of value-added (Table II.F 1 of the BEA database), which is the closest indicator to financial account profit and is not

subject to the double counting issue (see also Clausing (2020[15]) for a discussion). The BEA data also includes indicators of turnover ("Sales" in the income statement), tangible assets ("Property, plant and equipment" in the Balance sheet of affiliates in Table II.B 1-2 of the BEA database) and payroll ("Compensation of employees" in the decomposition of value-added).

## 5.3. Overview of the methodology underlying the matrices

491. To overcome the coverage limitations of the existing data sources, the approach is to combine data from different sources in a consistent framework (i.e. a set of matrices). The aim is to obtain a global geographic coverage of the profit and economic activity of MNEs, while using for each data point the most reliable data source available. Another key feature of the approach is to take advantage of cases where several data sources are available for the same data point, to benchmark sources against each other in order to enhance data quality and consistency.

### *5.3.1. Stylised example illustrating the methodology*

492. In practice, each matrix contains data across more than 200 jurisdictions of affiliate (matrix rows) and broken down across more than 200 jurisdictions of MNE ultimate parent (matrix columns). Each matrix therefore takes the form of a square table with more than 200 rows and more than 200 columns (the jurisdictions in rows and columns are the same). For example, the France-United States cell in the profit matrix contains the profit of US MNEs (i.e. MNEs with an ultimate parent in the United States) in France. Each matrix cell is filled with a certain data source, with a pre-defined order of preference when several sources are available, as discussed below.

493. As can be seen in Figure 5.1, which presents in a stylised way the data sources underlying the profit matrix, different data sources provide coverage of a different nature. In particular, CbCR data can be used to fill *columns* of the matrices, while ORBIS data can be used to fill *rows*. This is because CbCR data typically contain detailed information across affiliate jurisdictions, for a given jurisdiction of ultimate parent. In contrast, ORBIS unconsolidated account data contain, in the jurisdictions of affiliate with good ORBIS coverage, detailed information on MNE entities from any jurisdiction of ultimate parent.

Figure 5.1. Profit matrix: Stylised overview and underlying data sources

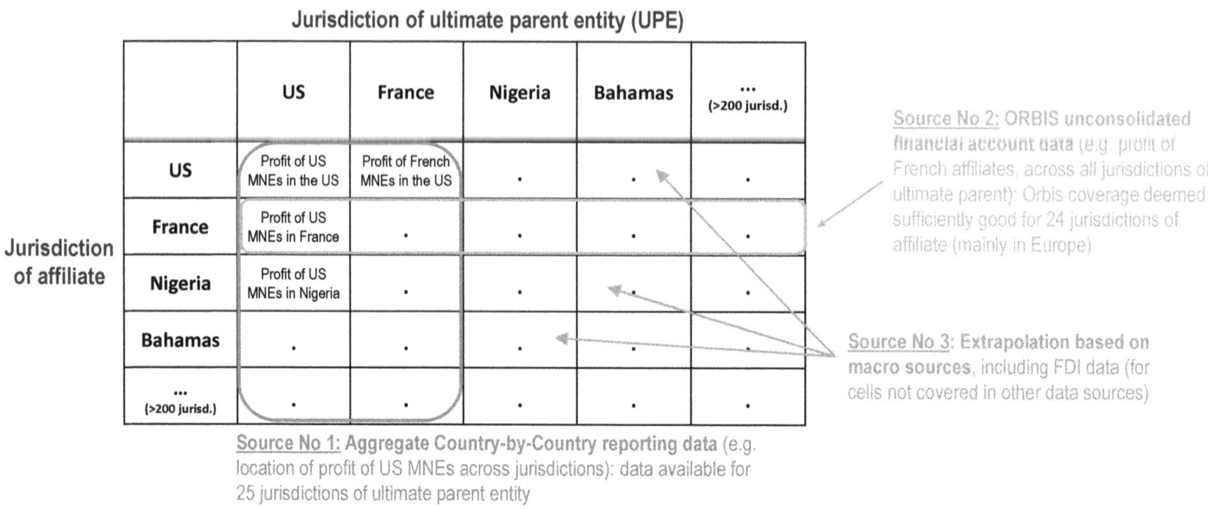


Note: CbCR data are used to fill *columns* of the profit matrix (e.g. profit of French MNEs across jurisdictions). ORBIS unconsolidated account data are used to fill *rows* of the profit matrix (i.e. MNE profit in France, split across ultimate parent jurisdictions). These two sources are used only where available, and in the case of ORBIS, where data coverage is sufficiently good. Other cells in the profit matrix are filled with extrapolations based on macroeconomic data, including FDI data. See Annex 5.A for the lists of jurisdictions where CbCR and ORBIS data are used.
Source: OECD Secretariat.

### *5.3.2. Definition of the variables included in the matrices*

494. The four variables considered in the matrices (profit, turnover, tangible assets and payroll) are defined in Table 5.1. These definitions were chosen based on the needs of the impact assessment of Pillar One and Pillar Two, also taking into account the constraints around existing data sources. In particular, all four variables are based on concepts from financial accounting data (as opposed to tax or national accounting data). The focus is on year 2016, which is the latest available year across the various data sources used.

495. The definitions presented in Table 5.1 are 'targets', in the sense that the four matrices are filled with variables that are as close to these definitions as possible. However, the exact values in matrix cells can deviate from these targets due to limitations in the available data used to fill the matrices (e.g. some intra-group dividends are included in CbCR data). The exact variables considered in each of the underlying data source are presented in Section 5.4.

Table 5.1. Definition of the variables considered in the four matrices

| Variable | Definition |
|---|---|
| Profit | Profit before tax, excluding dividends received from affiliates |
| Turnover | Revenues from sales to third-party and intra-group entities |
| Tangible assets | Property, plant and equipment, net of depreciation |
| Payroll | Expenditures for salaries and wages, including bonuses, social contributions and other employee benefits |

Note: The exact definitions of variables across matrix cells can deviate from the 'targets' presented in this Table due to limitations in the available underlying data (see Section 5.4). All four variables are based on financial accounting data. Data related to entities from the same MNE group are consolidated at the jurisdiction level. Only data for MNE groups with a positive profit in the jurisdiction considered are included, as discussed in Section 5.4.
Source: OECD Secretariat

### 5.3.3. Overview of data sources and their preference order

496. All four matrices are filled using the same overall methodology. However, given that certain variables are available in some sources and not in other (e.g. CbCR data contain information on profit, turnover and tangible assets, but not on payroll), the combination of sources is not exactly the same across the four matrices (Table 5.2). In all four matrices, a 'last resort' method based on extrapolations has been employed when no hard data is available. This ensures that all matrix cells can ultimately be filled, although the extrapolated values obviously come with a greater degree of uncertainty than values based on hard data.

Table 5.2. Overview and preference order of data sources underlying the set of matrices

| Data source (order of preference) | Profit matrix | Turnover matrix | Tangible assets matrix | Payroll matrix |
|---|---|---|---|---|
| 1 | CbCR data | CbCR data | CbCR data | ORBIS data |
| 2 | ORBIS data | ORBIS data | ORBIS data | OECD AMNE data |
| 3 | Extrapolations based on macro data (e.g. FDI) | OECD Analytical AMNE data | Extrapolations based on turnover matrix | Extrapolations based on turnover matrix |
| 4 | | OECD AMNE data | | |
| 5 | | Extrapolations based on macro data (e.g. gravity model) | | |

Note: The combination of sources differs across matrices, reflecting differences in the available variables across sources. The order of preference is necessary to decide on which source to use to fill the matrix cells for which several sources are available. The ordering is as consistent as possible across the matrices to ensure greater consistency across the matrices. Finally, there is for each matrix an extrapolation method (involving more uncertainty than hard data) that ensures that all matrix cells can ultimately be filled.
Source: OECD Secretariat

497. As several data sources can be available for the same data point, it is necessary to decide on an order of preference between data sources. To ensure consistency between the four matrices, the approach has been to order data sources in as consistent a way as possible across the four matrices. Another general principle is that hard data has been given priority over extrapolations. With these principles, several ordering choices remained possible, with no undisputable way to decide on the best ordering between sources that have different strengths and limitations (e.g. CbCR vs. ORBIS data). Ultimately, the choice has been made to make CbCR data the preferred source, reflecting that it is the available source with the widest geographic coverage across several variables considered. The second preferred source is ORBIS, which offers the benefit of covering the four variables considered. After these two sources come the OECD Analytical AMNE database (in the turnover matrix) and the OECD AMNE database (in the turnover and payroll matrices), and ultimately extrapolations specific to each matrix. Robustness checks are presented in Section 5.8.5 to illustrate the potential implications of different source ordering choices.

498. The fact that several data sources cover the same data points is very useful for the purpose of benchmarking sources against each other and more broadly assessing the quality of the data. The extensive benchmarking that was undertaken as part of the preparation of the matrices is presented in Section 5.8.

## 5.4. Methodology underlying the use of hard data

499. Four sources of hard data are used to fill the matrices: (i) CbCR data (in all matrices except the payroll matrix), (ii) ORBIS data (in all four matrices), (iii) OECD Analytical AMNE data (in the turnover matrix) and (iv) OECD AMNE data (in the turnover and payroll matrices). This section describes more precisely how each of these sources are used. The extrapolation methods to fill cells for which no hard data source is available are described in the following section.

### *5.4.1. Aggregated and anonymised CbCR data*

500. Aggregated and anonymised CbCR data have been used directly where available to fill cells in the profit, turnover and tangible assets matrices. Data are taken from Table I, 'Sub-groups with positive profits' panel. The variables used are respectively 'Profit (Loss) before Income Tax', 'Total Revenues' and 'Tangible Assets other than Cash and Cash Equivalents' (OECD, 2020[3]).

501. The data on 'sub-groups with positive profits' focus only on entities belonging to MNE groups that have positive profits in the jurisdiction considered, and therefore exclude entities from MNE groups that are in a loss position in the jurisdiction considered. An alternative option would have been to use the data for all MNE sub-groups regardless of their profit position. This would have led to lower profit amounts, as the profits of sub-groups with positive profits would have been netted of the losses of loss-making sub-groups. In contrast, it would have led to higher turnover and tangible assets, as the turnover and tangible assets of more MNE groups would have been included.[10]

502. The choice to focus on sub-groups with positive profits was driven by the aim of the matrices, which is to inform the impact assessment of Pillar One and Pillar Two. Given that both pillars would primarily affect the taxation of MNE groups in jurisdictions where they are in a profit position, the focus on sub-groups with positive profits makes the matrices more relevant tools for the impact assessment (see Chapters 2 and 3). This choice has been made consistently across the profit, turnover and tangible assets matrices to ensure consistency when the matrices are used in combination. To the extent possible, consistent assumptions to focus on sub-groups with positive profits have been made with other data sources (i.e. ORBIS) and implicitly in the extrapolations, as further discussed below.

503. The CbCR data have been used for 25 jurisdictions of ultimate parent, i.e. to fill *columns* in the matrices (see list of jurisdictions in Annex 5.A).[11] Certain jurisdictions of ultimate parent have reported the CbCR data at the level of each jurisdiction of affiliate, while others have reported the data for groups of jurisdictions (e.g. with groups by continent, or, in the most extreme cases of aggregation, only a split between their jurisdiction and foreign ones), or for a combination of individual jurisdictions and groups (e.g. with groups such as 'other European jurisdictions', 'other African jurisdictions'). The typical reason for this grouping is to avoid the potential breach of taxpayer confidentiality. For the purpose of filling the matrices, data for jurisdiction groups have not been used, since they cannot directly be attributed to individual jurisdictions. As a result, CbCR data have been considered missing for these cells, which have been filled based on the other available data sources (or extrapolations) following the order of preference presented in Table 5.2.

504. The CbCR data focus on year 2016, which is (for the moment) the only year available across a range of jurisdictions of ultimate parent, with the exception of the United States, which has already published 2017 CbCR data. The 2016 CbCR data in the United States was based on voluntary filing, while it was compulsory in 2017, leading to an increase by more than 40% in the number of reporting MNE groups.[12] Given this, the choice was made to use 2017 data for the United States instead of 2016 data. While this creates a small time inconsistency with the other sources of data in the matrices, it has been judged, on balance, to be an inconsistency worth accepting as it enables a better coverage of MNE groups.

505. CbCR data focus only on MNE groups with global revenues above EUR 750 million, since reporting is not compulsory for MNE groups below this threshold. In the context of the impact assessment of Pillar One and Pillar Two, the exclusion of smaller MNE groups from the data may be welcome, as it would provide more accurate estimates under the illustrative assumption that Pillar One and Pillar Two would include global revenue thresholds of the same order of magnitude as the CbCR threshold. However, the revenue threshold implies some inconsistency with some other data sources, where such a threshold cannot directly be applied. A detailed analysis based on consolidated account data from the ORBIS database (as described in Chapter 2) suggests that more than 90% of global MNE profit comes from MNE groups that have a turnover above the CbCR reporting threshold. The same holds for the other variables considered (turnover, tangible assets and payroll). Reflecting this, the overall impact on the matrices of the inconsistency created by the global revenue threshold in CbCR data is likely to be limited.

506. As discussed in section 5.2.1 above, CbCR data come with a number of limitations.[13] In particular, dividends from affiliates are potentially reported in profits in an inconsistent way (sometimes included and sometimes not). The extensive benchmarking of CbCR data against other sources presented below suggests that this does not seem to affect disproportionally the overall quality of CbCR data, although the issue may be more consequential in certain jurisdictions depending on the reporting guidance that was given and the importance of intra-company dividends across jurisdictions. The other main issue is that the profit and activity classified as 'stateless' in CbCR data may correspond to different situations, including 'pass-through' entities whose activities and profits are already included elsewhere in the data. Reflecting this, the profit and activity of 'stateless' entities have not been included in the matrices to avoid the risk of double counting.

507. The tangible assets variable in CbCR data includes property, plant and equipment, but it can also include inventories. As a result, it is not fully consistent with the definition of tangible assets in Table 5.1, nor with data from other sources, which exclude inventories. To address this issue, tangible assets values taken from CbCR data have been scaled down to exclude inventories, based on the share of inventories in the tangible assets of US MNEs (which are assumed to be representative of MNEs from other jurisdictions) computed using data from the US BEA.[14]

### 5.4.2. ORBIS data

508. ORBIS data have been used to fill cells in the profit, turnover, tangible assets and payroll matrices, using unconsolidated financial accounts of firms belonging to MNE groups (identified thanks to ORBIS ownership data, as detailed in Annex 5.B). The quality of coverage of ORBIS unconsolidated financial account data has been judged sufficient to use ORBIS as a data source to fill the matrices in 24 jurisdictions of affiliate (see list in Annex 5.A).[15] For each jurisdiction of affiliate, ORBIS contains financial information on MNE entities from any jurisdiction of ultimate parent (even when the ultimate parent is in a jurisdiction with poor ORBIS coverage of unconsolidated account data). As a result, ORBIS data can be used to fill the *rows* corresponding to these jurisdictions in the matrices. The variables used for the four matrices are respectively 'Profit and Loss before tax', 'Operating revenue turnover', 'Tangible fixed assets' and 'Cost of employees'.

509. ORBIS data have been cleaned and checked extensively before usage, building on OECD expertise from a range of past projects. Such cleaning is required to enhance data reliability because ORBIS data is not primarily collected for statistical analysis. A detailed cleaning of the ORBIS ownership data used in this project, including the identification of missing ownership links in the original ORBIS database, has been implemented by the OECD Directorate for Science, Technology and Innovation, following the methodology of Bajgar et al. (2019[16]). Regarding financial account data, the cleaning procedure is inspired by Gal (2013[17]), Johansson et al. (2017[18]) and Bailin et al. (2019[19]). The detailed cleaning procedure of ORBIS ownership and financial account data is presented in Annex 5.B.

510. ORBIS data contains two measures of profit: (i) profit before tax (PBT) and (ii) earnings before interest and tax (EBIT). The difference between the two measures is that PBT includes dividends received and is net of interest paid, while EBIT does not include dividends and is not net of interest. None of the two measures is exactly consistent with the concept of profit reported in CbCR data (which is net of interest and may or may not include dividends). While both measures are relevant indicators of profit, the choice was made to use PBT in the profit matrix as it is a more relevant indicator for the impact assessment of Pillar One and Pillar Two. For example, PBT is the measure of profit considered as the potential basis to define residual profit under Pillar One. Reflecting that EBIT data is also informative, consistency checks have been carried out with ORBIS data focusing on EBIT instead of PBT (see Section 5.8.2).

511. To enhance consistency with CbCR data, in which, as discussed above, the choice has been made to consider only sub-groups with positive profits (i.e. entities from MNE groups with a positive profit in the jurisdiction considered), the same assumption has been made in ORBIS data.[16] Also consistent with CbCR data, the identification of whether an entity belongs to a corporate group was based on a 50% ownership threshold. In contrast, the EUR 750 million global revenue threshold was not applied, reflecting that the consolidated financial information of the MNE group to which each entity belongs is not always available in the data.[17]

512. The coverage of tangible assets and payroll in ORBIS unconsolidated account data is less extensive than the coverage of turnover. Across the 24 jurisdictions where ORBIS data are used to fill the matrices, the turnover of MNE entities with missing information on tangible assets represents on average about 16% of the total turnover of MNE entities, with exact numbers depending on the jurisdiction considered. Coverage of payroll in ORBIS is generally weaker than coverage of the other variables considered in this chapter. As a result, ORBIS data are only used to fill the payroll matrix in 18 jurisdictions, against 24 jurisdictions for the other variables (see list in Annex 5.A). Across these 18 jurisdictions, the average share of missing information on payroll is 26%. To avoid that these gaps in coverage induce a negative bias in the data from ORBIS, tangible assets and payroll values taken from ORBIS have been scaled up in proportion to the estimated under-coverage rate in the jurisdiction and for the variable considered.[18]

### *5.4.3. OECD AMNE data*

513. Data from the OECD AMNE database were used to fill matrix cells in the turnover and payroll matrices, where they are used respectively as the fourth and second possible source (see Table 5.2). AMNE contains data on turnover ('turnover') and payroll ('personnel costs') for 'ultimate parent'-'affiliate' pairs of jurisdictions, mainly across OECD economies. The OECD AMNE database encompasses data from Eurostat FATS and US BEA AMNE databases. Both inward and outward AMNE data are used, and a preference was given to inward data in cases where both are available for the same matrix cell.

514. One issue is that OECD AMNE data do not always cover the full economy, as for example financial sectors are excluded in the inward statistics of European countries. In the case of turnover, AMNE data have been used to fill the turnover matrix only when they cover the full economy. In the case of the payroll matrix, where fewer alternative data sources are available, AMNE data have been used even when they do not cover the full economy, but they have been rescaled to make them as consistent as possible with full economy data. More precisely, the values from AMNE data have been multiplied by the ratio of turnover in the whole economy (taken from the relevant cell in the turnover matrix) to turnover in the sectors covered by AMNE data. For example, the payroll of US MNEs in France sourced from AMNE data has been multiplied by the ratio of turnover of US MNEs in France, sourced from the turnover matrix, to turnover of US MNEs in France, sourced from AMNE data. When AMNE and the data underlying the turnover matrix have the same sectoral coverage, the ratio is close to one and the adjustment is not consequential. When sectoral coverage is narrower in AMNE, the ratio is above one, and the rescaling ensures that the payroll

matrix is filled with data that focus – at least in an approximated way – on the whole economy and that is consistent with the turnover matrix.[19]

### 5.4.4. OECD Analytical AMNE data

515. OECD Analytical AMNE data were used only in the turnover matrix, where they are the third source in the preference order, after CbCR data and ORBIS data. At the level of disaggregation required for the matrices (i.e. jurisdiction-pair level), Analytical AMNE contains data on the gross output of MNEs, but not directly on turnover. The data available at a more aggregated level (i.e. jurisdiction level), which contain both gross output and turnover, suggest that these two variables are generally closely related to each other, except in certain specific sectors (in particular wholesale and retail trade, see Figure 2 in Cadestin et al. (2018[2])).

516. To 'convert' the data on gross output into a measure of turnover at the jurisdiction-pair level, gross output in a given industry and jurisdiction-pair was multiplied by the ratio of gross output to turnover for this industry and jurisdiction-pair, based on (non-published) data underlying the OECD Analytical AMNE database. For jurisdiction pairs where this ratio was not available, the average ratio of gross output to turnover at the 'market jurisdiction'-'industry' level, or at the industry level depending on data availability, was applied.

## 5.5. Methodology underlying the data extrapolations

517. The extrapolation methodology depends on the matrix considered, as the nature of the gaps in hard data and the available proxies that can be used for the extrapolation depend on the variable considered. For example, FDI data can be used to extrapolate profit location, but it is less well suited to extrapolating the other variables of interest.

518. Still, the general approach has important similarities across the four matrices. One common element is that the extrapolation methodology covers all cells in the matrix considered, to ensure that there is no data gap in the final matrices. In addition, the methodology often builds on the information contained in the matrix cells filled with hard data, which aims to ensure that extrapolated values are as consistent with these other matrix cells as possible. Finally, the extrapolations aim at making the data in the four matrices as comparable with each other as possible, reflecting that the matrices may need to be used in combination with each other. For example, the extrapolations in the tangible assets and payroll matrices are building on the data in the turnover matrix.

### 5.5.1. Extrapolations in the profit matrix

519. The extrapolation strategy in the profit matrix differs between 'diagonal' cells (i.e. the profit of MNEs in their jurisdiction of ultimate parent) and 'non-diagonal' cells (i.e. the profit of MNEs in foreign jurisdictions). This reflects differences in the available data. For non-diagonal cells, the extrapolation is primarily based on bilateral FDI data, which are not available in diagonal cells as FDI is, by definition, focusing on foreign investment. Reflecting this, the extrapolation methodology for diagonal cells is based on other macroeconomic aggregates, as discussed below.

#### *Extrapolations in 'non-diagonal' cells in the profit matrix*

520. Profit in non-diagonal cells is extrapolated using bilateral FDI positions and an assumption regarding the rate of return on FDI, which takes into account heterogeneities in the rate of return across both investing and recipient jurisdictions. An overview of the methodology is presented in this section, and a fully detailed description of all its components is included in Annex 5.C.

521. The FDI positions considered are based on the location of the *ultimate* (as opposed to *immediate*) investor into a jurisdiction, for consistency with the other data sources in the profit matrix, which are based on the concept of ultimate investor (i.e. the location of the ultimate parent of the investing MNE group). The ultimate investor is reported in the available OECD data for 15 jurisdictions. In other jurisdictions, the location of the ultimate investor is identified via repeated iterations on immediate FDI data, following and refining the methodology of Casella (2019[5])

522. This methodology is refined in two ways: (i) The probability that FDI from a certain jurisdiction is 'pass-through' (i.e. that the ultimate investor is not located in this jurisdiction), which is a central input to the methodology, is estimated based on the available OECD data on FDI by ultimate versus immediate investor, as explained in Annex 5.C. This is a more direct and geographically more widely available measure than the measure used by earlier studies (Damgaard and Elkjaer, 2017[4]; Casella, 2019[5]; Damgaard, Elkjaer and Johannesen, 2019[10]), which is based on the share of Special Purpose Entities (SPEs) in a jurisdiction's outward FDI investment. (ii) After identifying the ultimate investor corresponding to a given FDI position, the methodology eliminates from the data the intermediate positions corresponding to 'pass-through' (or 'conduit') FDI, as illustrated in Figure 5.2, which is an additional step compared to the methodology of Casella (2019[5]).

## Figure 5.2. Stylised example on 'immediate', 'ultimate' and 'pass-through' FDI

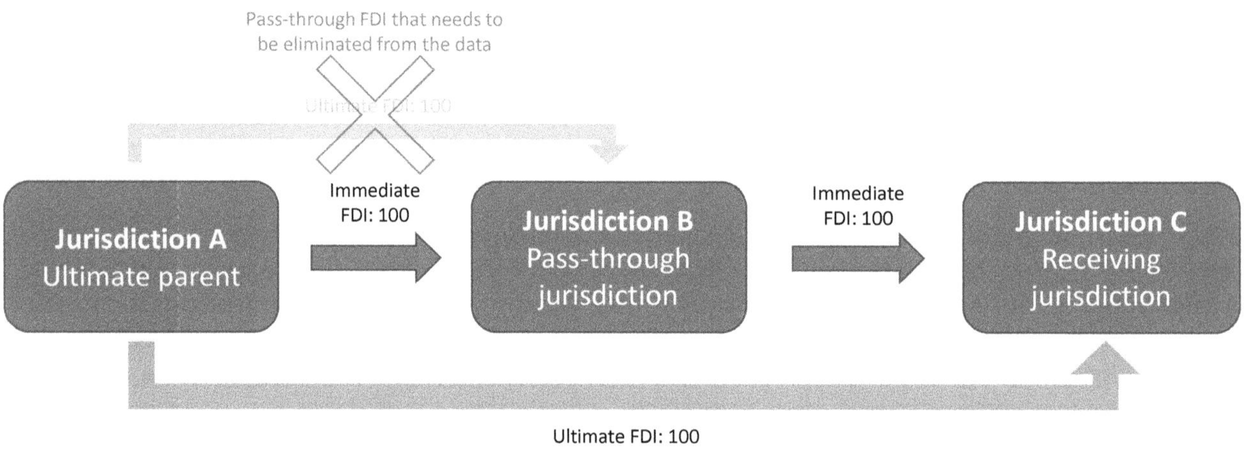


Note: In this stylised example, an MNE group with an ultimate parent in jurisdiction A has invested 100 into jurisdiction C, passing through jurisdiction B. FDI statistics by immediate investor report an FDI position from jurisdiction A into jurisdiction B, and a similar position from jurisdiction B into jurisdiction C. FDI statistics by ultimate investor in jurisdiction C report that the ultimate investor is jurisdiction A. However, when considering the ultimate investors into jurisdiction B, the FDI position of jurisdiction A into jurisdiction B is also considered as an ultimate investment (A being the ultimate parent), while it is only a 'pass-through FDI' that should be eliminated from the data.
Source: OECD Secretariat.

523. FDI data by ultimate investor is sourced from the OECD FDI statistics, and FDI data by immediate investor from the OECD FDI statistics and the IMF Coordinated Direct Investment Survey (CDIS). For the pairs of jurisdictions where no immediate FDI data are available, FDI positions are imputed using a standard gravity model relying on variables such as distance, GDP and GDP per capita of the investor and recipient jurisdictions. These imputations based on a gravity model ensure that the matrix of immediate FDI data is filled completely and, in turn, that the matrix of ultimate FDI estimates can also be filled completely. While these imputations based on a gravity model come with more uncertainty than hard FDI data, their overall impact is limited as they represent only about 2% of FDI positions in the final matrix of FDI by immediate investor.

524. Based on this methodology, two full matrices of FDI positions have been built: (i) FDI positions by *immediate* investor, and (ii) FDI positions by *ultimate* investor. The ultimate investor matrix is presented, for aggregated groups of jurisdictions, in Table 5.3 (the immediate investor matrix is presented in Annex Table 5.C.3). While these two FDI matrices have only been used as intermediate inputs for the extrapolations in the profit matrix in this chapter, they are interesting in their own right and could be the subject of (or useful tools for) future studies. For example, it is interesting to note that eliminating 'pass-through FDI' mainly reduces the relative importance of investment hubs (both as recipient and investor jurisdictions) in the FDI matrix (see Annex 5.C).

## Table 5.3. Matrix of FDI positions by ultimate investor, aggregated by broad jurisdiction groups

| | | Jurisdiction of ultimate investor | | | | |
|---|---|---|---|---|---|---|
| | (USD billion of 2016) | **High income** | **Middle income** | **Low income** | **Investment Hubs** | **Total** |
| **Jurisdiction of recipient** | High income (64 jurisd.) | 7787.9 | 591.0 | 1.4 | 2830.4 | **11210.8** |
| | Middle income (105) | 2559.7 | 367.9 | 2.2 | 2755.6 | **5685.4** |
| | Low income (29) | 11.1 | 7.2 | 0.1 | 2.3 | **20.7** |
| | Investment Hubs (24) | 4252.2 | 770.4 | 0.7 | 2228.8 | **7252.1** |
| | **Total** | **14611.0** | **1736.4** | **4.4** | **7817.2** | **24169.0** |

Note: Groups of jurisdictions (high, middle and low income) are based on the World Bank classification. Investment hubs are defined as jurisdictions with a total inward FDI position above 150% of GDP. The FDI positions considered in this matrix are based on the location of the *ultimate* (as opposed to *immediate*) investor into a jurisdiction. See methodology in Annex 5.C.
Source: OECD Secretariat.

525. The assumed rate of return on FDI is based on a global 'standard' return on FDI, which is computed as the median ratio of profit to FDI in the profit matrix cells filled with hard data (which yields a value of 7.9%). This approach offers the benefit of making the extrapolation methodology as consistent as possible with the hard data in the profit matrix. In addition to this 'standard' return, the rate of return takes into account how the average rate of return to FDI deviates (positively or negatively) from the global average across both investing and receiving jurisdictions. This deviation is computed based on the available data on FDI income[20] (see Annex 5.C for more details).

### *Extrapolations in 'diagonal' cells in the profit matrix*

526. Less data are generally available on the activity and profit of domestic-owned MNEs than on foreign-owned ones. This might reflect the fact that foreign-owned MNEs tend to generate more policy interest than domestic-owned ones. In addition, it may be difficult from a statistical collection point of view to disentangle the activity of domestic-owned MNE entities from that of non-MNE firms. Indeed, identifying a domestic-owned MNE entity requires knowing the location of its ultimate owner (to make sure that it is not foreign-owned) but also having information about the activities of other subsidiaries of this ultimate owner (to make sure that at least one of them is located abroad). Reflecting this, extrapolations in diagonal matrix cells are overall less refined than in non-diagonal cells, and can be assumed to come with greater uncertainty.

527. The starting point for the extrapolation in diagonal cells of the profit matrix is the total profit of domestic-owned firms (MNEs and non-MNEs) as estimated by Tørsløv et al. (2018[1]). To obtain the diagonal cells in the profit matrix (i.e. profit of domestic-owned MNEs), the profit of domestic-owned firms needs to be split between MNE and non-MNE entities. This is done based on a regression of the share of profit of domestic-owned MNEs in the total profit of domestic-owned firms, which is estimated over the approximately 30 jurisdictions where hard data are available in the profit matrix diagonal (i.e. based on

data from CbCR or ORBIS) for the numerator (i.e. profit of domestic-owned MNEs) and in Tørsløv et al. (2018[1]) for the denominator (i.e. total profit of domestic-owned firms), and using GDP and GDP per capita as explanatory variables.

528. For jurisdictions not covered in Tørsløv et al. (2018[1]), where even less data are available, the diagonal profit is directly extrapolated based on a regression on GDP and GDP per capita. The regression results suggest that in general, profit of domestic-owned MNEs is positively correlated with GDP per capita, in line with the intuition that richer countries have more MNE headquarters than poorer ones. Overall, these extrapolations in the diagonal of the profit matrix are based on relatively limited information (e.g. compared to extrapolations in non-diagonal cells), and the extrapolation methodology aims primarily to ensure that cells are filled with plausible values that are consistent with the hard data in the rest of the profit matrix.

### *5.5.2. Extrapolations in the turnover matrix*

529. With four available sources of hard data (CbCR, ORBIS, OECD Analytical AMNE and OECD AMNE), the turnover matrix is the one relying least on extrapolations across the four matrices. The extrapolation methodology follows a similar spirit as the extrapolations in the profit matrix, in the sense that the approach differs between diagonal and non-diagonal cells. In non-diagonal cells, turnover is extrapolated using a gravity model relating bilateral turnover to macroeconomic variables, the distance between countries and, where available, bilateral FDI data. In diagonal cells, turnover is extrapolated using macroeconomic variables in a way informed by the matrix diagonal numbers already available from the other data sources.

#### *Extrapolations in 'non-diagonal' cells in the turnover matrix*

530. The extrapolation of turnover in non-diagonal cells is based on a gravity equation. The level of bilateral MNE turnover is estimated using a Gamma pseudo-maximum-likelihood estimation (Santos Silva and Tenreyro, 2006[20]; Head and Mayer, 2014[21]), of the level of bilateral turnover on distance (mostly sourced from CEPII (Mayer and Zignago, 2011[22])), and both jurisdictions' GDP and GDP per capita. This estimation method, which is often used in a trade context, was chosen as it is well-suited to address the challenge arising from the fact that cells in the matrix of bilateral MNE turnover can take either positive or (frequently) zero values.[21] The results, which are reported in Table 5.4, are in line with intuition, in the sense that the size and income levels of both investor and recipient jurisdictions are positively related to bilateral MNE turnover, while distance is negatively related to it.

Table 5.4. Estimated gravity equation used for extrapolations in the turnover matrix

| | Dependent variable: Bilateral MNE Turnover (in levels) |
|---|---|
| | |
| GDP of investor (log) | 0.478*** |
| | (22.12) |
| GDP of recipient (log) | 0.635*** |
| | (23.81) |
| Distance (log) | -0.566*** |
| | (-9.51) |
| GDP per capita of investor (log) | 0.684*** |
| | (13.97) |
| GDP per capita of recipient (log) | 0.172*** |
| | (3.84) |
| Constant | -10.89*** |
| | (-14.74) |
| | |
| N | 6512 |

Note: T-statistics in parentheses. ***, **, *: denote significance at 1, 5, and 10% levels respectively.
Source: OECD Secretariat.

*Extrapolations in 'diagonal' cells in the turnover matrix*

531. Data on the diagonal of the turnover matrix are extrapolated in a similar fashion as in the profit matrix. The ratio of turnover of domestic-owned MNEs to GDP is regressed on GDP and GDP per capita over the approximately 30 diagonal matrix cells that were filled using CbCR and ORBIS.[22] The regression results are used to extrapolate diagonal cells where none of these data sources is available. Similar to the results on profit of domestic-owned MNEs, the ratio of turnover of domestic-owned MNEs to GDP is significantly positively correlated with GDP per capita, reflecting that richer countries tend to have more MNE headquarters than poorer ones.

### 5.5.3. Extrapolations in the tangible assets matrix

532. The extrapolations in the tangible assets matrix use the turnover matrix as a starting point. The idea is that tangible assets are generally an important input to production, meaning that turnover and tangible assets are likely to be correlated. Of course, capital intensity varies across firms, implying that the ratio of tangible assets to turnover will depend on the jurisdiction, the economic sector and the MNE considered.[23] To take this heterogeneity into account, at least to the extent possible with the available data, the approach considers how the average ratio of tangible assets to turnover varies across both ultimate parent and affiliate jurisdictions (i.e. across both *columns* and *rows* of the tangible assets matrix), as described in Figure 5.3.

Figure 5.3. Overview of methodology for extrapolations in the tangible assets matrix

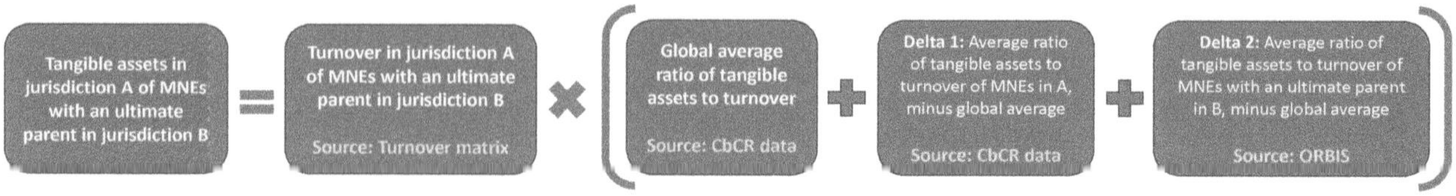


Note: The Figure summarises in a stylised way the methodology to extrapolate data in cells of the tangible assets matrix where no hard data is available. The methodology to extrapolate one cell in the tangible assets matrix starts from the value in the corresponding cell in the turnover matrix, and multiplies it with the global average ratio of tangible assets to turnover, adjusted for deviations of this ratio from the global average both by jurisdiction of affiliate (i.e. matrix row) and of ultimate parent (i.e. matrix column). The global average and the deviations are computed based on the available data in CbCR and ORBIS, as further discussed below.
Source: OECD Secretariat

533. For example, a jurisdiction A that has an economy mainly focused on capital-intensive sectors (e.g. commodity extraction, manufacturing) will likely have a relatively high ratio of tangible assets to turnover. This relatively high ratio will be visible in the data relative to affiliates in A from the CbCR data of the ultimate parent jurisdictions listed in Annex 5.A. When extrapolating the tangible assets in A of MNEs from other ultimate parent jurisdictions, the methodology assumes that these MNEs also have a relatively high ratio in A (implicitly assuming that the nature of their activities is similar to other MNEs in A). More formally, the component 'Delta 1' in Figure 5.3 will be positive for jurisdiction A. Similarly, if MNEs from a certain ultimate parent jurisdiction tend to have a high ratio of tangible assets to turnover, this will also be taken into account in the extrapolation, thanks to the 'Delta 2' component. This 'Delta 2' component is computed with consolidated account data from ORBIS, which have good coverage worldwide.[24]

534. The global average ratio of tangible assets to turnover, computed based on CbCR data (after adjusting for inventories, as discussed above), is 33%. This is also the average ratio in ORBIS unconsolidated accounts. To ensure that the adjusted ratio does not take extreme values as a result of the combination of 'Delta 1' and 'Delta 2' and potential noise in the underlying data, the adjustments are capped. Namely, the individual adjustments ('Delta 1' *or* 'Delta 2') are such that the imputed ratio of tangible assets to turnover that would occur after each adjustment cannot be outside of a range between 15% and 100%, and the final combined adjustment ('Delta 1' *plus* 'Delta 2') is then capped so that the final ratio cannot be outside of that range either.

### *5.5.4. Extrapolations in the payroll matrix*

535. The extrapolation methodology in the payroll matrix is very similar to the methodology in the tangible assets matrix. It starts from the turnover matrix, and applies to it an average ratio of payroll to turnover that takes into account heterogeneities across matrix rows and columns (Figure 5.4). The global average ratio of payroll to turnover, computed based on ORBIS unconsolidated data, is 15.3%.[25] Similar to the tangible assets matrix, the 'Delta 1' and 'Delta 2' parameters are capped both at the individual and combined level so that the imputed ratios are bounded between 5% and 25%.

### Figure 5.4. Overview of methodology for extrapolations in the payroll matrix

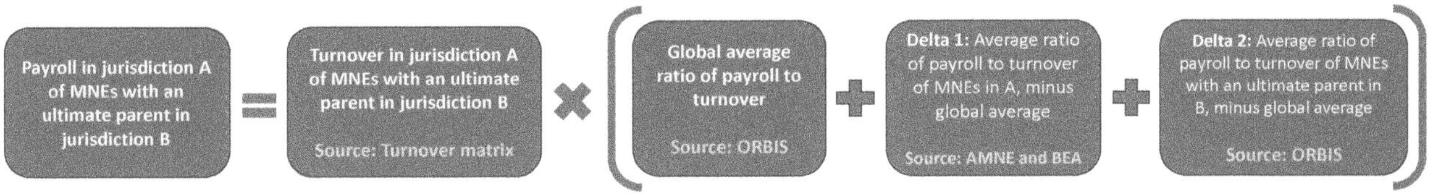


Note: The Figure summarises in a stylised way the methodology to extrapolate data in cells of the payroll matrix where no hard data is available. The methodology to extrapolate one cell in the payroll matrix starts from the value in the corresponding cell in the turnover matrix, and multiplies it with the global average ratio of payroll to turnover, adjusted for deviations of this ratio from the global average both by jurisdiction of affiliate (i.e. matrix row) and of ultimate parent (i.e. matrix column). The global average and the deviations are computed based on the available data in ORBIS and AMNE.
Source: OECD Secretariat

## 5.6. Overview of the matrices at an aggregated level

536. The full matrices have more than 200 rows and columns each. To have an overview of the matrices, it is useful to consider compact versions, aggregated by broad groups of jurisdictions, as presented in Table 5.5. The matrices in Table 5.5 are aggregated at the level of four broad groups of jurisdictions (high, middle and low income jurisdictions, and investment hubs). More disaggregated versions of the matrices, with jurisdiction groups combining the income-level dimension and the geographic dimension are presented in Annex 5.D.

### Table 5.5. The four matrices: Results aggregated by broad jurisdiction groups

**Panel A**: The profit matrix

| | | Jurisdiction of ultimate parent | | | | |
|---|---|---|---|---|---|---|
| | (USD billion of 2016) | **High income** | **Middle income** | **Low income** | **Investment Hubs** | **Total** |
| **Jurisdiction of affiliate** | High income (64 jurisd.) | 3569.1 | 44.1 | 0.1 | 171.3 | **3784.5** |
| | Middle income (105) | 366.2 | 821.8 | 0.1 | 167.9 | **1356.0** |
| | Low income (29) | 1.3 | 1.3 | 3.1 | 0.2 | **5.8** |
| | Investment Hubs (24) | 650.9 | 69.5 | 0.0 | 314.3 | **1034.7** |
| | **Total** | **4587.4** | **936.7** | **3.3** | **653.7** | **6181.1** |

**Panel B:** The turnover matrix

| | | Jurisdiction of ultimate parent | | | | |
|---|---|---|---|---|---|---|
| | (USD billion of 2016) | **High income** | **Middle income** | **Low income** | **Investment Hubs** | **Total** |
| **Jurisdiction of affiliate** | High income (64 jurisd.) | 37034.1 | 943.4 | 19.0 | 2602.3 | **40598.7** |
| | Middle income (105) | 4392.3 | 11281.2 | 11.5 | 1895.1 | **17580.1** |
| | Low income (29) | 50.4 | 22.4 | 45.4 | 11.3 | **129.6** |
| | Investment Hubs (24) | 3398.3 | 176.9 | 3.6 | 1487.3 | **5066.2** |
| | **Total** | **44875.1** | **12423.9** | **79.6** | **5996.0** | **63374.6** |

**Panel C:** The tangible assets matrix

| | (USD billion of 2016) | Jurisdiction of ultimate parent | | | | |
|---|---|---|---|---|---|---|
| | | **High income** | **Middle income** | **Low income** | **Investment Hubs** | **Total** |
| **Jurisdiction of affiliate** | High income (64 jurisd.) | 11463.1 | 314.5 | 6.2 | 614.8 | **12398.7** |
| | Middle income (105) | 1320.4 | 4357.9 | 5.0 | 757.4 | **6440.7** |
| | Low income (29) | 20.5 | 11.2 | 17.1 | 4.2 | **53.1** |
| | Investment Hubs (24) | 437.8 | 69.5 | 0.9 | 422.1 | **930.3** |
| | **Total** | **13241.8** | **4753.2** | **29.2** | **1798.5** | **19822.8** |

**Panel D:** The payroll matrix

| | (USD billion of 2016) | Jurisdiction of ultimate parent | | | | |
|---|---|---|---|---|---|---|
| | | **High income** | **Middle income** | **Low income** | **Investment Hubs** | **Total** |
| **Jurisdiction of affiliate** | High income (64 jurisd.) | 6967.3 | 153.6 | 3.0 | 472.2 | **7596.2** |
| | Middle income (105) | 497.8 | 1495.6 | 1.5 | 186.5 | **2181.4** |
| | Low income (29) | 7.0 | 3.1 | 6.8 | 1.8 | **18.7** |
| | Investment Hubs (24) | 225.3 | 18.2 | 0.4 | 170.3 | **414.2** |
| | **Total** | **7697.5** | **1670.5** | **11.8** | **830.7** | **10210.5** |

Note: Groups of jurisdictions (high, middle and low income) are based on the World Bank classification. The number of jurisdictions in each group is indicated in parentheses. Investment hubs are defined as jurisdictions with a total inward FDI position above 150% of GDP.
Source: OECD Secretariat.

537. The columns totals from the matrices in Table 5.5 confirm that MNE groups with ultimate parents in high income jurisdictions represent the majority of the global activity and profit of MNE groups worldwide (e.g. 71% of turnover, 74% of profit). The row totals in Table 5.5 show that most of the profit and activity of MNE groups worldwide is located in high income jurisdictions (64% of turnover, 61% of profit), and to a lesser extent in middle income jurisdictions (e.g. 28% of turnover, 22% of profit). Interestingly, the share of global MNE profit located in investment hubs (17%) is significantly higher than the share of MNE activity in investment hubs (8% of turnover, 5% of tangible assets, 4% of payroll), consistent with earlier evidence of profit shifting behaviour by MNEs (Johansson et al., 2017[18]; Beer, de Mooij and Liu, 2019[23]).

## 5.7. Relative importance of data sources in the matrices

538. The relative importance of each data source in each matrix is summarised in Table 5.6. It is presented both (i) as a percentage of the total number of cells in each matrix, and (ii) as a percentage of the total amount of the variable considered (e.g. as a percentage of all profit in the profit matrix). This second measure is generally more informative. This is because the total number of cells in each matrix is very high (almost 50,000 cells), reflecting the wide range of jurisdictions covered (222 in total, some of which are very small, see full list in Annex Table 5.D.2). As a result, a large majority of cells contain very small values and have limited importance, either because there are few MNEs with an ultimate parent in the ultimate parent jurisdiction considered (as is the case for many small and developing economies) or because the 'ultimate parent'-'affiliate' pair of jurisdictions considered in the cell have little economic relationship with each other (e.g. because of high geographic distance between the two jurisdictions). Consequently, even though more than 90% of the cells in the matrices are filled in by extrapolations, those represent only about 25% of the total amounts on average across the four matrices.

## Table 5.6. Relative importance of data sources in the matrices

| | Profit matrix | | Turnover matrix | | Tangible assets matrix | | Payroll matrix | |
|---|---|---|---|---|---|---|---|---|
| | % of cells | % of total profit | % of cells | % of total turnover | % of cells | % of total tangible assets | % of cells | % of total payroll |
| CbCR data | 2% | 63% | 2% | 58% | 2% | 60% | -- | -- |
| ORBIS data | 3% | 10% | 3% | 11% | 3% | 12% | 3% | 17% |
| Analytical AMNE data | -- | -- | 4% | 26% | -- | -- | -- | -- |
| AMNE data | -- | -- | 5% | 0% | -- | -- | 2% | 46% |
| Extrapolations | 95% | 27% | 86% | 4% | 95% | 28% | 96% | 36% |
| **Total** | **100%** | **100%** | **100%** | **100%** | **100%** | **100%** | **100%** | **100%** |

Note: For example, 2% of cells in the profit matrix are filled with CbCR data. These cells contain 63% of the total profit in the profit matrix. Cells filled with "-- " correspond to data sources not used in the matrix considered.
Source: OECD Secretariat.

539. The statistics in Table 5.6 indicate that CbCR data are the primary source of data in the profit, turnover and tangible assets matrices, representing about 60% of the total amount of each of these variables in their respective matrices. The share of extrapolations is much lower in the turnover matrix (4%) than in the three other matrices (27-36%), suggesting that the turnover matrix may be the most reliable of the four matrices.

540. The relative importance of extrapolations across jurisdiction groups is presented in Table 5.7. In general, the matrices rely to a relatively low extent on extrapolations for data relative to high income jurisdictions, both across matrix rows (i.e. MNE entities in high income jurisdictions) and columns (MNE entities with an ultimate parent in a high income jurisdiction). For example, extrapolations represent 14% of data in high income jurisdiction rows in the profit matrix, and also 14% in high income jurisdiction columns in the profit matrix. The share of extrapolations is much higher in middle income jurisdictions (above 50% for all variables except turnover, where it is below 10%) and it approaches 100% in low income jurisdictions, reflecting the wide gaps in the existing hard data in these jurisdictions. Finally, the share of extrapolated profit in matrix rows corresponding to investment hubs is below 40%. While still substantial, this number highlights the importance of the newly available CbCR data as a source of data on profit (and other variables) in investment hubs, as other data sources have generally poor coverage of investment hubs.

## Table 5.7. Relative importance of extrapolations in the matrices, by broad jurisdiction groups

**Panel A**: Share of extrapolated data by matrix rows

| | Profit matrix | Turnover matrix | Tangible assets matrix | Payroll matrix |
|---|---|---|---|---|
| High income (64 jurisd.) | 14% | 3% | 14% | 19% |
| Middle income (105) | 53% | 8% | 54% | 93% |
| Low income (29) | 77% | 94% | 93% | 97% |
| Investment Hubs (24) | 39% | 4% | 36% | 60% |
| **Global average** | **27%** | **4%** | **28%** | **36%** |

**Panel B:** Share of extrapolated data by matrix columns

| | Profit matrix | Turnover matrix | Tangible assets matrix | Payroll matrix |
|---|---|---|---|---|
| High income (64 jurisd.) | 14% | 3% | 15% | 22% |
| Middle income (105) | 72% | 9% | 64% | 95% |
| Low income (29) | 100% | 100% | 100% | 100% |
| Investment Hubs (24) | 51% | 5% | 31% | 49% |
| **Global average** | **27%** | **4%** | **28%** | **36%** |

Note: For example, 39% of data in *rows* corresponding to investment hubs in the profit matrix (i.e. profit of MNE affiliates in investment hubs) are extrapolated (Panel A), and 51% of data in *columns* corresponding to investments hubs in the profit matrix (i.e. profit of MNEs with an ultimate parent in an investment hub) are extrapolated (Panel B). Groups of jurisdictions (high, middle and low income) are based on the World Bank classification. Investment hubs are defined as jurisdictions with a total inward FDI position above 150% of GDP. The number of jurisdictions in each group is indicated in parentheses.
Source: OECD Secretariat.

## 5.8. Benchmarking and consistency checks

541. As the matrices combine data from a range of sources, as well as extrapolations, ensuring a sufficient degree of data consistency within and across the matrices is a key challenge. While the data sources used in the matrices all focus on measuring similar variables (e.g. MNE profits), there are inevitably some conceptual differences between them. In particular, the sources used can have different coverage (e.g. CbCR data includes only MNE groups with global revenues above the EUR 750 million reporting threshold, AMNE data excludes financial sectors), different variable definitions (e.g. profit in CbCR data may include some intracompany dividends received, while all dividends are included in the PBT measure from ORBIS and excluded in the EBIT measure) and different ownership rates to define multinationals (e.g. CbCR and ORBIS data are based on a 50% ownership threshold, while FDI data are based on a 10% threshold).

542. While the methodology to fill the matrices aims to address some of these inconsistencies (e.g. by using values in matrix cells filled with hard data in the procedures to extrapolate data to other cells, which enhances the consistency of the extrapolations with the available hard data), the persistence of some inconsistencies between sources is to some extent unavoidable. To gauge the magnitude of these inconsistencies, and to minimise their potential impact on final results, extensive benchmarking and quality checks have been undertaken. They are described in the following sections.

### *5.8.1. Correlation across the data sources used within the matrices*

543. The correlation of data across sources within each matrix has been systematically tested over the cells where several sources are available. As the extrapolation methodologies employed in this chapter produce values for all cells, all cells filled with hard data can be compared at least to the extrapolation results. In addition, there is substantial coverage overlap across the hard data sources, which provides the possibility to consider correlation across these sources as well.

544. The results, presented in Table 5.8 suggest that pairwise correlation of sources is good, especially among hard data sources. For example, correlation reaches 92% between CbCR and ORBIS data in the profit matrix, and 93% in the turnover matrix. Correlation between hard data and extrapolated values is generally lower, as could be expected (between 64% and 96% depending on the variable and data source considered) but still sufficiently high to consider the extrapolations relevant. Even in the profit matrix, where extrapolation is arguably more challenging than in the other matrices because identifying the location of MNE profit is complicated by the fact that it can differ from the location of MNE economic activity, the correlation of extrapolated values with hard data reaches 75%.

### Table 5.8. Pairwise correlation of sources in the matrices

Correlation between each pair of sources in each matrix, and number of observations where the sources overlaps

**Panel A**: Profit matrix

| | CbCR data | ORBIS data | Extrapolations |
|---|---|---|---|
| CbCR data | -- | 0.92<br>(252 obs.) | 0.75<br>(955 obs.) |
| ORBIS data | -- | -- | 0.75<br>(1483 obs.) |
| Extrapolations | -- | -- | -- |

**Panel B:** Turnover matrix

| | CbCR data | ORBIS data | Analytical AMNE data | AMNE data | Extrapolations |
|---|---|---|---|---|---|
| CbCR data | -- | 0.93<br>(254 obs.) | 0.75<br>(561 obs.) | 0.88<br>(417 obs.) | 0.73<br>(1064 obs.) |
| ORBIS data | -- | -- | 0.79<br>(941 obs.) | 0.92<br>(365 obs.) | 0.64<br>(1588 obs.) |
| Analytical AMNE data | -- | -- | -- | 0.95<br>(867 obs.) | 0.75<br>(2583 obs.) |
| AMNE data | -- | -- | -- | -- | 0.71<br>(1530 obs.) |
| Extrapolations | -- | -- | -- | -- | -- |

**Panel C:** Tangible assets matrix

| | CbCR data | ORBIS data | Extrapolations |
|---|---|---|---|
| CbCR data | -- | 0.84<br>(251 obs.) | 0.89<br>(1038 obs.) |
| ORBIS data | -- | -- | 0.87<br>(1493 obs.) |
| Extrapolations | -- | -- | -- |

| Panel D: Payroll matrix | | | |
|---|---|---|---|
| | ORBIS data | AMNE data | Extrapolations |
| ORBIS data | -- | 0.94<br>(598 obs.) | 0.95<br>(1171 obs.) |
| AMNE data | -- | -- | 0.96<br>(1321 obs.) |
| Extrapolations | -- | -- | -- |

Note: This table reports pairwise correlation of data sources in the four matrices, each panel corresponding to a matrix. For each pair of sources, the correlation is computed across the values in all matrix cells where both sources are available. For example, the correlation between the profit data from CbCR and ORBIS in the profit matrix, computed across the 252 profit matrix cells where both sources are available, is 92%. Given the extrapolation methodology employed, the extrapolations are available for comparison across all cells of all four matrices. Values are log-transformed before computing the correlations to avoid that extreme values have a disproportionate effect on the correlations. Correlations without this log-transformation are generally higher than those presented in this Table.
Source: OECD Secretariat.

545. Beyond the average correlation coefficients presented in Table 5.8, the consistency between data sources has been explored in more detail, based on an extensive set of comparison scatterplots. To remain readable, such scatterplots typically have to focus on comparing just one data source with another, in only one given matrix row or column. While these scatterplots would take too much space to be exhaustively reported in this chapter, illustrative examples are provided in Annex Figure 5.E.1, which compares CbCR data and ORBIS data in the columns of the profit, turnover and tangible assets matrices corresponding to ultimate parent jurisdictions where CbCR data have been reported for more than ten bilateral entries (payroll is not included in the Figure as it is not included in CbCR data).

546. This detailed exploration of the data has allowed the OECD Secretariat to identify a number of suspect values, defined as values for which several data sources were indicating very different outcomes. These values have been corrected manually, when necessary, after more detailed investigation to identify the most relevant data source – including via exchanges with jurisdiction representatives. As this exploration has primarily been based on a preliminary version of the CbCR data published in July 2020, it has allowed the identification of a few reporting errors in the CbCR data, which have been corrected before publication after exchanges with jurisdiction representatives.

### *5.8.2. Correlation with alternative data sources not used in the matrices*

547. A number of data sources have not been used directly to fill the matrices, but nevertheless represent useful benchmarks to assess data quality and identify potential data consistency issues in the matrices. Three alternative sources have been considered in this chapter:

- **EBIT instead of PBT as a measure of profit in ORBIS data**: As discussed in section 5.4.2, two measures of profit are available in ORBIS (EBIT and PBT). PBT has been preferred to EBIT as the variable used to fill the profit matrix when using ORBIS data, but EBIT offers an interesting comparison point. In particular, the fact that EBIT excludes dividends received makes the comparison with CBCR data (where intra-group dividends are partly included) and ORBIS PBT data (where they are fully included) illustrative of the influence of dividends in the profit matrix. As shown in Table 5.9 (row 1), the correlation of EBIT with CbCR data is high (92%) and the correlation with ORBIS PBT data (98%) even higher, suggesting that the inclusion of dividends (partial or total) in these sources has only limited average consequences on the overall profit matrix, even though certain cells may be more affected than others (e.g. dividends are likely to be larger in jurisdictions with a larger share of parent or holding companies).
- **OECD AMNE data on gross operating surplus**: As discussed in section 5.2.3, the (inward and outward) OECD AMNE database contains bilateral data on MNE gross operating surplus. This data

has not been used to fill in the profit matrix because it adds little coverage beyond CbCR data and ORBIS, does not always cover all economic sectors, and because gross operating surplus has conceptual differences with the measure of profit in financial accounts due notably to differences in depreciation rules. Still, data on gross operating surplus provide a useful comparison point. To enhance comparability with other sources, adjustments inspired by Tørsløv et al. (2018[1]) are applied to adjust for depreciation.[26] The correlation of the adjusted variable with CbCR data exceeds 80% for both inward and outward AMNE, and the correlation with ORBIS exceeds 85% (Table 5.9, rows 2 and 3). These correlations are overall lower than the CbCR/ORBIS correlation in Table 5.8 (i.e. 92%), which tends to confirm that adjusted gross operating surplus based on OECD AMNE data was less suitable than these two sources for the purpose of filling the profit matrix.

- **Data from the US BEA on US MNEs:** As discussed in section 5.2.6, the US BEA provides detailed data on the foreign activity of US MNEs. The BEA data on profit ('profit-type return'), turnover ('sales of US affiliates'), tangible assets ('property, plant and equipment'), and payroll ('compensation of employees') have been compared with US CbCR data (except for payroll, which is not available in CbCR) as well as ORBIS data on affiliates of US MNEs abroad. As BEA data does not distinguish 'positive' profits (i.e. profits from entities belonging to profit-making MNE sub-groups in the jurisdiction considered) from net profits, the comparison focuses on net profits (while only sub-groups with positive profits from CbCR and ORBIS are considered in the matrices). Overall, the correlation of CbCR and ORBIS data with the relevant BEA data is high (Figure 5.5). The comparison has also allowed for the identification of a few outlying values, corresponding to reporting errors or exceptional events in the data underlying the profit matrix, which have been corrected by replacing them with the corresponding values from the BEA data.

### Table 5.9. Pairwise correlation of the data used in the profit matrix with alternative measures of profit from other data sources

| | | Matrix sources | | |
|---|---|---|---|---|
| | | CbCR data | ORBIS (PBT) | Extrapolations |
| **Other sources** | ORBIS (EBIT) | 0.92 | 0.98 | 0.75 |
| | OECD AMNE (inward) | 0.84 | 0.86 | 0.76 |
| | OECD AMNE (outward) | 0.81 | 0.92 | 0.69 |

Note: This table reports pairwise correlation of data sources in the profit matrix (in column) and three alternative measures of profit from data sources which are not used in the profit matrix (in rows). The alternative measures considered are EBIT (sourced from ORBIS database), and gross operating surplus, adjusted for depreciation using data from Tørsløv et al. (2018[1]), in both inward and outward OECD AMNE data. For each pair of sources, the correlation is computed across all matrix cells where both sources are available. For example, the correlation between the profit data from CbCR and ORBIS EBIT data, computed across the profit matrix cells where both sources are available is 92%. Values are log-transformed before computing the correlations to avoid that extreme values have a disproportionate effect on the correlations. Correlations without this log-transformation are generally higher than those presented in this Table.
Source: OECD Secretariat.

## Figure 5.5. US MNEs: Comparison of CBCR and ORBIS data with data from the US BEA

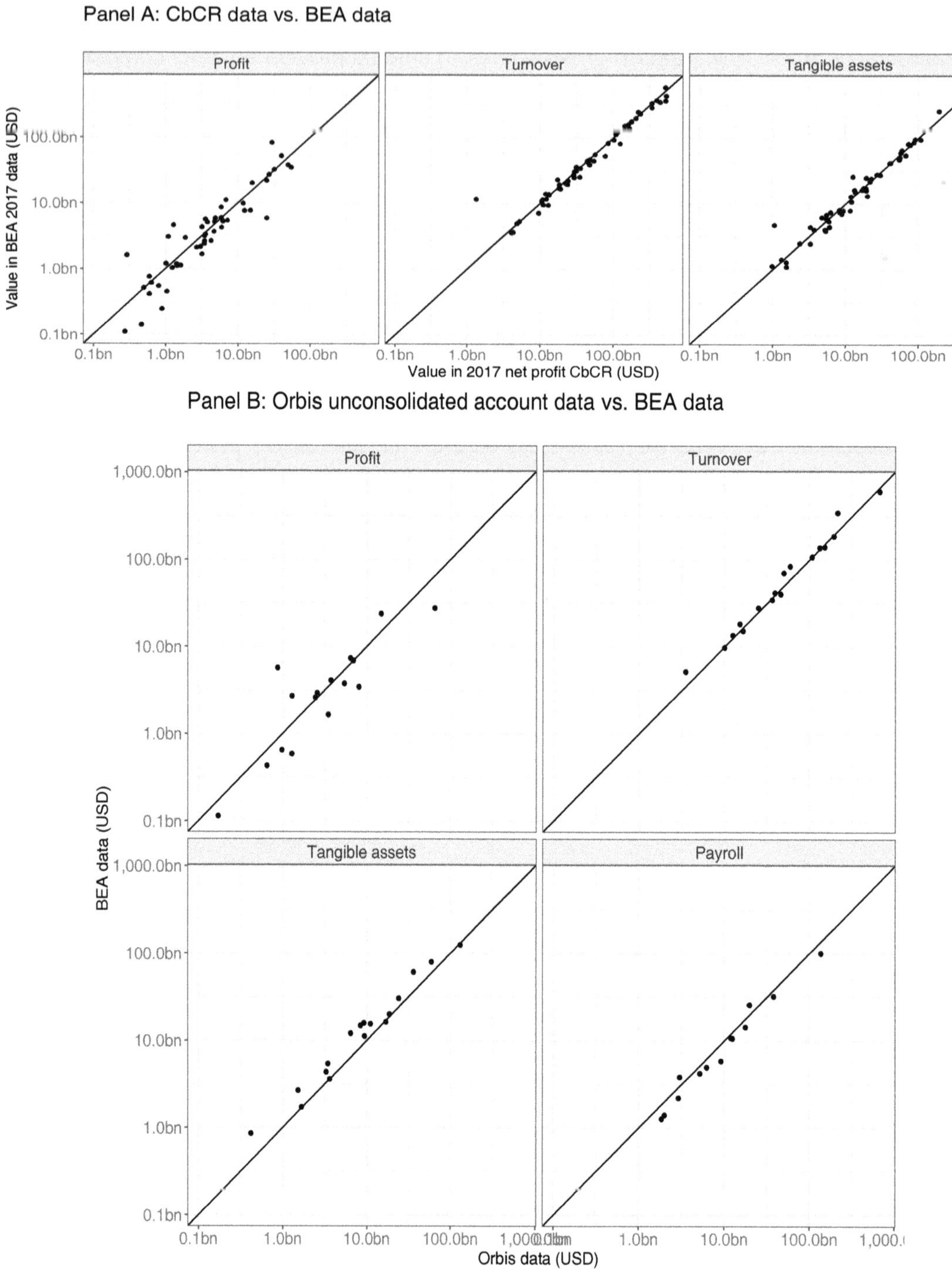


Note: These panels compare data from the US CbCR (Panel A) and ORBIS (Panel B) with data from the US BEA on the activity of multinationals. Data in Panel A relates to 2017 (the year for which US CbCR data are used in the analysis) and data in Panel B relates to 2016 (the year for which ORBIS data are used in the analysis). Each dot in the graphs corresponds to a jurisdiction where US MNEs have affiliates. A perfect correlation would imply that all dots are on the 45-degree line, which is overlayed on the graphs. The grey dots in the tangible assets panel for CbCR (Panel A), representing data for Luxembourg and Barbados, have been deemed outliers, suggesting reporting errors or exceptional events in the underlying CbCR data, and replaced manually by the corresponding values from the BEA data in the profit matrix. For greater comparability, the tangible assets variable considered in the BEA data includes inventories when comparing with CbCR data, and excludes inventories when comparing with ORBIS.
Source: OECD Secretariat.

### 5.8.3. Comparisons with financial data from MNE consolidated accounts

548. Column totals in the matrices have been benchmarked against information from consolidated financial accounts of MNE groups. For example, the total profit from US MNE groups – based on their consolidated financial accounts – should in theory correspond to the total in the US column of the profit matrix. However, there are several reasons why this comparison is imperfect: (i) the matrices focus on MNE sub-groups with positive profits (i.e. entities belonging to MNE sub-groups with positive profits in the jurisdiction considered), while data from consolidated financial accounts of MNEs consider all MNE entities regardless of their profit position in specific jurisdictions; as a result, overall profit is expected to be higher in the profit matrix than in consolidated financial accounts (where profit is net of the losses of loss-making entities); (ii) the turnover matrix focuses both on sales to third-party and related-party entities, while sales to related-party entities are not included in consolidated financial accounts.

549. Consolidated financial accounts from ORBIS have relatively good coverage of MNEs worldwide (contrary to unconsolidated accounts, where coverage is uneven across jurisdictions). To ensure even better coverage, the ORBIS dataset has been complemented by the OECD Secretariat with: (i) data from the Worldscope database, which contains the financial accounts of (mainly listed) firms worldwide; (ii) data from the EU Industrial R&D Investment Scoreboard, which covers the 2,500 companies with the highest level of R&D spending worldwide (Hernández et al., 2017[24]); and (iii) data from the Fortune Global 500 list (i.e. 500 firms with the highest turnover globally) (see Annex 2.A of Chapter 2 for more details).

550. Overall, there is a correlation between the column totals in the matrices and financial data from consolidated accounts, but it is imperfect for the reasons listed above (Annex Figure 5.E.2). While the differences between the two are generally moderate, they seem implausibly large in some jurisdictions of ultimate parent, even accounting for potential gaps in the coverage of consolidated account data. This may relate to fragilities in the extrapolation of diagonal cells in the profit and turnover matrices, which as discussed above entails a greater degree of uncertainty than data and extrapolations in other cells due to scarcer data availability. To address this issue, estimates in the profit and turnover matrix diagonal have been adjusted – when they relied on extrapolations, and when the difference between the column total in the profit matrix and the corresponding total from consolidated financial account data was deemed implausible – to bring back this difference to a more plausible level.[27] While inevitably imperfect due to data limitations, this adjustment aims to reduce the risk of implausible values in the matrices.[28]

### 5.8.4. Interactions with jurisdiction representatives

551. Bilateral interactions with jurisdiction representatives have helped refine the data in the matrices in two main ways. First, the data in the matrices has been benchmarked against tax and financial account data on the profit and activity of domestic-owned and foreign-owned MNEs provided to the OECD Secretariat on a confidential basis through a questionnaire filled by Delegates to Working Party No. 2 of the OECD's Committee on Fiscal Affairs in 2019. This has contributed to the identification of potential inconsistencies with data in the matrices.

552. Second, the values in some specific cells of the matrices have been the subject of bilateral discussions with jurisdiction representatives, either to identify the most relevant data source in the case of conflicting signals across sources (as discussed above), to eliminate from the data the effect of large one-off events (e.g. effect of large mergers and acquisitions on the amount and location of profit across jurisdictions) or to address limitations in the existing data sources (e.g. issues related to intra-company dividends in CbCR data). In this context, some representatives have been able to provide the OECD Secretariat with their estimates for specific matrix cells (e.g. diagonal cells in the profit matrix relative to their jurisdiction) based on detailed analysis of their national data. These estimates have been integrated in the relevant matrices, reflecting that, notwithstanding potential consistency issues with other data sources in the matrices, these estimates were deemed to be more accurate than the estimates based on the sources presented in this chapter.

### 5.8.5. Robustness check: Changing the order of preference between data sources

553. As the data sources underlying the matrices have a certain degree of overlap, the matrices are built with a preference order between sources, which is presented in Table 5.2. An interesting robustness check is to modify the ordering of sources and to compare the result with the original matrices. The result of this robustness check is presented in Annex 5.F, at a relatively aggregate level (i.e. the level of aggregation of the matrices presented in Table 5.5) for the experiment of inverting the order of preference between the first two data sources in each matrix. For example, in the profit matrix, the baseline order of preference is (i) CbCR data, (ii) ORBIS data, (iii) extrapolations. The experiment in Annex 5.F is to apply the following order instead (i) ORBIS data, (ii) CbCR data, (iii) extrapolations.

554. Overall, the results of this robustness check are reassuring, in the sense that most values (at the aggregate level presented in Annex 5.F) are modified by less than 10% with the alternative source ordering compared to the baseline.

## 5.9. Conclusion

555. This chapter describes the methodology and data sources underlying a set of matrices mapping the profit and activity of MNEs worldwide. These matrices have been central instruments in supporting the assessment of Pillar One and Pillar Two presented in this report. The matrices combine a range of existing data sources into a consistent framework, enabling a more accurate and comprehensive reform impact assessment than any individual source taken in isolation. While the matrices inevitably rely to some extent on extrapolations, sophisticated methods have been used to make the extrapolated values as accurate as possible. Another benefit of the methodology is to make these extrapolations explicit, which makes it possible to assess their quality.

556. Given the limitations of the underlying data sources, the methodology cannot go as far as offering a precise and certain estimate of each individual data point in each matrix. Rather, the aim of the methodology has been to ensure that the data points in the matrices have the right order of magnitude and offer a good level of consistency within and across matrices. For the purpose of the impact assessment in this report, overall consistency is even more important than the precise accuracy of individual points, as the assessment is generally based on combining data within and across matrices. To ensure the maximum level of consistency, extensive data checks and benchmarking have been undertaken, including via interactions with jurisdiction representatives.

557. Looking ahead, the matrices presented in this chapter could be used in the future for a range of other purposes. For example, they could be used for the analysis of MNE profit shifting behaviour, where they have potential to provide a more comprehensive and detailed picture of profit shifting than the earlier studies predating the publication of CbCR data (e.g. Johansson et al. (2017[18]) Tørsløv et al. (2018[1]) Beer et al. (2019[23])) or recent studies using the publicly available CbCR data of US MNEs (e.g. Clausing (2020[15])).[29] Preliminary estimates on profit shifting based on the matrices presented in this chapter and undertaken in the analysis of the potential MNE behavioural reactions to Pillar Two (presented in Chapter 3) suggest an overall intensity of profit shifting that is broadly consistent with these earlier studies, but offer a more detailed mapping of profit shifting flows. Another potential use of the matrices would be the analysis of potential fundamental corporate tax reforms. Beyond tax-related analysis, the matrices could also be used, in combination with data from the OECD Analytical AMNE database, to assess the links between global value chains and MNE profitability, for example to inform future analyses on the restructuring of those global value chains in a post-COVID-19 environment.

558. Another avenue for future work would be to update and refine these matrices as more data become available and to reflect the ongoing changes in the economic situation, including most prominently the COVID-19 crisis. The current matrices focus primarily on year 2016, which was the latest available year in

both CbCR and ORBIS data when the matrices were constructed. In particular, CbCR data are expected to gradually cover a wider set of ultimate parent jurisdictions in coming years, reflecting that 2016 was the first year where it was collected and that some jurisdictions were not yet in a position to compile and provide CbCR data for that year to the OECD for publication. The quality of CbCR data is also expected to improve in the future, since some issues related to its collection, which have been mentioned in this chapter, have been identified and are being addressed. As the quality and coverage of CbCR data improves, it may be possible to build more precise matrices in the future.

## References

Bailin, A. et al. (2019), "Like it or not? The impact of online platforms on the productivity of service providers", *OECD Economics Department Working Papers*, No. 1548, OECD Publishing, Paris, http://dx.doi.org/10.1787/080a17ce-en. [19]

Bajgar, M. et al. (2020), "Coverage and representativeness of Orbis data", *OECD Science, Technology and Industry Working Papers*, No. 2020/06, OECD Publishing, Paris, https://dx.doi.org/10.1787/c7bdaa03-en. [26]

Bajgar, M. et al. (2019), "Industry Concentration in Europe and North America", *OECD Productivity Working Papers*, No. 19, OECD, https://www.oecd-ilibrary.org/economics/industry-concentration-in-europe-and-north-america_2ff98246-en. [16]

Beer, S., R. de Mooij and L. Liu (2019), "International Corporate Tax Avoidance: A Review of the Channels, Magnitudes, and Blind Spots", *Journal of Economic Surveys*, pp. 1-29, http://dx.doi.org/10.1111/joes.12305. [23]

Blouin, J. and L. Robinson (2019), "Double Counting Accounting: How Much Profit of Multinational Enterprises Is Really in Tax Havens?", *SSRN Electronic Journal*, http://dx.doi.org/10.2139/ssrn.3491451. [14]

Bolwijn, R., B. Casella and D. Rigo (2018), *An FDI-driven approach to measuring the scale and economic impact of BEPS*, United Nations Conference on Trade and Development. [11]

Borga, M. and C. Caliandro (2018), "Eliminating the Pass-Through: Towards FDI Statistics that Better Capture the Financial and Economic Linkages between Countries", *NBER Working Paper*, No. 25029, http://dx.doi.org/10.3386/w25029. [12]

Cadestin, C. et al. (2018), "Multinational enterprises and global value chains: the OECD Analytical AMNE database", *OECD Trade Policy Papers*, No. 211, OECD Publishing, Paris, https://dx.doi.org/10.1787/d9de288d-en. [2]

Casella, B. (2019), "Looking through conduit FDI in search of ultimate investors-a probabilistic approach", No. 26(1), United Nations Conference on Trade and Development, https://unctad.org/en/PublicationChapters/diaeia2019d1a5_en.pdf. [5]

Clausing, K. (2020), "Profit Shifting Before and After the Tax Cuts and Jobs Act", *SSRN Electronic Journal*, http://dx.doi.org/10.2139/ssrn.3274827. [15]

Coppola, A. et al. (2020), "Redrawing the Map of Global Capital Flows: The Role of Cross-Border Financing and Tax Havens", *NBER Working Paper*, No. 26855, https://www.nber.org/papers/w26855. [27]

Damgaard, J. and T. Elkjaer (2017), “The Global FDI Network: Searching for Ultimate Investors”, *IMF Working Papers*, No. 17/258, https://www.imf.org/en/Publications/WP/Issues/2017/11/17/The-Global-FDI-Network-Searching-for-Ultimate-Investors-45414. [4]

Damgaard, J., T. Elkjaer and N. Johannesen (2019), “What Is Real and What Is Not in the Global FDI Network?”, *IMF Working Papers*, Vol. 19/274, http://dx.doi.org/10.5089/9781513521527.001. [10]

Eurostat (2008), “NACE Rev. 2 - Statistical classification of economic activities in the European Community”, *Eurostat Methodologies and Working papers*, Eurostat, Luxembourg, https://ec.europa.eu/eurostat/documents/3859598/5902521/KS-RA-07-015-EN.PDF. [9]

Gal, P. (2013), “Measuring Total Factor Productivity at the Firm Level using OECD-ORBIS”, *OECD Economics Department Working Papers*, No. 1049, OECD Publishing, Paris, https://dx.doi.org/10.1787/5k46dsb25ls6-en. [17]

Hanappi, T. and A. González Cabral (2020), “The impact of the pillar one and pillar two proposals on MNE’s investment costs : An analysis using forward-looking effective tax rates”, *OECD Taxation Working Papers*, No. 50, OECD Publishing, Paris, https://dx.doi.org/10.1787/b0876dcf-en. [6]

Head, K. and T. Mayer (2014), “Gravity Equations: Workhorse,Toolkit, and Cookbook”, *Handbook of International Economics*, Vol. 4, pp. 131-195, http://dx.doi.org/10.1016/B978-0-444-54314-1.00003-3. [21]

Hernández, H. et al. (2017), *The 2017 EU Industrial R&D Investment Scoreboard*, European Commission, https://ec.europa.eu/jrc/en/publication/eur-scientific-and-technical-research-reports/2017-eu-industrial-rd-investment-scoreboard. [24]

Johansson, Å. et al. (2017), “Tax planning by multinational firms: Firm-level evidence from a cross-country database”, *OECD Economics Department Working Papers*, No. 1355, OECD Publishing, Paris, https://dx.doi.org/10.1787/9ea89b4d-en. [18]

Mayer, T. and S. Zignago (2011), “Notes on CEPII’s Distances Measures: The GeoDist Database”, *CEPII Working Papers*, No. 2011-25, CEPII, http://dx.doi.org/10.2139/ssrn.1994531. [22]

OECD (2020), “Corporate Tax Statistics - Second Edition”, OECD Publishing, https://www.oecd.org/tax/tax-policy/corporate-tax-statistics-second-edition.pdf. [3]

OECD (2018), *Multinational enterprises in the global economy: Heavily debated but hardly measured*, OECD Publishing, Paris, http://www.oecd.org/industry/ind/MNEs-in-the-global-economy-policy-note.pdf. [8]

OECD (2015), *Implementing the latest international standards for compiling foreign direct investment statistics - FDI Statistics by the Ultimate Investing Country*, https://www.oecd.org/daf/inv/FDI-statistics-by-ultimate-investing-country.pdf. [13]

OECD (2015), *Measuring and Monitoring BEPS, Action 11 - 2015 Final Report*, OECD/G20 Base Erosion and Profit Shifting Project, OECD Publishing, Paris, https://dx.doi.org/10.1787/9789264241343-en. [7]

Santos Silva, J. and S. Tenreyro (2006), "The log of gravity", *Review of Economics and Statistics*, Vol. 88/4, pp. 641-658, http://dx.doi.org/10.1162/rest.88.4.641. [20]

Tørsløv, T., L. Wier and G. Zucman (2018), "The Missing Profits of Nations", *NBER Working Paper*, No. 24701, http://www.nber.org/papers/w24701.pdf. [1]

UNCTAD (2018), *World Investment Report 2018: Investment and New Industrial Policies*, https://unctad.org/en/PublicationsLibrary/wir2018_en.pdf. [25]

# Annex 5.A. List of jurisdictions covered by the main data sources

## Annex Table 5.A.1. List of jurisdictions of ultimate parent for which anonymised and aggregated CbCR data are used in the matrices

| | | |
|---|---|---|
| Australia | India | Norway |
| Austria | Indonesia | Poland |
| Belgium | Ireland | Singapore |
| Bermuda | Italy | Slovenia |
| Canada | Japan | South Africa |
| Chile | Korea | Sweden |
| Denmark | Luxembourg | United States (2017) |
| Finland | Mexico | |
| France | Netherlands | |

Note: Out of the 26 jurisdictions of ultimate parent included in the OECD publication of 2016 aggregated and anonymised CbCR data in July 2020, data from one ultimate parent jurisdiction (China) were not used in the analysis in this chapter. This is because Chinese CbCR data for 2016 are based only on a subsample of 82 CbCRs, while it is estimated that many more CbCRs were filed in China for the fiscal year 2016. CbCR data for Brazil have recently been added to the online CbCR database of the OECD, but was not available at the time when this analysis was undertaken. For all jurisdictions in this Table except the United States, CbCR data for 2016 are used, as 2017 data are not available yet. For the United States, CbCR data for 2017 are used, as they are more complete than 2016 data (in 2016, CbCR were filed on a voluntary basis in the United States).
Source: OECD Secretariat.

## Annex Table 5.A.2. List of jurisdictions of affiliate for which ORBIS unconsolidated account data are used

| Good coverage for both domestic-owned and foreign-owned MNE entities | | Good coverage only for foreign-owned MNE entities |
|---|---|---|
| Australia | Latvia | Bulgaria |
| Belgium | Lithuania | China |
| Croatia | Norway | |
| Czech Republic | Poland | |
| Denmark | Portugal | |
| Estonia | Russia | |
| Finland | Slovak Republic | |
| France | Slovenia | |
| Greece | Spain | |
| Italy | Sweden | |
| Korea | United Kingdom | |

Note: For each jurisdiction of affiliate, the quality of ORBIS coverage has been assessed based on a comparison with CbCR data and aggregate numbers from the Analytical AMNE database. Jurisdictions considered as having good coverage in ORBIS are those having at least 750 observations, where coverage of MNE turnover (assessed against Analytical AMNE data) is above 70%, and for which a comparison against available CbCR data (across all jurisdictions of ultimate parent where CbCR data are available to the OECD Secretariat) does not suggest major discrepancies. The coverage of the cost of employees variable is relatively poor in China, Greece, Latvia, Lithuania and Russia, and ORBIS data has not been used for this specific variable in these countries. In Korea, the definition of cost of employees in ORBIS may not be fully consistent with other jurisdictions, so ORBIS data have not been used for this specific variable.
Source: OECD Secretariat.

# Annex 5.B. ORBIS data cleaning

559. The ORBIS database, provided by Bureau van Dijk (BvD), is the largest cross-country database on ownership and financial accounts of firms worldwide. It relies on information from various underlying sources, and contains data for both publicly listed and privately owned companies.

560. Given that ORBIS data is not primarily collected for statistical analysis, important processing and cleaning work is required to enhance data reliability (e.g. eliminating duplicates and reporting errors). This concerns ownership data and financial data. The main data cleaning steps in each area build on OECD expertise with ORBIS and follow as much as possible procedures used in previous OECD studies, while adapting them when necessary to the needs of the current exercise. These main cleaning steps are detailed in the sections below.

## Cleaning of ORBIS ownership data

561. The ORBIS historical ownership database contains extensive information on ownership links between firms, which can be used to identify entities belonging to the same corporate group. Following Bajgar et al. (2019[16]), entities in ORBIS are assigned to corporate groups based on their Global Ultimate Owner (GUO), using a 50% ownership threshold, and considering GUOs of corporate nature (i.e. Industrial companies, Banks, Financial companies, Insurance companies, or Financial companies) to avoid for example assigning to the same group two independent firms owned by the same individual or government entity.

562. In turn, MNE groups are defined as corporate groups having entities in at least two jurisdictions. For each MNE group, only the consolidated accounts of the GUO are kept in the sample, to avoid potential double counting.

563. The procedure to clean and extend ownership links in ORBIS has been implemented by the OECD Directorate for Science, Technology and Innovation, following Bajgar et al. (2019[16]) and updating it for year 2016. The procedure focuses on all entities with a turnover of at least EUR 10 million, and focuses on ownership links above a 50% threshold. Missing links are identified, or (in a smaller number of cases) existing links are corrected, using the following steps:

- Using the BvD Zephyr database on Merger and Acquisition (M&A) to identify changes in immediate (rather than global ultimate) owners not available from ORBIS.
- Using ORBIS historic ownership linkages to identify changes in immediate owners not available from ORBIS.
- Translating the changes in immediate owners (from the first two steps above) to changes in ultimate ownership.
- Imputing missing ownership information by using data on M&A or changes in ownership in earlier or later years.
- Correcting ultimate owners that are in fact majority owned by another firm, since by definition they cannot be an ultimate owner.
- Removing temporary (one or two year) changes in ultimate owner that reverse themselves – as such cases seem highly unlikely to occur in reality and probably reflect gaps in in ownership data.
- Detecting missing linkages for large firms that change from having no subsidiaries to having a large number of subsidiaries one year to the next.

- Identifying missing links for large firms that never have any subsidiaries, and for large groups of subsidiaries that never have a parent with financials.
- Using name-matching algorithms to identify potential links, in combination with detailed manual inspection (e.g. against firms' annual reports) to check if these potential links are correct or not.
- Manually checking the 300 largest firms, using the subsidiary structure in their financial statements to cross-check the ownership data.

564. Overall, this procedure identified the GUO of about 50,000 entities for which it was not reported in the raw ORBIS data, and corrected the GUO of about 4,000 entities. Overall, these entities (added and corrected GUO) represent about 4% of global MNE turnover (as measured with the ORBIS dataset of consolidated MNE group accounts).

## Cleaning of ORBIS unconsolidated financial account data

565. The sample of unconsolidated account data is restricted to entities belonging to MNE groups, i.e. corporate groups that have entities in at least two jurisdictions, as identified with the ownership data cleaned with the procedure above.

566. The procedure for cleaning unconsolidated account data comprises the following steps, inspired by the cleaning steps in Gal (2013[17]), Johansson et al. (2017[18]) and Bailin et al. (2019[19]) that are relevant for this exercise:

- Selecting full-year accounts with closing date around December 2016 (from July 2016 to June 2017);
- Filtering duplicate firm-year observations, favouring those with non-missing key financial variables and with closing date equal to or closest to 31st of December;
- Eliminating implausible values: negative tangible assets, turnover, or cost of employees, implausibly high profit or turnover, tangible assets values above fixed assets or total assets values;
- Eliminating jumps in the turnover variable, i.e. situations where this variable is multiplied or divided by more than 5 in one year over 2014-2016;
- Eliminating implausible values: tax expenses higher than pre-tax profit, pre-tax profit minus tax expenditure inconsistent with post-tax profit;
- Eliminating outliers based on the following ratios of interest: EBIT to turnover, Profit before tax to turnover, Tangible assets to turnover and Cost of employees to turnover (keeping observations between the 2.5th and 97.5th percentiles of the distribution).

# Annex 5.C. Detailed methodology for the extrapolations based on FDI in the profit matrix

567. As described in the main text, the profit matrix is filled primarily with CbCR and ORBIS data. For matrix cells not covered by these sources, the approach is to rely on extrapolations based on macroeconomic variables (e.g. FDI positions). This annex describes in detail the sophisticated extrapolation procedure employed for non-diagonal cells of the profit matrix, i.e. for profit of MNEs outside of their jurisdiction of ultimate parent. This extrapolation consists of four steps, which are further described in the following sections:

- **Step 1**: building a full matrix of FDI positions by immediate investor, by (i) combining the available data in bilateral FDI statistics and (ii) extrapolating FDI positions to fill the data gaps in bilateral FDI statistics, based on a standard gravity model;
- **Step 2**: building a full matrix of FDI positions by ultimate investor jurisdiction. Existing OECD data on FDI by ultimate investor are used in the subset of jurisdictions where they are available. In other jurisdictions, estimates of FDI by ultimate investor are derived from the full matrix of FDI positions by immediate investor obtained in step 1, applying a methodology developed by Casella (2019[5]);
- **Step 3**: adjusting the matrix obtained in step 2 to eliminate double counting resulting from 'pass-through FDI' (also called 'conduit' FDI);
- **Step 4**: applying an estimated rate of return on FDI in each matrix cell, taking into account how the average rate of return to FDI deviates from the global average across both investing and receiving jurisdictions.

## Step 1: Building a full matrix of FDI positions by *immediate* investor jurisdiction

568. The bilateral FDI matrix by immediate investor jurisdiction is first filled with the existing bilateral FDI statistics from the OECD and the IMF, with the following order of preference: (i) OECD inward FDI statistics, (ii) OECD outward FDI statistics, (iii) IMF CDIS inward FDI, (iv) IMF CDIS outward FDI.

569. Even after combining these sources, there remain data gaps in the FDI matrix. These missing values are extrapolated using a standard gravity model. The gravity equation is estimated using a Poisson pseudo-maximum-likelihood estimation (Santos Silva and Tenreyro, 2006[20]) of the level of bilateral FDI on distance and both jurisdictions' GDP and GDP per capita, as well as the statutory CIT rate of the recipient jurisdiction. In the regression, all the independent variables have been transformed in logs. The results are reported in Annex Table 5.C.1. The results from the third column are the ones used for the extrapolation.

### Annex Table 5.C.1. Estimated gravity equation used to extrapolate bilateral FDI positions

| | Dependent variable: Bilateral FDI position (in levels) | | |
|---|---|---|---|
| GDP of investor (log) | 0.380*** | 0.551*** | 0.551*** |
| | (4.03) | (40.86) | (41.25) |
| GDP of recipient (log) | 0.370*** | 0.506*** | 0.525*** |
| | (6.71) | (34.06) | (29.37) |
| Distance (log) | -1.121*** | -0.770*** | -0.766*** |
| | (-15.46) | (-33.03) | (-33.12) |
| GDP per capita of investor (log) | | 0.725*** | 0.725*** |
| | | (25.56) | (25.75) |
| GDP per capita of recipient (log) | | 0.164*** | 0.148*** |
| | | (7.74) | (6.47) |
| Statutory CIT rate of recipient | | | -0.963** |
| | | | (-2.50) |
| Constant | 10.68*** | -2.934*** | -2.685*** |
| | (9.03) | (-6.78) | (-6.30) |
| N | 20151 | 19742 | 19602 |

Note: T-statistics in parentheses. ***, **, *: denote significance at 1, 5, and 10% levels respectively.
Source: OECD Secretariat.

570. The amount of FDI derived from each of the sources in the FDI matrix by immediate investor is presented in Annex Table 5.C.2. For example, 61% of the FDI matrix was filled with OECD inward FDI data, while only 2% was filled with the gravity model. Annex Table 5.C.3 presents an aggregated version of the FDI matrix by immediate investor. The global level of FDI is found to be slightly above USD 35.3 trillion, which is comparable to the 2016 numbers from Damgaard et al. (2019[10]).[30]

## Annex Table 5.C.2. Sources of bilateral FDI data by immediate investor

| Source of immediate FDI data | Total FDI (USD billion) | Share |
|---|---|---|
| OECD inward | 21654 | 61% |
| OECD outward | 6659 | 19% |
| IMF inward | 5137 | 15% |
| IMF outward | 1240 | 4% |
| Extrapolation (gravity model) | 638 | 2% |
| **Total** | **35329** | **100%** |

Source: OECD Secretariat.

## Annex Table 5.C.3. FDI by *immediate* investor matrix, aggregated by broad jurisdiction groups

| | | Jurisdiction of investor | | | | |
|---|---|---|---|---|---|---|
| | (USD billion of 2016) | **High income** | **Middle income** | **Low income** | **Investment Hubs** | **Total** |
| **Jurisdiction of recipient** | High income (64 jurisd.) | 7218 | 512 | 4 | 5231 | **12965** |
| | Middle income (105) | 2320 | 381 | 5 | 3487 | **6193** |
| | Low income (29) | 32 | 18 | 1 | 20 | **72** |
| | Investment Hubs (24) | 7241 | 1109 | 6 | 7743 | **16099** |
| | **Total** | **16811** | **2021** | **16** | **16480** | **35329** |

Note: Groups of jurisdictions (high, middle and low income) are based on the World Bank classification. The number of jurisdictions in each group is indicated in parentheses. Investment hubs are defined as jurisdictions with a total inward FDI position above 150% of GDP.
Source: OECD Secretariat calculations, based on OECD and IMF FDI statistics, complemented with extrapolations based on a gravity model.

### Step 2: Building a full matrix of FDI positions by *ultimate* investor jurisdictions

571. For the purpose of filling the profit matrix, it is preferable to use FDI positions by *ultimate* rather than *immediate* investor, i.e. based on the jurisdiction of the ultimate parent of the MNE investing in a jurisdiction (Annex Figure 5.C.1). This is because the profit matrix is structured by jurisdiction of ultimate parent. For example, each column in the profit matrix corresponds to MNEs from a given jurisdiction of ultimate parent. Other sources used to fill the profit matrix (e.g. CbCR data, ORBIS) are consistent with this 'ultimate investor' approach.

Annex Figure 5.C.1. Stylised example on FDI by ultimate versus immediate investor

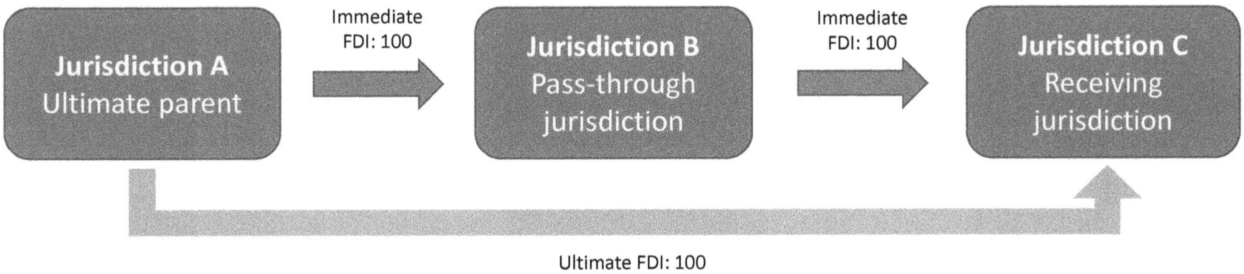


Note: In this stylised example, a MNE with an ultimate parent in jurisdiction A has invested 100 into jurisdiction C, passing through jurisdiction B. FDI statistics by immediate investor report a FDI position from jurisdiction A into jurisdiction B, and a similar position from jurisdiction B into jurisdiction C. FDI statistics by ultimate investor in jurisdiction C report that the ultimate investor is jurisdiction A.
Source: OECD Secretariat.

572. While FDI data are traditionally reported by "immediate investing country", the OECD recently started publishing inward FDI statistics by ultimate investor for a subset of 15 receiving jurisdictions,[31] whose combined inward FDI represents 23% of global FDI.

573. There are important differences between inward FDI data by immediate versus ultimate investor, which reflect that some FDI may pass through a jurisdiction before reaching its final destination.[32,33] For instance, in 2018, OECD FDI data indicate that the United States accounted for 3.2% of immediate investors in Iceland (USD 0.3 billion out of USD 9.5 billion) but 28.6% of the ultimate investors (USD 2.7 billion out of the same USD 9.5 billion), reflecting that most investment from the United States to Iceland were channelled through third-party jurisdictions.

574. To build a full matrix of FDI positions by ultimate investor jurisdiction, the approach in this chapter is to use the available OECD data for the jurisdictions where it is available, and to complement it with extrapolations using data on FDI positions by immediate investor, applying the methodology developed by Casella (2019[5]).

575. Casella (2019[5]) uses a probabilistic method in order to obtain the distribution of ultimate investors in a given jurisdiction based on data on immediate investors. The intuition is the following. The first step is to assess if an FDI position is "pass-through" or not (or, more precisely, the probability that it is "pass-through"). If a position is not "pass-through", the immediate investor is considered to be the ultimate investor. If it is "pass-through", the second step is to go up in the investing chain, based on FDI data by immediate investor, to try to find the ultimate investor. This procedure is repeated until the ultimate investor is found. Identifying the ultimate investor may require going up several steps in the investing chain if the investment has been channelled successively through several jurisdictions. In practice, this procedure is implemented by using absorbing Markov chains (see Casella (2019[5]) for more details).

576. For example, in Annex Figure 5.C.2, jurisdictions B1 and B2 are immediate investors into jurisdiction C. Jurisdiction B2 is identified as a pass-through jurisdiction (based on assumptions described below), while jurisdiction B1 is not. Therefore, jurisdiction B1 is considered to be the ultimate investor into jurisdiction C for the investment observed from B1 to C in the statistics by immediate investors. In the case of jurisdiction B2, one needs to go one step up in the investing chain to identify the ultimate investor(s), which are here A1 and A2. Ultimate investors into C are finally found to be B1 (investment of 50), A1 (30) and A2 (20). If A1 had itself been a pass-through jurisdiction, one would have needed to look at the jurisdictions investing into A1 to identify the ultimate parent.

## Annex Figure 5.C.2. Stylised example on the methodology to identify ultimate investors

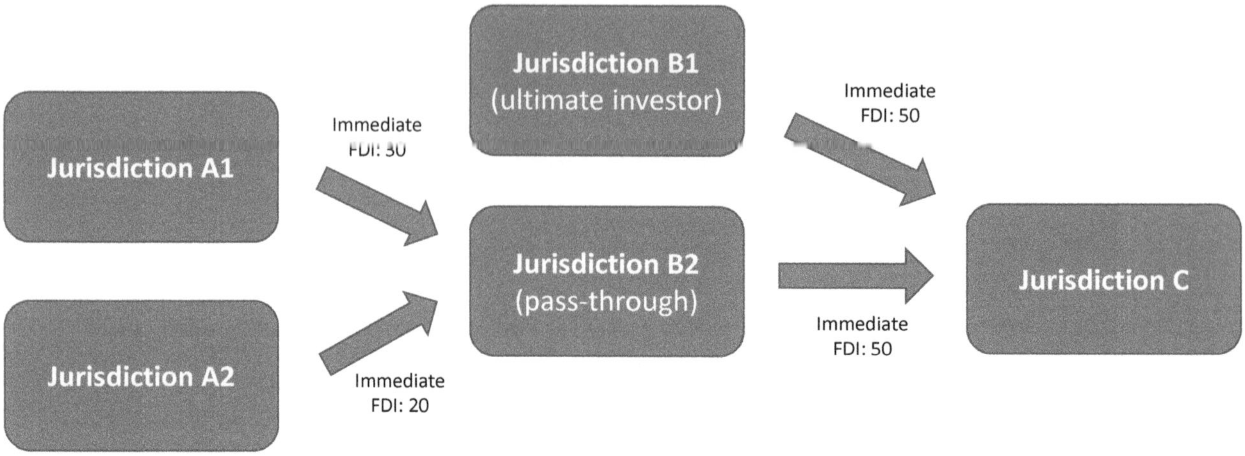


Note: In this stylised example, both jurisdictions B1 and B2 are immediate investors in jurisdiction C, and both jurisdictions A1 and A2 are immediate investors in jurisdiction B1. However, the immediate investment observed from B2 to C is identified as being a "pass-through" investment corresponding to the immediate investments made by A1 and A2 into B. The "ultimate investors" in C are thus B1, A1 and A2 and the respective levels of ultimate investments are 50, 30 and 20.
Source*:* OECD Secretariat.

577. In this simplified example, B1 is fully an ultimate investor jurisdiction and B2 is fully a pass-through jurisdiction. In practice however, many jurisdictions are simultaneously ultimate investors (for certain positions) and pass-through (for other positions). The methodology therefore relies on the *probability* that an FDI position from a jurisdiction is pass-through. For example, if the probability that positions from jurisdiction B are pass-through is 40%, 60% of positions from B are considered as having B as ultimate investor, and one looks one step up in the investing chain to identify the ultimate investor for the remaining 40%.

578. A key input to the procedure is therefore the probability that a FDI position is "pass-through". Several approaches have been proposed to assess this probability. In particular, Bolwijn et al. (2018[11]), Casella (2019[5]), Damgaard et al. (2019[10]) suggest using the share of Special Purpose Entities (SPEs) in a jurisdiction's outward FDI investment.[34] However, an issue with this approach is that only around 30 jurisdictions report FDI statistics for SPEs separately, and that extrapolating the share of SPEs beyond these jurisdictions entails important uncertainties.

579. As an alternative, the present analysis assesses the probability that investment from a given jurisdiction is pass-through based on the available data on inward FDI by ultimate versus immediate investor, across the subset of 15 recipient jurisdictions where it is available. The intuition is that if a jurisdiction is often an immediate investor without being an ultimate investor, an important share of its outward FDI is likely to be pass-through. Reflecting this, it is assumed that the share of investment from a jurisdiction that is *not* pass-through corresponds to the ratio between this jurisdiction's outward FDI as an *immediate* investor and its outward FDI as an *ultimate* investor.[35] To ensure that the numerator and denominator of the ratio are comparable, only FDI into the subset jurisdictions reporting FDI statistics by ultimate investor is included. Finally, if the ratio exceeds one, it is assumed that the jurisdiction is never pass-through.

580. For example, in Annex Figure 5.C.3 below, jurisdiction group C is assumed to be the set of jurisdictions reporting FDI data by ultimate investor. Outward FDI of jurisdiction B as an *immediate* investor into C is 110, out of which jurisdiction B is the ultimate investor for 10, and a pass-through jurisdiction for investment from A for 100. The probability that jurisdiction B is *not* "pass-through" is estimated to be 10/110 = 9%, and therefore the probability that it is pass-through is 91%. Hence, for 9% of observed FDI positions

from jurisdiction B, jurisdiction B will be deemed to be the ultimate investor. For the other 91%, the procedure will assume that jurisdiction B is not the ultimate investor, and go up one step in the investment chain to search for an ultimate investor, based on the data on immediate investors into jurisdiction B.

### Annex Figure 5.C.3. Stylised example on probability to be "pass-through"

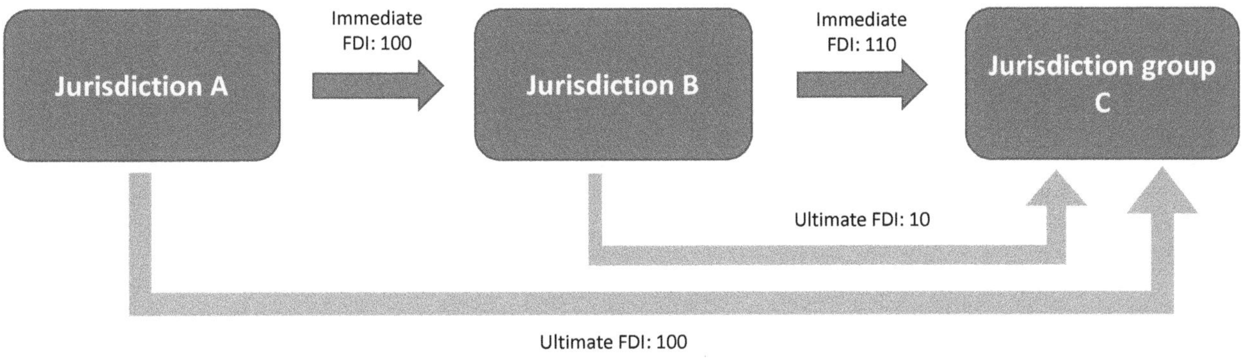


Note: In this stylised example, jurisdiction group C is the group of jurisdictions reporting FDI data by ultimate investor. Based on data from these jurisdictions, it appears that jurisdiction B is often an immediate investor without being an ultimate investor. This happens for 100/110=91% of jurisdiction B's immediate investments into C. As a result, it is assumed that jurisdiction B is a pass-through jurisdiction 91% of the time.
Source: OECD Secretariat.

581. The resulting FDI matrix by ultimate investor jurisdiction based on the methodology described above is presented for aggregate jurisdiction groups in Annex Table 5.C.4. The main difference compared to Annex Table 5.C.3 reflects the fact that investment hubs are more often intermediate than ultimate investors. The aggregate level of FDI is slightly lower than in Annex Table 5.C.3, which is mainly due to the elimination of 'self FDI', where a jurisdiction is the ultimate investor of foreign direct investment into itself (while the immediate investor is in another jurisdiction).[36] Annex Table 5.C.4 excludes this 'self-investment'. However, the difference in global FDI between Annex Table 5.C.4 and Annex Table 5.C.3 is relatively small given the scale of 'pass-through FDI'. This is because pass-through FDI has not been fully dealt with at this stage, which is why Step 3 is required.

### Annex Table 5.C.4. FDI by *ultimate* investor matrix, aggregated by broad jurisdiction groups

| | | **Jurisdiction of ultimate investor** | | | | |
|---|---|---|---|---|---|---|
| | (USD billion of 2016) | **High income** | **Middle income** | **Low income** | **Investment Hubs** | **Total** |
| **Jurisdiction of recipient** | High income (64 jurisd.) | 8281 | 655 | 1 | 3114 | **12051** |
| | Middle income (105) | 2841 | 462 | 3 | 2863 | **6169** |
| | Low income (29) | 40 | 18 | 1 | 13 | **72** |
| | Investment Hubs (24) | 9137 | 1335 | 2 | 5159 | **15632** |
| | **Total** | **20299** | **2470** | **7** | **11148** | **33924** |

Note: Groups of jurisdictions (high, middle and low income) are based on the World Bank classification. The number of jurisdictions in each group is indicated in parentheses. Investment hubs are defined as jurisdictions with a total inward FDI position above 150% of GDP.
Source: OECD Secretariat calculations, based on OECD FDI statistics and estimates based on the FDI matrix by immediate investor (Annex Table 5.C.3) and a methodology following Casella (2019[5]).

## Step 3: Eliminating double counting from "pass-through FDI"

582. Considering FDI data by jurisdiction of ultimate investor as done in Step 2 addresses some issues related to "pass-through FDI" (also called "conduit FDI") compared to FDI data by jurisdiction of immediate investor, but not all of them. This is illustrated by the example in Annex Figure 5.C.4. In this example, the ultimate investor into jurisdiction C is correctly identified to be jurisdiction A. However, when considering the ultimate investors into jurisdiction B, the FDI position of jurisdiction A into jurisdiction B is still considered as an ultimate investment, while it should be eliminated as it is "pass-through FDI" for which jurisdiction B is not the final destination.

### Annex Figure 5.C.4. Stylised example on "pass-through FDI"

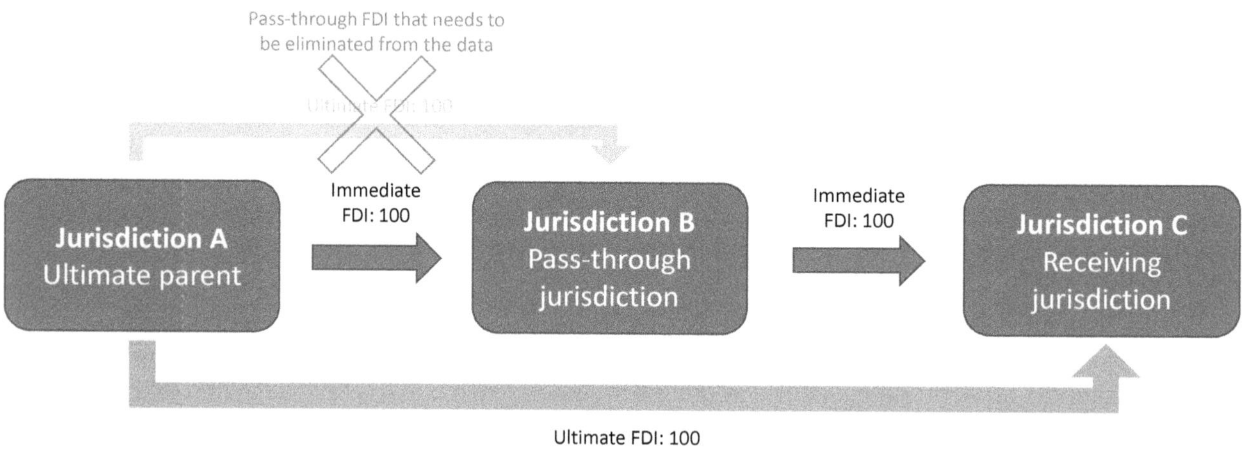


Note: This stylised example shows that FDI data by ultimate investor jurisdiction contain redundant FDI positions resulting from pass-through FDI that needs to be eliminated to avoid double counting. In this example, the ultimate investor into jurisdiction C is correctly identified to be jurisdiction A. However, when considering the ultimate investors into jurisdiction B, the FDI position of jurisdiction A into jurisdiction B is still considered as an ultimate investment, while it is only a "pass-through FDI" that should be eliminated from the data.
Source: OECD Secretariat.

583. The underlying reason for this issue is that FDI data by ultimate investor does not consider whether a given FDI position stops in jurisdiction B or is pass-through to another jurisdiction (in this case, jurisdiction C).

584. Another way to see this double counting issue is that the global total of FDI positions by jurisdiction of *immediate* investor is only slightly lower than the global total of FDI positions by jurisdiction of *ultimate* investor (see Annex Table 5.C.3 and Annex Table 5.C.4), while global FDI positions by jurisdiction of *ultimate* investor should be substantially lower if pass-through FDI were fully dealt with (see also Damgaard et al. (2019[10])).

585. To address the issue, the approach in this chapter is to adjust downwards the FDI positions into a jurisdiction in proportion to its probability to be pass-through. For example, if a jurisdiction is deemed to be pass-through for 91% of FDI positions into it (as was the case of jurisdiction B in the example of Annex Figure 5.C.3 above), FDI positions into jurisdiction B are reduced by 91%, reflecting that jurisdiction B is the ultimate *destination* of the FDI in only 9% of the cases.

586. The resulting FDI matrix is presented in Annex Table 5.C.5. As expected, total global FDI is reduced, from USD 35.3 trillion in the immediate investor matrix, to USD 24.2 trillion in Annex Table 5.C.5. This represents a 32% reduction, which can be interpreted as suggesting that 32% of global FDI is pass-through. This is broadly consistent with estimates by Damgaard and Elkjaer (2017[4]) and Damgaard et al.

(2019[10]), who both use data on FDI towards Special Purpose Entities to identify pass-through FDI. Damgaard and Elkjaer (2017[4]) assess that 34% of FDI is pass-through, and Damgaard et al. (2019[10]) assess that the share of "phantom" (i.e. pass-through) FDI was about 30% in 2009 and increased to almost 40% in 2017.

### Annex Table 5.C.5. FDI by *ultimate* investor matrix, after adjustment for "pass-through FDI", aggregated by broad jurisdiction groups

| | | Jurisdiction of ultimate investor | | | | |
|---|---|---|---|---|---|---|
| | (USD billion of 2016) | **High income** | **Middle income** | **Low income** | **Investment Hubs** | **Total** |
| **Jurisdiction of recipient** | High income (64 jurisd.) | 7788 | 591 | 1 | 2830 | **11211** |
| | Middle income (105) | 2560 | 368 | 2 | 2756 | **5685** |
| | Low income (29) | 11 | 7 | 0 | 2 | **21** |
| | Investment Hubs (24) | 4252 | 770 | 1 | 2229 | **7252** |
| | **Total** | **14611** | **1736** | **4** | **7817** | **24169** |

Note: Groups of jurisdictions (high, middle and low income) are based on the World Bank classification. The number of jurisdictions in each group is indicated in parentheses. Investment hubs are defined as jurisdictions with a total inward FDI position above 150% of GDP.
Source: OECD Secretariat.

587. An interesting way to assess the quality of the methodology to identify ultimate investors is to compare the predicted distribution of ultimate investors to their actual distribution in the jurisdictions where this distribution is observed in the data, i.e. in the 14 jurisdictions reporting FDI data by ultimate investor and a global aggregate inward FDI position.[37] The predicted values in these 14 jurisdictions are not used to build the matrix in Annex Table 5.C.5 given that actual data is available (and therefore used) in these jurisdictions, but comparing these predicted values to actual data is a way to test the performance of the methodology to identify ultimate investors.

588. This comparison is done by computing the "distance" between the predicted and the actual distribution of ultimate investors into a jurisdiction. This distance is measured, for each recipient jurisdiction, by the sum of the absolute deviations in the shares of each ultimate investor in the total FDI into this recipient jurisdiction considered (i.e. the so-called "L1 norm") as done by Casella (2019[5]). The results are presented in Annex Table 5.C.6 (column 2). These distances are positive, reflecting that the predicted distributions differ from the actual distributions, but they are substantially lower than the distances between the distribution of immediate investors and the distribution of ultimate investors (column 1). This suggests that the methodology clearly improves the identification of ultimate investors compared to a methodology that would simply assume that the distribution of ultimate investors is the same as the distribution of immediate investors. The median improvement across the 14 jurisdictions in Annex Table 5.C.6 is 34%.

Annex Table 5.C.6. Distance between predicted and actual distribution of ultimate investors

| Recipient jurisdiction | (1) Distance between distribution of immediate and ultimate investors | (2) Distance between actual and predicted distribution of ultimate investors | % difference between (1) and (2) |
|---|---|---|---|
| Canada | 0.46 | 0.45 | -3% |
| Czech Republic | 0.31 | 0.21 | -32% |
| Estonia | 0.16 | 0.16 | -2% |
| Finland | 0.25 | 0.23 | -8% |
| France | 0.25 | 0.14 | -46% |
| Germany | 0.32 | 0.21 | -35% |
| Hungary | 0.75 | 0.48 | -36% |
| Iceland | 0.99 | 0.55 | -45% |
| Italy | 0.31 | 0.24 | -23% |
| Lithuania | 0.22 | 0.19 | -12% |
| Poland | 0.28 | 0.18 | -38% |
| Switzerland | 0.46 | 0.24 | -48% |
| Turkey | 0.09 | 0.18 | 96% |
| United States | 0.21 | 0.12 | -41% |
| | Median difference | | -34% |

Note: This table presents, for the 14 recipient jurisdictions reporting FDI data by jurisdiction of ultimate investor and a global inward position in the OECD data, the "distance" between the distribution of ultimate FDI investors into the recipient jurisdiction considered with (i) the distribution of immediate FDI investors into the recipient jurisdiction considered (column 1), and (ii) the predicted distribution of ultimate FDI investors into the recipient jurisdiction considered, as computed with the methodology described in this annex (column 2). Distance is measured as the sum of the absolute deviations in the shares of each investor in the total FDI of the recipient jurisdiction considered (i.e. the so-called "L1 norm") similar to Casella (2019[5]). Recipient jurisdictions do not always report the jurisdiction of the ultimate investor for 100% of their inward FDI (e.g. due to confidentiality concerns) and the sum is computed only over the jurisdictions of ultimate investor covered on the data. As a result, the *level* of the distances are not necessarily comparable across jurisdictions, but the relative differences between columns 1 and 2 are comparable.
Source: OECD Secretariat.

## Step 4: Computing jurisdiction-specific rates of return to FDI

589. The final step to obtain a measure of profit that can be used to fill cells in the profit matrix is to apply a rate of return to the bilateral FDI positions obtained in Step 3. The rate of return on FDI can vary across both investing and receiving jurisdictions for a range of reasons, such as the sectoral composition of investment, the riskiness of investments and tax planning schemes (e.g. returns on FDI generated by profit shifting strategies can differ from returns on 'real' investments). For instance, average rates of return have been relatively low in low income jurisdictions over the last five years compared to other jurisdiction groups (UNCTAD, 2018[25]).

590. The approach in this chapter takes into account that average rates of return can differ from the global average both at the investor and receiving jurisdiction level. The method is first to compute a global average rate of return to FDI, and then to apply to this average (i) a (positive or negative) delta corresponding to the difference between the average rate of return on FDI of the *investing* jurisdiction and the global average (Delta 1), and (ii) a (positive or negative) delta corresponding to the difference between the average rate of return on FDI in the *receiving* jurisdiction and the global average (Delta 2) (Annex Figure 5.C.5).

Annex Figure 5.C.5. Assumption on the rate of return to FDI

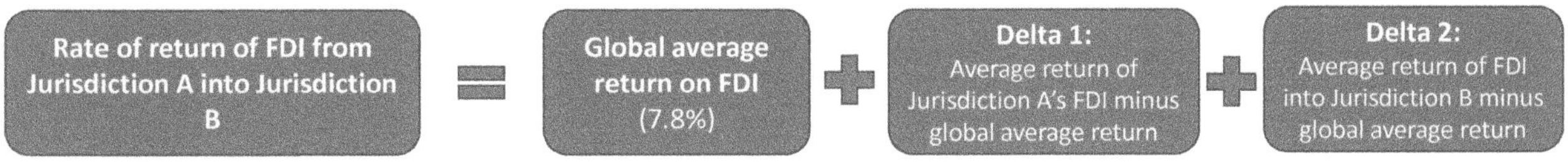


Source: OECD Secretariat.

591. For example, in the case of FDI from a jurisdiction A into a jurisdiction B, if global FDI from jurisdiction A has an average return that is 3 percentage points above the global average, but that global FDI into jurisdiction B has an average return that is 1 percentage point below the global average, the rate of return on FDI from jurisdiction A into jurisdiction B is assumed to be equal to the global average plus 3-1=2 percentage points. To avoid potential noise from extreme observations, both deltas are bounded at +/- 5 percentage points, and the sum of the two deltas as well.

592. For consistency with the other data sources used in the profit matrix (CbCR and ORBIS data), the global average rate of return on FDI is computed based on the cells of the profit matrix that are already filled with these sources. In each of these cells, profit (measured with CbCR or ORBIS) is divided by the bilateral FDI position obtained in Step 3. After excluding cells with outlying rates of return from the sample (based on the Cook's distance of each observation in the regression of profit on FDI), a "standard" rate of return is computed by taking the median ratio of bilateral profit to bilateral position across remaining matrix cells. This results in a standard rate of return of 7.8%.

593. Return differentials at the level of both investing and receiving jurisdictions (Delta 1 and Delta 2) are computed based on statistics on FDI positions and FDI income in the OECD FDI statistics.[38] For each investing and each receiving jurisdiction, a differential is computed for each year between 2013 and 2016 by comparing the rate of return of the jurisdiction to the global rate of return. The jurisdiction-specific differential is the median of the differential over the four years to reduce volatility, capped between -5 and +5 percentage points to avoid generating extreme values, as mentioned above.

# Annex 5.D. Matrices aggregated by broad income groups and regions

## Annex Table 5.D.1. Matrices aggregated by broad income groups and regions

**Panel A**: The profit matrix

| In USD billion | A. Americas - High income | B. Europe & Central Asia - High income | C. East Asia & Pacific - High income | D. Middle East & North Africa - High income | E. Latin America & Caribb. - Middle and low income | F. Europe & Central Asia - Middle and low income | G. East Asia & Pacific - Middle and low income | H. Middle East & North Africa - Middle and low income | I. South Asia - Middle and low income | J. Sub-Saharan - High and middle income | K. Sub-Saharan - Low income | L. Americas invest. hubs | M. Europe invest. hubs | N. Other invest. hubs | Total |
|---|---|---|---|---|---|---|---|---|---|---|---|---|---|---|---|
| A. Americas - High income | 1527 | 126 | 53 | 4 | 12 | 1 | 5 | 0 | 3 | 1 | 0 | 5 | 52 | 2 | **1791** |
| B. Europe & Central Asia - High income | 158 | 884 | 34 | 5 | 2 | 3 | 4 | 1 | 3 | 1 | 0 | 11 | 74 | 3 | **1184** |
| C. East Asia & Pacific - High income | 63 | 28 | 605 | 2 | 1 | 0 | 3 | 0 | 0 | 0 | 0 | 2 | 10 | 4 | **720** |
| D. Middle East & North Africa - High income | 14 | 7 | 2 | 56 | 0 | 1 | 1 | 1 | 1 | 0 | 0 | 0 | 5 | 1 | **89** |
| E. Latin America & Caribbean - Middle and low income | 49 | 33 | 4 | 0 | 110 | 1 | 1 | 0 | 0 | 0 | 0 | 3 | 18 | 1 | **221** |
| F. Europe & Central Asia - Middle and low income | 10 | 27 | 3 | 2 | 1 | 109 | 1 | 0 | 1 | 0 | 0 | 6 | 42 | 1 | **203** |
| G. East Asia & Pacific - Middle and low income | 52 | 37 | 89 | 1 | 0 | 2 | 472 | 0 | 2 | 1 | 0 | 49 | 11 | 21 | **736** |
| H. Middle East & North Africa - Middle and low income | 5 | 8 | 0 | 2 | 0 | 0 | 0 | 15 | 0 | 0 | 0 | 0 | 1 | 0 | **31** |
| I. South Asia - Middle and low income | 15 | 8 | 3 | 1 | 0 | 0 | 1 | 0 | 80 | 0 | 0 | 0 | 3 | 3 | **114** |
| J. Sub-Saharan - High and middle income | 8 | 10 | 1 | 0 | 0 | 0 | 1 | 0 | 0 | 24 | 0 | 2 | 4 | 1 | **52** |
| K. Sub-Saharan - Low income | 0 | 0 | 0 | 0 | 0 | 0 | 0 | 0 | 0 | 1 | 2 | 0 | 0 | 0 | **4** |
| L. Americas Investment hubs | 115 | 11 | 2 | 0 | 5 | 1 | 0 | 0 | 1 | 0 | 0 | 31 | 19 | 10 | **196** |
| M. European Investment hubs | 265 | 115 | 14 | 4 | 3 | 6 | 2 | 0 | 1 | 1 | 0 | 4 | 136 | 7 | **558** |
| N. Other Investment hubs | 78 | 28 | 18 | 2 | 5 | 3 | 39 | 0 | 2 | 1 | 0 | 34 | 16 | 56 | **281** |
| Total | **2358** | **1322** | **829** | **78** | **140** | **128** | **529** | **17** | **94** | **30** | **2** | **150** | **391** | **112** | **6181** |

**Panel B:** The turnover matrix

| In USD billion | A. Americas - High income | B. Europe & Central Asia - High income | C. East Asia & Pacific - High income | D. Middle East & North Africa - High income | E. Latin America & Caribb. - Middle and low income | F. Europe & Central Asia - Middle and low income | G. East Asia & Pacific - Middle and low income | H. Middle East & North Africa - Middle and low income | I. South Asia - Middle and low income | J. Sub-Saharan - High and middle income | K. Sub-Saharan - Low income | L. Americas invest. hubs | M. Europe invest. hubs | N. Other invest. hubs | Total |
|---|---|---|---|---|---|---|---|---|---|---|---|---|---|---|---|
| A. Americas - High income | 13909 | 1364 | 1153 | 45 | 121 | 14 | 50 | 13 | 56 | 17 | 3 | 82 | 826 | 36 | **17686** |
| B. Europe & Central Asia - High income | 1589 | 9162 | 530 | 115 | 54 | 93 | 159 | 42 | 63 | 39 | 7 | 111 | 1236 | 56 | **13254** |
| C. East Asia & Pacific - High income | 521 | 340 | 7534 | 37 | 16 | 16 | 91 | 12 | 15 | 17 | 2 | 78 | 97 | 42 | **8818** |
| D. Middle East & North Africa - High income | 77 | 68 | 22 | 564 | 8 | 14 | 8 | 14 | 17 | 5 | 1 | 2 | 30 | 7 | **840** |
| E. Latin America & Caribbean - Middle and low income | 489 | 363 | 125 | 20 | 1576 | 13 | 31 | 7 | 6 | 8 | 1 | 32 | 126 | 8 | **2804** |
| F. Europe & Central Asia - Middle and low income | 114 | 315 | 73 | 32 | 38 | 1316 | 19 | 10 | 6 | 8 | 1 | 68 | 342 | 24 | **2367** |
| G. East Asia & Pacific - Middle and low income | 544 | 411 | 1253 | 24 | 15 | 76 | 7058 | 9 | 18 | 8 | 2 | 808 | 119 | 248 | **10594** |
| H. Middle East & North Africa - Middle and low income | 32 | 85 | 24 | 32 | 8 | 15 | 9 | 171 | 2 | 4 | 1 | 2 | 30 | 6 | **420** |
| I. South Asia - Middle and low income | 96 | 78 | 52 | 16 | 6 | 7 | 15 | 4 | 653 | 3 | 1 | 6 | 26 | 9 | **970** |
| J. Sub-Saharan - High and middle income | 61 | 123 | 31 | 14 | 9 | 7 | 12 | 4 | 4 | 155 | 1 | 6 | 32 | 5 | **464** |
| K. Sub-Saharan - Low income | 5 | 18 | 6 | 6 | 3 | 3 | 2 | 2 | 2 | 5 | 32 | 1 | 6 | 2 | **92** |
| L. Americas Investment hubs | 184 | 6 | 6 | 1 | 2 | 1 | 1 | 0 | 1 | 0 | 0 | 36 | 4 | 1 | **243** |
| M. European Investment hubs | 1100 | 747 | 114 | 24 | 19 | 15 | 17 | 11 | 9 | 9 | 2 | 37 | 1041 | 15 | **3160** |
| N. Other Investment hubs | 694 | 210 | 303 | 9 | 7 | 4 | 59 | 2 | 16 | 5 | 0 | 24 | 110 | 220 | **1663** |
| Total | **19415** | **13289** | **11226** | **940** | **1881** | **1593** | **7531** | **302** | **867** | **280** | **55** | **1293** | **4024** | **679** | **63375** |

**Panel C:** The tangible assets matrix

| In USD billion | A. Americas - High income | B. Europe & Central Asia - High income | C. East Asia & Pacific - High income | D. Middle East & North Africa - High income | E. Latin America & Caribb. - Middle and low income | F. Europe & Central Asia - Middle and low income | G. East Asia & Pacific - Middle and low income | H. Middle East & North Africa - Middle and low income | I. South Asia - Middle and low income | J. Sub-Saharan - High and middle income | K. Sub-Saharan - Low income | L. Americas invest. hubs | M. Europe invest. hubs | N. Other invest. hubs | Total |
|---|---|---|---|---|---|---|---|---|---|---|---|---|---|---|---|
| A. Americas - High income | 4567 | 360 | 290 | 19 | 46 | 7 | 20 | 5 | 19 | 17 | 1 | 39 | 185 | 19 | **5594** |
| B. Europe & Central Asia - High income | 348 | 2674 | 97 | 29 | 15 | 23 | 30 | 11 | 16 | 9 | 2 | 35 | 249 | 22 | **3559** |
| C. East Asia & Pacific - High income | 162 | 80 | 2443 | 13 | 6 | 7 | 29 | 4 | 8 | 7 | 1 | 17 | 17 | 17 | **2810** |
| D. Middle East & North Africa - High income | 32 | 26 | 10 | 312 | 4 | 7 | 4 | 7 | 13 | 2 | 1 | 1 | 10 | 3 | **433** |
| E. Latin America & Caribbean - Middle and low income | 143 | 130 | 39 | 10 | 703 | 7 | 12 | 3 | 2 | 3 | 1 | 238 | 42 | 4 | **1335** |
| F. Europe & Central Asia - Middle and low income | 39 | 93 | 17 | 12 | 13 | 695 | 7 | 4 | 4 | 2 | 0 | 23 | 97 | 6 | **1013** |
| G. East Asia & Pacific - Middle and low income | 123 | 90 | 255 | 8 | 5 | 42 | 1900 | 3 | 4 | 2 | 0 | 197 | 23 | 65 | **2717** |
| H. Middle East & North Africa - Middle and low income | 16 | 50 | 11 | 19 | 5 | 9 | 5 | 108 | 1 | 2 | 1 | 1 | 15 | 4 | **245** |
| I. South Asia - Middle and low income | 25 | 51 | 41 | 12 | 4 | 5 | 12 | 3 | 672 | 2 | 0 | 1 | 17 | 5 | **851** |
| J. Sub-Saharan - High and middle income | 45 | 73 | 17 | 10 | 6 | 5 | 7 | 3 | 2 | 110 | 1 | 1 | 16 | 4 | **300** |
| K. Sub-Saharan - Low income | 2 | 6 | 2 | 3 | 1 | 1 | 1 | 1 | 1 | 2 | 10 | 0 | 2 | 1 | **34** |
| L. Americas Investment hubs | 28 | 2 | 2 | 1 | 1 | 0 | 0 | 0 | 1 | 0 | 0 | 18 | 1 | 2 | **57** |
| M. European Investment hubs | 99 | 148 | 34 | 7 | 12 | 4 | 4 | 3 | 2 | 4 | 1 | 10 | 221 | 4 | **554** |
| N. Other Investment hubs | 50 | 35 | 29 | 3 | 2 | 2 | 16 | 1 | 15 | 2 | 0 | 26 | 12 | 126 | **319** |
| Total | **5679** | **3819** | **3286** | **457** | **823** | **814** | **2049** | **156** | **760** | **165** | **18** | **608** | **908** | **282** | **19823** |

**Panel D:** The payroll matrix

| In USD billion | A. Americas - High income | B. Europe & Central Asia - High income | C. East Asia & Pacific - High income | D. Middle East & North Africa - High income | E. Latin America & Caribb. - Middle and low income | F. Europe & Central Asia - Middle and low income | G. East Asia & Pacific - Middle and low income | H. Middle East & North Africa - Middle and low income | I. South Asia - Middle and low income | J. Sub-Saharan - High and middle income | K. Sub-Saharan - Low income | L. Americas invest. hubs | M. Europe invest. hubs | N. Other invest. hubs | Total |
|---|---|---|---|---|---|---|---|---|---|---|---|---|---|---|---|
| A. Americas - High income | 3704 | 219 | 109 | 5 | 16 | 2 | 8 | 2 | 11 | 2 | 0 | 7 | 136 | 4 | **4226** |
| B. Europe & Central Asia - High income | 279 | 1653 | 58 | 11 | 9 | 20 | 15 | 9 | 18 | 9 | 1 | 22 | 257 | 11 | **2373** |
| C. East Asia & Pacific - High income | 60 | 46 | 710 | 4 | 2 | 2 | 12 | 1 | 1 | 4 | 0 | 7 | 15 | 5 | **870** |
| D. Middle East & North Africa - High income | 14 | 12 | 3 | 81 | 1 | 2 | 1 | 2 | 2 | 1 | 0 | 0 | 6 | 1 | **127** |
| E. Latin America & Caribbean - Middle and low income | 55 | 54 | 11 | 2 | 198 | 2 | 5 | 1 | 1 | 1 | 0 | 3 | 21 | 1 | **354** |
| F. Europe & Central Asia - Middle and low income | 12 | 45 | 7 | 4 | 5 | 136 | 3 | 1 | 1 | 1 | 0 | 4 | 44 | 3 | **265** |
| G. East Asia & Pacific - Middle and low income | 48 | 55 | 100 | 2 | 2 | 7 | 938 | 1 | 2 | 1 | 0 | 51 | 17 | 22 | **1246** |
| H. Middle East & North Africa - Middle and low income | 4 | 13 | 3 | 4 | 1 | 2 | 1 | 23 | 0 | 0 | 0 | 0 | 5 | 1 | **58** |
| I. South Asia - Middle and low income | 22 | 17 | 10 | 3 | 1 | 1 | 3 | 1 | 137 | 0 | 0 | 1 | 6 | 2 | **203** |
| J. Sub-Saharan - High and middle income | 7 | 18 | 3 | 2 | 1 | 1 | 2 | 0 | 0 | 20 | 0 | 0 | 5 | 1 | **61** |
| K. Sub-Saharan - Low income | 1 | 2 | 1 | 1 | 0 | 0 | 0 | 0 | 0 | 1 | 5 | 0 | 1 | 0 | **13** |
| L. Americas Investment hubs | 4 | 1 | 1 | 0 | 0 | 0 | 0 | 0 | 0 | 0 | 0 | 2 | 0 | 0 | **8** |
| M. European Investment hubs | 52 | 83 | 9 | 2 | 2 | 2 | 2 | 1 | 1 | 1 | 0 | 2 | 137 | 1 | **296** |
| N. Other Investment hubs | 33 | 22 | 19 | 1 | 1 | 0 | 7 | 0 | 1 | 0 | 0 | 1 | 12 | 13 | **111** |
| Total | **4294** | **2240** | **1041** | **122** | **239** | **178** | **997** | **43** | **175** | **42** | **8** | **102** | **664** | **64** | **10211** |

Note: The composition of the jurisdiction groups is presented in Annex Table 5.D.2.
Source: OECD Secretariat

## Annex Table 5.D.2. Jurisdiction groups in the aggregated matrices

**Panel A**: Jurisdiction groups A to G

| A. Americas - High income | B. Europe & Central Asia - High income | C. East Asia & Pacific - High income | D. Middle East & North Africa - High income | E. Latin Am. & Caribbean - Middle and low income | F. Europe & Central Asia - Middle and low income | G. East Asia & Pacific - Middle and low income |
|---|---|---|---|---|---|---|
| Antigua and Barbuda | Andorra | Australia | Bahrain | Argentina | Albania | American Samoa |
| Aruba | Austria | Brunei Darussalam | Israel | Belize | Armenia | Cambodia |
| Bonaire | Belgium | Cook Islands | Kuwait | Bolivia | Azerbaijan | China (People's Republic of) |
| Canada | Croatia | French Polynesia | Oman | Brazil | Belarus | DPRK |
| Chile | Czech Republic | Guam | Qatar | Colombia | Bosnia and Herzegovina | Fiji |
| Curaçao | Denmark | Japan | Saudi Arabia | Costa Rica | Bulgaria | Indonesia |
| Montserrat | Estonia | Korea | United Arab Emirates | Cuba | Georgia | Kiribati |
| Panama | Faroe Islands | Macau (China) | | Dominica | Kazakhstan | Lao PDR |
| Puerto Rico | Finland | New Caledonia | | Dominican Republic | Kosovo | Malaysia |
| Saint Kitts and Nevis | France | New Zealand | | Ecuador | Kyrgyzstan | Micronesia |
| Sint Maarten | Germany | Northern Mariana Islands | | El Salvador | Moldova | Mongolia |
| Trinidad and Tobago | Greece | Palau | | Grenada | Montenegro | Myanmar |
| United States | Greenland | Chinese Taipei | | Guatemala | North Macedonia | Nauru |
| United States Virgin Islands | Iceland | | | Guyana | Romania | Papua New Guinea |
| Uruguay | Italy | | | Haiti | Russia | Philippines |
| | Latvia | | | Honduras | Serbia | Samoa |
| | Liechtenstein | | | Jamaica | Tajikistan | Solomon Islands |
| | Lithuania | | | Mexico | Turkey | Thailand |
| | Monaco | | | Nicaragua | Turkmenistan | Timor-Leste |
| | Norway | | | Paraguay | Ukraine | Tonga |
| | Poland | | | Peru | Uzbekistan | Tuvalu |
| | Portugal | | | Saint Lucia | | Vanuatu |
| | San Marino | | | Saint Vincent and the Grenadines | | Viet Nam |
| | Slovak Republic | | | Suriname | | |
| | Slovenia | | | Venezuela | | |
| | Spain | | | | | |
| | Sweden | | | | | |
| | United Kingdom | | | | | |

**Panel B:** Jurisdiction groups H to N

| H. Middle East & North Africa - Middle and low income | I. South Asia - Middle and low income | J. Sub-Saharan - High and middle income | K. Sub-Saharan - Low income | L. Americas investment hubs | M. European investment hubs | N. Other investment hubs |
|---|---|---|---|---|---|---|
| Algeria | Afghanistan | Angola | Benin | Anguilla | Bailiwick of Guernsey | Hong Kong (China) |
| Djibouti | Bangladesh | Botswana | Burkina Faso | Bahamas | Cyprus | Liberia |
| Egypt | Bhutan | Cabo Verde | Burundi | Barbados | Gibraltar | Malta |
| Iran | India | Cameroon | Central African Republic | Bermuda | Hungary | Marshall Islands |
| Iraq | Maldives | Comoros | Chad | British Virgin Islands | Ireland | Mauritius |
| Jordan | Nepal | Congo | DRC | Cayman Islands | Isle of Man | Mozambique |
| Lebanon | Pakistan | Côte d'Ivoire | Eritrea | Turks and Caicos Islands | Jersey | Singapore |
| Libya | Sri Lanka | Equatorial Guinea | Ethiopia | | Luxembourg | |
| Morocco | | Eswatini | Gambia | | Netherlands | |
| Palestinian Authority | | Gabon | Guinea | | Switzerland | |
| Syria | | Ghana | Guinea-Bissau | | | |
| Tunisia | | Kenya | Madagascar | | | |
| Yemen | | Lesotho | Malawi | | | |
| | | Mauritania | Mali | | | |
| | | Namibia | Niger | | | |
| | | Nigeria | Rwanda | | | |
| | | Sao Tome and Principe | Sierra Leone | | | |
| | | Senegal | Somalia | | | |
| | | Seychelles | South Sudan | | | |
| | | South Africa | Tanzania | | | |
| | | Sudan | Togo | | | |
| | | Zambia | Uganda | | | |
| | | Zimbabwe | | | | |

Note: The groups are based on World Bank classifications of jurisdictions by income levels and geographic regions. Certain categories are grouped to ensure a sufficient number of jurisdictions in each group in order to preserve confidentiality of the jurisdiction-specific data. Investment hubs are defined as jurisdictions with a total inward FDI position above 150% of GDP.
Source: OECD Secretariat

# Annex 5.E. Additional figures on benchmarking across data sources

Annex Figure 5.E.1. Comparison between CbCR data and ORBIS unconsolidated account data, by jurisdiction of ultimate parent

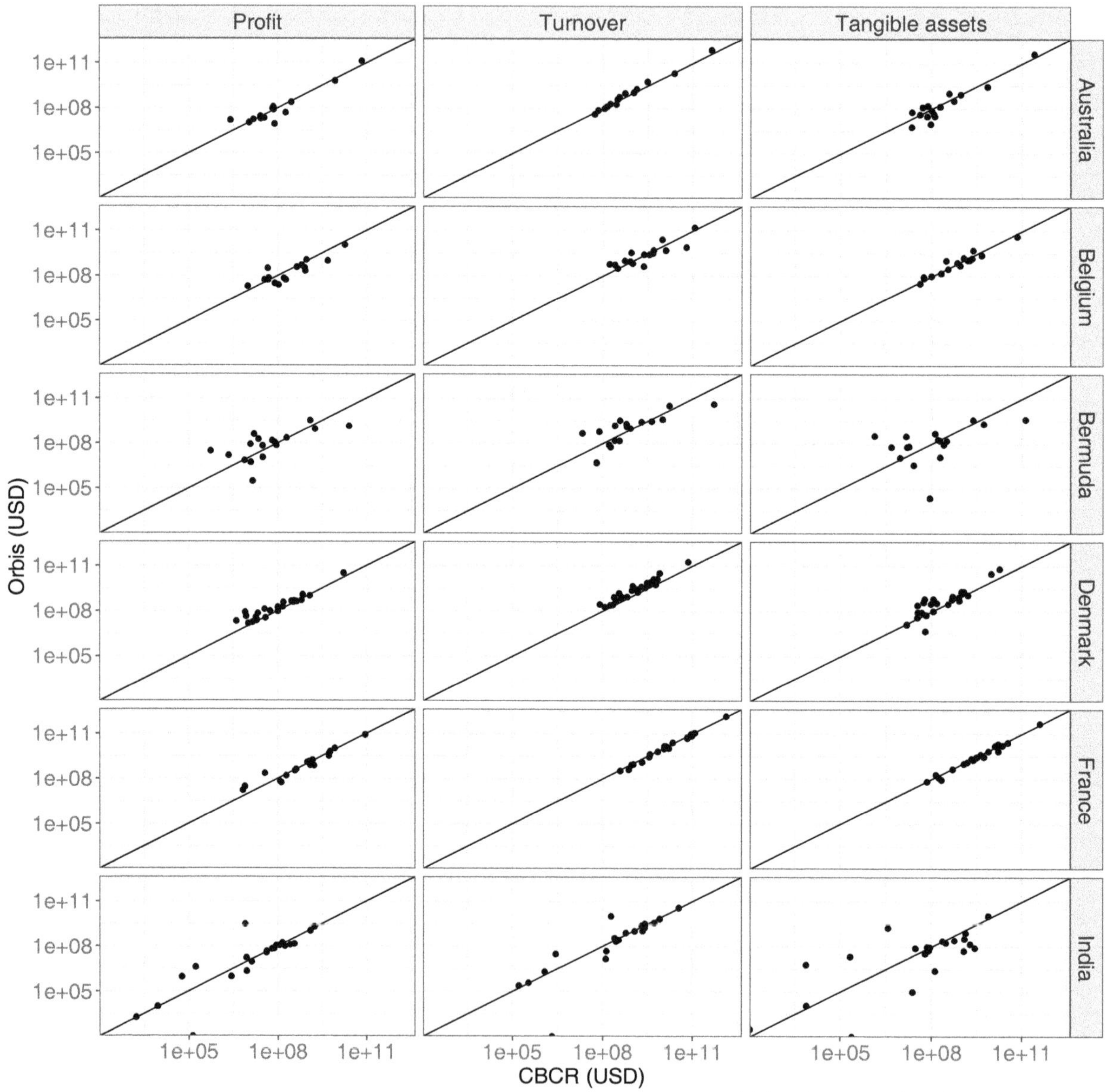


Jurisdictions with more than 10 bilateral entries in their CbCR

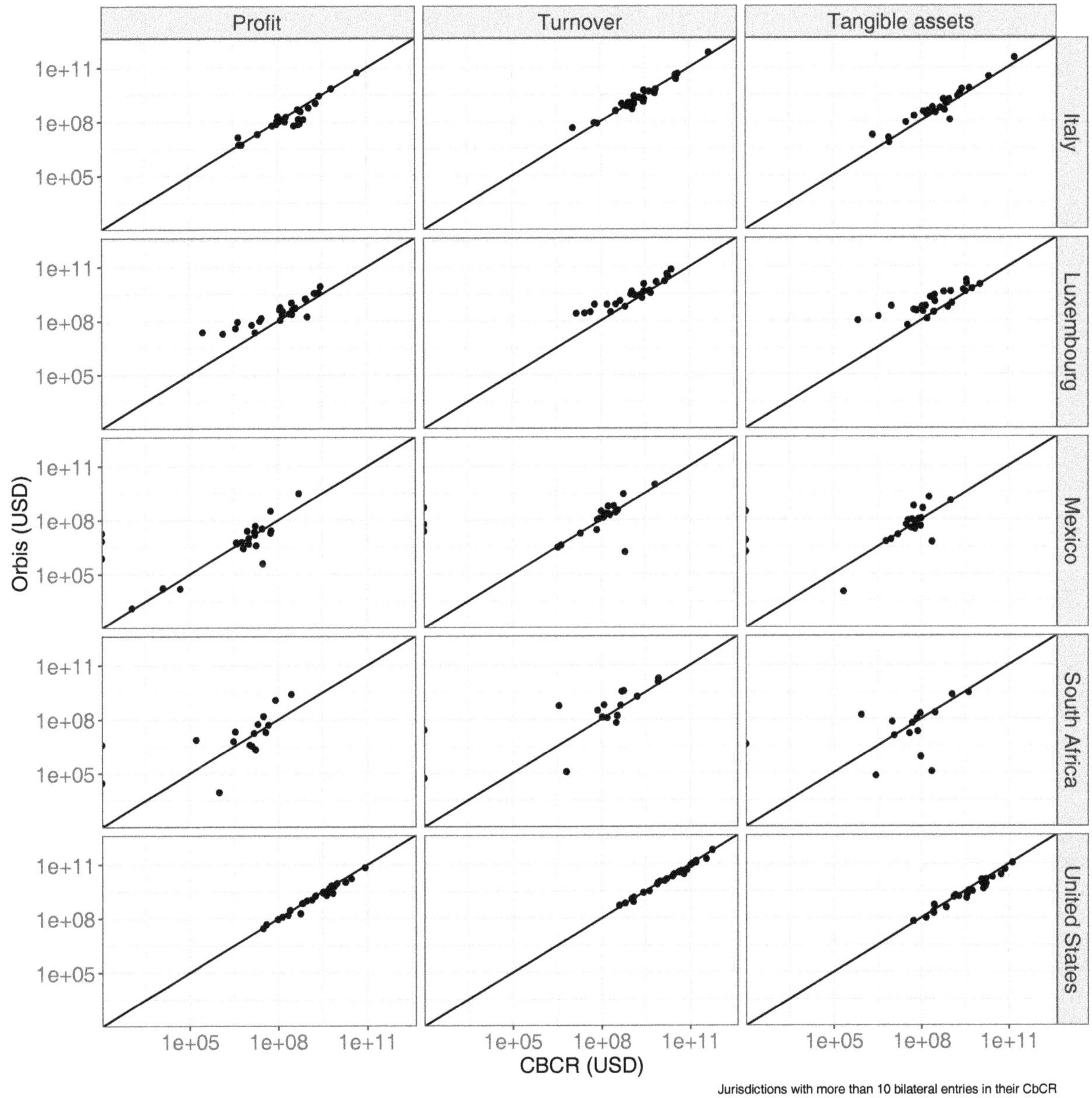


Note: These figures compare data on profit, turnover, and tangible assets, of MNEs with an ultimate parent in a given jurisdiction across a range of affiliate jurisdictions, from two sources: CbCR data and data from ORBIS (unconsolidated financial accounts). For comparability, both data sources focus on 'sub-groups with positive profits' in 2016, except for the US data which is from the 2017 CbCR. Each dot corresponds to one jurisdiction of affiliate. The comparison is restricted to jurisdictions of affiliate with sufficiently good coverage of unconsolidated accounts in ORBIS (see list in Annex 5.A), and to ultimate parent jurisdictions that reported more than ten bilateral entries in their CbCR data (i.e. a subset of the list in Annex 5.A). The line corresponds to the 45-degree line.
Source: OECD Secretariat calculations based on ORBIS and CbCR data.

## Annex Figure 5.E.2. Comparison between the column totals in the matrices and consolidated financial account data

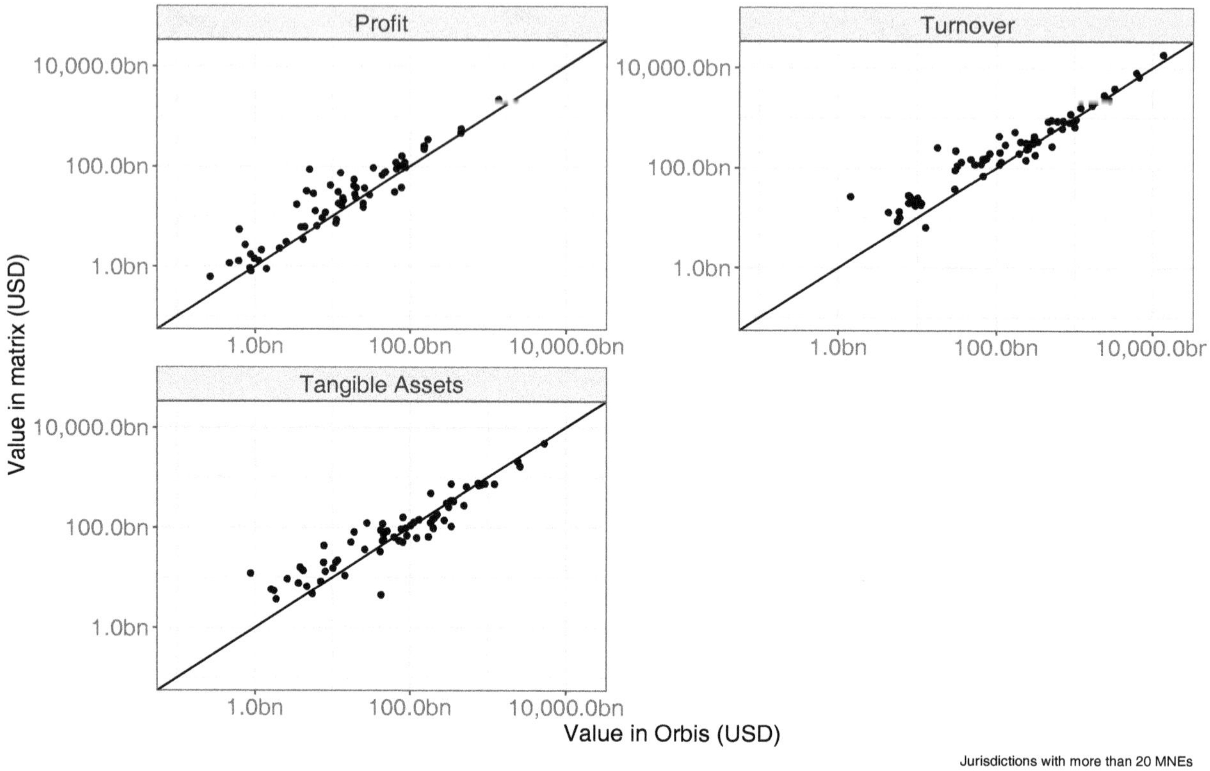


Note: These figures compare data on total profit, turnover, and tangible assets of MNEs by jurisdiction of ultimate parent (each dot corresponds to a jurisdiction of ultimate parent), from two sources: totals by column (i.e. by jurisdiction of ultimate parent) in the profit, turnover, and tangible assets matrices, and consolidated financial account data from ORBIS combined with other sources such as Worldscope (total of consolidated financial accounts by jurisdiction of ultimate parent). Only jurisdictions with at least 20 observations of MNE consolidated accounts in ORBIS are included. In the case of turnover, data in the matrix includes intra-group transactions, while they are netted out in consolidated ORBIS data, explaining why turnover tends to be relatively higher in the data from the matrix. Likewise, in the case of profits, data in the matrix focus on 'sub-groups with positive profits', while profits are net in consolidated ORBIS data, explaining why profit tends to be relatively higher in the data from the matrix. The coverage of payroll in consolidated account data from ORBIS was judged insufficient to include payroll in the comparison.
Source: OECD Secretariat.

# Annex 5.F. Robustness of the matrices to a different data source ordering rule

### Annex Table 5.F.1. Alternative order of data sources to fill the matrices: Differences with the baseline matrices

Differences with the amounts in the baseline matrices when the order of preference of the first and second preferred data sources are inverted

**Panel A**: Profit matrix

| | | Jurisdiction of ultimate parent | | | | |
|---|---|---|---|---|---|---|
| | | High income | Middle income | Low income | Investment Hubs | Total |
| Jurisdiction of affiliate | High income (64 jurisd.) | +2% | +23% | +6% | +11% | **+3%** |
| | Middle income (105) | -12% | -3% | +5% | -15% | **-7%** |
| | Low income (29) | +3% | +2% | +9% | +4% | **+6%** |
| | Investment Hubs (24) | +1% | +3% | +6% | +2% | **+1%** |
| | **Total** | **+1%** | **-1%** | **+9%** | **+0%** | **+1%** |

**Panel B:** Turnover matrix

| | | Jurisdiction of ultimate parent | | | | |
|---|---|---|---|---|---|---|
| | | High income | Middle income | Low income | Investment Hubs | Total |
| Jurisdiction of affiliate | High income (64 jurisd.) | +2% | +4% | +1% | +6% | **+2%** |
| | Middle income (105) | -6% | -0% | +0% | -26% | **-4%** |
| | Low income (29) | -0% | -0% | -21% | -0% | **-7%** |
| | Investment Hubs (24) | +0% | +0% | +1% | +0% | **+0%** |
| | **Total** | **+1%** | **+0%** | **-11%** | **-5%** | **+0%** |

**Panel C:** Tangible assets matrix

| | | Jurisdiction of ultimate parent | | | | |
|---|---|---|---|---|---|---|
| | | High income | Middle income | Low income | Investment Hubs | Total |
| Jurisdiction of affiliate | High income (64 jurisd.) | +3% | +1% | -0% | +9% | **+3%** |
| | Middle income (105) | -5% | -0% | -1% | -19% | **-3%** |
| | Low income (29) | -0% | +0% | +0% | +1% | **-0%** |
| | Investment Hubs (24) | -0% | +0% | +6% | -0% | **+0%** |
| | **Total** | **+2%** | **+0%** | **-0%** | **-5%** | **+1%** |

| Panel D: Payroll matrix | | | | | | | |
|---|---|---|---|---|---|---|---|
| | | Jurisdiction of ultimate parent | | | | | |
| | | High income | Middle income | Low income | Investment Hubs | Total |
| Jurisdiction of affiliate | High income (64 jurisd.) | -1% | -6% | 0% | -8% | **-2%** |
| | Middle income (105) | -0% | 0% | 0% | 0% | **-0%** |
| | Low income (29) | 0% | 0% | 0% | 0% | **0%** |
| | Investment Hubs (24) | 0% | 0% | 0% | 0% | **0%** |
| | **Total** | **-1%** | **-1%** | **0%** | **-5%** | **-1%** |

Note: For example, when the first and second data sources (i.e. CbCR and ORBIS) are switched in the preference order rule to fill the profit matrix, the amount of profit in the 'high income'-'high income' cell is increased by 2% compared to the amount in the baseline matrix presented in Table 5.5. Groups of jurisdictions (high, middle and low income) are based on the World Bank classification. The number of jurisdictions in each group is indicated in parentheses. Investment hubs are defined as jurisdictions with a total inward FDI position above 150% of GDP.
Source: OECD Secretariat.

## Notes

[1] In the rest of this chapter, anonymised and aggregated Country-by-Country Report (CbCR) data are simply referred to as CbCR data.

[2] In this report, groups of jurisdictions (high, middle and low income) are based on the World Bank classification of jurisdictions by income group. Investment hubs are defined as jurisdictions with a total inward FDI position above 150% of GDP.

[3] For a detailed discussion of these issues, see OECD (2020[3]) and https://www.oecd.org/tax/tax-policy/anonymised-and-aggregated-cbcr-statistics-disclaimer.pdf.

[4] For example, a potential source of inconsistency across sources is that CbCR data focuses only on MNE groups with global revenues above EUR 750 million, which is not the case for the other data sources in this report. As more than 90% of the worldwide profit and turnover of MNE groups is generated by groups that are above this revenue threshold, this difference is assumed not to be overly consequential, which is confirmed by the benchmarking undertaken in this report.

[5] More specifically, the turnover matrix was used as a proxy measure to identify where revenues from the 'undertaxed payments rule' would accrue. The potential recipients of revenues from the 'income inclusion rule', which would accrue to the jurisdiction of ultimate parent of the MNE, have been identified directly based on the information in the profit matrix.

[6] A potential formulaic substance-based carve-out would imply that the amount of low-taxed profit subject to the minimum tax would be reduced in relation to the level of economic activity of the MNE in the jurisdiction where this profit is located. The amount of economic activity could be measured based on criteria including tangible assets depreciation and payroll (see Chapter 3).

[7] See discussion in Box 3 of OECD (2020[3]) and also https://www.oecd.org/tax/tax-policy/anonymised-and-aggregated-cbcr-statistics-disclaimer.pdf.

[8] For a detailed discussion on ORBIS coverage and representativeness, see Bajgar et al. (2020[26]).

[9] See more details on FDI data and methodology, see http://www.oecd.org/corporate/mne/statistics.htm.

[10] In a relatively small number of cells, data are missing in the panel on 'sub-groups with positive profits', but not missing in the panel focusing on all sub-groups. For these cells, data from the latter panel were used instead of the former, except in the few cases where the reported amount of profit in the panel focusing on all sub-groups was negative. In these cases, CbCR data have been considered missing for the purpose of building the matrices.

[11] Out of the 26 jurisdictions of ultimate parent included in the OECD publication of 2016 CbCR data, data from one ultimate parent jurisdiction (China) has not been used in the analysis in this chapter. This is because Chinese CbCR data for 2016 are based only on a subsample of 82 CbCRs, while it is estimated that a significantly larger number of CbCRs were filed in China for the fiscal year 2016.

[12] In 2016, 1 101 US MNE groups reported CbCR, against 1 575 in 2017. The total turnover of these groups was respectively USD 16.3 trillion and USD 21.6 trillion.

[13] See discussion in Box 3 of OECD (2020[3]) and also https://www.oecd.org/tax/tax-policy/anonymised-and-aggregated-cbcr-statistics-disclaimer.pdf.

[14] This calculation was based on Table II.B 1-2 from the BEA data on the activity of MNEs, which provides data on the balance sheet of foreign affiliates of US MNEs and in particular separates inventories from property, plant and equipment. Inventories are found to represent on average 24% of the total of inventories, property, plant and equipment of US MNEs in 2016 and in 2017. As a result, the CbCR data in the tangible assets matrix has been scaled down by 24%, except for US MNEs where the adjustment was based on the exact share of inventories of US MNEs in each market jurisdiction, when available in the BEA data.

[15] The quality of ORBIS coverage has been assessed based on benchmarking of key variables against CbCR data and aggregate numbers from the Analytical AMNE database. For 22 jurisdictions, ORBIS is used both for domestic-owned and foreign-owned MNE entities. For two jurisdictions, it is used only for foreign-owned entities. See detailed lists in Annex 5.A.

[16] This selection has been done in the following way. For each MNE group, the total profit of the group in a given jurisdiction has been computed by summing the profit of all entities belonging to the group in that jurisdiction, based on ORBIS data. All entities from MNE groups in a loss position in a given jurisdiction have been eliminated from the final ORBIS dataset used as a data source for the four matrices.

[17] A possible future refinement would be to apply a EUR 750 million global revenue threshold to entities belonging to MNE groups where the necessary information on global revenues at the group-wide level is available in ORBIS.

[18] For example, if the value of tangible assets is missing for 10% of MNE entities (weighted by turnover) in a jurisdiction, the total estimate of tangible assets of MNE entities in this jurisdiction has been scaled up by 1/(1-10%)=11.1%.

[19] This approach was inspired by Tørsløv et al. (2018[1]) who apply the ratio of gross operating surplus to labour compensation in FATS to the compensation of employees in national accounts. The main limitation

of the approach is that the ratio of payroll to turnover may vary across industries, which cannot be accounted for with the available data.

[20] An alternative approach to the whole extrapolation methodology would have been to use data on FDI income instead of FDI positions as a starting point. While this would a priori have seemed a more direct approach, it would have posed significant challenges for extrapolation (FDI income being more volatile than FDI positions) and, more importantly, it would have made it difficult to identify ultimate investors, because the available data on FDI by ultimate investor focus only on FDI positions and not on FDI income.

[21] The recent literature using pseudo maximum-likelihood methods in gravity models has often used a method based on a Poisson distribution (PPML) as first described by Santos Silva and Tenreyro (2006[20]). Head and Mayer (2014[21]) compare different methods trying to achieve the same goals (in particular a better handling of zeroes in the variable of interest) and suggest that methods based on the Poisson distribution (PPML) and the Gamma distribution (GPML) perform best, and that there is no obvious reason to prefer one method over the other since their relative performance will depend on the structure of the error term. Without any strong *a priori* on this structure, the GPML method has been chosen for the extrapolation of turnover in this chapter because it provided a better fit with the available benchmarks (i.e. alternative data sources such as CbCR data and US BEA data) among the type of jurisdictions for which extrapolations play an important role (e.g. low income jurisdictions). The two methodologies yield broadly similar coefficients in the estimation, and broadly similar aggregates: for instance, global turnover in the matrix is 0.6% higher after using GPML compared to PPML.

[22] AMNE data and Analytical AMNE data were not included in this regression because AMNE does not include diagonal terms and the diagonal terms in Analytical AMNE are generally based on imputations.

[23] An additional difficulty is that turnover can be distorted by profit shifting behaviour, in which case it may not give a good indication of the level of economic activity, and, in turn, of tangible assets in a jurisdiction. This is a limitation of the approach that is difficult to fully address with the available data.

[24] In jurisdictions with less than ten MNE groups in ORBIS consolidated account data, the data is considered to be insufficiently representative and no adjustment is made (i.e. 'Delta 2'=0). Similarly, in jurisdictions present in less than three ultimate parent jurisdictions in CbCR data, it is assumed that 'Delta 1'=0. For the purpose of computing 'Delta 2', turnover in ORBIS consolidated account data is rescaled to take into account the fact that consolidated turnover does not include intra-group sales, while these sales are included in the turnover matrix. This rescaling is done based on the global ratio of unrelated to total revenue in CbCR data, which is 69%.

[25] The ratio of payroll to turnover computed on the aggregate inward and outward AMNE data (13.5%) is broadly similar to the average in ORBIS. Differences might be explained by the restricted sectoral coverage in AMNE (which often excludes the financial sectors), the different geographical coverage in the two sources, and the fact that the ORBIS ratio is computed on subgroups with positive profits while this distinction is unavailable in AMNE.

[26] More precisely, the adjustment is based on the share of depreciation in gross operating surplus by market jurisdiction, as computed by Tørsløv et al. (2018[1]). In jurisdictions where no data are available in Tørsløv et al. (2018[1]), the ratio for the "Rest of the world" is used.

[27] In practice, when the total of a column in the profit matrix for a given jurisdiction of ultimate parent was less than 50% of the total consolidated profit of MNE groups from this jurisdiction of ultimate parent, as observed in the ORBIS consolidated account dataset, the diagonal cell for jurisdiction in the matrix (when based on extrapolation) has been adjusted upwards to cap the difference at 50%. In addition, when the

diagonal cell in the profit matrix for a jurisdiction was above 100% of the total consolidated profit of MNE groups from this jurisdiction of ultimate parent, as observed in the ORBIS consolidated account dataset, the diagonal cell has been adjusted downwards, to 100% of this total. Similar adjustments were made in the turnover matrix. These adjustments mainly focus on smaller jurisdictions, where data quality issues may be more frequent and where the matrices rely more on extrapolations than in larger jurisdictions. In the turnover matrix, this adjustment affects 48 jurisdictions (out of 222) and the total turnover in the cells affected represents 0.5% of the total turnover in the turnover matrix. In the profit matrix, this adjustment affects 51 jurisdictions, and the total profit in the cells affected by the adjustment represents 4.4% of the total profit in the profit matrix.

[28] No similar adjustment is made in the tangible assets and payroll matrices since the imputed values in those matrices rely on the turnover matrix, which has already been adjusted.

[29] One limitation of the matrices for the analysis of profit shifting is that they focus only on MNE sub-groups with positive profits, and therefore do not reflect potential loss-shifting behaviour.

[30] The authors only report an exact number for 2017, but their Figure 6 suggests a level of global FDI positions slightly below USD 35 trillion.

[31] Austria, Canada, Switzerland, Czech Republic, Germany, Estonia, Finland, France, Hungary, Iceland, Italy, Lithuania, Poland, Turkey, and the United States.

[32] For example, Borga and Calandro (2018[12]) define "pass-through capital [as] capital that flows into one economy and that is subsequently invested in another economy".

[33] In a recent paper, Coppola et al. (2020[27]) show that similar patterns occur when considering the issuance of securities. For instance, they find that classifying securities by the ultimate issuer (the parent) instead of the immediate issuer (an affiliate) increases substantially the level of portfolio investment from developed economies to emerging economies.

[34] SPEs are entities that have little or no employment, physical presence, or operations in a jurisdiction but that do provide important services to the MNE, such as holding assets and liabilities or raising capital (see https://www.oecd.org/daf/inv/How-MNEs-channel-investments.pdf).

[35] Here, "outward" FDI is not used as the "reporting" principle under which the data is reported since the FDI data by ultimate investor is only available in the reports that some jurisdictions make about their inward FDI. The term "outward" is used here to specify the direction of the flow: for instance, the inward FDI reported by France from the United States is an outward flow from the United States to France.

[36] For instance, OECD data shows that in 2016, France was the ultimate investor for USD 42 billion of FDI positions in France, or 6.1% of its global inward FDI; while the United States was the ultimate investor for USD 73 billion FDI positions in the United States, or 1.9% of its global inward FDI.

[37] Among the 15 jurisdictions reporting FDI data by ultimate investor, Austria does not report an aggregate inward FDI position in the OECD data.

[38] Jurisdiction-level results are similar when considering data from the IMF balance of payment statistics for FDI income and the IMF CDIS dataset for FDI positions.

www.ingramcontent.com/pod-product-compliance
Ingram Content Group UK Ltd.
Pitfield, Milton Keynes, MK11 3LW, UK
UKHW051458290926
15471UKWH00008B/1286

9 789264 495074